Reeling Roosters
and Dancing Ducks

Celtic Mouth Music

Heather Sparling

For Rod C. MacNeil
and in loving memory of Helen.

Cape Breton University Press recognizes the support of the Province of Nova Scotia, through the Department of Communities, Culture and Heritage and the support received for its publishing program from the Canada Council for the Arts Block Grants Program. We are pleased to work in partnership with these bodies to develop and promote our cultural resources.

FILM & CREATIVE INDUSTRIES
NOVA SCOTIA

Canada Council   Conseil des Arts
for the Arts   du Canada

Cover image: Golden Mouth Boat, by Onni Norden, Sydney, NS
Cover design: Cathy MacLean Design, Chéticamp, NS
Layout: Mike Hunter, Port Hawkesbury and Sydney, NS
Editing: Laura Bast, Toronto, ON
First printed in Canada.

Library and Archives Canada Cataloguing in Publication

Sparling, Heather, 1972-, author
       Reeling roosters and dancing ducks : Celtic mouth music
/ Heather Sparling.
Includes bibliographical references and index.
Issued in print and electronic formats.
ISBN 978-1-927492-98-7.--ISBN 978-1-927942-12-3 (pdf).--
ISBN 978-1-927492-13-0 (epub).--ISBN 978-1-927492-14-7 (mobi)

       1. Mouth music--History and criticism. 2. Celtic music--
History and criticism. I. Title.

ML3655.S736 2014   781.62'9163   C2014-904136-5
                                           C2014-904137-3

Cape Breton University Press
PO Box 5300, 1250 Grand Lake Road
Sydney, NS B1P 6L2 CA
www.cbupress.ca

Reeling Roosters & Dancing Ducks

Heather Sparling

CAPE BRETON UNIVERSITY PRESS
SYDNEY, NOVA SCOTIA

Table of Contents

viii   List of Figures

ix   Acknowledgements

xiii   Foreword by Mary Ann Kennedy

1   Introduction: Why Study Puirt-a-Beul?

25   1 Mouth Music: A Global Phenomenon

55   2 "Chuirinn air a' Phìob e": Origin Theories

97   3 "Ciamar a Nì Mi an Ruidhle Bhòidheach": Musical Features

139   4 Nonsense, Innuendo and Twisted Tongues: Puirt-a-Beul Lyrics

182   5 From the Tip of the Tongue to the Tips of the Toes: Puirt-a-Beul and Dance

245   6 Quit Fiddling Around! Puirt-a-Beul's Other Functions

279   7 Keeping Things in Line: The Role of Puirt-a-Beul in Gaelic Society

315   Appendix

319   Glossary

322   Notes

331   References

350   Index

List of Figures

28   Fig 1. Curwen notation ("Calum Crùbach"/"Miss Drummond of Perth")

48   Fig 2. Canntaireachd vowels and pitch equivalents

48   Fig 3. Canntaireachd "hin" and "tro"

106   Fig 4. "Am Muileann Dubh" (port-a-beul)

107   Fig 4a. "Am Muileann Dubh" (fiddle tune)

111   Fig 5. "Cairistìona Chaimbeul" (as sung by Hugh Duncan)

116   Fig 6. "Cairistìona Chaimbeul" (as it appears in K. N. MacDonald's *Puirt-a-Beul*)

118   Fig 7. "Christie Campbell" (fiddle tune)

121   Fig 8. "Fear an Dùin Mhòir" (port-a-beul)

124   Fig 9. "Lord Dunmore" (fiddle tune)

126   Fig 10. "A Sheana Bhean Bhochd"

135   Fig 11. "Tha Mis' air Uisg' an Lònain Duibh"

249   Fig 12. "'S ann an Ìle"

293   Fig 13. "Còta Mòr Ealasaid"

Puirt-à-Beul: Faireadair na Gàidhlig Gatekeeper of Gaelic Culture

Now, there's a great claim for a small, and considered by some an insignificant, genre in Gaelic music and song. If they are even to be considered songs. "Get some real songs!" was one person's exhortation on first hearing of Heather Sparling's passion for and research into puirt-à-beul. Children's amusements, simple mnemonics, teaching aids, nonsense verses, the diminutives applied to these Gaelic-language dance songs are endless, and yet, they have taken on a central position in the continuum of Cape Breton and Scottish Gaelic music. Who would have thought that "reeling roosters and dancing ducks" would be germane to the politics of minority culture?

Heather Sparling's survey of Gaelic puirt-à-beul offers a new perspective on a subject about which relatively little has been written, and that mostly from the perspective of the Scottish side of the Atlantic. Her overview puts the genre in the context of other song and music cultures, of vocabelization in performance and transmission, and of the wider genre of Celtic mouth musics.

She addresses the various creation theories and myths with which puirt have been saddled for more than two-and-a-half centuries, and tackles the various roles of puirt in dancing, instrumental and singing contexts. And while puirt, as Heather shows, fulfill many different functions in social and performance contexts, of particular interest here is the evidence of the relationship between fiddlers and singers in Nova Scotia and in Prince Edward Island, where singers can be heard "jigging" or "tuning" the dances along with, or in the absence of, an instrumentalist.

Puirt-à-beul today are valued as performance repertoire by contemporary vocalists who might at the same time denigrate their value as songs; instrumentalists see their obvious connection to dance-tune repertoire, but see them as singers' territory. Small wonder they have struggled at various times to find an acknowledgement or affirmation from either side. Interesting too that, for all that, they can also elicit strong and oft-times emotional opinions on classification, history, purpose and performance!

I have perhaps a different perspective on puirt-à-beul than many other Gaelic singers, having been brought up in a family of pipers and singers who also loved to dance, and for whom puirt-à-beul was the natural crossing-point for the different disciplines. Growing up with Gaelic-speaking aunts, uncles and grandparents who sang and played, my sister Wilma and I learned to appreciate the intricacy of language in these vocal musical miniatures; we bibbed our way through Highland dancing practice to the sounds of "Gille Calum" and "Siuth'd a Bhalachaibh," the classic puirt tunes for the Sword Dance and the Highland Fling; we could hear when an exceptional musical ear had absorbed the rhythms of language into a multi-nuanced playing style.

And here is where Heather has taken a bold step, addressing issues of language and expressive arts in a minority culture where there is as rapid a decline in speakers of one of its core languages as there is a flourishing of many aspects of its performance genres. The number of fluent and native Gaelic speakers continues to diminish, still lower is the number for whom the natural idiom, rhythms and cadences of the language comes as second nature.

For each person who picks up a fiddle and starts to learn the tunes of the likes of the late, great Joe Peter MacLean, there is always the question of where Gaelic sits as an ingredient to the "secret recipe" of Cape Breton fiddle style. For that matter, for every person who decides they want to sing Gaelic songs—on either side of the Atlantic—there is ever the same query about fluency, competence and confidence in the language. To be with or without Gaelic raises conflicting emotions, philosophies and rationales and a need for a delicate cultural diplomacy.

This study achieves two vital objectives. It asserts a spectrum of existence which allows puirt-à-beul a relevance across a wide expanse of Scottish and Cape Breton traditional music rather than trying to pigeonhole through narrow definition. But more than this, if this book achieves anything, it is to identify a continuum of cultural, musical and linguistic reference and evolution for a musical genre and wider tradition in which the Gaelic language is a vital element. It recognizes that music, language, tradition and heritage are not fixed points in any book or archival recording, but living entities which of necessity move on and evolve. Current innovation today may yet be the revered and touch-me-not cornerstones of tradition for generations hence.

As Heather states: "puirt-à-beul remain important in Gaelic culture because they function as a 'cultural linchpin' ... connecting and integrating diverse strands of expressive culture, including language, music, dance and storytelling." For this reason alone, this genre of Gaelic vocal music punches away above its weight, and I hope this book will go some way to re-asserting the value of the "small but perfectly formed."

Màiri Anna NicUalraig / Mary Ann Kennedy
Àrd Ghobhair, Loch Abar
Sultainn 2014

Acknowledgements

As with any kind of scholarly book, particularly one based on ethnographic fieldwork, there are many, many people to thank. I am grateful for the assistance and support of the following people, without whom this book would not have been possible. My thanks appear in no particular order.

I am very grateful to all the people who have allowed me to interview them over the years, and to those who have spent time discussing Gaelic song with me. This book would not be possible without engaged community members willing to share their knowledge, opinions and insights. I am especially grateful to Rod C. and the late Helen MacNeil for hosting me on many early visits to Cape Breton and treating me as a member of their family. We had many discussions about puirt-a-beul, Gaelic song, and community in general that positively shaped my understanding of Gaelic culture in Cape Breton. There are several people whose names have not been used in this book but who were generous with their time: thank you. I would like to thank Christine Primrose, Wilma Kennedy and David Livingston-Lowe in particular for reading sections of the book and reaffirming comments they initially made many years ago.

Many thanks to all the people who offered constructive feedback on earlier drafts—namely Ian Brodie, Stephanie Conn, Kate Dunlay, Burt Feintuch, Meghan Forsyth, John Gibson, Jeff

Hennessy, Sherry Johnson, Mats Melin and Michael Newton. I am grateful to Mary Ann Kennedy for writing the foreword and for offering helpful comments on several chapters. Thanks to John Alick MacPherson for an engaging interview about the book, recorded for CBU Press. Special thanks to Laura Bast, editor, and Mike Hunter, editor-in-chief, at Cape Breton University Press.

Thank you, Mary Campbell and Carla White, for getting innumerable books from other libraries for me—I probably single-handedly kept you busy full-time during the peak weeks of writing and research! Thanks to all the CBU library staff who have helped me to find missing books, access books in the special collections, retrieved interlibrary loan books for me, and generally assisted me with my research.

I would also like to thank the many colleagues, administrators and staff at Cape Breton University who have supported and encouraged my research in various ways. I feel very grateful to be working at an institution that values the research I do.

Thank you to the creators of two invaluable online resources: Andrew Kuntz (*The Fiddler's Companion*, http://www.ibiblio.org/fiddlers/index.html, and its associated wiki, http://www.tunearch.org/wiki/TTA) and Jeremy Keith (*The Session*, http://thesession.org). The first provides a list of tunes with known recordings listed for each and extensive annotations from various sources, many of which are otherwise hard to access. The second provides a list of tunes with notation for each and a forum for discussion. Although both involve "crowd-sourced" information—and so I am also grateful to all who have contributed to these resources to ensure their success—I also know the time it takes to conceive and manage such a resource. I have benefited immensely from the time that these two individuals have taken to create such extensive online resources for the free use of anyone interested in traditional "Celtic" tunes.

Thank you to ethnomusicologist and Irish singer Lillis O' Laoire for recommending recordings with examples of Irish *portaireacht* and to Caroline Murphy for helping me to get copies of them.

Thank you to Mats Melin for feedback, particularly regarding traditional Scottish dance, and to Michael Newton, for conversations about the history of dance and Gaelic song in the Highlands, which directly led to my rethinking how to trace the history of puirt-a-beul.

Thank you to Anita MacDonald for looking up innumerable fiddle tunes associated with puirt-a-beul, and to Anita and Maile Graham-Laidlaw for tune transcriptions.

Thank you to Gillebride MacMillan for opinions from a Scottish Gaelic speaker's and singer's perspective.

Thank you to Margaret Stewart for suggestions and feedback regarding puirt-a-beul lyrics.

Thank you to Hector MacNeil for his assistance with lyric transcriptions, encouragement and feedback.

Thank you to Barry Shears and Kate Dunlay for their help differentiating marches and strathspeys.

Thank you to Mary Ann Kennedy for providing me with a copy of her thesis on puirt-a-beul.

Finally, thanks to my husband, Chris McDonald, for support throughout the writing process—which at times seemed interminable! I am particularly grateful for the assistance provided with many of the musical transcriptions. I could not have written this book without your love and encouragement. Even though.

Introduction:
Why Study Puirt-a-Beul?

I didn't start out researching *puirt-a-beul*. My original intention was to research Cape Breton dance music for my Master's thesis in ethnomusicology. As a flute player with barely competent singing abilities and a lover of dance, I was interested in instrumental traditions. But because I lived far from Cape Breton, in Toronto at the time, and had limited access to (and, to be perfectly honest, little knowledge of) Cape Breton musicians, I decided to start my research by conducting a few interviews on the subject of Scottish Gaelic dance songs. I had enrolled in Gaelic classes in Toronto and thus knew a few people who would be able to speak on the subject. Since my understanding of puirt-a-beul was that they were vocal dance tunes used in the absence of instruments, and because I had a few recordings of puirt-a-beul by Cape Breton artists, it seemed like a reasonable place to start my investigation of Cape Breton dance music. My first two interviews changed the direction of my research completely.

My first interview was with a native-Gaelic-speaking woman from the Hebrides of Scotland who had immigrated to Canada in 1967. She fondly recalled learning puirt-a-beul from her grandmother who performed them at weddings and, while visiting in someone's home, would "dandle" a child on her knee to their accompaniment. She herself sang puirt-a-beul in a band and she recalled that they would be used to accompany Scottish country dancing. She stated that "everyone loves puirt-a-beul."

My second interview was with an advanced Gaelic learner from Toronto with family connections to Cape Breton. Her attitude to puirt-a-beul was radically different. She explained that most serious Gaelic singers don't like puirt-a-beul because they are "just tunes" rather than real songs. She noted that puirt-a-beul seem to appeal mostly to Gaelic learners rather than to fluent or native speakers. She suggested that lots of singers would know them and find them amusing, but they would never volunteer to sing one if they could sing another kind of song instead. She made it clear that puirt-a-beul were not particularly valuable as songs in Cape Breton.

I was taken aback at the almost completely opposite attitudes articulated in these two interviews. What could explain this difference? My surprise that puirt-a-beul were not valued as songs in Cape Breton was all the greater since the few commercial Cape Breton recordings I had that included Gaelic song almost invariably contained puirt-a-beul, including recordings by the Rankin Family, the Barra MacNeils, Mary Jane Lamond and Ashley MacIsaac. If puirt-a-beul were so negligible in Cape Breton, why were they being recorded, particularly on albums aimed at large, non-local audiences? Surely if puirt-a-beul were of such limited value they would not be ideal representatives of Gaelic song culture? I decided that it would be worth investigating the disconnect between these two interviews.

I went to Cape Breton for the first time in 1998. I continued to find puirt-a-beul everywhere I looked. They were regularly included on CDs that incorporated Gaelic songs. There were whole workshops devoted to puirt-a-beul. I discovered that one of the most revered Gaelic tradition-bearers within living memory, Joe Neil MacNeil (1908-1996), recorded more than 100 for collector and ethnologist John Shaw in the late 1970s even though he was not even a singer! John Shaw collected dozens more from other community members. And yet, people, when they found out what

I was researching, were often ambivalent. One Gaelic teacher warned me that I wouldn't find many puirt-a-beul. A fluent Gaelic learner advised me to "get some real songs." And one Gaelic singer mused that I might be able to write a short essay about puirt-a-beul but would be unable to write a whole thesis on the subject.

Such negative attitudes are not entirely surprising for a number of reasons. As will be discussed in Chapter 6, puirt-a-beul have been popularized in Scotland via the Royal National Mod and mass media. This hasn't been the case in Cape Breton. Language revivalists necessarily and understandably tend to focus their efforts on preserving and highlighting linguistic expressions of particular value, and the ones in Cape Breton have consequently tended to dismiss puirt-a-beul, since they are not deemed as valuable as other linguistic expressions. I suggest why puirt-a-beul tend to be devalued and ignored in Chapter 7.

It would also seem that I am not alone in experiencing reactions of surprise and resistance to the study of mouth music. Although Scottish ethnomusicologist Kim Chambers does not deal with puirt-a-beul in her analysis of vocables in Scottish mouth music (mainly because so few actually consist primarily or exclusively of vocables), in researching Scottish songs containing vocables, she also met with resistance: "The insignificant status of the genre in some contexts led to a mild reluctance on the part of some informants to vocabelise and articulate ideas about vocables to the exclusion of what they felt to be their more significant musical contribution" (Chambers 1980: 241n11). K. N. MacDonald likewise felt the need to justify his early and unique collection of puirt-a-beul:

> Many Highlanders of the advanced school may consider that the foregoing "Puirt a Beul" mouth tunes, or articulate music, were not worth preserving. Certainly as far as the poetry is concerned there may be some truth in the statement, but we do not claim the rhymes as poetry. (1931 [1901]: 50)

MacDonald's assertion that puirt-a-beul are not woth preserving as poetry but may be worth preserving as music raises an important point about the difficulty of classifying them, a point to which I'll return shortly.

I discovered that it was going to be hard to contextualize my Cape Breton discoveries within existing scholarship because puirt-a-beul scholarship is almost non-existent. Small collections of puirt-a-beul texts and sometimes music exist in a handful of print sources (e.g., Tolmie 1910-1913; M. F. Shaw 1977 [1955]; Comunn Gaidhealach Leodhais 1998 [1982]; Mhàrtainn 1994). The aforementioned K. N. MacDonald did publish an entire book of puirt-a-beul (1931 [1901]; this book was republished with extensive annotations by Lamb in 2012). But these and other sources rarely give more than a passing mention of puirt-a-beul beyond their lyrics and music. They offer tantalizing tidbits about their origins, their composition, their associated stories, or their uses, but usually without much elaboration and without any supporting evidence. Many of the details provided are speculative at best and whimsical at worst. In MacDonald's book devoted to puirt-a-beul, he writes of their texts as remnants of a long-lost Druidic language (1931 [1901]: 3) even though we have little knowledge about the Druids due to very few surviving artifacts, written materials or other tangible resources. It is therefore hard to know what their language was like. Of course, due to the lack of evidence, we cannot actually *dis*prove MacDonald's claim, no matter how unlikely it may be. Other sources provide limited, if any, information. For example, although Margaret Fay Shaw includes a whole section of puirt-a-beul in her Gaelic song collection, *Folksongs and Folklore of South Uist*, she does not mention them even once in her introduction. Although she translates puirt-a-beul as "vocal dance music," her only reference to musical dance accompaniment in the book's introduction is instrumental (Shaw 1977 [1955]: 16). Why include so many in the body of the book but ignore them in the introduction?

Even books devoted to Scottish (and particularly Highland or Gaelic) dance and dance music barely mention puirt-a-beul, if they do at all (e.g., Rhodes 1964; Emmerson 1971; Flett and Flett 1964; 1996). This struck me as especially odd given that puirt-a-beul are usually associated with dance. However, the problem with puirt-a-beul is that it falls in the cracks between song and music, and it is often missed by language, song and music scholars alike. Gaelic literary and song scholars tend to prefer to study and analyze "heavier" Gaelic poetry, a preference that is evident from the absence of puirt-a-beul in many major Gaelic poetry and song collections (e.g., N. MacDonald 1863; Mac-na-Ceàrdadh 2004 [1879]; D. J. MacDonald and Innes 1998; Black 1999, 2001). Many song collections omit puirt-a-beul altogether or, if they do include them, they do not explicitly identify them as puirt-a-beul (e.g., Creighton and MacLeod 1964; Campbell and Collinson 1969-1981; Fergusson 1977; Campbell 1990). Piper and Celtic scholar Joshua Dickson describes a conversation that highlights the tendency for song scholars to omit puirt-a-beul from their studies:

> Dr John Shaw, Senior Lecturer in Celtic and Scottish Studies, University of Edinburgh, has suggested in conversation that *puirt-à-beul* may not really be classified as "songs" under the traditional Gaelic point of view; that a "song," in Gaelic culture, is meant primarily to perform narrative—to tell a story—whereas *puirt-à-beul* are sung to provide music for step-dancing and thus any narrative component is minimal. (2006: 241n11)

Because puirt-a-beul lyrics are not as literary as those of other song genres, and because they are associated with instrumental music and dance, they tend to be ignored by song and poetry scholars.

Meanwhile, scholars of instrumental music often overlook puirt-a-beul, partly because they are vocal music, but also likely due to the language factor. There have been very few, if any, musicologists or ethnomusicologists who have been fluent enough in Gaelic to take on a study of Gaelic songs. Francis Collinson is the only musicologist I know who has included puirt-a-beul in his studies of Scottish music (1966), but it is unclear to what degree he could understand or speak Gaelic, if at all. However, the fact that he grew up in Edinburgh; the fact that his Gaelic song–related publications, including his major contribution to Gaelic song scholarship (Campbell and Collinson 1969-1981), were co-authored with John Lorne Campbell, a fluent Gaelic speaker, suggest that he had little, if any, Gaelic fluency. The majority of scholars investigating Scottish-derived instrumental music in Cape Breton have focused on fiddling (e.g., Spielman 1972; Garrison 1985; McKinnon 1989; Doherty 1996; Dunlay and Greenberg 1996; Feintuch 2004; Graham 2006; Hennessy 2008; Herdman 2008) or piping (Gibson 1998, 2002; Fatone 2002; Shears 2008) and they, like their Scottish counterparts, have not given much attention to puirt-a-beul.

If books specializing in music or dance rarely mention puirt-a-beul, there should be no surprise, then, that more general reference works seldom mention them either. For example, there is no mention of puirt-a-beul in Purser's *Scotland's Music* (1992) and only the briefest of mentions in Thomson's *Companion to Gaelic Scotland*, under "music, of Gaelic Scotland," itself a very short entry (1983). The *Garland Encyclopedia of World Music* mentions puirt-a-beul in passing in the Europe volume but the term does not appear in the index or glossary of foreign terms, nor does it appear in the U.S./Canada volume. The only reference work to provide more than a cursory reference to puirt-a-beul is the *New Grove Dictionary of Music and Musicians*, under "Scotland."

There are a couple of other reasons why puirt-a-beul may have been afforded little attention by scholars. One is gender. Until relatively recently, scholarship in many fields, including ethnomusicology, musicology and folklore, has focused on male tradition-bearers and male-dominated music genres. This is true of Gaelic culture too. There are more studies of fiddling and piping (traditionally dominated by male players) than of harping (now strongly associated with women despite once being the domain of men); more research about male bards than female ones; and more collections of songs associated with male bards than with female singers. As I will discuss in Chapter 1, puirt-a-beul seem most often to be the preserve of women. It is therefore not entirely surprising that it has been thus far overlooked by academics.

At the same time, I would be remiss if I did not acknowledge that Gaelic scholarship has hardly excluded studies of women or women's repertoire. Indeed, there have been of late many collections of female bards' repertoire (e.g., Craig 1949; Watson 1965; Douglas 1971; Meek 1977; Ó Baoill 2009), female collectors of Gaelic song (e.g., Kennedy-Fraser and MacLeod 1909; Tolmie 1910-1913; Shaw 1977 [1955]; Landin 2009) and female scholars of Gaelic song (e.g., Bassin 1977; M. MacLeod 1984; Bennett 1998). Scholars have also paid considerable attention to particular types of women's repertoire, especially waulking songs (e.g., Campbell and Collinson 1969-1981; J. MacInnes 1969-1970). Waulking songs were sung by Scottish women to accompany the beating of newly woven wool in order to shrink it and make the weave tighter. The waulking tradition continues to this day in Cape Breton, where it is known as "milling" instead. Interestingly, although once an exclusively female context, in Cape Breton the milling frolic has come to be dominated by male singers and tradition-bearers. All in all, however, and despite increasing representation of female bards and repertoire, Gaelic song scholarship is still dominated by male scholars studying the repertoire of male bards.

Another reason that puirt-a-beul may have been overlooked by scholars is that, until very recently, the only musics considered worth studying would have been "art," "elite" or "learned" musics. This is obvious in university music programs that generally focus almost exclusively on Western art (or "classical") music. Even when the discipline of ethnomusicology entered post-secondary institutions, the emphasis at first was on the art musics of non-Western cultures. Likewise, Celticists, when they have turned to Gaelic song at all, have tended to focus on "high" Gaelic art at the expense of more common expressions. Although folklorists provided a welcome alternative by studying vernacular ("folk") music, they tended initially to focus on lyrical analysis while generally ignoring the music itself, the social context in which music existed, and music-related processes (such as learning, transmitting, practising, rehearsing and performing).

Part of the reason for the emphasis on high art forms of poetry and music was that these forms were the most likely to be documented in written form. Written sources of course made it much easier to study music and poetry, but written history and tangible documents also came to be privileged by scholars over other forms of information, such as oral histories (see, for example, Perks and Thomson 2006; C. James 1988). Thus, song forms not documented in writing have been overlooked and even dismissed. Until the rise of scholarship based on oral sources (such as folklore, anthropology, oral history and ethnomusicology), oral sources were considered suspect because memory is notoriously unreliable and there is always the potential for a source to skew information deliberately for personal or other reasons. Indeed, they remain suspect in many disciplines. And yet oral sources allow scholars to study cultural forms, including mouth music, not otherwise documented. If we keep in mind the limitations of oral sources, there is no reason they cannot be effectively used. Their increasing prevalence as areas of valid scholarly inquiry is evident in the rise of ethnography as a method in several disciplines, including anthropology, ethnomusicology and folklore.

Another reason that "high art" forms have been studied at the expense of more common forms is that our society values cultural products—whether antique furniture, visual art or musical compositions—that have withstood time. Written sources can be dated, proving that the music and songs recorded are several centuries old. Vernacular forms of music and poetry, particularly those dating prior to the 18th century, tend not to be documented in writing. This may be because the cultural expressions of the common people were not deemed worthy of being recorded and also because the people who practised them were illiterate or had no access to writing materials or publishing venues. As a result, it is difficult to trace these expressive forms back very far, even if they were, in fact, practised just as long as high-status forms of expressive culture.

With improved education, increasing literacy rates, and cheaper publications, it became easier to document vernacular culture in written form. It also became desirable to do so for nationalist reasons. The extremely influential German philosopher Johann Gottfried Herder (1744-1803) argued in the 18th century that every country should have its own distinct culture rooted in its own distinct language and practised by its common people. Herder's philosophies sent scholars throughout Europe on a search for vernacular songs, music and dances, which were subsequently published in large numbers (see, for example, S. James 1999; Bohlman 2004). Consequently, we may well have access to written sources and documentation of vernacular culture dating back a couple of centuries, but rarely further back than that. As it happens, puirt-a-beul seem to have emerged in the 18th century (see Chapter 2). A history that is something like 300 years old is certainly nothing to sneeze at! But it doesn't compare with some much older Gaelic song traditions, which is likely why it wasn't documented much. Moreover, while we can today certainly recognize "erudite" versus "vernacular" forms of Gaelic song, such distinctions were not necessarily relevant or apparent to collectors and scholars in the 18th and 19th centuries. During the height of European colonization and imperialism, there was a common belief among dominant European populations, including English, French, Dutch, Spanish, German and Portugese, that their cultures were the most highly evolved in the world. All other cultures were seen as less evolved and less civilized. There was therefore a tendency to disregard cultural nuances within "other" cultures. At the same time, as I discuss elsewhere in this book, there was a need for minority cultural groups to convince dominant groups of their cultures' value, which needed to be asserted using criteria that would make sense to the dominant group. Scottish Gaelic culture was certainly a minority culture within the U.K. by the 18th century. It is therefore not entirely surprising that Gaelic song collections would have emphasized songs whose lyrics could compare with valued English-language songs. The issues are complicated, and there are other reasons that puirt-a-beul have not conventionally been documented in writing. I explore this topic in Chapter 4.

Today, scholars in many disciplines, including ethnomusicology and popular music studies, are turning to the music that everyday people make and listen to in their everyday lives. After all, surely the most popular music among a population can tell us as much about the significance and role of music in a particular society as the study of a few specialized genres. It is therefore appropriate to take the opportunity to examine and evaluate a Gaelic song genre such as puirt-a-beul alongside the more erudite bardic poetry that has generally received the most attention in Gaelic song studies.

Who Am I? Who Are You?

Although I now live in Cape Breton, I am originally from Toronto, Ontario. I first discovered Gaelic when I took a Gaelic-language course while living for a year in Edinburgh in the mid-1990s. After my year in Scotland and after completing an undergraduate degree in music, I decided to enroll in a Master's program in ethnomusicology, which allowed me to pursue my interests in both music and Celtic culture. I continued studying Gaelic while undertaking graduate studies in Toronto. When the Toronto Gaelic teachers all retired in 1999 and no other teachers stepped forward to replace them, I wound up teaching Gaelic with two fellow students in order to maintain the classes. Although my level of Gaelic was still not very advanced, teaching the language forced me to learn vocabulary and grammar quickly and thoroughly. To improve my own fluency, I enrolled in several week-long Gaelic immersion courses at the Gaelic College in Cape Breton and I met weekly with the two other local Gaelic teachers to speak the language over coffee. I supplemented my studies with occasional workshops in Toronto but also in Cape Breton while conducting fieldwork. I returned to Cape Breton almost annually after spending several months there in the summer of 1998. But my Gaelic fluency improved most after I spent a year studying at Sabhal Mòr Ostaig, the Gaelic-medium college on Skye in Scotland, in the early 2000s. When I moved permanently to Sydney, Nova

Scotia, in 2005, I was fortunate enough to be able to continue my Gaelic teaching career with the Gaelic Society of Cape Breton, An Comunn Gàidhlig Cheap Breatuinn. I continue to be involved in developing my own Gaelic skills while actively working in the Cape Breton and wider North American Gaelic communities.

I initially planned this book to be the publication of my slightly edited MA thesis about puirt-a-beul (2000). However, in revisiting my thesis, I realized that I had much more to say about puirt-a-beul now than I did then, and that there were many aspects of the structure of the thesis that I wanted to change. And so although a significant amount of data for this book was first elicited in preparation for my thesis, this book is really a completely different manuscript.

I have written for a general audience interested in Gaelic or Celtic culture. I have tried to keep the academic jargon to a minimum, and I have made a point of explaining what an ethnomusicologist does and how this has influenced the research that underlies this book. I have assumed that most readers will be North Americans or Scots and have therefore incorporated comparisons to mainstream Anglo-American culture to make understanding Gaelic culture a little easier for readers. Given that Gaels are "bi-cultural" in that they are all—today—fluent in English as well as Gaelic and live in an English-dominated world as well as a Gaelic one, Gaels may themselves make these same comparisons in their own minds as they absorb what puirt-a-beul are and their roles in Gaelic society (I discuss some of the implications of such a practice in Chapter 7). I have also tried to give examples from my personal experience wherever appropriate. They will hopefully help the audience to better understand who I am as the author, including my point of view and possible biases.

What do I Mean by "Celtic"?

This book is about Celtic mouth music. I will elaborate extensively on what I mean by "mouth music" and, more particularly, the Gaelic term "puirt-a-beul," in the next chapter. However, I would like to spend a little time here explaining what I mean by "Celtic." Although many readers will probably have a sense of what "Celtic" means, it is by no means a straightforward term, as much recent scholarship has attested.

Definitions of Celtic are usually based on one or more of the following: language, geography and/or ethnicity. There is a group of languages known as Celtic. They form a branch of the Indo-European language tree. The Indo-European language tree was first theorized in the late 18th century. The theory posits that many very different languages actually have their origins in a single language, is supported by the existence of some very similar words across languages. For example, the French word for "morning" is *matin* and in Gaelic it is *madainn* (pronounced *MAH-teen*). The Gaelic word *doras* (pronounced *DORE-uss*), is quite similar to its English equivalent, "door." Over time, this single Indo-European language was lost as it evolved into numerous languages spoken in various areas. The Indo-European language tree is organized so that there are branches of similar languages. For example, the Latin branch includes the so-called Romance languages: French, Italian and Spanish. The German branch includes German, Dutch, English, Danish and Norwegian. The Celtic branch is further divided into two sub-branches. The Brythonic languages include Welsh, Cornish and Breton (spoken in Brittany, France). The Goidelic languages include Irish Gaelic, Scots Gaelic and Manx (once spoken on the Isle of Man and, like Cornish, undergoing a revival).

A linguistic definition of Celtic suggests that anything in a Celtic language is Celtic. By this account, puirt-a-beul can be labelled "Celtic" since their lyrics are largely in Scottish Gaelic. The problem, however, is that many other forms of mouth music do not use semantically meaningful words at all, as we shall see in the next chapter. How does one define a song genre linguistically if it doesn't use "real" words? Even puirt-a-beul sometimes incorporate vocables, and I have occasionally come across an example containing English. So, while a linguistic definition of

Celtic generally works—at least in the case of puirt-a-beul—it doesn't always.

A geographical definition of Celtic suggests that anything emerging from a region defined as Celtic is therefore also Celtic. Specific places are defined as Celtic based on the presumption that people sharing a Celtic identity (identified by various common or similar practices and beliefs) and/or language live there and have lived there, usually for such a long time that they are considered the indigenous population. Celtic regions include Wales, Cornwall, Brittany, Scotland, Ireland and the Isle of Man. Galicia in Spain is sometimes controversially included (controversially because a Celtic language was never spoken there, although various artistic styles and practices can be linked to those in the other Celtic regions). According to this definition of Celtic, puirt-a-beul are Celtic because of their association with Scotland. However, the definition is difficult to uphold in the face of my emphasis on puirt-a-beul in Cape Breton, Nova Scotia.

One could argue, of course, that Cape Breton itself is a Celtic region due to the large number of Scottish immigrants who settled there in the 18th and 19th centuries. But if we define Cape Breton as a Celtic region along these lines, we should define many other areas of the New World as Celtic as well, since numerous places throughout North America were settled by large numbers of Scottish immigrants. Moreover, while Cape Breton was indeed settled by large numbers of Gaelic-speaking Scots, they shared the island with Acadians, English, American Loyalists, Irish and, later, people from various eastern and southern European countries, not to mention the Mi'kmaq. There is just as much reason to call Cape Breton, say, an Acadian island as a Celtic one.

Perhaps someone would argue that Cape Breton counts as a Celtic region because Gaelic is still spoken there. There are, of course, Gaelic learners scattered throughout North America, and there are pockets of learners in particular places. There are also native Gaelic speakers from Scotland who immigrated to Canada or the U.S. relatively recently. But Cape Breton is unique because there the language has been transmitted through the generations among descendants of the original Gaelic-speaking settlers, whereas it is no longer passed on anywhere else in North America as a first language. Cape Breton is widely recognized as the only *Gàidhealtachd* (Gaelic-speaking region) outside of Scotland. And yet Gaelic as a mother tongue currently has only the most tenuous hold in Cape Breton and it is already the case that the majority of Gaelic speakers there are learners. We certainly cannot consider Celts to be the indigenous populations of any place in North America, since Celtic settlers encountered indigenous peoples (also known as First Nations, Aboriginal Peoples, Native Canadian or Americans and North American Indians) upon their arrival.

Even if we accept that Cape Breton is a Celtic region without labelling any other former colony as such, it is still difficult to define puirt-a-beul geographically since puirt-a-beul are now sung wherever there are Gaelic learners, which includes most of North America as well as England, Australia, New Zealand and beyond. Puirt-a-beul is listened to in even more areas, thanks to recordings and the Internet, both of which can reach people in very remote areas. Puirt-a-beul has long overflowed its Celtically defined geographic boundaries.

If we exclude Cape Breton from our Celtic regions, we could arguably still label puirt-a-beul "Celtic" because they at least originated in Scotland, even if they are no longer restricted to Scotland. And it is true that many puirt-a-beul known in Cape Breton appear to have been brought over by immigrants. But it is also true that new puirt-a-beul have been composed in Cape Breton. We should expect no less since puirt-a-beul tend to be composed by average people (they are not dependent upon skilled poets) and tend to commemorate local events and people (more about this in Chapter 4).

Finally, we come to a definition of Celtic based on ethnicity, the most complex definition of the three. According to this definition, anything produced by a Celtic people—regardless of language spoken or where they are located—can be considered

Celtic. The troublesome issue is how to define a Celtic people. Greeks and Romans wrote about the Celts several centuries before the Common Era. According to Roman records, the Celts spread throughout Europe and even threatened the Roman Empire. However, the Romans ultimately succeeded in pushing them westward so that all that remains of them today are the Celts found in the peripheral regions of Europe defined above. By this definition, puirt-a-beul are Celtic because they were and are generated by Celts.

However, as anthropologist Malcolm Chapman points out (1992), we should not assume that just because the Romans and Greeks labelled a group of people as Celts that the people so labelled used the term for themselves, or that they even considered themselves a unified group. Chances are good that Romans ethnocentrically lumped disparate groups together as "Celts" just as people today might label a person as "African" or "Oriental" or "European" despite the rather sweeping, generalized nature of such categories or the fact that such terms rarely align with how people might choose to label themselves. These broad terms also ignore the fact that they tend to represent large numbers of countries that are quite different from one another culturally, linguistically, economically, politically and so on. It is quite likely that the people whom the Romans defined as Celts actually consisted of multiple groups of people who may have worked together to conquer particular territories or who may have shared some features with one another, but who otherwise saw themselves as quite different groups.

Archaeologist Simon James argues that although a Celtic ethnicity can certainly be said to exist today, it can really only be said to have emerged in the 18th century when it was politically expedient for particular marginalized groups of people in the British Isles to differentiate themselves from Anglo-Saxons in England (1999). The 1707 *Act of Union* joined Scotland to England and the 1800 *Act of Union* added Ireland to the United Kingdom, turning Scots and Irish into an undifferentiated mass of Britons. The process of "making" the contemporary Celts began with

Welsh linguist Edward Lhuyd's discovery of the linguistic links between Welsh, Breton, Cornish, Scots Gaelic, Irish Gaelic and Manx Gaelic; he labelled these languages "Celtic" for reasons not entirely understood. Regardless, Lhuyd essentially gave these languages a pedigree that predated that of the English language:

> Lhuyd's forerunners and contemporaries at Oxford and elsewhere had been studying early documents and the language in which they were written to build up a picture of the early English, not least for political reasons: to give English identity a good historical pedigree. As a Welsh patriot as well as a talented linguistic scholar, Lhuyd sought to do the same for his own country, and for its non-English neighbours…. Lhuyd's work was instrumental in providing the non-English peoples with an academically authoritative, shared historical pedigree far deeper than their individual national histories, and older by a thousand years than that of the English. (S. James 1999: 50)

Although Lhuyd's argument was strictly a linguistic one, it didn't take long for people to decide that where there were linguistic connections, there must also be cultural connections that stretched back as far as the languages themselves did.

Thus, previously distinct groups of people, such as the Irish, Scots and Welsh, came to see and label themselves as unified Celts. James shows how a lengthy and robust Celtic history came to be constructed and believed, so that we tend now to think of the Celts as having a continuous 2,000-year-old history despite their much more recent origins, and many people justify the value of Celtic culture on these grounds. Even if we accept that Celts as a homogenous group did exist in Roman times and that they did eventually come to inhabit the western outreaches of the British Isles and Ireland, it is difficult to argue that this ethnic group and its cultural output has managed to survive largely unchanged until the modern day. These Celts encountered many different peoples, languages and cultures through invasion, trade and travel, and so there is no doubt that intercultural contact happened on a regular basis. Intermarriage occurred. People adopted words, skills, practices, values and beliefs from one another. As Chapman puts it, "Any individual today in the British Isles, wherever he or she lives, and whatever language he or she speaks, is as likely to be descended from a Roman solider, a German mercenary, or a Viking raider, as from any prototypical Celt" (1992: 81).

As part of the desire to believe and prove that Celts have successfully passed their culture down over millennia, ancient origins are sometimes claimed for puirt-a-beul. However, as will be discussed in Chapter 2, most puirt-a-beul cannot be traced back before the 19th century. It is difficult to claim that puirt-a-beul are Celtic based on their association with an ancient Celtic people since the very notion of a Celtic people has been called into question. Even if we accept that the Celts, as we understand them today, only emerged in the 18th century (along with puirt-a-beul), we run into problems in labelling puirt-a-beul "Celtic" when we observe that puirt-a-beul are now listened to, studied and performed by people with many different—and often mixed—ethnic backgrounds and associations. The difficulty of this association is illustrated by the story of David Greenberg. A classically trained American violinist, David Greenberg is widely accepted, both within Cape Breton and without, as a highly competent Cape Breton fiddler. His ability to learn and perform the Cape Breton fiddle style despite not being from Cape Breton or even having a Cape Breton or Scottish heritage, indicates how problematic it is to assume that certain cultural expressions can only be mastered and transmitted by people from specific cultural groups.

Having just demonstrated how problematic it is to label puirt-a-beul or mouth music "Celtic," I am going to proceed to do just that. Whatever the academic limitations of the term, we don't really have a particularly useful alternative. I cannot call it "Scottish" because Gaelic song was only ever practised in parts of Scotland, not the entire country. Moreover, as I have explained, it is no longer limited to Scotland. I could call it "Gaelic," but as I noted earlier, puirt-a-beul lyrics are not always limited to words found in the Gaelic language but instead draw on vocables and sometimes even other languages. "Celtic" is thus a broad enough term to address these issues. At the same time, it narrows our focus in useful ways. Celtic mouth music may be practised throughout the world but it is not practised universally. It may share features with other forms of mouth music from around the world, as discussed in the next chapter, but it also has unique features. I suggest that puirt-a-beul can be considered Celtic largely because that is how it is commonly understood, and that, in the majority of cases, it is able to be defined as such along all three definitional parameters (linguistic, geographic and ethnic), no matter how problematic such a definition is upon closer inspection.

Scope and Chapter Outline

The emphasis in this book is on puirt-a-beul, a particular type of Celtic mouth music. Its relationship to other types of Celtic and global mouth music is introduced in the next chapter. Briefly, puirt-a-beul tends to be defined as vocal mouth music, or tunes, used to accompany dancing in the absence of instruments. As will also be detailed in the next chapter, puirt-a-beul appear to be uniquely Scottish Gaelic (although there are interesting parallels with Irish *portaireacht*, which is more likely to be translated as "lilting" or "humming" than as "mouth music") and, as such, it has travelled to areas where Scottish Gaelic speakers emigrated, including Cape Breton, Nova Scotia. Although this book is meant to be a study of puirt-a-beul in general, it must be understood as a study coming from a North American perspective generally, and from a Cape Breton perspective more particularly. This is the result of having spent most of my research time in Cape Breton, and of being involved in the North American Gaelic community. I have been participating in these communities much more actively and intimately than I have in Scotland, and for longer. At the same time, I have also spent some time in Scotland and have worked with Scottish Gaelic singers and scholars to try to ensure that what I write about puirt-a-beul applies to the Old World as well as the New.

I remain humbly aware that my understanding of Gaelic culture generally, whether in Cape Breton or Scotland, and of puirt-a-beul specifically, have always been limited if for no other reason than that I am coming to Gaelic culture from an outsider's perspective. What I bring to this book is the methods and analytical skills of an ethnomusicologist combined with years of investigating puirt-a-beul. However, my insights will almost certainly differ from those, say, of a respected singer of puirt-a-beul in Scotland or of a Gaelic-language activist from central North America. I am confident in my research. But I am also confident that this is not the final or only word to be said on puirt-a-beul. My own understanding will increase and mature with continued involvement in the Gaelic world, and others will no doubt bring additional insights to bear.

As an ethnomusicologist, my research is based primarily on fieldwork, which includes participant observation (learning by watching as well as learning by doing) and interviews. I have conducted formal interviews with dozens of people active in the Gaelic communities of Toronto, Scotland and especially Cape Breton. This formal interviewing is supplemented with informal conversations and observations over many years. At the time of writing this book, I had been living in Cape Breton for nine years, and had been conducting research here for sixteen. In addition to fieldwork, I have compiled the often very short, passing references to puirt-a-beul made in many sources in order to identify any patterns or dissimilarities. It is in bringing these many sources and references together that a rich picture of puirt-a-beul emerges. I also do some basic musical analysis in Chapter 3 and lyric analysis in Chapter 4 to reveal typical features. To ensure the accuracy and validity of my claims in this book, many of the chapters were circulated to members of the Gaelic community, as well as to instrumental music scholars and other ethnomusicologists (these generous individuals are gratefully recognized in this book's acknowledgements) for comments, corrections and suggested revisions.

Although chapters have been arranged so that their order facilitates a growing understanding of puirt-a-beul as the reader goes through them, each chapter has also been designed to stand on its own, with references to other chapters for readers who want further information about a particular topic. I have included examples of puirt-a-beul as often as possible, and noted for each any recorded examples on commercially available CDs. However, readers are also encouraged to visit Sruth nan Gàidheal (Gael Stream, a website containing archival recordings of Nova Scotia Gaelic songs recorded mostly in the 1970s and early 1980s [http://gaelstream.stfx.ca]) and Tobar an Dualchais (Kist o Riches, a website containing archival recordings of Scottish Gaelic songs recorded throughout the 20th century, particularly mid-century [http://www.tobarandualchais.co.uk]). Many of the songs discussed in this book can be heard on one or both sites.

The next chapter contextualizes puirt-a-beul within a global phenomenon of mouth music for, despite what some may assume, Gaelic mouth music is not the only mouth music to exist in the world. In fact, mouth music exists in many cultures. I begin by discussing some of the most common roles of diverse types of mouth music. This global context is designed to highlight not just how puirt-a-beul are consistent with other types of mouth music, but also which of its features are distinctive. From there, I discuss different types of Celtic mouth music, for there is more than one. I discuss how puirt-a-beul are different from, for example, diddling and *canntaireachd*.

Chapter 2 considers where puirt-a-beul came from and why. I start with an examination of the two most common origin stories: 1) that puirt-a-beul emerged in the wake of a proscription of the Highland bagpipes after the 1746 Battle of Culloden or 2) that puirt-a-beul developed when 19th-century priests and ministers discouraged dancing and encouraged the destruction of instruments, particularly fiddles. I also review other origin theories and explore which came first: instrumental music or puirt-a-beul?

Chapter 3 focuses on the musical features of puirt-a-beul, starting with a description of the basic structure of the form of most puirt-a-beul and explaining the differences between the three most common types: jigs, strathspeys and reels. I also explain why puirt-a-beul are difficult to perform well.

Chapter 4 partners with the previous one by focusing on the lyrical features of puirt-a-beul. In addition to discussing their typical characteristics, I address processes of composition and creation, including an overview of who creates puirt-a-beul and why, the use of vocables in puirt-a-beul and associations of puirt-a-beul with humour and bawdry. I conclude the chapter with a discussion of the role of puirt-a-beul in language learning and learner identity. In Chapters 3 and 4 especially, I refer to many examples of puirt-a-beul and I identify some of the recordings on which they can be found for interested readers. References to other puirt-a-beul are scattered throughout the book, usually with reference to recordings on which they can be found. For those readers who do not have an extensive Gaelic song recording library, I recommend searching for some of the tunes on YouTube, which includes a growing collection of Gaelic songs. Note that puirt-a-beul are often named, quite simply, "puirt-a-beul" rather than by their tune names, so if a YouTube search does not yield a tune by name, try searching by the more generic label. It may also be possible to hear tunes online using other means, such as iTunes or by using ABC notation and a midi player (ABC notation converts ASCII text—the letters you type on a standard keyboard—into musical notation; just search for "ABC notation" online to find a number of free tools and tune collections). I strongly encourage readers to try listening to puirt-a-beul by whatever means they have available. Not only do I suspect that most people will really enjoy them, but a familiarity with the sounds and texts of at least some puirt-a-beul will make this book more useful and comprehensible. There is only so much that one can learn about music by reading about it.

Puirt-a-beul are almost invariably defined as vocalized dance tunes, and so Chapter 5 considers the relationship between puirt-a-beul and dance. I review various types of Scottish dance as well as their appearance in Cape Breton before turning to the music associated with them and an exploration of the types of dances associated with puirt-a-beul, particularly step dancing.

Although puirt-a-beul are strongly associated with dance, they actually perform other functions too, the subject of Chapter 6. Indeed, many of the other functions played by puirt-a-beul are reminiscent of the roles mouth music plays in many world cultures, as outlined in Chapter 1: transmitting and learning instrumental tunes, learning the Gaelic language and as vocal showpieces.

Finally, Chapter 7 is another chapter about puirt-a-beul's functions, but about less obvious ones: it is about the social roles that puirt-a-beul play. In this chapter, I discuss the controversial debate about whether an instrumentalist needs to speak Gaelic and know puirt-a-beul in order to play in an authentic Gaelic style. I also suggest that puirt-a-beul function as a cultural "linchpin," linking many different Gaelic expressive forms together. Finally, I discuss how puirt-a-beul provide an entry point to Gaelic culture and how this can be a double-edged sword.

Terminology

A number of Gaelic terms appear in this book. I have retained Gaelic spellings but not accents when the words are commonly heard in English. For example, "puirt-a-beul" should properly be spelled "puirt-à-beul," for *à* (with an accent) means "from" whereas an *a* (without an accent) has quite a few other meanings and functions, depending on its place in a sentence. However, puirt-a-beul are commonly referenced in the English language, both orally and in writing, typically without the accent. I have followed this general practice. Similarly, the word "cèilidh" should have an accent but I have typically spelled it "ceilidh."

When introducing a Gaelic word, I generally provide an approximate phonetic pronunciation based on standard Canadian English. Although IPA (International Phonetic Alphabet) transcription would provide a more accurate pronunciation guide, I have not used it here since so few people are familiar with it. Since this book is aimed at a general audience, it seemed appropriate to use easily comprehensible pronunciation guides whenever possible. For those readers more linguistically inclined, I recommend the online Gaelic-English dictionary, *Am Faclair Beag* (The Little Dictionary), which can be found at http://faclair.info. Many of the words are given with IPA pronunciations. I also recommend Michael Bauer's comprehensive guide, *Blas na Gàidhlig: The Practical Guide to Scottish Gaelic Pronunciation* (2011). Note that I have notated the sound of "ch" in Gaelic (as in the Scots word "loch")—a sound not heard in English—as "kh."

A note also about the terms "native Gaelic speaker," "fluent speaker" and "Gaelic learner," which appear deceptively simple but can be quite complex. When referring to a "native speaker," I generally refer to people who learned Gaelic informally as a child in the home as a primary language, rather than through formal instruction. However, "native speakers" can vary in their fluency depending on how often they spoke Gaelic in their youth, with how many people and in how many different contexts, and also whether they had the opportunity to continue speaking Gaelic throughout their lives. Thus, "native speakers" are not necessarily experts on all aspects of Gaelic language, whether grammar or vocabulary, although they very often have more idiomatic expressions and vocabulary, as well as insights into Gaelic "ways of being" and culture.

Gaelic learners can likewise vary tremendously in their understanding of the Gaelic language and Gaelic culture. Some learners become extremely fluent, sounding "native" in their accent, idioms, grammar and vocabulary. Others never learn much beyond a few phrases. Most could be placed somewhere on a continuum between these two poles. I use the word "fluent" speaker to refer to a person—often a learner, but it could also refer to a native speaker—who is capable of having a Gaelic conversation on a range of topics with little difficulty understanding or being understood orally by other fluent speakers.

Finally, I'd like to acknowledge the challenge of speaking about Gaelic culture within the context of the West. The term "the West" is often used as a shorthand to refer to common histories, cultures and worldviews shared by countries in western Europe and North America. "The West" offers a convenient and effective means of referring to a whole slew of shared characteristics, particularly in comparison to, say, Asian or Middle Eastern cultures. However, although the Scottish Gàidhealtachds in both Scotland and Canada are geographically part of "the West," they often exhibit beliefs and musical characteristics not typical of other Western traditional musics and cultures. Some of these differences will become evident over the course of this book. At the same time, it's a useful term because it encapsulates dominant cultural and musical ideas that are likely familiar to most readers. I therefore reluctantly use the term "the West" occasionally in this book. More often, I refer to the "Anglo-American mainstream," by which I mean dominant English-speaking society, whether in Britain (the "Anglo-" part of Anglo-American) or North America (the "American" part of Anglo-American). Although every Gaelic speaker is also an English speaker today, and although every Gaelic speaker today participates in mainstream Anglo-American society, this was not always so, and Gaelic culture developed in many ways in reaction to the Anglo-American mainstream and dominance. The term "Anglo-American mainstream" is therefore helpful, if lacking grace.

Chapter 1
Mouth Music: A Global Phenomenon

Global Mouth Music

Mouth music is just what it sounds like: music made with the mouth. Most often, what differentiates mouth music from other kinds of song is the use of vocables. Vocables are sometimes defined as nonsensical words, but "nonsensical" isn't really the appropriate term. They may be residual words, as ethnomusicologist Ida Halpern argues with respect to vocables in songs of the Pacific Northwestern First Nations peoples (1976: 17-36). Alternatively, as Hinton points out, "some vocables carry a little bit of meaning, even though they are not words. Just as the vocables 'tra la la' in English carry the slight connotation of happiness, so do some vocable phrases in Havasupai carry connotations of emotion" (Hinton 1980: 284). Jazz scholar Brent Hayes Edwards argues that scat singing can be meaningful in many ways, from its ability to quote other melodies to the potential "multitude of meanings" arising from textlessness, opening up many possible meanings where text would limit them (2002). A better definition of vocables is "non-lexical syllables," which acknowledges that they do not make immediate or obvious lexical sense while not denying the potential for linguistic meaning to be conveyed.

Vocables are quite common in many musical traditions, not just Celtic ones. A particularly well-known example in English is the use of the "fal la la" vocables in the Christmas carol "Deck the Halls." Indeed, mouth music itself is found around the world and can fulfill many different functions. The purpose of this chapter is to provide a context in which to understand puirt-a-beul. To start, I briefly introduce a number of "vocabelizing" traditions (Chambers 1980) from around the world organized according to their function. As an ethnomusicologist, I am interested in understanding how puirt-a-beul might fit into a broader global phenomenon of mouth music and in comparing, contrasting and relating puirt-a-beul with other forms of vocabelizing. After considering selected international forms of mouth music, I narrow my focus to Celtic mouth music, discussing different types such as jigging (also known as "diddling," "lilting" and other terms) and *canntaireachd*. Although puirt-a-beul are sometimes equated with other types of Celtic mouth music, they are more often understood as something unique. Having an awareness of the features of different types of Celtic mouth music will clarify what features make puirt-a-beul distinct, but also how puirt-a-beul fit within a larger conception of Celtic vocal music.

I should add that the global traditions I discuss are not necessarily known as "mouth music" within their home communities. However, because they are song forms connected to instrumental traditions through vocables, and because they have parallel functions, I find them interesting to compare to puirt-a-beul and other types of Celtic mouth music. I should also add that mouth music and vocables may have other functions than those listed below. For example, the Navajo use vocables in spiritual contexts (Frisbie 1980). However, I have restricted the list to mouth music and vocable traditions that share functions associated with Celtic mouth music. I also realize that it is somewhat artificial to divide mouth music traditions according to function because any one of them may perform multiple functions, often simultaneously. For example, syllables that function as a kind of "vocal notation" are almost always implicated in teaching and transmission: a music teacher can use the vocal syllables to teach a piece of music or a particular style to a student. However, breaking the functions into discrete topics of discussion enables clearer description and analysis.

Vocal "Notation"

Vocables are sometimes used to symbolize particular pitches in both oral and written musical representations. In the heading above, I have placed "notation" in quotation marks because the idea of "vocal notation" is something of an oxymoron; "notation" generally refers to something written. However many music cultures have developed ways of representing music orally rather than, or in addition to, with written notation. In Western European music, for example, we use solfa syllables to represent the notes of the scale, a system perhaps made most famous by the *Sound of Music* song "Do-Re-Mi." Part of my undergraduate training in music involved sight singing, which we did with solfa syllables. To this day, when I'm trying to "hear" a new piece of written music, I will use solfa. Oral solfa ultimately became a means of written notation as well. Before it became relatively easy and inexpensive to print staff notation, and in order to make music accessible for those not literate in music notation, for example, solfa syllables were regularly published together with rhythm symbols in a system called "Curwen notation" (see Fig. 1).

Many other music cultures have their own solfa systems. Indian ragas, which are something like complex musical scales, can be represented with syllables much like Western solfa, called *sargam*. Each note of the scale or *raga* has its own syllable. These syllables can be used in a teaching or learning situation and are both sung and used as part of Indian written musical notation. For example, in South Indian classical music performances, a solo vocalist may improvise using sargam syllables. This form of improvisation is particularly impressive because the singer does not simply sing an improvised selection of vocables (as in scat singing), but vocables that are tied to the pitches being sung. Therefore, the singer needs to be able not only to sing appropriate

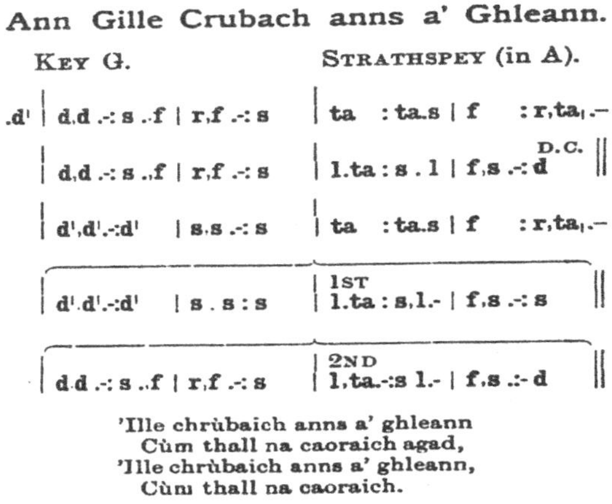

Ann Gille Crubach anns a' Ghleann.

Key G.   Strathspey (in A).

.d' | d,d .-: s ..f | r,f .-: s | ta   : ta.s | f   : r,ta,.–

| d,d .-: s ..f | r,f .-: s | l.ta : s . l | f,s .-: d D.C. ||

| d',d'.-:d' | s.s .-: s | ta   : ta.s | f   : r,ta,.–

| d'.d'.-:d' | s . s : s | 1st
                              | l.ta : s,l.- | f.s .-: s ||

.| d d .-: s ..f | r,f .-: s | 2nd
                              | l,ta.-:s l.- | f.s .:- d ||

'Ille chrùbaich anns a' ghleann
Cùm thall na caoraich agad,
'Ille chrùbaich anns a' ghleann,
Cùm thall na caoraich.

Fig. 1. Example of Curwen Notation. From Puirt-a-Beul *by K. N. MacDonald (1931 [1901]: 17). This tune is known as "Miss Drummond of Perth." The port-a-beul is known as "Calum Crùbach" (see Chapter 4 for further discussion of this port, and Appendix A for multiple sets of lyrics).*

notes, but to name them while performing (see Viswanathan and Allen 2004: 43, 66; Kassebaum 2000: 98-99). A similar system exists in Korea: *kuŭm* is a system of "mouth notes" and it is the oldest system of notation in Korean music (Um 2002: 817). In the realm of Celtic music, a highly developed oral notation system known as canntaireachd developed around piping, and it is discussed further below.

Teaching and Learning

Most solfa systems are used for pedagogical reasons. Teachers use them to help students grasp some musical aspect such as melody, but it could also extend to rhythm, emphasis, ornamentation or something else. Japanese *syôga* is similar to the solfa systems described above:

> A special means of teaching and learning instrumental melodies, *syôga* uses syllables (often onomatopoeic) that have no lexical meaning. Unlike Western solmization [solfege], these syllables do not necessarily correspond to absolute or relative pitches. Furthermore, each genre and instrument

has its own system of *syôga*. *Syôga* is considered the first and vital step in learning any traditional instrument, and one or more *syôga* transmit information about tone color, melodic ornamentation, patterned movement, and playing techniques. As a means of musical communication, *syôga* bridges the oral and literate worlds: it exists in both sung and written forms. In addition, it functions as a means of communication—a kind of invisible score—when two or more musicians perform together. By knowing the *syôga* of each instrumental part as well as that of his or her own instrument, a musician can use *syôga* as a frame of reference, either out loud when rehearsing or silently when performing. (Haruko and Mihoko 2002: 573)

Thus syôga conveys information not just about melody but also about tone colour, also known as "timbre." In most music cultures, if not all, good musicians do not simply play notes in a particular rhythm; rather, they can generally vary the sound quality of the notes. As a flute player, I can get a rich, brassy tone quality or I can aim for a purer, gentler tone. It is worth noting that the Western written musical system is ill-equipped to notate tone quality, and so it is of particular interest that some vocal notation systems are designed to do just that.

Although solfa or equivalent syllables are used in some cultures to represent particular scalar pitches in the melodic realm of music, vocables can also be used as a means of representing particular drum strokes in the rhythmic realm. Ethnomusicologist David Locke has written about the use of vocables for the teaching and learning of Dagomba drumming in northern Ghana. He describes his teacher and research colleague's use of vocables:

Vocables are a way to "play the drum with your mouth." The sounds have no lexical meaning in the Dagbani language, but to call them "nonsense syllables" would be misleading since they precisely symbolize the drumming music. Vocables are a verbal notation system that captures the pitch, timbre, melody, rhythm, dynamics, and articulation of notes in a drum phrase.... When he teaches a new drum phrase, Alhaji [Abubakari Lunna] usually has students begin with vocables. After they learn to chant the drumming phrase, he instructs, "Now make the exact same sound on the drum." Although Alhaji emphasizes that drumming is based in the Dagbani language, he does not start by teaching the Dagbani texts that go with the drum phrases. He explains that students should first know how to make the sound of the phrase in vocables and on the drum. Only then have they earned the right to gain advanced knowledge does [*sic*] Alhaji feel comfortable to reveal the inner meaning. (Locke 2007)

In Northern India, all musicians (not just drummers) learn and communicate different categories of rhythm and their variations through the use of drum syllables (Ruckert 2004: 44). Tabla drum rhythms can be represented vocally with *bols*. Each bol is meant to represent a particular type of drumstroke, but they can also be combined to create a kind of musical grammar. In an online music lesson, tabla master Ashwin Batish writes:

The bols can be compared to your learning the alphabets (the bols [themselves]), forming from these words (bol combinations of 2, 3, 4 beats etc.), then with these words making sentences (tukadas, mukhadas, tihais, etc.), weaving these into paragraphs and stories (Kaidas, Kaida prakars, gats, parans, etc).... The vocalization of the tabla bols is very important. Your learning will be stunted if you don't master this process. (Batish 2003)

As with the Ghanaian drum tradition, drummers recite bols as they practise in order to help them learn patterns and develop techniques. Cape Breton Gaelic singer Mary Jane Lamond found the parallels between Gaelic mouth music and Indian bols so compelling that she incorporated them into a recording of "Mo Ghille Mòr Foghain'each," a port-a-beul on her album *Làn Dùil* (1999).

Mnemonics

One of the reasons that teachers use vocables to teach music, whether instrumental or vocal, is that they can then be used as a memory aid, helping musicians to recall a composition as a whole or specific features of a composition more specifically. Throughout East Asia

> mnemonics [vocables] are used for both melodic and percussion instruments. Some percussion mnemonics are for ensembles and designate not only rhythms but specific instruments or combinations of instruments. Chinese percussion notation developed into a type of mnemonics called *luogujing* that is used to denote specific instrumental ensembles and overall rhythm patterns. Using onomatopoeic syllables for each instrument, and composite syllables for a combination of instruments, it is capable of recording playing techniques, instrumentation, and the contour of a melody. (Lau 2002: 55)

Mnemonics are memory aids that help a person to remember otherwise difficult-to-recall information. Mnemonics are often used in Anglo-American classrooms to help students remember particular information, often technical in nature, or having a particular structure. For example, readers may have used a mnemonic phrase in science class to recall biology's taxonomy of living things (Domain, Kingdom, Phylum, Class, Order, Family, Genus, Species). One example is "Did King Phillip Cry Out, 'For Goodness' Sake'"? Music students often learn a phrase such as "Father Charles Goes Down And Ends Battle" using the first letter of each word to remember the order in which sharps are notated in a key signature (F# - C# - G# - D# - A# - E# - B#). It can be difficult to remember the order of sharps because the order can seem quite arbitrary to a learner—all the pitches may seem equally viable as the "first" sharp to notate. The mnemonic encodes the order of the pitches in an easily memorable phrase. As I discuss in Chapter 6, puirt-a-beul are also sometimes used to help a musician to remember a tune.

Instrumental Substitute

Just as puirt-a-beul are often defined as vocal tunes performed in the absence of instruments, the voice is used to substitute for an instrument in a number of other cultures too. In Korea, "a singer may actually perform as a musical instrument in an ensemble; indeed, in a technique known as susŏng karak, the voice leads the melody for the instrumental accompaniment" (Um 2002: 817). In Tibet, "the instrumental line [of *nangma*, or 'Western songs'] could also be performed vocally if there were not instruments available, at least for the fast part of the Western songs" (Samuel 1976: 410).[1]

Perhaps the most well-known Western form of mouth music in which the voice replaces an instrument is scat singing in jazz, although it is important to recognize that scat singing is not necessarily simple and, like puirt-a-beul, has had many meanings and has played many roles (Edwards 2002). Scat singing is jazz improvisation using vocables and was made famous by Louis Armstrong in the 1920s and 1930s. Armstrong's recording of "Heebie Jeebies" brought scat singing into the mainstream. It is particularly interesting to note that it is a song about a dance, so that Armstrong's scat singing becomes a kind of vocal dance music, just like puirt-a-beul.

Scat singing pre-existed Louis Armstrong. Its origins are uncertain, although many theories have been suggested, as is true also of puirt-a-beul (I discuss the origins of puirt-a-beul in the next chapter). Some suggest that scat singing began with the vocal representation of drum strokes in West Africa (OnMusic Dictionary 2013). Others argue that it began when a singer forgot the words (Edwards 2002: 624). Still others say that because New Orleans jazz musicians were taught that they should be able to sing something before playing it, they were able to move easily between instrument and voice (see Berliner 2009: 181). Whatever the original catalyst for scat singing's existence, it became popular and continues to be practised today.

An interesting variation of scat singing was the development in jazz of vocalese, a word that combines the root "vocal" with the suffix "ese," which denotes a language. Unlike scat singing, which is based on vocables, vocalese uses real words set to improvised instrumental solos (see Berliner 2009: 99-101). This is a particularly interesting parallel to puirt-a-beul since, as we shall see, puirt-a-beul consist primarily of words, despite their reputation for being made of vocables.

Onomatopoeia

Because vocables are not words, they can be used to represent other non-lexical sounds. In Navajo culture, for example, some vocables are meant to represent "the sounds, calls, cries, and barks of deities, animals, and birds" (Frisbie 1980: 356). A fascinating and humorous Appalachian tradition, known as "eephing," uses the voice to imitate farm animals. This "hiccupping rhythmic wheeze" managed to make it into the American musical mainstream as part of a few novelty hits, the most famous of which is probably "Little Eefin' Annie" (1963) by Joe Perkins and featuring the eephing talents of Jimmie Riddle. Jimmie Riddle's eephing was later featured on CBS's television program, *Hee Haw* (Sharpe 2006).

Part of the reason that we can call vocables "mouth music" is that they are often not just designed to substitute for an instrumental part, but can actually sound like an instrument—or at least they're supposed to. In other words, it's not the equivalent of using a clarinet to play a saxophone part. Instead, it is like substituting the clarinet part with a vocal imitation of the clarinet. We have already seen this in the use of vocables to represent drum strokes in African and Indian traditions. But the voice can do more than imitate drums:

> [In Korea,] various other instruments can be imitated. For example, in *p'ansori* the singer's ornaments and vibrato recall stringed instruments such as the *kayagum* (a long twelve-stringed zither) and the *ajaeng* (a seven-stringed zither), and wind instruments such as the *p'iri* (a double-reed pipe) and the *taegŭm* (a large transverse bamboo flute). The voice can even imitate percussion instruments: thus

certain sung syllables resemble the rhythmic patterns of the *kkwaenggwari* (a small gong) and the *changgu* or *changgo* (and hourglass drum), played in traditional Korean farmers' bands. (Um 2002: 817)

Likewise, puirt-a-beul are sometimes said to imitate piping or fiddling, particularly their ornamentation, leading to the controversial assertion that fiddlers and pipers playing in Scottish Gaelic–based styles (as opposed to Lowland, Shetland or Orkney styles) must know puirt-a-beul and Gaelic in order to play their instruments authentically, a debate I discuss in Chapter 7.

Celtic Mouth Music

Having seen a variety of vocable-based mouth musics from around the world and their various functions, we now turn our attention to forms of Celtic mouth music. Despite the great variety of vocabelizing forms to be found globally, a Google search for "mouth music" almost exclusively returns sites referring to the Scottish Gaelic tradition of puirt-a-beul. And yet there is more than just puirt-a-beul in traditional Celtic mouth music. Christine Chambers, in her dissertation about vocables in Scottish traditional music (1980), identifies the following types of "vocabelizing":

- plain diddling ("singing with a selection of vocables which do not represent any specific musical instrument or genre");
- instrumental diddling ("representing in vocables a tune as it would be played on an instrument other than the bagpipe");
- cantering ("singing with a selection of vocables, some of which have drifted in from individual and formal canntaireachd, representative, either by imitation or association, of highland bagpipe music");
- individual canntaireachd ("a method of representing *ceòl mòr* and *ceòl beag* [two broad types of pipe music] in vocables ... used by traditional pipers and by non-pipers who are exposed to or influenced by piping tradition");

- formal canntaireachd ("the systematic representation of *ceòl mòr* in written vocable notation, i.e., in vocables with consistent assigned or associative meaning"); and
- vocable refrains ("arrangements of pre-composed vocables appearing regularly between the lines or verses of the narrative body of a song"). (Chambers 1980: 17-36)

Despite the multiple types of vocabelizing identified, this list does not include puirt-a-beul, which Chambers excludes because of the inconsistency with which vocables appear within them (more about this soon). She also does not include any vocable traditions from outside Scotland, such as Irish *port-a-béil* or lilting. Clearly, there are many types of mouth music within Celtic traditions. The fact that there are so many types of mouth music within Scottish and broader Celtic traditions suggests their importance.

This great variety of vocabelizing and mouth music has led to much confusion, especially among those who have only a passing familiarity with Celtic traditional musics. It is important to recognize that different people, including singers, musicians and Gaelic speakers, have varying degrees of knowledge about these traditions, which will affect the ways they define them and how much detail they are able to provide about them. So, a piper who has learned to play through canntaireachd will have a different understanding of it from a non-piper. Pipe Major John Stewart explains:

> A lot of these diddlers [...] may not be pipers themselves, but they're hearing ... the same sort of note-syllables, as it were, and they're putting them into their own form of diddling ... but [it's] certainly not canntaireachd ... there's no name for it really, it's just something that you grow up with in piping. (Qtd. in Chambers 1980: 22)

The non-piper may well believe that she or he is performing canntaireachd, but it would not be recognized as such by a piper familiar with the tradition.

A related problem is that different people use different terms to refer to the same thing (or use the same term to refer to different things). For example, Father John Angus Rankin, a promoter of Cape Breton musical and dance traditions, notes:

> A lot of the old tunes had Gaelic words to them, and quite a few of the stepdancers learned to dance by the canntaireachd—the old people singing the words of the tune. Then, when they'd get up on that stage, the fiddlers would play those old tunes the way they had heard the Gaelic of them. So you'll hear the old folks saying, "God, that fellow's got a lot of Gaelic in his music!" Of course, when they were growing up, a lot of the dancers had violin players to dance to, but somebody in the house might also be good at "tuning" (i.e., jigging tunes) and you could learn to dance to that as well. (Qtd. in MacGillivray 1988: 152)

Father Rankin starts by describing what sounds like puirt-a-beul, but then calls it canntaireachd, although references to canntaireachd in Cape Breton are rare, and I have never otherwise heard it referring to anything but the piping tradition, nor have I ever heard it described as having words rather than vocables. He also uses the term "tuning" where most other Cape Breton fiddlers would use the term "jigging"; Scots would use "diddling"; and Irish would use "lilting." Given the many terms used and sometimes confused when discussing Celtic mouth music, I would like to discuss a number of traditions that are often mistaken for puirt-a-beul in order to clarify what I mean by puirt-a-beul throughout the remainder of this book.

Jigging, Diddling and Lilting

"Jigging" is the improvisation of vocables to represent an instrumental tune. It is extremely common in the musics of Ireland (where it is most often known as "lilting"); Scotland (where it is called "diddling"); and Cape Breton. The vocables are usually believed to be random and made up on the spot, although Christine Chambers has shown that actually only a very restricted number of vocables are acceptable, at least in the Scottish diddling tradition (Chambers 1980: 89-149; Vallely suggests the same with respect to lilting [1999]). In a study of thousands of vocables used in various forms of Scottish traditional vocabelizing, Chambers tracked how often particular consonants and vowels were used, how they were combined into vocables and how the vocables were combined into vocable "texts." She discovered the following tendencies: 1) only a limited number of "formulae" for combining consonants and vocables is acceptable; 2) diddling uses some vocables not used in other Celtic mouth musics (such as canntaireachd); 3) where specific vocables are common to both diddling and other mouth musics, some tend to dominate in one or the other; and 4) some vocables are restricted for use in either musically stressed or unstressed positions. For example, a significant number of vocables in diddling start with "d" whereas "h" is more common in canntaireachd. Chambers found seven consonants that are peculiar to canntaireachd and unheard in diddling. Overall, she found that diddlers are more restricted in the vocables they use compared to singers of canntaireachd. The vocable "rules" help to differentiate the sounds of diddling from the sounds of canntaireachd and other forms of Celtic mouth music.

Jigging and its Irish and Scottish counterparts are widespread partly because of their great flexibility. They are used in many different contexts for a variety of purposes. Many of these purposes are shared with those of puirt-a-beul, which helps to further explain why puirt-a-beul are so often confused with jigging. In order to make these connections, and in order to demonstrate the value of jigging (despite the sometimes negative attitudes attached to it), I spend a little time here describing some of the main uses of jigging.

Jigging in Teaching and Transmission

Perhaps one of the most common and important uses of jigging is teaching. In Virginia Garrison's study of how Cape Breton fiddlers learn their instruments, she notes that "the mother's influence as a singer of Gaelic songs and by 'jigging' fiddle tunes" was one of the factors that apparently helped motivate fiddlers to learn to play as young children (Garrison 1985: 180). She also found that 80 per cent of the twenty-three fiddlers she interviewed were ear-players (in other words, they did not read music), and therefore learned their playing skills and repertoire by observing and listening to other fiddlers, but also by "listening to relatives and non-relatives sing Gaelic songs, or sing nonsense syllables in vocal renditions of fiddle tunes, a practice known in Cape Breton as 'jigging,' and making 'mouth music'" (Garrison 1985: 185).

The late, great Cape Breton fiddler Angus Chisholm learned all his tunes by ear in the beginning and "compiled a modest repertoire of tunes by mastering the ones which his sisters used to 'jig' for him" (MacGillivray 1981: 20). Ken Perlman tells us that Prince Edward Island fiddlers also used jigging in this way: "Many fiddlers report that they learned their first tunes by listening to the jigging of family members" (1996: 13). Christine Chambers provides examples from Ireland and Scotland:

> I'd run over a part on the practice chanter, and then he'd say, "You're not doing that right, it should be: [fragment of vocabelising] ... it was just a shortcut for playing the tune as it should be played. (Piper Ruarí Somers qtd. in Chambers 1980: 39)

> The only way you can really teach style ... if they don't get it off the fiddle, you can get 'em to sing it with you. Then they'll put it onto the fiddle. (Fiddler Tom Anderson qtd. in Chambers 1980: 39)

Vocabelizing is useful in teaching contexts for several reasons. By using particular vocables, the teacher can indicate whether the music ought to be particularly emphasized or de-emphasized (for example, using a more explosive consonant, such as "p," to emphasize part of the music, or using a more liquid consonant, such as "l," to de-emphasize part of the music). The teacher can also use the same string of vocables to clarify repeated phrases or cadences (cadences are harmonic formulae that mark the ends of phrases) in the music, thus clarifying the overall structure of the piece, particularly in cases where there is considerable repetition and variation within a section of music. The teacher can also use vocables to illustrate how to ornament a melody. Cape

Bretoner Sandy MacInnis explains how he learned to ornament fiddle tunes: "Ever since I started playing I've done exercises with bowing. At home, they always talked about bowing and cuts. My mother would jig 'Devil in the Kitchen' with all the cuts, and I tried to get it that way" (qtd. in MacGillivray 1981: 125).

Chambers notes that one of the most helpful aspects of vocabelizing is that it frees the teacher's hands to gesture:

> The importance of the body gestures of the teacher should not be under-emphasised as they can be of great importance not only in amplifying (or as is the case with pibroch, clarifying) phrasing and accents in the music, they may also signal changes in the teacher's attitude, marking approval or displeasure, so that a pupil who is not sensitive enough to receive these subtle signals may not reap the full benefit of his teacher's presence. (Chambers 1980: 50)

The instrumentalist's hands are free and, in the case of a wind instrument such as the bagpipes, the mouth becomes visible, enabling the musician to use facial expressions, hand gestures and arm movements to suggest volume, phrasing, expression, articulation or other musical elements. The music literally becomes embodied so that the listener does not simply hear the music but sees it and feels it as well.[2]

Jigging is not restricted to teachers and students. It is also used among established musicians to "discuss" music:

> The vocables [can] be used as a vehicle to convey one musician's concept of a tune to another musician. Instead of using words, or lexical communication, they use music conveyed in vocables for direct musical communication. Instead of trying to describe a non-verbal medium verbally, musicians "speak" about music *in* music, thus dispensing with the cumbersome intermediary of words. (Chambers 1980: 51)

In the words of one popular proverb that has been attributed to various people, "Writing [or talking] about music is like dancing about architecture." While discussing music may not be very efficient, jigging can be, for musical information is still conveyed through music rather than through words.

Jigging provides a means of swapping tunes at a moment when musicians might not have access to their instruments:

> And he'd call me aside and say, "I want you to hear this new tune, Jesus, it's a great tune, ye must learn it." And he'd be lilting it. And I'd lilt it back to him. (Ruarí Somers qtd. in Chambers 1980: 51)

> Visitors would just come around—uninvited but always welcome. You'd pick up tunes by ear; the older people had them and would jig them in Gaelic. (Joe MacLean qtd. in MacGillivray 1981: 136)

Jigging also provides a means for non-instrumentalists to transmit tunes. Many older Cape Breton fiddlers have talked about how they learned their repertoire from the jigging of non-fiddling family members:

> I was always hearing my sister, Maybelle, playing Scotch music on the piano, and that had a definite influence on me. She showed me tunes, and so did my father who could "jig" them correctly. (Cameron Chisholm qtd. in MacGillivray 1981: 96)

> [Our father] could jig any tune and correct me in any way, though he himself couldn't play the violin. (Margaret [Chisholm] MacDonald, Cameron Chisholm's brother, qtd. in MacGillivray 1981: 114)

> Encouraged by his mother, who could "jig" tunes, Hughie [Angus Jobes] soon acquired the skills necessary to become a good dance player. (MacGillivray 1981: 108)

Perlman also documents this tendency in Prince Edward Island:

> Making music in old island *districts* (communities) was not just the province of the fiddler. Most residents knew at least the more common tunes by heart, and a fair percentage

excelled at an activity known as *tuning* or *jigging*—singing dance tunes with full rhythmic nuance using abstract vocables or nonsense lyrics. In fact, many Islanders jigged in full voice as they went about their daily chores. (Perlman 1996: 13)

Thus anyone in the community could participate in musicmaking. This was especially important for women who, until relatively recently, tended not to be instrumentalists. I discuss the link between puirt-a-beul and women further below.

Jigging to Remember Tunes

Just as is the case with other forms of mouth music found around the world, jigging functions as a valuable mnemonic tool. Although literate musicians can use staff notation to remember tunes (and many traditional Celtic musicians today are musically literate and regularly make use of both published and unpublished tune sources), many musicians feel that the tradition is best served if written notation is used as sparingly as possible. Although staff notation is reasonably well equipped to represent the basic melody and rhythm of a tune, it is not generally adequate to represent subtle variations in rhythm and timing, ornamentation, bowing or other stylistic and musical features, as discussed earlier. Jigging—and puirt-a-beul even more so (as I will discuss later)—provides an oral/aural means of remembering a tune without having to refer to a printed page. Musicians can also use jigging to jog another musician's memory. In asking a musician if he or she knows a particular tune, one could jig a part of it to demonstrate how the tune "goes" or sounds. As Cape Breton step dancer Angus Archie Gillis explains, he used jigging to tell a musician what tunes he wanted: "And the fiddler was 'Little' Jack MacDonald. I jigged my tunes for him—'Calum Crùbach' and 'Lord MacDonald' for a fast figure—and he played them" (qtd. in MacGillivray 1988: 59).

Jigging is also used as a means of practising tunes, perhaps in a context where playing a tune is not possible. Cape Breton fiddler Brenda Stubbert remembers that she "used to sit in school and jig tunes instead of listening to the teacher" (qtd. in MacGillivray 1981: 164). Buddy MacMaster recalls: "I used to 'jig' tunes every morning in bed and would pretend I was tuning the violin for 'Lord MacDonald's Reel'" (qtd. in MacGillivray 1981: 150). Dan MacKinnon didn't have an actual instrument when he first began showing an interest in fiddling. Instead, "his fiddling career began in rough fashion on an old shingle strung with horse hair; he would 'jig' tunes out behind the barn while pretending to play" (MacGillivray 1981: 52).

Jigging, Dancing and Children

Another important aspect of jigging has been its association with dancing, although this may be more true of the past than of the present. Jigging could be used to accompany a dancer in the absence of any available instrumental accompaniment. This was especially common in relatively informal contexts. For example, Gussie MacLellan of Cape Breton remembers: "If I went into a neighbour's house [at an early age] and anyone wanted to see me dance, they'd jig a tune and I'd give them a little step" (qtd. in MacGillivray 1988: 116).

It did come to pass occasionally, however, that a need arose for dance music in a more formal context where no instrumentalist was available. In a 1953 interview, Scottish folklorist Hamish Henderson interviewed Robin Hutchison, an ex-farm servant and diddler:

> Henderson: Did ye ever see the tinkers dancin' when they were haein' a spree, man?
>
> Hutchison: Oh, aye, aye.
>
> Henderson: And what did they use for music?
>
> Hutchison: Oh well, they used bagpipes, but if they had no bagpipes, they used ti, they gied the mouth music.
>
> Henderson: Oh aye? And how did it go?
>
> Hutchison: Oh, it went [and sings]. (Qtd. in Chambers 1980: 71)

In other cases, instruments were available but the instrumentalists needed a break, which was provided by jigging:

> My grandmother was one of these people who sang when there was a shortage of fiddlers ... and it happened that there were dances and the fiddler would be tired, or there was fiddlers wanting a rest, and they would get up 'n sing this. Oh, there were various people, Jean Pole, another old fiddler, she did the same thing. She played the fiddle and she also sang the tunes. (Tom Anderson qtd. in Chambers 1980: 72)

In another instance, the melodeon breaks down, leaving a fiddler on his own to provide dance music. Melodeons (as well as accordions) became popular dance instruments in Scotland during the 20th century because they could be heard in large halls over the sound of many feet. Two "jiggers" help the grateful fiddler out:

> Oh aye ... the melodeon went, ah, we struck up, Jimmy Cameron and I ... him and I used ti diddle quite a lot in the both—And we were ... at this open air dance, and, oh, somehow or other the melodeon went phut, just finished with a sheeze, so, poor fiddler, we, we went up and started diddling along with the fiddler. He was quite glad o' the help, really, because 't was hard work ... oh, he enjoyed it ... he asked us if we could keep goin' so's he could get another melodeon. (Willie Fraser qtd. in Chambers 1980: 72)

Ethnomusicologist Katherine Campbell cites a 1904 Scots song by John Christie that refers to diddling being used to accompany dancing while the fiddler takes a turn on the floor:

> But Backies noo laid doun his fiddle,
> An' grup't a pairtner by the middle,
> An' cried on "Trunk" tae come an' diddle,
> An' he wad dance at Drachlaw. (Campbell 2007: 89)

Many, many Cape Breton step dancers learned to step dance to the accompaniment of jigging. Maryann Currie Gouthro explains: "I'd sit down and start to jig for [my daughter] and she'd get on the floor" (qtd. in MacGillivray 1988: 71). Kay MacPherson Handrahan recalls, "My mother used to jig tunes and we'd dance" (qtd. in MacGillivray 1988: 78). And Natalie MacMaster's mother, Minnie Beaton MacMaster, used the same method to teach her daughter to dance: "I taught Natalie and she knows quite a few steps. I jigged the tunes for her and now she does it herself" (qtd. in MacGillivray 1988: 123). Sadie MacMullin MacNeil describes how she learned to dance and jig tunes from her father:

> [My father] would get my sister Kay and I on the floor, and he always told us to keep the tune in our minds: "Remember the tune!" He'd whistle or jig a strathspey and we'd dance…. After my father showed me my first few steps, well, then I got out on my own…. I knew the tunes in my head and I could jig them. (Qtd. in MacGillivray 1988: 128-29)

Although Sadie's father jigged tunes for her and her sister, the other stories all refer to women jigging tunes for their children. Indeed, jigging and puirt-a-beul tend to be associated with women more often than men, probably because women jigged tunes so often for their children. There is also a long history of parents vocabelizing while "dandling" a child on their knees. Scottish Gaelic singer Christine Primrose talked to me about the use of puirt-a-beul with children:

> [Puirt-a-beul] started, or developed, in the home, a lot of them, making up wee ditty songs, you know … especially when they have children on their knee. I know that they're called dandling songs, officially, but I remember my Granny, she'd have wee kids on her knee and she'd be singing to them. Maybe a verse or two of [sings a verse of the port-a-beul, "M'eudail air mo shùilean donna"], things like that. That's the kind of song that I always remember being associated with children, being on their knee and dandled on their knee. (Interview, July 12 and 13, 1998)

Many lullabies include vocables just as jigging does; vocables are not only used to reproduce upbeat instrumental tunes.

The association between jigging and women may also be the result of the tendency, until recently, for men to be fiddlers and pipers, while women, if they played any instrument at all, played piano accompaniment. Jigging would have provided a means for women to participate in the fiddling repertoire without actually playing a fiddle. Even if some women did not play the fiddle, they could clearly be very knowledgeable about fiddle tunes, having heard them frequently in their homes or as accompanists.

Having been exposed to jigging and dancing at home, children themselves learned to jig:

> Christine Chambers: When do you think you learned to diddle?
>
> Betsy Brown: Oh, my father could diddle fine.
>
> Chambers: Did he? And you just heard him—
>
> Brown: Oh yes, just heard him, I didnae know I could do it as well. (Qtd. in Chambers 1980: 75)

> Willie Fraser: I'd been hearing diddling all the time, you see.
>
> Chambers: From your parents, and just the people about—
>
> Fraser: Aye, well, from the folk about, oh, 't was not only my parents that diddled, I mean the folk round about all diddled. (Qtd. in Chambers 1980: 75)

Chambers notes that diddling was an important tool in a child's musical development since they could vocabelize long before being physically big or dexterous enough to handle an actual instrument, and they could learn a tune without having to worry about remembering lyrics as well (Chambers 1980: 76).

Having learned to jig and dance, children were then able to entertain themselves. Children could jig for each other, instead of relying on adults, as the following examples from Prince Edward Island and Cape Breton indicate:

> School children in many communities would spend their lunch recess jigging tunes and step-dancing to jigged accompaniment; they would also make a game out of imitating the jigging styles of community adults. What's more, when no instruments were available, *tuners* [people who

jigged tunes] were sometimes called upon to provide music for square dancing. (Perlman 1996: 13)

When we were kids going to school, every day at recess we'd go out to an old building that they had there and we'd dance—every time there was a break. Someone would be humming a tune and someone prompting the sets. (Peggy MacDonald Beaton qtd. in MacGillivray 1988: 39)

And when our father and mother would go away to North Sydney or Sydney selling stuff from off the farm, we'd be jigging for one another and we'd be dancing. (Christena Campbell MacKinnon qtd. in MacGillivray 1988: 41)

In this brief section, I have illustrated a few of the most important ways in which jigging is used: for teaching, discussing or transmitting tunes, remembering tunes and accompanying dancing, whether for adults or children. As we shall see, jigging shares all of these contexts with puirt-a-beul, which is part of the reason why they are often confused (see my discussion of puirt-a-beul, below, for more on this issue). Jigging, diddling and lilting are pervasive in Celtic music.

Canntaireachd

I now turn to "canntaireachd" (pronounced "COUNT-er-ukhk") which, like jigging, is the vocal rendition of instrumental tunes through the use of vocables—in this case, pipe tunes in particular.[3] However, unlike jigging, canntaireachd uses a formal system of vocables somewhat like the solfa systems discussed earlier:

> "*Canntaireachd*" (literally "chanting" or "singing") refers broadly to all forms of vocabelising connected to or associated with the bagpipes. Within the self-contained world of piping in Scotland the term *canntaireachd* is used by pipers of differing backgrounds to denote different kinds of pipe-oriented vocabelising. Most commonly it refers to the systematic and formal solmization system found in books and manuscripts of pibroch and to pipers' somewhat less

systematic singing of that genre. Pipers divide on the question of whether their singing of *ceòl beag* ("small music,"
i.e. jigs, reels, marches, strathspeys, airs, etc.) is or is not
canntaireachd. (Chambers 1980: 11)

By "formal system," I mean that each canntaireachd vocable
or sound has a specific meaning, such as a particular pitch or grace
note. This does not seem to be true of the vocables in other types
of mouth music. However, it is important also to note that there
are several historical canntaireachd systems, and what seems to be
more important today is that the canntaireachd employed by any
given piper be *internally* consistent, but not necessarily consistent
from one piper to another (Fatone 2002: 114-15).

Pibroch (*piobaireachd* in Gaelic), known also as ceòl mòr or
"big music," is the classical music of the Highland bagpipes. It
consists of a theme and variations played in free time. The variations become increasingly technically difficult. The best pipers
include subtle variations in note lengths and will perform in a
manner that highlights the pibroch's structure. This is difficult
to do on the bagpipes. Unlike other wind instruments, the piper
cannot use the mouth, lips and tongue to give a particular attack
to a note. There is also no dynamic variation possible on the pipes,
and the piper therefore uses rhythm and ornamentation to give
expression to the music.

Because of pibroch's rhythmic flexibility and the complexity of pipe ornaments, pipe music is difficult to notate using
Western staff notation. Canntaireachd provides both a written
and oral means of notating it, although it is important to note
that canntaireachd vocables are generally considered ineffective at
conveying phrasing or, more fundamentally, note durations and
rhythm, although some would argue otherwise (see, for example,
K. N. MacDonald 1931 [1901]: 50-51; A. A. MacDonald 1995: 70;
Donaldson 2000: 452).

Each note of the bagpipe scale is assigned a vowel and, in the
case of the lowest notes, a nasal stop as well (the airflow through
the mouth is "stopped" by a nasal consonant such as "m" or "n,"
sounds that are produced by directing air through the nose). The

vowels (pitches) are combined with different preceding consonants to indicate grace notes. (See Figs. 2 and 3.)

These vocables are combined into "words" to represent the complex chains of grace notes that tend to occur in later variations within pibroch. But despite how formalized and structured this system may seem, the reality is that pipers don't really have to remember which vowel represents which note since the intended pitch can be heard when sung. Pipers generally insist that canntaireachd must be heard rather than read. Many pipers also tend to finger a practice chanter while singing canntaireachd, demonstrating what ornaments are intended regardless of the vocables actually used. Canntaireachd is therefore rarely performed strictly "correctly," although vocable precision is obviously necessary for printed tune collections (Chambers 1980: 28).

When canntaireachd is used today, it is almost always either in the context of teaching or as a mnemonic aid, although it is difficult to determine how much this has been historically true (Fatone 2002: 98). Canntaireachd is particularly valuable in teaching contexts because its performance can convey musical elements difficult for a student to perceive in the actual playing of the pipes. In singing canntaireachd, a teacher can emphasize particular notes dynamically, through physical gesture (since the

Fig. 2. Canntaireachd vowels and pitch equivalents

Fig. 3. Canntaireachd "hin" and "tro," illustrating how consonants dictate grace notes while vowels indicate pitch.

singer's hands are not necessarily occupied with an instrument), or by the choice of vocable. As with jigging, a singer can convey emphasis through the use of "harder" consonants (e.g., "p" or "t") and de-emphasis through the use of "softer" consonants (such as "l" or "m"). Alternatively, musical stress and unstress can be conveyed by the choice of vowel. It can be difficult to perceive note emphasis in piping due to the pipes' inability to perform dynamic contrasts. The vocal emphasis in canntaireachd is generally translated onto the pipes as a lengthened note. Regularly recurring vocable "phrases" also help to clarify musical structure.

There are numerous printed canntaireachd collections, demonstrating that canntaireachd can be used as a written as well as oral notation system. Publishers seem to have been largely motivated either to preserve pipe tunes or to provide a mnemonic for them. However, because of the written form's limited ability to convey rhythm, most pipers insist that it must be learned from oral sources.

In many ways, canntaireachd is quite similar to both jigging and puirt-a-beul. Jigging and canntaireachd both use vocables while puirt-a-beul is often assumed to do so. At the very least, puirt-a-beul often seems nonsensical even when the lyrics do consist of actual words. All three involve the vocal representation of instrumental tunes. And all are used in teaching contexts and as mnemonic devices.

However, there are some substantial differences. Canntaireachd is a formalized system, whereas jigging and puirt-a-beul are not. It has a "respectable" history given that it is associated with the most reputable piping families and formal piping institutions. Puirt-a-beul and jigging have no such institutional ties or family connections. In fact, they tend more often to be associated with average people and are often performed by non-musicians (or at least non-instrumentalists). Where canntaireachd is most often associated with ceòl mòr (great or big music), the classical music of the pipes, jigging and puirt-a-beul are most often associated with ceòl beag (little music), instrumental dance tunes. Where pipers themselves will often speak of the necessity of canntaireachd for learning pibroch properly, rarely do musicians say the same about jigging or puirt-a-beul (although the debate regarding the need for Gaelic fluency to play the fiddle is an exception; see Chapter 7). Finally, those most familiar with Scottish traditional music view the ability to perform canntaireachd as a specialized skill, whereas they do not generally view puirt-a-beul and jigging as such, although some singers or musicians are known to be particularly adept at them. Ultimately, puirt-a-beul and jigging are not granted as much status as canntaireachd: "pipers award pibroch canntaireachd the highest status that any musician awards to any form of vocabelising in Scotland" (Chambers 1980: 84).

Puirt-a-Beul and Portaireacht

Puirt-a-beul (pronounced "POORSHT-uh-BEE-uhl") is a Scots Gaelic term and literally translates as "tunes from the mouth," but is more commonly translated as "mouth music." What makes puirt-a-beul different from the other types of mouth music discussed here is that, contrary to popular belief, they consist of actual words (rather than vocables) most of the time. Puirt-a-beul texts are also fixed, which means that they are deliberately composed and must be performed as learned. It is not generally appropriate for the singer to make up new words, not even where vocables are used. Puirt-a-beul is not improvised as jigging is, nor is it a system like canntaireachd where particular consonant and vowel combinations are used to represent particular musical sounds.

I should emphasize that the manner in which I define puirt-a-beul is not necessarily the way that others would define it, nor should my definition be considered the most correct. There are others who define it differently. I have already quoted Father Rankin, who seems to have used the term "canntaireachd" to refer to what I would call puirt-a-beul. Here are some other references to puirt-a-beul that suggest a different definition from the one I am proposing:

> Puirt-a-beul in Gaelic involves the singing of Gaelic words, called vocables, to certain melodies, those often being marches, jigs, strathspeys and reels played on the pipes and

the fiddle. The Gaelic vocables don't have to make sense, but they must (and always do) convey the lively qualities of Gaelic speech. (Graham 2006: 62)

In Prince Edward Island's North Shore Gaelic communities the singing of puirt-a-beul (referred to in English as "jigging tunes" throughout the Scottish Canadian Maritimes) was a regular feature of weddings and dances where two people would be hired to sit on either side of the fiddler and sing the tunes as they were played; people also regularly jigged tunes unaccompanied at home for children to dance to. (Shaw 1992-1993: 44)

Puirt-a-beul, or mouth music, is essentially a combination of Gaelic words ... usually with vocables or nonsense syllables. (Doherty 1996: 179)

Interestingly, in the last case, the author includes a footnote meant to clarify: "The term 'jigging' refers to a practice resembling puirt-a-beul, although generally consisting of nonsense syllables only."

It is not that any of these authors is wrong about what puirt-a-beul are or are not. However, the conflation of puirt-a-beul with other Celtic mouth music traditions and the inconsistency with which puirt-a-beul is defined makes it hard to see the differences (and similarities) between puirt-a-beul, jigging and canntaireachd. I am proposing a definition that clearly differentiates between these three terms in order, I hope, to make it easier to recognize when each is used and why. In other words, my definition works for me and this book but I would not want to suggest that it should be used by anyone else, nor that it is a better definition than anyone else's. As an ethnomusicologist, I want to respect the terminologies used by people within Scottish Gaelic song culture, not impose my own upon them.

There is an equivalent term to "puirt-a-beul" in Irish: *portaireacht*. As with puirt-a-beul, it seems often to be equated with lilting rather than with songs that have fixed texts:

> Lilting, or *portaireacht bheil* as it is known in Irish, played a dominant role in Irish dancing and music tradition. (Uí Ógáin 1995: 84)

> Until the mid-20th century, music for dancing was sometimes provided by lilters, men or women who vocalized dance tunes, solo or in unison duet, to standard vocables. Also known as dydeling, mouth-music or in Irish as *portaireacht bhéil*, lilting is sometimes still performed to entertain listeners. (Carolan 2001)

> When instruments were unavailable, skilled individuals (often women) provided music for dancers by *portaireacht* (lilting or "puss" music). (Ó Laoire 2005: 272)

These definitions suggest that portaireacht consist of improvised vocables. However, I have occasionally come across songs that I would consider puirt-a-beul if they were in Scottish—rather than Irish—Gaelic, often because they are highly repetitive lyrically and musically, they have humorous or nonsensical lyrics, and they are performed jig time, which is associated with dancing (I discuss the musical and lyrical characteristics of puirt-a-beul more in Chapters 3 and 4). Wonderful examples can be heard on the recording *Dual* with Scottish Gaelic singer Julie Fowlis and Irish Gaelic singer Muireann Nic Amhlaoibh (Machair Records 2008). On this album, the two singers perform sets of tunes that include puirt-a-beul as well as Irish songs that seem awfully similar. However, they never go so far as to actually label them portaireacht.

A set of songs that are quite similar to puirt-a-beul appears on a recording by Irish sean-nós singer Peadar Ó Ceannabháin (*Mo Chuid den t-Saol / Traditional Songs from Connemara* 1997). Here are the lyrics of the first tune, taken directly from the CD liner notes:

An Rógaire Dubh
Tá mo stoca is mo bhróga ag an rógaire dubh (x3)
Mo naipicín póca le bliain sa lá inniu

Portaireacht

Tá nead insa sliabh ag an rógaire dubh (x3)
Ní ghabhfaidh sé an bóthar ach cóngar an chnoic

Dá bhfeicteása Máire taobh eile den tsruth (x3)
Is a dhá chois in airde ag an rógaire dubh!

The Black Rogue
The black rogue has taken my socks and shoes (x3)
And my pocket handkerchief, a year ago today.

Portaireacht

The black rogue has a nest in the mountain (x3)
He won't travel by road, but takes the shortcut over the
    hill.

If you were to see Máire on the far side of the stream
    (x3)
And the black rogue's two legs high up in the air!

Where the word "portaireacht" appears, Ó Ceannabháin lilts, once again making the equation between lilting and portaireacht, even within a song that otherwise looks a lot like puirt-a-beul thanks to its brief lyrics, repetition and silly—even bawdy—theme. The liner notes, however, do not label any of the three songs in the set as portaireacht, although they do indicate that "these songs in double and slip jig time are often played by musicians," features that further parallel the puirt-a-beul tradition. In fact, all of the (admittedly few) examples I have of Irish songs that look like puirt-a-beul are in jig time. Indeed, while "port" means "tune" in both Irish and Scottish Gaelic, it is more often today translated as "jig" in Ireland. The frequency of jig-time songs in Ireland is not particularly surprising since jigs are strongly associated with Ireland. But it does suggest that these puirt-a-beul-like songs developed independently in Ireland. If puirt-a-beul had originated in Ireland, one would expect to find more jigs borrowed into the Scottish tradition, but, while jigs do exist, they are one of the rarest types of puirt-a-beul. On the other hand, assuming that puirt-a-beul originated in Scotland, one might expect to see more examples of puirt-a-beul reels borrowed into the Irish tradition, since reels are by far the most common type of puirt-a-beul. But this does not appear to be the case.

Another question that these songs raise is where the line is between a "song" (which is usually called an *òran* in Scottish Gaelic, or an *amhrain* or a *dàn* in Irish Gaelic) and a "tune" (a *port* in Irish or Scottish Gaelic)? Does the lack of the portaireacht label indicate that the songs that Muireann Nic Amhlaoibh and Peadar Ó Ceannabháin sing are better understood as songs than as puirt (tunes)? The metrical shifts between and within Ó Ceannabháin's songs, together with pauses at the ends of some lines, suggest that Ó Ceannabháin's songs are not associated with dancing, or at least that they are no longer performed as though they were dance music. The beat would have to be much steadier to accompany dancers. Gaelic song scholar Alan Bruford agrees and therefore implies that these types of Irish songs cannot really be considered the equivalent of puirt-a-beul. Instead, he suggests, "there is a range of comic or nonsensical songs in Irish which are popular today simply because you can't sing slow songs all night, though these faster songs can hardly have formed five per-cent of the old traditional repertoire" (Bruford 1978b: 7).

If there is little written about Scottish puirt-a-beul, there seems to be even less about Irish portaireacht. I claim no expertise on the subject. But I do want to highlight the Irish tradition because of its intriguing similarities to puirt-a-beul, and express the hope that someone will research it further.

Puirt-a-beul, as mouth music, is not unique in the world. There are many forms of instrumental music delivered vocally in diverse cultures, and many share similar functions, including orally "notating" instrumental music, transmitting tunes, substituting for an instrument or even imitating an instrument. But puirt-a-beul is distinct. For one, it is among the few Western European forms of mouth music. It is unusual for its use of "real" words (instead of vocables) and fixed lyrics. They also have wonderful stories associated with them that have captured the imaginations of many. I turn to some of those stories in the next chapter, as I explore their origins.

Chapter 2
"Chuirinn air a' Phìob e":
Origin Theories

After contextualizing puirt-a-beul and providing a working definition, it would seem appropriate to discuss their origins.[1] Where did they come from? Even more important is the question of when they originated, for there is a tendency—in the West certainly, and likely elsewhere too—to grant status to cultural forms that are verifiably "old" (although how old something has to be to be considered old is a whole other question). Also, why did they emerge? The unfortunate answer is that there really is no definitive answer to any of these questions. We simply lack the evidence to make any claims with certainty. As the *New Grove Dictionary of Music and Musicians* tells us, there is "little direct contemporary evidence concerning traditional music in Scotland before the 18th century" and "Gaelic musical culture was exclusively oral until the early 18th century" (Duesenberry and Collinson 2001: 909, 912). However, several theories of the origins of puirt-a-beul have been bandied about over the years, and I will look at each of these in turn to discuss their merits and limitations. I will also offer some tentative explanations for their popularity and persistence. I start with the two most popular: the belief that puirt-a-beul emerged in the wake of the Jacobite Rebellion of 1745-1746 in order to maintain pipe tunes during the proscription of the bagpipes, and the belief that they emerged in the 19th century to protect fiddle tunes at a time when zealous religious leaders discouraged secular music and actually burned instruments.

Proscription of the Bagpipes

The most romantic origin story is one that assumes that puirt-a-beul originated when the bagpipes were banned after the Battle of Culloden in 1746. The Battle of Culloden was a watershed moment in Highland history. Charles Edward Stuart, more commonly known as Bonnie Prince Charlie, wanted to pursue his right to the Scottish throne. Until King James VI of Scotland became King James I of England (r. 1603-1625), effectively uniting the Scottish and English thrones, England and Scotland had been distinct kingdoms, each with its own king (or, occasionally, queen). But when Queen Elizabeth I (r. 1558-1603) died without an heir, the English crown went to King James of Scotland. So in order to assert his claim on the Scottish throne, Stuart had to advance on London, not just Edinburgh. The Bonnie Prince was supported by the Jacobites, most of whom were Highlanders, although it's important also to note that not all Highlanders were Jacobites and that some Scottish Lowlanders were also Jacobites. Despite relatively limited numbers fighting for his cause, Bonnie Prince Charlie was surprisingly—and, for the supporters of the reigning British monarch King George II (r. 1727-1760), terrifyingly—close to success. In the latter half of 1745, he won a number of battles in Scotland. He came within 200 kilometres of London but, advised by Lord George Murray to return to Scotland in the face of approaching government forces and the lack of promised English support, he reluctantly agreed to a retreat. This gave the Hanoverians (supporters of King George II) time to improve their previously ineffective resistance, and it also gave them the courage to pursue the Jacobites as they withdrew northward. The Prince had lost his pride, and his supporters gradually deserted him while others died from hunger and disease. The Jacobites took their last stand at Culloden on April 16, 1746, where they were utterly destroyed.

King George II and his military council were appalled that the Jacobites had been so nearly successful in their bid for the English throne. Mindful that Prince Charles's rising was the second major Jacobite rebellion (the first having been led by his father in 1715), and that only mild consequences had been visited upon the traitorous Jacobites the first time around, the government resolved on a response that would prevent any further Jacobite uprisings. The Hanoverians were especially determined to stamp out any thoughts of further rebellion because Bonnie Prince Charlie managed to escape Culloden and there were fears that he could initiate yet another insurrection. Hundreds of suspected rebels were jailed or killed in the days after Culloden. For months afterwards, estates of "rebellious" clan chiefs were destroyed, with buildings burned, livestock run off and possessions stolen; and people suspected of treason or found with weapons were killed. Lawlessness, chaos and violence persisted for years.

After the first Jacobite Rising of 1715, the *Disarming Act* was enacted, which forbade the bearing (but not the possession) of arms. It was largely ineffectual. Consequently, after the Jacobite Rebellion of 1745-1746, the *Act of Proscription* was enacted. Having more severe punishments than the *Disarming Act* and being more rigorously enforced, it forbade the ownership of arms. It also forbade Highland dress, seen as a symbol of rebellion, for civilian men. The consequences of wearing Highland dress were either six months in prison without bail or, upon subsequent offences, transport beyond Britain's borders.

The *Act* also called for the surrender of all "warlike weapons." Some have suggested that this included the bagpipes since they were known to be played during battle as a means of rallying the troops. One such person is James Logan (ca. 1794-1872), secretary of the Highland Society of London in the 1830s. He wrote, "some of the unfortunate pipers who were taken on the suppression of the rebellion, thought they could effectually plead that, being only pipers, they had not carried arms against his Majesty, but it was decided that their pipe was an instrument of war" (1831 qtd. in Gibson 1998: 29). Although Logan wrote within living memory of Culloden and certainly within memory of the *Act of Proscription*, his claims must be taken with a grain of salt. After all, Logan has also been implicated in publishing information of questionable validity with respect to the tradition of clan tartans (Trevor-Roper 1983: 38-39). It is possible that Logan liberally interpreted something written by Edinburgh piper Donald MacDonald (b. 1749): "after the Battle of Culloden the Bag-Pipe was almost completely laid aside. In this interval much of the Music was neglected or lost" (qtd. in Gibson 1998: 29; from *A Collection of Ancient Martial Music of Caledonia called Piobaireachd*, Edinburgh, ca. 1822). Or perhaps he was influenced by Samuel Johnson's famous account of his 1773 trip to Scotland: "The solace which the bagpipe can give, they have long enjoyed; but among other changes, which the last revolution introduced, the use of the bagpipe begins to be forgotten" (Johnson and Macdonald 1983: 131). Regardless, after Logan's account, subsequent publications reinforced the story of the proscription of the bagpipes. Although authors today tend to be a little more cautious in their claims about the treatment of bagpipes under the *Act of Proscription*, many still suggest that bagpipes were frowned upon and discouraged in the years after Culloden, even if not officially and legally outlawed.

Piping scholar John Gibson argues that the belief that the bagpipes were outlawed or discouraged largely hinges on the 1746 hanging of Jacobite piper James Reid of Ogilvie's Regiment. The court at York ruled with these words: "no regiment ever marched without musical instruments such as drums, trumpets and the like; and that a highland regiment never marched without a piper; and therefore his bagpipe, in the eye of the law, was an instrument of war" (qtd. in Gibson 1998: 33). Although Reid was hanged more than three months after the *Act of Proscription* officially went into effect on August 1 of that year, Gibson argues that the part of the *Act* pertaining to "warlike weapons" was not applied to Gaelic Scotland until the summer of 1748, almost two years *after* Reid was hanged. Gibson instead argues that Reid, as an active rebel, was hanged for treason and not for anything to do with the *Act of Proscription*—that is, the hanging was a case of judicial revenge rather than a legal precedent:

> The proponents of the idea that the Reid case set a precedent for the *Disarming Act* enforcers erroneously link what was a post-rebellion trial in an English city for the capital crime of high treason with the application of a calculated, extremely explicit sixteen-page act of the British government that had nothing whatever to do with proscribing the Highland bag-pipes and was not enforced until after the Treaty of Aix-la-Chapelle ended the duke of Cumberland's European war in 1748. Not only is there no mention of bagpipes or bagpipers in the act but no pipers were convicted as such under any of the act's published stipulations. (Gibson 1998: 33-34)

Most scholars today agree that the bagpipes were unlikely to have been systematically sought out and destroyed, although some argue instead that the *Act* encouraged a widespread anti-Highland attitude, which impacted Highland culture. Historian John MacLeod, for example, writes: "the Disarming Acts banned the bagpipes—'engines of war'—and the wearing of tartan. How rigidly these provisions were enforced is doubtful; psychologi-cally, however, the message was clear. The Gaelic culture itself was condemned" (MacLeod 1996: 183). But Gibson scoffs even at the belief that "the Disarming Act all but destroyed traditional bag-piping, or that a cultural 'crisis' doomed most piping to a speedy death and the rest to artificial and military-sponsored resuscita-tion" (Gibson 1998: 36). He argues that the military presence in Scotland was limited, as was their effectiveness in catching and prosecuting offenders. Gibson cites events, documents and songs indicating that the Highlanders maintained their "*hauteur* and feistiness" throughout this period (48). At the same time, it is clear that Gaelic culture declined precipitously after this time. This is evident especially in the decline in the number of Gaelic speakers in Scotland, the large numbers of Gaelic speakers who emigrated even before the Clearances of the 19th century and the increasing number of songs that lament the loss of traditional lands, ways of life and dress.

But for our purposes here, the important question is whether the bagpipes were outlawed and whether puirt-a-beul emerged in their absence. By this logic, if the bagpipes were never outlawed, there was never any need to create puirt-a-beul as a means of preserving the tunes. On the other hand, if one accepts that the bagpipes were discouraged as part of an overall and pervasive anti-Highland sentiment at the time, puirt-a-beul may have emerged as an important substitute. However, I think that it is the story's flair and romance that makes it so likable as a theory. How wonderful to imagine that puirt-a-beul arose in defiant resistance to harsh Hanoverian laws, preserving the traditional music of the Gaels against the Hanoverians' best efforts.

At the same time, I am surprised at how rarely this theory was mentioned by the people I interviewed in Cape Breton and even in Scotland, although it seemed more common there. Only one Canadian interviewee mentioned it, and only skeptically. As something of a self-educated Gaelic scholar, neither his awareness of the theory nor his doubt is surprising:

> I suppose the stereotype of puirt-a-beul was that it was after the so-called "proscription" of the pipes and musical instruments and trappings of Gaelic culture. So they were forced to come up with vocables that would allow them to dance. That's the story. But maybe the truth is more likely that you wouldn't always have a musical instrument nearby and maybe people always did this kind of mouth music. Who knows? Perhaps with the discouragement of traditional instruments mouth music became more necessary. But I'm kind of skeptical about all that. I think a number of factors came together. I don't want to overemphasize one of them. (Interview with David Livingston-Lowe, March 10, 1998)

His doubt echoes that of musicologist Francis Collinson, who writes:

the *puirt-a-beul* tradition is of uncertain origin. Some believe it arose as a substitute for the bagpipe when that instrument was proscribed after the 18th-century Jacobite risings; but this could only be likely if other musical instruments, such as the harp or fiddle, had also been forbidden, which they were not. (1980: 73)

Perhaps another reason to doubt the theory is that a very similar one exists in Ireland, where it is believed that lilting was developed to resist English domination "when both Irish Gaelic and vernacular music were proscribed" (Atherton 2007: 17). The striking parallels suggest that there were rhetorical and ideological reasons for promoting these theories that were perhaps not based on historical evidence. Anthropologist Malcolm Chapman (1992) and archaeologist Simon James (1999) have persuasively suggested that the Celts are not actually a continuous 2,000-year-old race of people, but rather the Celts of today were largely invented in 18th-century Britain as a means of opposing Anglo-Saxon political and cultural pressures. Music and song offered 18th- and 19th-century Celts an important means of resisting Anglo-Saxon cultural dominance by asserting distinctive musical practices and, by extension, distinct cultural (Celtic) groups who practised them.

It strikes me as no coincidence that the belief that puirt-a-beul—or lilting, for that matter—emerged in 18th-century Scotland (or Ireland). After all, it was a time when considerable effort was being made to counter British-imposed cultural restrictions. Not only does such a theory suggest that Scottish Gaelic musical and linguistic culture persisted despite anglophone Britain's best efforts (the beloved plot in which the underdog somehow "pulls one over" on the larger, more powerful bully), it also provides Scotland with a musical form for which there is no equivalent in English musical culture. Part of the means by which the "Celtic" regions claimed independence from England, as well as political and cultural legitimacy, was through difference. As long as the so-called Celtic peoples spoke the same language, ate the same foods, wore the same clothes and practised the same religion as the English, it was hard to understand why they should be recognized and treated as anything other than a single group of people. The English understood this and worked very hard to encourage (sometimes more forcefully than not) a common culture. The non-English-speaking peoples of the area who resisted hegemony likewise understood this and sought as many examples of difference in as many different realms as possible. Puirt-a-beul and other forms of Celtic mouth music such as lilting likely contributed to this effort.

None of this is to say, of course, that puirt-a-beul didn't exist or that they didn't indeed emerge as a result of British-imposed cultural pressures during the mid- to late 18th century. It is to say, however, that the historical evidence for such a theory is lacking, making it far from a foregone conclusion. It is further undercut by another very similar theory that places puirt-a-beul's origins about a hundred years later.

Fiddles and Religion

A second popular origin theory suggests that puirt-a-beul emerged during the 19th century in response to religious, rather than political, proscription. Authors regularly refer to the belief that Presbyterian ministers denounced secular musics because of their association with drink and dance. Drinking's potential ills are self-evident, but dancing was considered dangerous because physical contact could lead to sexual temptation. More than simply discourage secular music, stories emphasize that clergy actually physically destroyed or, psychologically worse, encouraged the musicians themselves to destroy, instruments. These stories persist in both Scotland and Cape Breton. Alexander Carmichael, collector and compiler of the multi-volume *Carmina Gadelica: Hymns and Incantations* (1928 [1900]), writes evocatively about the loss of music and dance in Protestant areas of the Highlands. Because his work is widely known and influential, he is worth quoting at length:

"And have you no music, no singing, no dancing now at your marriages?" "May the Possessor keep you! I see that you are a stranger in Lewis, or you would not ask such a question," the woman exclaimed with grief and surprise in her tone. "It is long since we abandoned those foolish ways in Ness, and, indeed, throughout Lewis. In my young days there was hardly a house in Ness in which there was not one or two or three who could play the pipe, or the fiddle, or the trump. And I have heard it said that there were men, and women too, who could play things they called harps, and lyres, and bellow-pipes, but I do not know what those things were." "And why were those discontinued?" "A blessed change came over the place and the people," the woman replied in earnestness, "and the good men and the good ministers who arose did away with the songs and the stories, the music and the dancing, the sports and the games, that were perverting the minds and ruining the souls of the people, leading them to folly and stumbling." "But how did the people themselves come to discard their sports and pastimes?" "Oh, the good ministers and the good elders preached against them and went among the people, and besought them to forsake their follies and to return to wisdom. They made the people break and burn their pipes and fiddles. If there was a foolish man here and there who demurred, the good ministers and the good elders themselves broke and burnt their instruments, saying:—

Is fearr an teine beag a gharas
la beag na sithe,
Na'n teine mor a loisgeas
la mor na feirge.

> Better is the small fire that warms on
> the little day of peace,
> Than the big fire that burns on the
> great day of wrath.

The people have forsaken their follies and their Sabbath-breaking, and there is no pipe, no fiddle here now," said the woman in evident satisfaction. "And what have you now instead of the racing, the stone-throwing, and the caber-tossing, the song, the pipe, and the dance?" "Oh, we have now the blessed Bible preached and explained to us faithfully and earnestly, if we sinful people would only walk in the right path and use our opportunities." (Carmichael 1928 [1900]: xxix-xxx).

Carmichael then gives the pathetic story of a fiddler who is convinced to give up his fiddle:

A famous violin-player died in the island of Eigg a few years ago. He was known for his old style playing and his old-world airs which died with him. A preacher denounced him, saying:— "Tha thu shios an sin cul na comhla, a dhuine thruaigh le do chiabhan liath, a cluich do sheann fhiodhla le laimh fhuair a mach agus le teine an diabhoil a steach"— Thou art down there behind the door, thou miserable man with thy grey hair, playing thine old fiddle with the cold hand without, and the devil's fire within. His family pressed the man to burn his fiddle and never to play again. A peddlar came round and offered ten shillings for the violin. The instrument had been made by a pupil of Stradivarius, and was famed for its tone. "Cha b'e idir an rud a fhuaradh na dail a ghoirtich mo chridhe cho cruaidh ach an dealachadh rithe! an dealachadh rithe! agus gu'n tug mi fhein a bho a b'fhearr am buaile m'athar air a son, an uair a bha mi og"— It was not at all the thing that was got for it that grieved my heart so sorely, but the parting with it! the parting with it! and that I myself gave the best cow in my father's fold for it when I was young. The voice of the old man faltered and a tear fell. He was never again seen to smile. (Carmichael 1928 [1900]: xxxii)

It is worth noting that the association of instrumental music and dance with the Devil and evil was not new in Scotland at this time. Robbie Burns's (1759-1796) poem "Tam O'Shanter" portrays the Devil as a piper accompanying a witches' dance, an image illustrated in an edition of the book by artist John Faed (1819-1902):

> Warlocks and witches in a dance;
> Nae cotillion brent-new frae France,
> But hornpipes, jigs strathspeys, and reels,
> Put life and mettle in their heels.
> A winnock-bunker in the east,
> There sat auld Nick, in shape o' beast;
> A towzie tyke, black, grim, and large,
> To gie them music was his charge:
> He scre'd the pipes and gart them skirl,
> Till roof and rafters a' did dirl.

Bagpipe scholar Hugh Cheape observes that the pipes were denounced as the Devil's instrument during the time of the European witch hunts of the 16th and 17th centuries (2000: 49). Although these earlier associations were between the bagpipes—rather than the fiddle—and the Devil, they set a precedent for denouncing instruments, instrumental music and dance as evil. It is interesting, however, that the emergence of puirt-a-beul is not tied to these early denouncements, but only to those that emerged in the 19th century.[2]

As with the bagpipe proscription theory, the demise of fiddles did not necessarily mean the loss of tunes or the eradication of dancing. Ethnomusicologist Katherine Campbell, for example, quotes a Scots song, "A Country Weddin'" by Jamie McQueen (ca. 1852-1928), in which the minister's authority is respected as long as he is present, but there are plans to have a dance as soon as he leaves:

> In wedlock noo they baith were joined—
> A' drank their health in sparklin' wine;
> The reverent man then bless'd the pair,
> An' shook them by the hand' sae kin'.
> Wi' this the fiddler hove in sicht—
> The green bag in his han' did hing—
> The best man ran oot tae the door,
> An' bade him pit it 'neath his wing.

He said, "The parson's nae awa'—
Ye canna touch't until he gang;
Gae ben an' hide it in the bed,
He winna bide noo vera lang." (2007: xv-xvi)

One means of continuing to dance despite the lack of fiddles—
or so the story goes—was through the use of puirt-a-beul as dance
accompaniment. Scottish Gaelic song scholar James Ross agrees
that puirt-a-beul evolved during the 19th-century Presbyterian
persecution of instruments and secular song:

it is unlikely, however, that the mouth-music was widely used
as an accompaniment to the actual dance. Its origin is more
likely to lie in the desire of instrumentalists to perpetuate
their favourite tunes after the destruction or banning of
their instruments. (1957: 133)

Puirt-a-beul were believed to be particularly effective because, if a
minister was seen to approach a gathering, a singer could simply
stop with no physical evidence of music-making to hide. Moreover,
a singer's voice would not carry as well as an instrument, making
it less likely to be overheard by the minister from a distance:

A Highland clergyman informed me that some of these
dance songs lingered long in the outskirts of the Highlands
after their day as an institution was over, on account of a
class of preachers who denounced as sinful all secular music
and dancing, especially instrumental music. The enormity
of the lapse from the precepts of the preacher would probably lie more lightly on the consciences of the dancers when
the music was that of the human voice, and the risk of detec-
tion and denunciation would also be reduced. (Mackintosh
ca. 1910: 288)

What is particularly interesting about this latter statement is
that it was made in the second decade of the 20th century. On
the one hand, this particular belief has clearly persisted for over
a century, for it is still mentioned today. On the other hand, it
indicates that the idea that clergy destroyed instruments was an
undocumented fact circulating only in oral tradition even in the

early 20th century. It does not seem to have been recent history. Mackintosh's statement that "a Highland clergyman informed me" suggests a lack of familiarity with this religious "history" prior to being informed of it. His paper was originally given orally to the Gaelic Society of Inverness—an organization one could reasonably expect to be familiar with Highland history and customs—and only later published in their *Transactions*. If the Presbyterian clergy's active discouragement of secular dance music was recent or familiar history in Gaelic Scotland, one wouldn't expect him to have to make his point explicitly to his audience. His source also suggests that the denouncement of secular music and dance had happened at some earlier point in history, rather than in the recent past.

A medical doctor from Edinburgh who took an interest in traditional Scottish lore made a fascinating claim at the turn of the 20th century about the origins of puirt-a-beul that I have not heard anywhere else:

> These ports, in Gaelic *Puirt-a-bheoil* (vocalised tunes), are really mnemonics for particular airs, and recall them just as the first verse of the Old Hundred would recall the air to any one with an ear for music. Music seems to have been taught in a primitive way by associating words not necessarily conveying any meaning with the air to be remembered, and so an old minister of the parish of Kilchoman in Islay is said to have taught his people sacred music, but, for fear of secularising the proper words of the Psalms, to have invented ports for the purpose of instruction. (MacLagan 1901: 108)

What makes this claim so interesting is that it still ties the origins of puirt-a-beul to the rise of Protestant pressures on secular cultural practices, but it situates the origins of puirt-a-beul with the clergy themselves, rather than in a kind of defiance of them. Rather than pitting sacred song against secular puirt-a-beul, this story turns puirt-a-beul into something that enables the integrity of both to be preserved simultaneously.

Joshua Dickson, a piping scholar, has written about the differences between Roman Catholic and Calvinist views of secular music and dance in the Outer Hebrides (Dickson 2006: 38-56). Radical evangelicalism was embraced in the Church of Scotland Free, established when 451 clergy walked out of the General Assembly of the Church of Scotland Reformed in 1843, an event known as the Disruption. These ministers were concerned that too much importance was being placed on earthly rather than spiritual matters:

> Piety, restraint and a turning away from worldliness are the basic aims of Calvinism in the form of the Free Church; the obstacles to these things are anything that can be deemed a worldly excess, such as drinking, dancing, and merry-making in general. The "people's melodies" are returned "purified and baptised in Christian seriousness." Hebridean areas in which this religious climate prevails would find the merry-making that goes on "in the saloon or in the street"—and by extension the *taigh-céilidh* [the ceilidh house]—contrary to the dignity that comes with the observance of that faith's principles. (Dickson 2006: 53)

Dickson provides several examples of active musicians who gave up their music after conversion. Donald Munro, a blind Skye fiddler, gave up his instrument after converting in the early 19th century. Sinclair Thomson, the "Shetland Apostle," likewise gave up fiddling after his conversion around 1816. John MacDonald of Ferintosh, the "Apostle of the North," gave up his pipes after conversion; his father subsequently "applied the axe" to them.

It is worth nothing that Protestant radicalism affected secular music elsewhere in the British Isles as well:

> The development in Wales of both the Methodist and the Nonconformist Puritanical Protestant Churches in the eighteenth century, which condemned the performance of non-religious music, had a diminishing effect on secular music and dance. In fact, the dance tradition never fully recovered from its suppression in the name of religion. Instruments were banned and burned, even as recently as 1905, in a series of Methodist revivals. (Williams 2009: 93)

The 18th-century movement in Wales foreshadowed and likely influenced the 19th-century one in Scotland. That Methodists and other Welsh Protestants took a strong stance against secular music and dance also lends strength to accounts of similar attitudes and actions taken in Scotland.

At the same time, Dickson suggests that new converts were the most zealous and therefore the most likely to change their behaviours radically. They were not necessarily representative of all musicians in the Protestant Hebrides. John Gibson suggests that because there was a limited number of Free Church ministers, their cultural impact was not necessarily always absolute or pervasive (Gibson 1998: 325n28). Moreover, negative musical attitudes applied only to secular music, not sacred music. Music therefore continued to exist in the Protestant Highlands as evidenced in both the celebrated psalm singing in the churches as well as in the formation of the Lewis Pipe Band in 1904 (Dickson 2006: 52). "The moderates" of the Church of Scotland Reformed tended to be more accepting of folk culture. However, the Free Church's general attitude toward secular music and pastimes is clear, and it is also obvious that it had an impact on local music-making, even if that impact was not as widespread or as absolute as has sometimes been asserted.

Meanwhile, the Roman Catholic view in the southern Hebrides was that "religious occasions were a time not for ascetic solemnity, but for earthly jubilation" (Dickson 2006: 54). Dickson cites several examples of songs that refer to both religious themes and secular music or dancing; he also identifies a tale in which a priest plays a fiddle and makes a woman dance in order to cure her of some ill. Writing in the late 18th century, Samuel Johnson also noted the tendency for traditional culture to persist better in the Roman Catholic Hebrides, even though he himself did not travel to the Catholic islands:

> Popery [Catholicism] is favourable to ceremony; and among
> ignorant nations, ceremony is the only preservative of tradi-
> tion. Since Protestantism was extended to the savage parts
> of Scotland, it has perhaps been one of the chief labours of

the ministers to abolish stated observances, because they continued the remembrance of the former religion. We therefore who came to hear old traditions, and see antiquated manners, should probably have found them amongst the Papists. (Johnson and Macdonald 1983: 148)

Although there are exceptions in which priests discourage dance and secular music, Dickson argues that these stories generally identify priests concerned with Sabbath temperance rather than broad doctrinal intolerance (Dickson 2006: 250n73). More often, priests in Scotland have actively promoted traditional Gaelic culture. For example, Fr. Allan McDonald (1859-1905) is a well-known and widely celebrated priest in both South Uist and Eriskay who was an avid folk collector and assisted many folklorists with their research.

Scottish music and dance scholar George S. Emmerson argues that strict Protestant values flourished among immigrants from Protestant communities in the new world:

Many emigrants took this puritan zeal with them to Canada—to Nova Scotia, Upper Canada, and Manitoba, where the privations of pioneer life put a premium on the philosophy of unremitting "useful" work and the introspection encouraged by Calvinistic precepts. It is easy to exaggerate this attitude and its regressive influence on the folk music, dancing, and lore of the Gaels at home and abroad—whatever it did for science and philosophy—for the most outrageous examples of suppression are the most widely publicized; but there is no doubt that it has left some legacy of loss in the Protestant communities. (Emmerson 1972: 224)

Gibson's research supports the belief that 19th-century Presbyterian ministers in Scotland actively discouraged music and dance, but he suggests that Presbyterian Puritanism had minimal effect on music and dance in Nova Scotia:

It may be that overt cultural exuberance was more muted in the Free Church parishes, but only marginally.... Evaluating the impact of the Presbyterian Disruption [after 1843] on traditional bagpiping, fiddling, and dancing in the Gaelic communities of Nova Scotia, it is fair to say that where the Disruption church emerged, there tended to be a growth in serious piety and in temperance. There is a temptation to believe that there was a downturn in traditional music, dance, and story telling, but in the case of the Presbyterian area from Strathlorne to Headlake via the east side of Lake Ainslie in Cape Breton, any downturn was slight. Protestant musicians and dancers did not disappear when the Church moved from establishment status (and doubtless those who preferred to shun music and dance continued in their ways). Many very musical Presbyterian families had emigrated from Scotland, some of whom certainly had no compunction about continuing to foster musical tradition. (Gibson 1998: 200-201)

Indeed, one of Gibson's informants, Neil Dan MacInnis of Glenville, said that "one minister who used to visit the MacInnis home used discreetly to leave if people began to gather, knowing that the musical instruments were coming out and dancing was about to begin" (Gibson 1998: 248). Of course, the limited impact of the Free Church on music-making in Nova Scotia makes sense given that the majority of Scottish immigrants settled in Cape Breton prior to the Disruption. The Disruption was felt most keenly in Scotland and among Scottish emigrants who had experienced it personally; it was felt less strongly elsewhere.

Intriguingly, it would seem that restrictions on fiddle music and dancing in Nova Scotia came not from the Presbyterian Church, but from the Roman Catholic one, largely as a result of temperance efforts. This is particularly striking given the strong role that several recent and well-known priests have played in the Cape Breton fiddle revival. But present-day philosophies and actions do not necessarily reflect those of the past.

Throughout the 19th century, Nova Scotia bishops advocated temperance, reinforced by Canadian law, such as the *Temperance Act* of 1878 and the prohibition of distilling by the 1860s at the latest (Gibson 1998: 202). Numerous priests furthered the temperance movement in their parishes. A particularly notorious example is Father Kenneth MacDonald, first Pastor at Mabou 1865-1894, who was apparently a very strict and conservative religious leader:

> Father Kenneth MacDonald was one of the most earnest workers of his time in the cause of temperance. So bitterly did he regret the harm done by drinking that nothing short of total abstinence, [sic] could be regarded by him as a proper attitude towards drink. Because he found that dances, picnics and such outings lent themselves to drinking he strenuously opposed them, and those whom he found indulging in intoxicating liquors had to pay the penalty. (Rankin 1944-1945: 114)

Father MacDonald is infamous for encouraging the destruction of fiddles in order to quell secular music and dance (McDavid 2009). When speaking of religious efforts to suppress secular music in Nova Scotia, he is regularly named as an example, whether in oral accounts or written papers. Donald Angus Beaton, nephew of fiddler Johnny "Ranald" Beaton (1862-1928), tells of his uncle's attempt to foil Father MacDonald:

> Fr Kenneth came looking for fiddles to destroy.... Johnny had two, and so he gave Fr Kenneth the worst one and secretly kept the other. However, the priest got wind of the ruse and eventually tore the violin right from Johnny Ranald's hands and smashed it. (Qtd. in MacGillivray 1981: 11)

Although Fr. MacDonald emerged victorious in the end of this story, it illustrates that his parishioners did not always agree with his philosophy on fiddles and fiddle music. Fiddler Lauchie Meagher (1881-1942) also apparently refused to surrender his fiddle to Father MacDonald (MacGillivray 1981: 70). As Gibson wryly observes, "throughout his pastorate fiddlers and pipers and traditional dancers were everywhere, however many were the violins that he confiscated" (Gibson 1998: 203). Indeed, other priests in nearby parishes, such as Fr. MacLean in Judique, were musicians and dancers themselves. It was very unlikely that Fr. MacDonald had much success eradicating secular music and dance from his parish.

Although Fr. MacDonald is usually seen as representing an extreme reaction, he was apparently not the only Catholic priest to take a negative view of secular music and dance. Celticist Ken Nilsen collected and wrote about the stories of Danny Cameron, a Gaelic-speaking Nova Scotian. Many of Danny Cameron's stories involve priests, such as the one about Father Andrew MacGillivray, Pastor at Lismore, Pictou County, 1871-1897:

> Fr Andrew, like many of the priests of the last century, seems to have been quite severe and strict.... Like Fr Kenneth, Fr Andrew seized all the violins belonging to his parishioners, but unlike Fr Kenneth he did not break them into pieces— he just kept them and as a result had a house full of violins. We may note here that Fr Andrew played the violin himself. Like Fr Kenneth, he was against dances because of the drinking and courting that followed. On one occasion, he complained to a parishioner that after a dance young couples walked home together in the dark. The parishioner turned to him and said, *Dh' fhaodadh iad an aon rud a dheanamh a' trusadh suibheagan preas* [They could do the same thing gathering raspberries]. (Nilsen 1996-1997: 185-86)

Another Mabou priest, Fr. (Dr.) John Francis MacMaster (1894-1937), also advocated temperance and took particular umbrage with square dances:

> Fr MacMaster's preoccupation with the drinking problem was coupled with the threat to his parishioners' morals, as he saw it, of the quadrille, a new group dance in which there was body contact. However, he was much more obviously in favour of Scotch music than Fr Kenneth, particularly piping, and appears never to have discouraged traditional step-dancing to traditional music. He organized picnics and bazaars and counted on local musical talent to put on

a show. But, he would not brook public quadrille dancing. (Gibson 1998: 203)

As Gibson notes, strict views on the consumption of alcohol and on dance did not necessarily mean that priests were against secular music. For example, Danny Cameron tells a story about Bishop Fraser (whose Episcopal term ran 1827-1851), which indicates his love of music even though he was one of the bishops most in favour of temperance:

> [A] group of people come to the Bishop with news that a man of ill repute is about to arrive at Pictou from Scotland. They want the Bishop to go to Pictou and prevent the man from landing in Nova Scotia. The Bishop says that he has no knowledge of the man and cannot judge him on mere hearsay. The Bishop accompanies the group to Pictou where the boat has just arrived. They see the man in question dressed in *an deise Ghaidhealach* [the Highland dress], playing the pipes, making his way to the shore. When they see him, they turn to the Bishop and say—"There he is, Bishop Fraser. That's him. Make him go back to Scotland." The Bishop calmly turned to his companions and said—"I can't do that. I don't know anything about the man. But I do know this, *tha lùdag aige cho milis is a chuala mi riamh!*" [he has the sweetest little finger I've ever heard]. The Bishop made no attempt to interfere with the man and so we learn that in addition to his sense of fair play, the Bishop also had a good ear for music and, in fact, is reported to have been an excellent singer as well. (Nilsen 1996-1997: 183)

What is relevant about all these accounts of fiddle-burning ministers and priests is that they never suggest that the repression of fiddling or fiddles results in the creation of puirt-a-beul. Jodi McDavid argues that accounts of Mabou's "fiddle burning priest" are as important for their illustration of the survival of the Cape Breton fiddle tradition against all odds as they are for their expressions of resistance to possible priestly abuses of power (2009).

As an iconic symbol of Cape Breton, the fiddle is important, and its survival is the necessary moral of the story.

As with the theory that puirt-a-beul emerged in response to post-Culloden pressures on the bagpipe a century earlier, it is difficult to consider the theory that puirt-a-beul developed in the wake of religious pressures on secular music and dance likely. After all, some puirt-a-beul seem to pre-date this period. Moreover, many puirt-a-beul came from Roman Catholic regions of Scotland where Presbyterianism had little impact. Since these regions did not suffer the same restrictions on secular music, they would have little reason to create, sing or otherwise perpetuate puirt-a-beul. Finally, we might also note the persistence of puirt-a-beul in Cape Breton where the pressure to give up secular music-making seems to have been rather weak and highly localized. If puirt-a-beul existed as a sneaky way to make secular music in the face of religious constraints, why would they continue, especially in significant numbers, in a place where the religious constraints were minimal (or at least felt minimally)?

Puirt-a-Beul, Druids, Ossian and Highlandism

If puirt-a-beul did not develop in response to the loss of either the bagpipes or the fiddles, where did they come from and why were they created? K. N. MacDonald asserts in *Puirt-a-Beul* that vocable lyrics indicate that the genre derives from an ancient, and now lost, Druidic language (1931 [1901]: 3). Although MacDonald's allegations may seem fanciful, they are unsurprising given the interest at the time in old songs, particularly in Britain. James Francis Child's collection of 305 ballads (and approximately 1,000 variations) from England and Scotland published between 1882 and 1898 was especially influential. Although most of Child's ballad sources date from the 17th and 18th centuries, a handful can be traced back much further, and many of the ballads he documented were probably in oral circulation for some time before being notated (Pound 1932; see also Buchan 1972: 10; Gerould 1957 [1932]: 193; Bronson 1976: xxx-xxxi, xliv-xlv). Child's collection included North American variants of his British "originals," which inspired many North American collectors to seek other Child ballad variants. Not long after, English scholar Cecil Sharp made a name for himself by collecting Child ballads in the United States, especially in Appalachia, suggesting that while the old British ballads were foundering in the United Kingdom, they were flourishing in the New World. Other collectors eagerly followed suit. Many collectors of the early 20th century focused so much on finding and publishing surviving Child ballad variants that they ignored many other types of songs, especially those of more recent origin. It is not surprising, consequently, that MacDonald would emphasize the age of puirt-a-beul as a means of positioning them as equal to the more prestigious and better-known Child ballads, despite substantial differences in their lyric conventions and poetry.

Keith Norman MacDonald published many books, including the fiddle tune compilations *The Skye Collection* (1986 [1887]) and *The Gesto Collection* (1895), both of which are still used by fiddlers today. His interest in fiddle tunes explains his interest in puirt-a-beul. But so does his book *In Defense of Ossian* (1906). The Gaelic songs and poems of Ossian were at the centre of considerable debate throughout the late 18th and 19th centuries. James MacPherson published in the 1760s what he claimed to be a cycle of Gaelic poems narrated and authored by Ossian, the son of Finn MacCumhaill, a figure in Gaelic mythology. The poems, as published by MacPherson, were wildly popular not just in Scotland but throughout the world, with fans as famous as Napoleon, the German writer Goethe, nationalist scholar Johann Gottfried Herder, and Scottish author Sir Walter Scott. Ossian's poems were hailed as the Scottish equivalent of Classical works by authors such as Homer. He pretty much single-handedly changed the international view of Scottish Gaelic culture from a second-rate, diluted descendant of Irish culture to the apex of Western European culture.

But the veracity of MacPherson's texts was debated from the beginning, with Samuel Johnson being the most famous of their detractors. The controversy centred on the sources of Ossian: were they based on Gaelic oral tradition and Scottish manuscripts as MacPherson claimed? Were they based on Gaelic fragments incorporated into MacPherson's own composition as Johnson argued? Were they based on Irish or Scottish or even English sources? The debate continued for well over a century not least because MacPherson was unwilling or unable to show the sources he claimed had informed his work. In the 1950s, Gaelic scholar Derick Thomson demonstrated that MacPherson had combined a number of Gaelic oral and written sources but had altered and adapted them while introducing his own ideas and materials (1951).

The possibility of Ossian's authenticity helped to give rise to the world's love affair with all things Highland, augmented by Sir Walter Scott's Waverley novels. Written in the 1810s about the "Forty-five," Bonnie Prince Charlie's Jacobite rebellion, the novels were internationally successful. Inspired by the Waverley novels, King George IV travelled to Scotland in 1822, the first reigning monarch to do so since 1650. He arrived dressed to the nines in what became known as the Royal Stuart tartan, and Walter Scott encouraged clan chiefs and various Highland and Celtic societies to dress in tartan regalia too. This was a bit of a farce. Although tartan had long existed in Scotland, the proliferation of clan *setts* (tartan patterns) at this time was largely the result of creative writers catering to a national and international audience keen to define "Scottishness," visually and culturally as much as by any other means (see Cheape 2010; Trevor-Roper 1983). The world was enamoured. Queen Victoria and Prince Albert acquired Balmoral Castle in Scotland's Aberdeenshire in 1852 after enjoying a holiday there. Nineteenth-century Romantic composers throughout Europe were inspired by Scotland, as exemplified by Felix Mendelssohn's *Hebrides Overture* (1830) and Franz Schubert's *lieder* (German songs) based on Ossian's poems (composed 1815-1817 and first published in 1830).

K. N. MacDonald's position within the Ossian debate indicates that he considered at least part of Scottish Gaelic oral expression to be pedigreed, valuable and worthy of scholarly study. His book of puirt-a-beul, published only a few years before his defense of Ossian, may have been intended to introduce a broader array of Gaelic song to a public fascinated by Scotland. His acceptance of Ossian's poetry also explains his interest in positioning puirt-a-beul as ancient. Their association with the Druids gives puirt-a-beul an authenticity of age and also an element of mystery that is appealing. He does his best to give puirt-a-beul the same pedigreed history as the poems of Ossian:

> The cultivation of poetry and music were the chief amusements of the Gael, and connected with both was dancing. There are frequent references to this pastime by the earliest historians as having been practised by almost every people. It formed, in fact, part of the religious ceremonies of almost all nations, and the gods are said to have been not only pleased but were themselves emulous in the dance! Lycurgus, the celebrated Spartan legislator, who flourished in the 9th century before the Christian era, instituted dancing from a conviction of its utility in making the youth strong, agile, and expert in the use of weapons. Homer, also, the greatest poet of Greece, and the ancient world, who lived in the 8th century before Christ, mentions the art as a diversion at entertainments, and numerous others mention it with approbation, such as Socrates, about B.C. 469; Xenophon, B.C. 450; Plato, B.C. 427; Aristotle, B.C. 384; Polybius, B.C. 204; Pliny, A.D. 23; Diodorus, A.D. 50; Lucian, A.D. 52; Tacitus, A.D. 54; Plutarch, A.D. 66; and several others. It is not surprising therefore, that "puirt-a-beul"—dancing songs—were in frequent requisition both in ancient and modern times. (1931 [1901]: 4)

Generally speaking, MacDonald's theory is highly unlikely. Perhaps the most damning evidence is the fact that the vast majority of known puirt-a-beul consist of real words rather than vocables. It is hard to argue that puirt-a-beul perpetuate the remains of a long-lost Druidic language when the examples recorded by

MacDonald are clearly in Gaelic. Secondly, as MacDonald himself admits, many of the tunes are known to be of relatively modern composition, and some of the lyrics, by way of reference to particular modes of dress or events, also indicate relatively recent creation. Third, while it is true that some Gaelic songs are known to have circulated orally for centuries, it is hard to imagine that this is the case for puirt-a-beul, given their silly lyrics and often highly personal references. They do not appear to have been meant to be remembered for long periods. Instead, puirt-a-beul seem to have been meant to be reinvented by each generation (see Chapter 4).

Interestingly, and perhaps tellingly, similar claims that song vocables preserve the traces of "real" words exist in other cultures. Musicologist Ida Halpern studied the music of the First Nations peoples of British Columbia's northern coastal areas. She argues that many of their vocables are modified, variant or distorted forms of real words:

> Sometimes ... if [song lyrics are] not translatable, they are referred to as words of archaic status because the singer no longer knows their meaning. This occurs especially among peoples whose songs are orally transmitted through many generations, during which time the knowledge of the language is gradually lost or substantially altered. (Halpern 1976: 253)

Ethnomusicologist Charlotte Frisbie published studies of the vocables found in songs of the Navajo, a Native people from the southwestern United States. Although working with an indigenous people located across the continent from those of northern BC, Frisbie identifies a similar theory explaining vocables:

> The most popular and most frequently cited theory is that vocables derive from words that through time have lost their meaning, either to all Navajos or just non-ceremonialists. A comment (in English) from CS, while working on Corn Grinding Songs, exemplifies this idea clearly. "Parts of the songs have been forgotten. Probably what are now tones

[vocables] had some meaning once, but as the songs were passed down to generations, the people forgot their meaning." (Frisbie 1980: 354)

While these studies could be used to bolster MacDonald's claims by suggesting that there is a "natural" or "universal" process by which archaic song lyrics gradually morph into untranslatable vocables, they could also be used to argue that the very claim itself is what is "natural": faced with inexplicable vocables transmitted across time, perhaps anyone would wonder if they were the remnants of a long-lost language. Without additional evidence, we cannot be sure whether vocables relate to semantically meaningful language or not.

At the same time, there's nothing to say that, even if specific examples of puirt-a-beul tend to be much more recent than Druidic or Roman times, the concept of mouth music or dance songs hasn't existed for centuries. Moreover, none of this is to suggest that puirt-a-beul are not worthy of study or maintenance, regardless of their age. Besides, several seem to have survived since at least the 18th or 19th centuries, which is certainly nothing to sneeze at. It's only to argue that they are not demonstrably quite as ancient as MacDonald would have liked to believe.

Which Came First?

Which came first: the instrumental tunes or the puirt-a-beul related to them? This question animated many people's responses to my questions about the origins of puirt-a-beul, and an answer would help determine when puirt-a-beul may have first emerged. The following comments were made during interviews I conducted in 1998.

I'm sure puirt-a-beul have been sung from the beginning of Celtic society, because of the dual nature of the slower, more melancholic kind of song that is full of longing and at the same time, this immense, instinctive desire to dance and do music that is this joyful, fun. So I'm sure it's been around always. (Gaelic speaker and singer from Scotland who emigrated to Nova Scotia)

I don't think there's any way to really know what the origins were or what it originally was exactly for.... You know, the fiddle and the pipes. I mean, which came first, the song or the instrument? Maybe it is the song, maybe it is the voice that's the original instrument. (Gaelic learner and singer from Christmas Island in Cape Breton)

You don't know what to believe. It's a chicken and egg problem. It's hard to say because I think that a lot of the songs that we know are [tunes by] Dow and Gow and Marshall.... A lot of tunes we know come from the 18th century so that's only as far back as we're going in many cases. So if you're talking about those tunes, the classics of Scottish fiddling and Cape Breton fiddling, coming from the 18th century and really composed by these men, then obviously the tune came first. If they really did make the tunes, then the tune really did come first and then someone put words to it [and] why not? They were doing that all the time in the classical music world in the 18th century. There's lots of tunes; in *The Beggar's Opera,* there's tunes by Geminiani and Purcell and Handel that existed as instrumental pieces first and they put [words] to them because the tune was a hit already and, if the tune's a hit already, why not have words to it and then you can sing it as a showpiece? ... You've got to wonder about those stories about pipes and fiddles being banned. Does that mean that they had these tunes already and so they wrote words to them to remember or were there words already with them for the same reason as they were in the 18th century? ... Often, there's so many different sets of words that go with the tune, it leads me to believe that this tune was popular and various people at various times made words to go with it so they could sing it either because they didn't have a fiddle or because it was just fun. (Gaelic learner and singer from Toronto)

[When] it was first used here, there was somebody going to dance and they had no [instrumental] music. And instead of just using the sounds, there was words put to it. (Gaelic speaker and singer from Barra Glen in Cape Breton)

On the one hand, the voice is humankind's first instrument. It existed before instruments and we generally learn to use our voices before we learn to use instruments. Surely all people have sung to accompany dancing, no matter how informally or poorly executed. Tunes get stuck in our heads and we hum to ourselves while shuffling our feet in time. We sing nursery rhymes and encourage our children to dance. It is not hard to imagine something like puirt-a-beul arising to accompany dance, especially in times before the technologies of today that make personal, informal and amateur singing less and less necessary or even desirable. Moreover, there is a long history of connections between Gaelic song and instrumental music in Scotland; there wasn't always a sense of a clear divide between the two such as we have today. Indeed, much of European society danced to song rather than instrumental music right through the Middle Ages and even when instrumental music began being used to accompany dancing, instruments played song melodies (Emmerson 1971: 4-6, 12). It was common in Europe for an instrument such as the violin to double the voice in a song and it is no surprise that, eventually, instruments began playing song melodies independently (Boyden 1965: 52-53). In other words, the connection between instrumental music and puirt-a-beul song is hardly unique to 18th-century Scotland, and obviously has roots in earlier European musical traditions.

On the other hand, just because we can imagine that singing pre-existed instrumental dance music, the puirt-a-beul we know today didn't necessarily pre-exist it. As various people have noted, puirt-a-beul can sound quite "pipey," suggesting that they emulate the instrument rather than the other way around (see Chapter 3). Even K. N. MacDonald, despite arguing for the ancient, pre-instrumental origins of puirt-a-beul, acknowledges that some puirt-a-beul so nearly "approach the rhythm of the music ... that in many instances one can tell whether the music was a pipe-set or not" (MacDonald 1931 [1901]: 4-5). To hear pipey-sounding puirt-a-beul, I recommend the recordings of Kenna Campbell, who is perhaps the most celebrated puirt-a-beul singer anywhere. She herself argues that "puirt-a-beul aren't songs at all, but *instrumental* tunes whose lyrics power their rhythms" (paraphrased in Kopka 1997: 18; emphasis in original). In 1998, I interviewed a Scottish Gael living in Toronto who played me a recording she had of a BBC interview with Kenna Campbell in which Campbell indicated that although she was aware of the belief that puirt-a-beul developed after Culloden, she believed that the battle did not so much give rise to puirt-a-beul as simply increase the opportunity to sing puirt-a-beul already in existence. Kenna argued that puirt-a-beul and piping were developed simultaneously.

The uncertainty regarding "the chicken or the egg" question extends to scholars as well. Gaelic scholar William Lamb argues that "there were times that Gaelic speakers chose *not* to use instruments for dancing, actually preferring puirt-à-beul," making the point that puirt-a-beul were not necessarily substitutes for instrumental tunes but existed independently (Lamb 2012: 22; emphasis in original). In an even more recent article, Lamb argues that Scottish instrumental dance tunes, particularly strathspeys and their rhythms, began as Gaelic song, although not necessarily as puirt-a-beul as we know them today (2013). George S. Emmerson is ambivalent regarding the origins of puirt-a-beul. On the one hand, Emmerson accepts that puirt-a-beul could have ancient origins. Citing Bruno Nettl's *Music in Primitive Culture* (1956), he asserts that ethnomusicologists have found that "most primitive peoples seem to conceive of the words and melody of a song as an indivisible unit, are rarely able to differentiate between them and cannot ordinarily give either text or music alone without difficulty" (Emmerson 1971: 5). Emmerson concludes that "Puirt-a-beul ... [are] the product of a primitive impulse to associate all music with words, or rather, with uttered syllables, whether they make sense or not" (9). On the other hand, Emmerson indicates that puirt-a-beul may have evolved from instrumental music:

"The term mouth music is not used of song; it has the meaning of instrumental music made by the mouth and thus would appear to date from a period after the introduction of instrumental music" (Emmerson 1971: 5).

Alan Bruford, a renowned Celtic folklorist, was somewhat vague about the origins of puirt-a-beul, but unromantic: "very often each verse and each refrain is sung twice over, just like the repeats in instrumental dances … this is [therefore] one indication that the mouth music must be copied from fiddle or pipe tunes rather than the other way about" (Bruford 1979: 11). James Ross, a Gaelic song scholar, did not deny the possibility that puirt-a-beul as a genre was old, but he did deny the age of much of the present-day repertoire: "The *raison d'être* of this song type is the memorizing of dance tunes…. The practice of singing dance tunes such as strathspeys and reels appears to be of modern origin" (1957: 133). Likewise, Collinson concurs that "the general opinion is … that as a form of music puirt-a-beul is of comparatively modern date—probably as late as the eighteenth century" (1966: 94).

Indeed, the earliest description of what seems to be puirt-a-beul comes from none other than Bonnie Prince Charlie himself during the 1745-1746 Jacobite uprising. Upon seeing some Highland women at a shieling, he purportedly said, "Come, my lasses, what would you think to dance a Highland reel with me? We cannot have a bag-pipe just now, but I shall sing you a Strathspey reel" (Forbes, *The Lyon in Mourning*, 1895 qtd. in Newton 2014). The Prince's reference to singing a "strathspey reel" to accompany a "Highland reel" dance certainly implies that he planned to sing a port-a-beul, although he does not use the term. For that matter, he might have planned to "jig" the tune with improvised vocables rather than sing actual lyrics.

The earliest documented port-a-beul exists in a late-18th-century document. The MacDiarmid manuscript, dated 1770, is a song "scrapbook" of sorts made by a minister (Rev. Eoghan Macdhiarmid) interested in Gaelic songs and poems. The manuscript contains a mix of songs, including songs of known authorship and many anonymous songs. Celtic scholar Derick Thomson published a book transcribing and annotating the manuscript's songs of unknown authorship, including one port-a-beul-like song from a St. Kilda source (Thomson 1992: 156-157). It is the only port-a-beul in the manuscript (although it is not labelled as such) and it is not found in any other written sources, although it was recorded two centuries later by the School of Scottish Studies from a Harris woman (Newton 2009: 253).

Tha iolairean a' chaolais
A' caoineadh a' choilich dhuibh
Iolairean a' chaolais
A' caoineadh a' choilich dhuibh
Tha iolairean a' chaolais
A' caoineadh a' choilich dhuibh
A' caoineadh, ag eughach
A' rànaich a' choilich dhuibh.

A' caoineadh, ag eughach
A' rànaich a' choilich dhuibh
A' caoineadh, ag eughach
A' rànaich a' choilich dhuibh
A' caoineadh, ag eughach
A' rànaich a' choilich dhuibh
Tha iolairean a' chaolais
A' caoineadh a' choilich dhuibh.

The eagles are shrieking
The hollering of the black cocks
The eagles are shrieking
The hollering of the black cocks
The eagles are shrieking
The hollering of the black cocks
Hollering, shouting
The bawling of the black cocks.

Hollering, shouting
The bawling of the black cocks
Hollering, shouting
The bawling of the black cocks
Hollering, shouting
The bawling of the black cocks

The eagles are shrieking
The hollering of the black cocks.

Angus Cumming's *A Collection of Strathspeys* (1782) is a collection of 60 tunes, all but one of which have English titles. However, 27 titles also have Gaelic names. Lamb believes that the Gaelic titles imply their Gaelic origins (Lamb 2013). Newton, however, observes that only 5 of the 27 strathspeys can be found in other Gaelic sources—we might expect them to appear more often in contemporary Gaelic sources if they were indeed of Gaelic origins—suggesting that "these titles ... depict a musical genre still maturing and not yet corresponding to the surviving repertoire of *puirt-à-beul*" (Newton 2014). In other words, this collection, which neither uses the term "puirt-a-beul" nor provides Gaelic lyrics for any tunes, may be an indicator that the late 18th century was the time of puirt-a-beul's consolidation as a recognizable and distinct genre.

Alexander Campbell, writing more than thirty years after Cumming's collection was published and almost fifty years after the MacDiarmid manuscript was created, describes the use of puirt-a-beul as dance accompaniment in Lochmaddie, South Uist. His is the first recorded instance of using the term "puirt-a-beul" that I know of:

> While here, I witnessed for the first time, persons singing at the same time they dance: and this is called dancing to port-na-beul, being a succedaneous [substitute] contrivance to supply the want of a musical instrument. This effect is droll enough; and gives an ideal of what one might conceive to be customary among tribes but little removed from a state of Nature. What renders the illusion more probable is the mode in which these merry Islanders perform the double exercise of singing and dancing:—thus the accent and *rhythms* quite accurately—the effect is animating: and having words correspondent to the characters of the measure—there seems to be a 3-fold species of gratification arising from the union of song and dance—rude, it is confessed—but such as pleases

the vulgar; and not displeasant to one who feels disposed to join in rustic pleasures, or innocent amusement. (1815, "Slight Sketch" qtd. in Dickson 2006: 18)

Scottish fiddle scholar Katherine Campbell makes the intriguing point that fiddle tunes were once sung at the same time they were played, a practice common throughout Europe since at least the Medieval period, and this was no less true in Scotland. She labels it a "lost art" and explains why it probably fell out of favour:

Much of the fiddler's repertoire consisted of songs in the early period, so it is very easy to see why people sang as they played. When the potential of the modern violin was explored through the more sophisticated compositions that came in during the eighteenth century, the tradition of singing while playing would likely have seemed old-fashioned. Many accounts show that the tradition carried on in the unskilled minstrel class of musicians. For those making a living, it was important to be heard above the cacophony of street life if one wanted to earn a copper or two and the sound of the fiddle could be boosted by the addition of voice. (2007: 36)

Although Campbell does not mention puirt-a-beul directly, it is certainly possible that puirt-a-beul emerged as part of the "singing fiddling" tradition. Indeed, John Shaw has documented just such an occurrence in the Canadian province of Prince Edward Island: "Jigging, called puirt-a-beul in Gaelic, was a frequent feature of wedding and dances on the North Shore, where two people would be hired to sit on either side of the fiddler and jig the tunes as they were played" (Shaw 1987).

One might disagree that puirt-a-beul evolved with the fiddle for the repertoire is not limited to fiddle tunes; there are several pipe-related puirt-a-beul as well. However, there is no reason why the tradition might not have started with fiddle tunes and later expanded to include tunes from other instrumental repertoires. This is, in fact, Celtic historian Michael Newton's perspective:

> When the modern violin arrived in Scotland in the sev-
> enteenth century it came with a new style of dance music
> which, once reshaped by native musical sensibilities, evolved
> into distinctively Scottish forms, particularly the reel and
> strathspey. These tunes, primarily instrumental and played
> specifically for dancing, are referred to in Gaelic as *puirt*
> (plural, singular *port*). As they became "verbalised" in song
> form (known as *port-à-beul* "mouth-tune") for the purposes
> of memorising and teaching, they acquired the rhythms and
> cadences of Gaelic speech. These ditties, however, are not
> considered true poetry according to the high standards of
> Gaelic poetry (such as found in the genres of dàn, laoidh,
> etc.), but mnemonic verbalisations, sung for dancers if in-
> struments are not available. (2009: 253)

Newton argues that puirt-a-beul emerged in tandem with the music that accompanied the new styles of dance that migrated to Scotland from the European continent. After a body of puirt-a-beul repertoire was created for these dances, and once the genre had become established, new puirt-a-beul began to be created without direct connection to dancing (Newton 2009: 253).

Returning to Katherine Campbell, I'd like to draw attention to her interesting point that singing and fiddling continued among amateur musicians, a continuation that parallels the puirt-a-beul tradition in that puirt-a-beul are generally believed to be the products of lay-people rather than the creations of bards. Campbell describes a particular fiddler known to make up (English) songs on the spot for audiences, which also echoes what we know about puirt-a-beul. As I will discuss in Chapter 4, puirt-a-beul were often created to commemorate local characters or events. Rather than emerging before or after instrumental traditions, perhaps puirt-a-beul emerged in tandem with one.

Another way to investigate the origins of puirt-a-beul is to investigate the origins of their form. As I explain in Chapter 3, virtually all puirt-a-beul are in binary form (two sections of equal length, each repeated). While both the harp and bagpipes may well have accompanied dance, we have little knowledge of the kinds of music they might have played to do so. The music that we *do* know initially played each instrument was not, in either case, binary-form dance tunes. Harps are quiet instruments and therefore not particularly suited to accompanying large groups of dancers anyway. Highland harpers originally accompanied Gaelic syllabic verse, although the nature of this accompaniment is not known (Sanger and Kinnaird 1992: 172). Instrumental music for its own sake (not for the accompaniment of song or dance) became increasingly popular in western European art music circles from the late 15th century, and by 1600 it was strongly represented. As part of this trend, the "port" type of harp tune emerged and flourished in Scotland (it seems to have never been known in Ireland) from around the mid-16th century until about a hundred years later (Sanger and Kinnaird 1992: 174). The word "port" would suggest a connection with "port-a-beul," but while the word means the same in both instances ("tune"), the music is completely different. In the case of harp puirt, their irregular phrasing suggests they were not used as music for song or dance but instead indicate a kind of harp music designed to be listened to and appreciated for its own sake. In fact, harp scholars Keith Sanger and Alison Kinnaird argue that the theme and variations format of classical bagpipe music may have had its roots in harp music such as the puirt (1992: 186).

Michael Newton argues that when the bagpipes made their way to Highland Scotland by the 16th century, the harp (*clàrsach*) tradition was already well entrenched and, consequently, bagpipes were not initially used as a musical instrument so much as a military tool, used to "lead soldiers, intimidate enemies, and send battle signals" (Newton 2009: 263-64). Eventually, the harp tradition declined while bagpipes became increasingly popular, adapting techniques and repertoire from the harp tradition (Sanger and Kinnaird 1992: 186-90). Consistent with the history of harp music, and with general trends in continental European instrumental music, some early bagpipe music is linked to Gaelic song, particularly commemorative clan songs (MacNeill and Richardson 1987: 20; Newton 2009: 269). Classical bagpipe music is called pibroch

("pibroch" is the Anglicized version of the original Gaelic word *pìobaireachd*, but more accurately called ceòl mòr, or "big music" in Gaelic), and it is based on a theme-and-variations form and features increasingly intricate and challenging playing techniques that were clearly intended to be the focus of attention rather than subsidiary to dancing. Interestingly, as in the harp tradition, the term "port" seems to have been used at one time to refer to pipe music, but used for its generic meaning of "tune." To avoid confusion with terms like "port-a-beul," some Gaelic writers of the late 19th and early 20th centuries—when the term "port-a-beul" was already well established and in common use—actually used the term *port mòr* (big tune) to refer to a pibroch (Cannon 2002: 46). *Ceòl beag* ("little music") is the term used to refer to the binary dance tune repertoire, but the first collection of these tunes for bagpipes did not appear until 1829, in Edinburgh bagpipe maker Donald Macdonald's *A Collection of Quicksteps, Strathspeys, Reels and Jigs* (Collinson 1966: 197). The origins of the term "ceòl beag" are uncertain, and it is not clear that it was a traditional term; piping scholars generally believe that pibrochs are the older form of pipe music (Cannon 2002: 46). It would seem that prior to the 19th century, all pipe music was considered "pìobaireachd." It was only during the Victorian era that pipe music came to be divided into types, including ceòl mòr and ceòl beag (Shears 2008: 28).

We know that the binary dance tunes that have come to be so strongly associated with Celtic musical traditions were never limited to Scotland and Ireland. They were played elsewhere in Europe too. J. S. Bach (1685-1750), for example, composed dance suites that incorporated numerous binary dance tune types, each associated with a different country (e.g., the allemande from Germany, the courante from Italy and France, the sarabande from Spain and Italy, and the gigue from England and Ireland). Although his compositions were based on dance music, they were designed for listening, not as dance accompaniment. It's clear that by Bach's time these binary dance tunes had long been played by the peasantry of continental Europe. Unfortunately, this vernacular dance music had not been deemed worthy of collection and notation, both because of its lower social and musical status and because most dance players would have been musically illiterate, learning to play through oral transmission and therefore not requiring notated music.

The earliest examples I can find of binary dance tunes in continental Europe are some French dances called *branles* or *bransles*, from the French word *branler*, meaning to swing from side to side (Dolmetsch 1959: 55), popular from early in the 16th century. These apparently were also known in the Scottish Highlands. The dance scholar Mabel Dolmetsch tells us that sometime around 1924 she was performing 16th-century dances when she met a Gaelic-speaking woman from Sutherland in Scotland:

> The brawl, she told me, was still danced in those parts as "the brail." I asked her whether our steps and gestures nearly resembled those of the present-day dance, to which question she replied that they did; "only," she added apologetically, "we do more *shouting*." (1959: 71; emphasis in original)

Indeed, there was a suite of branles called the Branles d'Écosse, and Arbeau, famous for his late-16th-century dance textbook *Orchesographie*, assures us that branles named after regions were drawn from these regions. However, Emmerson is not entirely convinced:

> Whatever the facts, there is not much evidence of a characteristic Branle in Scotland, unless it came under the name of round, which is very likely. One suspects that the Branle d'Écosse is a French creation based upon a step or steps used in some Scottish rounds. (1972: 42)

We really have no way of knowing when the "brail" first came to be practised in Scotland, let alone how much originated in Scotland versus how much came from foreign dances that were adopted and danced by Scots.

Documented and elite music from the earlier Medieval period (pre-1400) used *formes fixes* (fixed forms) and was not in binary form. However, that does not mean that binary dance tunes were not being played by the peasantry during the Middle Ages; it only means that we have no record of them. Ultimately, we do not know where and when binary dance tunes first developed or how they spread. We only know from notated sources that they existed by the early 1500s in continental Europe.

This also means that we have no incontrovertible evidence of when binary dance tunes entered Scottish repertoire. We do know, however, that the violin developed as a European instrument from about 1520, about the same time as branles were being documented and printed. The violin had two basic functions until at least 1600: to double the voice in song, and to accompany dancing (Boyden 1965: 50). The first Scottish manuscript of tunes specifically for the violin, the Newbattle Manuscript, dates from 1680 (Alburger 1983: 24), suggesting that the violin was commonplace in (Lowland) Scotland by that point. Prior to the arrival of the violin in Scotland, the fiddle existed, arriving in Scotland by no later than 1497 (Alburger 1983: 11). Although the terms "fiddle" and "violin" are today used to refer to the same instrument, the fiddle was, at one time, a different instrument altogether. The fiddle was subsequently replaced by viols; despite the similarity in name to "violin," viols were different instruments again. Unfortunately, we have no written music for the Scottish fiddle or viol and therefore are uncertain whether they played binary dance tunes or not.

Although violin and fiddle historians indicate that these instruments became commonplace in Scotland, it is difficult to say how quickly they permeated Scottish society, how the instruments spread (from Lowlands to Highlands, for example, or from cities to rural areas?), and what class of people played them (did they start among the gentry and gradually make their way to the peasantry?). Part of the problem is that vernacular music—the music of everyday people—was not generally deemed worthy of documenting until relatively recently, and the peasantry were often either musically and literally illiterate or, even if they were literate, had little use for notating music or writing about it. Therefore, most of the earliest documentary evidence of the fiddle and violin in Scotland refers to upper-class music-making in major cultural centres such as Edinburgh. This does not mean that these instruments were not known elsewhere; it only means that we often lack evidence to prove it. There are, however, some early indications of the popularity of the fiddle among the peasantry, as in a declaration dated November 17, 1587, in which unemployed musicians of Edinburgh are ordered to leave:

> Ordanis proclamatioun to be maid chairgeing all menstrallis, pyperis, fidleris, commoun sangsteris, and specially of badrie and filthy sangs, and siclyke all vagabounds and maisterles persouns quha hes na seruice nor honest industrie to leif be, remoue and depairt furth of this burgh incontinent, and be nocht fund within the samyn heirafter vnder the payne of imprysonment in the thevis hoill and pvnesing of thair persouns at the will of the magestrats. (Edinburgh Burgh Records, 1882, qtd. in Campbell 2007: xiv)

Mary Alburger documents Gaelic place names that indicate the pervasiveness of the fiddle in Gaelic culture as well as Lowland culture, place names like:

> Carn an Fhidhleir (Carn Ealar), "fiddler's rock," on the borders of Aberdeenshire, the Highlands and Perth and Kinross; Sgurr an Fhidhleir, "fiddler's peak," on Ben Mòr Coigeach, Wester Ross; and Binnein an Fhidhleir, "fiddler's pinnacle" (now called Stob Coire Creagach), Argyll and Bute. (Alburger 2007: 238)

Michael Newton notes that the first reference to the fiddle can be found in a manuscript dating from about 1160. Although he observes that "there is scant surviving evidence about this instrument ... so it is unlikely to have played a prominent role in élite Gaelic society" (2009: 258), there is nothing to say that it wasn't prominent among peasant Gaels. Evidence from elsewhere in Europe indicates that peasant fiddlers were common, and there is no reason to disbelieve that the same was the case in Scotland. The fiddle and later violin were and are portable instruments and rudimentary versions could be made relatively easily and inexpensively, making them ideal instruments for the peasant classes.

The earliest printed collections of instrumental tunes in Scotland did not appear until the early 1600s and they seem to consist predominantly of binary tunes, suggesting that these kinds of tunes were already well established in Scotland by then, at least in the Lowlands. Michael Newton argues that binary tunes and the modern violin did not become popular in Gaelic Ireland or Scotland until somewhat later, in the 17th century (2009: 258). The earliest known tune collections did not typically target particular instruments; they were meant to be played on a range of instruments.

Alburger suggests that as long as the King of Scotland resided in Edinburgh, the court there was the centre of music-making. Court music would have reflected the continental European fashions of the day, and music printed in other countries would have circulated in Scotland's capital and beyond. But when King James VI of Scotland became King James I of England in 1603 and moved to London, taking his court and its music with him, elite Edinburgh society looked around for new musical inspiration and discovered the music of their own citizenry, and this is what led to the relatively late development of printed collections of Scottish tunes (1983: 15-16).

The Scottish Reformation also likely played a role in limiting the collection and printing of dance music, for Protestant Reformers denounced most dancing throughout the late 16th and 17th centuries. At the same time, the fact that there are many records of people being brought before the Kirk Session and fined or punished for dancing indicates that dancing persisted even so.

Due to the lack of early written records of vernacular music not just in Scotland but anywhere in Europe, it is really impossible to know when and where binary dance tunes emerged and were popular. But we do know that by the time the earliest known port-a-beul shows up in 1770, binary dance tunes were well-established in Scotland. The first use of the term "puirt-a-beul" doesn't appear until 1815. By then, the harp was largely extinct, the bagpipes were on the decline, and the fiddle was the primary instrument of social music and dance accompaniment. It is significant also that there appears to be only a very limited equivalent of puirt-a-beul in Ireland, which certainly suggests that puirt-a-beul was a primarily Scottish Gaelic genre and likely of more recent origins. If it were otherwise, we would expect to find more examples of Irish portaireacht and more information and stories about them than we do.

The disappointing reality is that no one really knows when and why puirt-a-beul were invented. My husband and I are both musicians and, consequently, we often make up silly words to well-known tunes and songs. Our lyrics are designed to be sung and heard within the family where the references will be understood. Our lyrics usually centre on our cat's activities, occasionally on a humorous slip-of-the-tongue or faux-pas, and sometimes on bawdy subjects. We occasionally share them with close friends who will appreciate their humour. But they would surely be considered ridiculous and trivial by anyone outside our close circle of friends and family. Puirt-a-beul are generally much the same and probably have similar origins. As far as we know, they tended to be made by lay-people, that is to say, by average people rather than by bards. Their silly, sometimes nonsensical lyrics and ridiculous topics suggest that they too were created for a small audience rather than as poetry designed to withstand the tests of time.

Such an origin theory, however, is relatively banal and doesn't make a great story. And people like good stories. The stories explaining the origins of puirt-a-beul, whether in response to the purported proscription of the bagpipes, the religious fervour of fiddle-burning priests and ministers, or the ancient inclinations of Druids, make this genre stand out as unique in the world of traditional music. And despite quite a variety of origin theories, puirt-a-beul's origin stories almost always explain how Gaelic song and music have persevered against all odds, the heroic cultural underdog. It is therefore no real surprise that such stories have flourished, whatever their actual likelihood.

The origins of puirt-a-beul are likely much more ordinary and diffuse. They likely emerged in unremarkable ways for fairly mundane reasons. Scottish music scholar and Whistlebinkies concertina player Stuart Eydmann notes, "Although it is commonly held that [puirt-a-beul] resulted from the political or religious proscription of indigenous cultural practices, I prefer an explanation based on economic reality and recognition of the highly participative nature of the musical culture of the period" (Eydmann 2007: 194-95). There is no question that there is a long history of accompanying dance with song, not just in Scotland but throughout Europe as well. However, these dance songs were not known as puirt-a-beul, nor were they in binary form. But puirt-a-beul, as vocal dance accompaniment, were clearly not an odd or unusual development. Rather, they seem to have emerged as a new form based on an established tradition.

It is quite possible, even likely, that puirt-a-beul flourished after Culloden and during Scottish Presbyterianism's strictest days. Certainly puirt-a-beul seem to have stabilized as a definitive and recognizable genre during those particular periods. But it is difficult to assert with any confidence that puirt-a-beul were actually invented in response to either situation. Puirt-a-beul probably emerged in an organic way, perhaps with variations emerging in different places at the same time, gradually developing into the genre we label puirt-a-beul today. Post-Culloden political and later religious tensions likely helped to spur puirt-a-beul's visibility, popularity and new repertoire creation, but they are unlikely to have been the direct cause of their invention.

Chapter 3
"Ciamar a Nì Mi an Ruidhle Bhòidheach": Musical Features

In this chapter, I describe the musical characteristics of puirt-a-beul. It is aimed primarily at an audience unfamiliar with Scottish traditional music.[1] I have tried to make it as accessible as possible to those who may not be musically literate, although I have also provided several notated examples to help illustrate the characteristics I describe in the text.

There are several different types of puirt-a-beul. By far and away the most common are reels and strathspeys. However, there are also a few jigs and the occasional march. The prevalence of the former two and existence of the latter two raise some interesting questions about the relationship between puirt-a-beul and dance, especially what kinds of dances might have been accompanied by puirt-a-beul, an issue that I explore further in Chapter 5.

While reels, jigs and marches are known and played in both Irish and Scottish musical traditions, reels are generally ascribed Scottish origins whereas jigs are most strongly associated with Ireland. Meanwhile, strathspeys are unique to Scotland and Cape Breton; they are generally not played in Ireland. The fact that there are numerous strathspeys in the puirt-a-beul repertoire and comparatively few jigs is consistent with the strong profile of puirt-a-beul in Scotland versus the relatively minimal emphasis on the parallel tradition in Ireland. Meanwhile, puirt-a-beul-like Irish songs tend to be in jig time.

Form and Structure

Given that puirt-a-beul seem to have emerged at about the same time that particular forms of European dance tunes began to be played in Scotland (as discussed in the previous chapter), it is not surprising that they share their structure. Generally speaking, dance tunes consist of two melodic sections called "turns" in Cape Breton. We could call these sections A and B. Each section is usually 4 or 8 bars long and each is repeated, resulting in an overall form of AABB. The entire piece is then repeated, giving us: AABB AABB. This symmetrical and repetitious form is known as "binary" in classical music scholarship.

After playing the tune through twice, a Cape Breton musician would today move on to a second tune, linking together multiple tunes into sets or groups, as they are known in Cape Breton. Sets can be extended as long as needed (i.e., as long as the dance being accompanied) or desired and the incorporation of different tunes keeps the music interesting and inspiring for both musicians and dancers. In Ireland and Scotland, the tune might be repeated a third time before moving on to the next tune. The same can be done with puirt-a-beul although it depends on the number of verses (I describe set creation further below).

To differentiate between the tune and the lyrics and to clarify their relationship, I use the term "sections" to refer to the parts of the tune and the terms "verses" and "choruses" to refer to the lyrics. In the case of a port-a-beul with multiple verses, the verses are all separated by the chorus. Most puirt-a-beul only have a single verse and chorus, which correspond to the two tune sections (such that the verse is sung to the tune of the first section and the chorus is sung to the tune of the second section). In these cases, each port-a-beul would be repeated once through in its entirety, just like an instrumental tune, and then the singer would move on

to another port-a-beul. However, some puirt-a-beul have two or
more verses, in which case the singer would continue to alternate
between verse and chorus until the song is complete. The chart
below illustrates what happens given a port-a-beul with a single
verse and chorus, two verses and a chorus, and three verses and
a chorus:

    Port-a-beul with one verse, one chorus
        Verse = A
        Chorus = B
        Performance: AABB AABB
    Port-a-beul with two verses, one chorus
        Verse 1 = A1
        Verse 2 = A2
        Chorus = B
        Performance: A1A1BB A2A2BB
    Port-a-beul with three verses, one chorus
        Verse 1 = A1
        Verse 2 = A2
        Verse 3 = A3
        Chorus = B
    Performance: A1A1BB A2A2BB A3A3BB (note the
    extended form in this case)

In very simple terms, music can be analyzed according to contrast and repetition. As we will see in the next chapter, the lyrics
include repetition both within a turn and across turns. Likewise,
the melodic material of the two sections includes both contrastive
and related material. The start of the B section usually contrasts
quite clearly with the A section. Typically, it will suddenly involve
singing in a higher register to contrast with the lower notes of the
previous turn. Sometimes it's the other way around: the B section
suddenly drops in register in contrast to the higher A section. This
contrast helps to define the musical structure of dance tunes and
also provides musical interest. But while the B section may start
quite differently from the A section, it often contains, especially at
the end, musical material drawn from the A section. This repetition helps to unite the two sections and leads the musician (and

listener) back to the A section for a repeat of the tune. Watch for these repetitions and contrasts in the examples I provide below.

Reels

By far the most common type of puirt-a-beul is a reel. The word "reel" comes from the Anglo-Saxon *rulla*, meaning "to whirl" (Collinson 2001).[2] Reels are in 4/4 time (also known as "common time" because it is such a frequently occurring time signature). This means that they have four beats per bar (the top number in the time signature) with each beat lasting a quarter of the bar (the bottom number in the time signature). The first beat gets the strongest accent and the third beat gets a moderate accent. The second and fourth beats are normally unaccented. This pattern of accented and unaccented beats is known as *metre*. Once this regular pattern of accented and unaccented beats is established, it is possible for a composer to deliberately thwart the expected pattern, creating an accented note in a spot normally unaccented. Known as *syncopation*, this creates a lot of excitement and drive.[3] Reels are often the most popular tune type with audiences due to their quick tempos and fast, dense rhythms, as well as their frequent syncopations.

Reels are often played in "cut time," which means that a half note ("minim" in British English) gets the beat, rather than the quarter note (or "crotchet"), because the tempo is too fast to count shorter notes. In essence, this means that each bar sounds as though it only has two beats instead of four. However, there are still four beats—they're just so fast that we don't register them as such. Fiddle scholar Kate Dunlay argues that reels almost invariably felt in two (cut time), at least in Cape Breton, with fiddlers tapping either twice per bar, or four times per bar using a rocking motion of the foot such that the heel marks the strong beats (beats 1 and 3) and the ball of the foot marks weak beats (beats 2 and 4; personal communication, December 31, 2013). Reel tempos are more consistent than strathspey tempos (see the next section for a discussion of strathspeys), normally registering around 120 beats per minute in cut time (that would be 240 beats per minute in regular 4/4 time!), although tempos vary according to fiddle style, musician and context. In Ireland, for example, where notes are often slurred (several pitches are played by the fiddle bow moving in one direction), tempos can be faster. In Cape Breton, where slurring is less common (the bow changes direction for each pitch), tempos tend to be a little slower. The sound of a reel is most identifiable by the dominance of eighth ("quaver") notes. The density of these relatively short note durations, especially when played at a quick tempo, gives the impression of speed. The consistency and density of short note durations also creates a smooth sound. This smooth sound is similar to that of a jig but contrasts significantly with strathspeys and many marches, as will become clear later.[4]

A particularly popular reel in both Scotland and Cape Breton is "Am Muileann Dubh" ("The Black Mill"), which goes by its Gaelic name in English circles as well (although it has various spellings). This tune dates from at least the late 1700s, appearing in McGlashan's *A Collection of Reels* (1786) as "The Mullin Du." The title suggests that Gaelic lyrics were already associated with it at the time it was published although we don't know whether it was known first as a tune or as a port-a-beul.[5] Traditionally in Gaelic culture, songs were tied to stories that contextualized their lyrics (the connection between puirt-a-beul and stories is discussed in more detail in the next chapter), and this tune is no exception. In fact, there are several associated with it. In telling the stories about this port-a-beul, I move away from a focus on its sonic and musical properties. However, I offer them here in order to acknowledge that puirt-a-beul (and their associated fiddle tunes) are more than musical texts; they are part of cultural complexes that include contextual and historical information.

In 1900, *The Celtic Monthly*, an English-language magazine, published three letters about "Am Muileann Dubh," each with a different set of lyrics. One writer, Gregor MacGregor, suggests that the song is about an illicit whisky still. He had learned "Am Muileann Dubh" as a child but never understood the lyrics' meaning. He had also been to an illicit still but did not know it to be named anything in particular until he met a Professor Mackinnon, who told him that an illicit still was known as a "Muileann Dubh," a black mill. For Mr. MacGregor, the song suddenly made complete sense with each line "pregnant with meaning" (MacGregor 1900: 159-60).

Sèist
Tha muileann dubh air bhogadan
Air bhogadan, air bhogadan
Tha muileann dubh air bhogadan
Se togairt dol a dhannsa.

Rannan
Bha nead na circe-fraoiche
Sa mhuileann duibh, sa mhuileann duibh
Bha nead na circe-fraoiche
Sa mhuileann duibh bhon t-samhradh.

Bha gobhair agus caoraich
[*pattern follows that of the first verse*]

Bha crodh a' breith nan laugh

Bha tombac agus snaoisein

Bha rud nach eil sibh saoilsinn

Bha cur 'us cathadh 's gaoth

Shaoil leam gun robh min eorna
Sa mhuileann duibh, sa mhuileann duibh
Shaoil leam gun robh min eorna
Sa mhuileann duibh 's gun deann ann.

Bha Diobhol-dubh-nan-adhaircean

Refrain
A black mill has shaken
Has shaken, has shaken
A black mill has shaken
It has started to dance.

Verses
The nest of the moorhen
Was in the black mill, in the black mill
The nest of the moorhen
Was in the black mill since the summer.

Goats and sheep
[*pattern follows that of the first verse*]

Cattle birthing calves

Tobacco and snuff

A thing you wouldn't imagine

Snow and drifts and wind

I thought there was barley
In the black mill, in the black mill
I thought there was barley
In the black mill and that there was snuff.

The black-devil-of-the-horns

I leave it to the reader to decide whether the interpretation of the black mill as an illicit still is as obvious in the lyrics as Mr. MacGregor seemed to suppose.

Although "Am Muileann Dubh" is an example of a port-a-beul having multiple verses, only two are commonly heard in Cape Breton today, and they vary slightly from those above:

Sèist
Tha 'm muileann dubh air thuraman
Tha 'm muileann dubh air thuraman
Tha 'm muileann dubh air thuraman
Se togairt dol a dhannsa.

Rannan
Tha nead na circe-fraoiche
Sa mhuileann dhubh, sa mhuileann dhubh
Tha nead na circe-fraoiche
Sa mhuileann dhubh bhon t-samhradh.

'S iomadh rud nach saoil sibh
[*pattern follows that of the first verse*]

Refrain
The black mill is moving around
The black mill is moving around
The black mill is moving around
It has started to dance.

Verses
The nest of the moorhen has been
In the black mill, in the black mill
The nest of the moorhen has been
In the black mill since the summer.

Many's the thing you wouldn't believe
[*pattern follows that of the first verse*]

One Cape Bretoner recently agreed that *am muileann dubh* was a code, but suggested a different interpretation:

"Mullin Dubh" means the "Black Mill." Though a pipe tune, it was first a song (as with most of our native music). Specifically, it was a Gaelic Jacobite "code" song. (The name refers to the exiled monarch, the dark-haired James Stewart VII and II). The first verse says: "The nest of the moor hen (another Stewart code name) is in the Black Mill," and goes on to list some extremely unlikely things that are in "the Black Mill of the Summer." The chorus says: "The Black Mill is turning (spinning), lifting to go to the Dance." This refers to the return of the Stewarts from abroad, and the beginning of a Rising. (The motif of the return of the true king bringing summer, and the analogy of the Rising as a "dance" is common in both Gaelic and Broad Scots Jacobite songs.) (S. Taylor 1998: 26)

Yet another Cape Breton story suggests that the lyrics have a double-entendre, but in this account, they are a veiled insult to a particular local family:

In the Margaree district, where the MacDougalls are very numerous, it was highly inadvisable to play the tune known by the innocent title, "Am Muileann Dubh" (The Black Mill), for a [curious] reason.... One line of a stanza set to this tune runs: "Tha nead na circe fraoiche 's a' muileann dubh" (in the black mill is the heather-hen's nest); and the MacDougalls of Margaree, because of some joke about hens once told at the expense of their clan, were so sensitive that they could not tolerate a reference to poultry of any kind and were likely to regard even the playing of the tune as a veiled insult. (Dunn 1991 [1953]: 102)

Dr. Seósamh Watson and Dr. John Shaw collected variations of yet another Cape Breton story about this tune (J. Shaw 2007: 184-87; S. Watson 2005-2006: 14-15). Essentially, the story goes like this: an elderly member of the community was very ill and another man was sent to fetch the priest to deliver last rites. The two hurried back but as they passed a mill, they heard such a compelling melody that they had to stop. They waited for the melody to end, but it never did. It just went on and on. Suddenly, the priest came out of his reverie and cried, "Get going! It's the devil trying to prevent us from reaching the sickbed!" And so the two raced on, but they were too late: the elderly man had died before they reached their destination. The melody stayed with the two men and they called it "Muileann Dubh a' Logadair" ("The Devil's Mills"). Dr. Watson, who collected the story in 1982, speculates that the word "Logadair" is a corruption of the Lochaber place name, Auclaucharach, in Glen Roy, Scotland.

Will Lamb has identified other theories about the meaning of "Am Muileann Dubh," including that it's a smuggling bothy (Mackintosh ca. 1910: 294) or that it's phallic (MacLagan 1905: 457). Lamb continues:

> [MacLagan] suggests that the word *muileann* "mill" has been mistaken for *mulan*, meaning a corn stack, hillock, or small field. This certainly seems plausible given the lines of the song. Another interpretation is that *Am Muileann Dubh* is essentially a satirical double entendre about—as one would say in Gaelic—*boireannach a bha car fosgailte*, a woman who was rather "accessible." This suggestion comes from John MacInnes, who said that he remembers it being said in his youth, as well as having heard it from the well-known Tiree tradition bearer *Dòmhnall Chaluim Bàin* (Donald Sinclair). (2012: 153)

Despite the variety of stories associated with "Am Muileann Dubh," the overall tune has remained quite consistent and has been well documented in published collections over the years (which perhaps contributed to the tune's relative stability). Note in Fig. 4 that, typical of reels, almost every single note is an eighth note and that the melodic motion is predominantly "conjunct" (stepwise or consisting of small jumps between notes) with only a few slightly larger intervals placed to provide some melodic interest. Interestingly, instrumental versions of the tune do often include considerable leaps between notes, as in Fig. 4a (note especially the second bar, as well as the B section). The overall tune is still identifiably the same because the leaps usually occur on notes between beats or on offbeats and using pitches from the same chord (so that the implied harmony remains constant). These leaps, particularly when they occur on unaccented beats, create considerable excitement. It is possible that the port-a-beul is a simplified version of a more disjunct[6] fiddle tune, for it would be difficult to sing some of the leaps that a fiddler can manage with relative ease. But it is equally possible to imagine that the

Fig. 4. "Am Muileann Dubh" (transcribed by Heather Sparling from the singing of Mary Jane Lamond on Bho Thìr nan Craobh, ca. 1994).

original tune was simple, and that instrumentalists introduced melodic leaps to vary it, make it more interesting, and to create a more challenging tune to play.

Note the musical features I described earlier. The tune is in "cut time" (the "C" with a line through it indicates this), which means common time (4/4) cut in two. In cut time, the tempo is fast enough that it's easier to think of it as two beats instead of four per bar. There are four bars per section and each is repeated. Interestingly, there is no strong contrast in register between the A and B sections of this tune; the contrast is more subtle with one

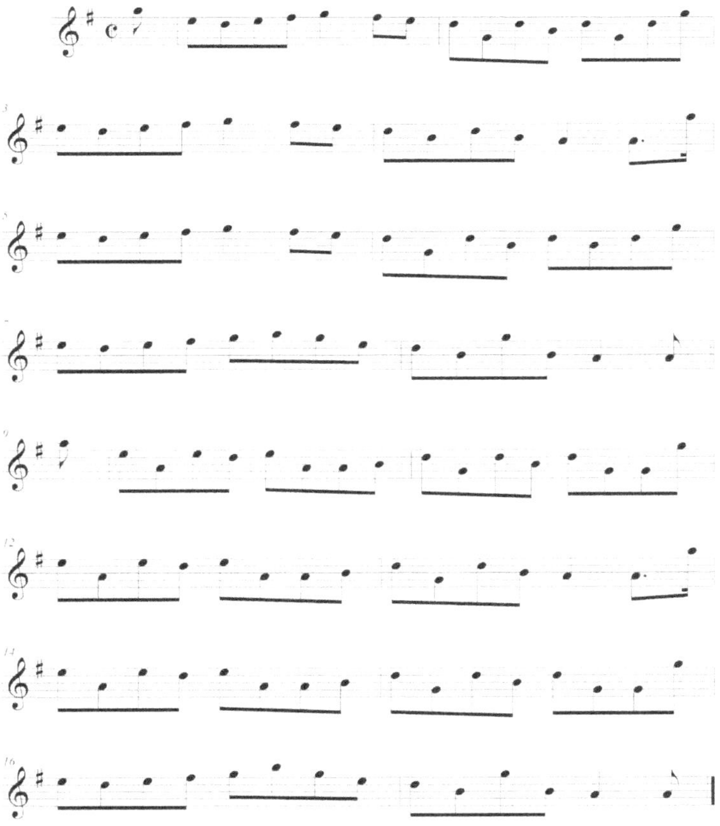

Fig. 4a: "Am Muileann Dubh," from Kuntz's The Fiddler's Companion, transcribed from Stewart-Robertson's The Athole Collection (1884).

section featuring notes moving in a scalar (scale-wise) manner while the other starts with repeated notes. But you can see that the final bar of the second section is the same as the final bar of the first, and the penultimate bars are very similar too. It is this repetition that connects the two sections together into a single coherent tune.

Strathspeys

Strathspeys are unique to the Scottish musical tradition. No one is certain where and when strathspeys were first developed. The first tune labelled a strathspey doesn't show up in a printed collection until James Oswald's *Caledonian Pocket Companion* (eventually, the *Companion* consisted of twelve volumes published between ca. 1743 and 1749). In the entire collection of some 550 tunes, there are only two tunes labelled strathspeys and both are Oswald's own compositions (Alburger 1983: 45). From that point on, there are many references to strathspeys, strathspey reels, strathspey minuets, and so on. It is generally believed that the strathspey was developed by fiddlers in Speyside, Scotland, although William Lamb has recently argued that it may have much older Gaelic roots.[7]

Like reels, they are in duple time, although reels, as noted above, tend to be felt in two whereas strathspeys are felt in four. The first beat of each bar in both tune types receives the strongest emphasis, but part of what makes strathspeys distinctive is the strong emphasis on every beat (albeit not as strong as the first), a feeling that is reinforced by instrumentalists' tendencies to tap their foot to each and every beat. In Cape Breton, the foot tap can be more of a foot stomp! Strathspeys exhibit a far greater range of tempos than do reels. Strathspeys used to accompany Highland dance tend to be much slower, clocking in around 108 beats per minute, than step dance strathspeys, which tend to be played faster, often around 160 beats per minute. Scottish players seem to play strathspeys a little slower, on the whole, than Cape Breton musicians. But as Kate Dunlay and David Greenberg show in *Traditional Celtic Violin Music of Cape Breton* (1996), there is a wide range of acceptable tempos, at least in Cape Breton: they documented fiddlers playing strathspeys as slow as 118 beats per minute, and as fast as 202!

What differentiates a strathspey from a reel, aside from how their tempos and accents are played, is the dominant rhythms. Strathspeys are defined by the inclusion of a significant number of "dotted rhythms." Dotted rhythms are so called because one note of a pair is dotted, making it longer than the note with which it is paired.[8] The pair of notes therefore sounds rhythmically asymmetrical, with one note longer than the other. In strathspeys, this usually involves a dotted eighth note paired with a sixteenth note (dotted quaver and a semi-quaver) or its reverse, a sixteenth note paired with a dotted eighth note (semi-quaver and a dotted quaver). The latter is quite unusual in most Western European music, particularly the frequency with which this rhythm is found in strathspeys. When a short note is followed by a long note in Western European musics (whether elite or folk), the short note almost always sounds like an unaccented "pick up" to the following longer note, acting as a driver to the longer note rather than as an independently significant note. In the case of strathspeys, the short note quite surprisingly gets the accent and is clearly the most important note rhythmically. One theory is that this short–long rhythmic pattern derives from the rhythms of the Gaelic language, in which emphasis is almost always on the first syllable of a word, even when the first syllable is short. Regardless, the short–long rhythm pair is strongly associated with Scottish traditional music and therefore is known as the "Scotch snap."

Strathspeys also tend to feature melodic leaps (gaps between two adjacent notes) which contrast with the smaller, stepwise melodic intervals of puirt-a-beul reels.[9] Stepwise melodies and the lack of large melodic leaps, together with their regular, symmetrical rhythms (reels tend to have few, if any, dotted rhythms), help to create the sense of "flow" and speed in a reel. The strathspey's intervals are not so large as to make them hard to sing. But they do contrast with the predominant intervals in a reel, helping to differentiate the two tune types and providing yet another element of contrast in sets involving both strathspeys and reels. The prevalence of dotted rhythms paired with melodic leaps make a strathspey sound "jumpy" or "angular" compared to the smoothness of the reel. "Cairistiona Chaimbeul" illustrates these elements well (see Fig. 5).[10]

The time signature is "common time." In this tune, there are 8 bars in each of the A and B sections. As with "Am Muileann Dubh," melodic repetition helps to unify the tune. Once again, the last lines of sections A (bars 7-8) and B (bars 15-16) are almost identical except for a few minor rhythmic variations to accommodate the different lyrics.

At the same time, we also have some melodic contrast. The first three lines of the A section start with notes in the lower range of the tune and climb higher toward the ends of the lines. By contrast, the first three lines of the B section start quite high and stay there or descend slightly. The fourth and eighth lines, being melodically identical (and only slightly different rhythmically), traverse almost the entire range of the tune, starting high, descending to one of the lowest pitches of the tune, and finishing on the same note with which the tune started (the "tonic").

The "jumpy" elements of this tune should be quite clear. Not only are there many examples of dotted rhythms, there is also just generally a variety of rhythms in this strathspey compared to the earlier reel which consisted almost exclusively of one rhythm (eighth notes/quavers) with the occasional longer note (quarter note/crotchet). "Cairistiona Chaimbeul" doesn't just feature a variety of rhythmic durations but also constantly switches them up. These varying and jumpy rhythms complement the almost constant disjunct melodic motion. There is little stepwise or scalar movement in the first section, whereas such movement is predominant in "Am Muileann Dubh" (except in the last bar of each section, which provides a bit of melodic interest and excitement through contrast).

At the same time that "Cairistiona Chaimbeul" illustrates some typical strathspey features that clearly differentiate it me-

Fig. 5. "Cairistiona Chaimbeul," transcribed by Heather Sparling from the singing of Hugh Duncan, recorded by Calum I MacLean in 1953 and available on Tobar an Dualchais.[11]

lodically and rhythmically from a reel, it also illustrates how there can be exceptions to these features. Most tunes are not perfect exemplars of the characteristics I've described in this chapter. The fact that tunes do not always neatly match defining criteria helps to keep the tunes interesting and unexpected even within a relatively predictable framework. In this case, the B section is marked by a stepwise descending melody rather than by melodic leaps. The smooth downward melodic arc helps to provide contrast with the jumpier A section.

This tune has a number of lyrical variations. The most basic and common set of words consists of two "parts" to coincide with each section of the tune. In these lyrics, Cairistìona (Christina) is described positively. Note how the considerable repetition within the lyrics matches the repetition within the melody.

> Tha i tighinn air an rathad,
> Cairistìona Chaimbeul.
> Tha i tighinn air an rathad,
> Cairistìona Chaimbeul.
> Tha i tighinn air an rathad,
> Cairistìona Chaimbeul.
> Cairistìona Curstaidh Anna,
> Cairistìona Chaimbeul.

> Tha i bòidheach, tha i laghach,
> Cairistìona Chaimbeul.
> Tha i bòidheach, tha i laghach,
> Cairistìona Chaimbeul.
> Tha i bòidheach, tha i laghach,
> Cairistìona Chaimbeul.
> Cuimir dìreach anns an ruidhl' i
> 'S cinnteach anns an danns' i.

> > She's coming along the road,
> > Christina Campbell.
> > She's coming along the road,
> > Christina Campbell.
> > She's coming along the road,
> > Christina Campbell.
> > Christina Christy Annie
> > Christina Campbell.

> > She is pretty, she is pleasant,
> > Christina Campbell
> > She is pretty, she is pleasant,
> > Christina Campbell
> > She is pretty, she is pleasant,
> > Christina Campbell
> > Keep her straight in the reel
> > And sure-footed in the dance.

K. N. MacDonald has different lyrics (MacDonald 1931 [1901]: 27):

> Pòsaidh mi thu air an t-Sàmhuinn,
> 'Chairistìona Chaimbeil.
> Pòsaidh mi thu air an t-Sàmhuinn,

'Chairistìona Chaimbeil.
Pòsaidh mi thu air an t-Sàmhuinn,
'Chairistìona Chaimbeil.
'S ged a tha do chasan caola,
'S e mo ghaol gun taing thu!

Dh'ith thu 'n ràc 's an tunnag odhar,
Chairistìona Chaimbeil.
Dh'ith thu 'n ràc 's an tunnag odhar,
Chairistìona Chaimbeil.
Dh'ith thu 'n ràc 's an tunnag odhar,
Chairistìona Chaimbeil.
Chairistìona Chiorstaidh Anna,
Chairistìona Chaimbeil.

Cailleach as mios' air an t-saoghal,
Chairistìona Chaimbeil.
Cailleach as mios' air an t-saoghal,
Chairistìona Chaimbeil.
Cailleach as mios' air an t-saoghal,
Chairistìona Chaimbeil.
Chairistìona, Chiorstaidh Anna,
Chairistìona Chaimbeil.

> I'll marry you on Halloween,
> Christina Campbell.
> I'll marry you on Halloween,
> Christina Campbell.
> I'll marry you on Halloween,
> Christina Campbell.
> Although your legs are thin,
> You're my love in spite of yourself.

> You ate the drake and tawny duck,
> Christina Campbell.
> You ate the drake and tawny duck,
> Christina Campbell.
> You ate the drake and tawny duck,
> Christina Campbell.
> Christie Anna's Christina,
> Christina Campbell.

The worst old woman in the world,
Christina Campbell.
The worst old woman in the world,
Christina Campbell.
The worst old woman in the world,
Christina Campbell.
Christie Anna's Christina,
Christina Campbell.

This set of lyrics is a little harder to make sense of (an issue I discuss in the next chapter). We don't know, for example, the significance of the eating of the drake and duck. However, the Cairistiona described in this second version is clearly not as lovely and pleasant as in the more common version provided above. In the first verse, there's a hint that she's not very attractive but she's apparently still worth marrying. The last verse suggests that she's a horrible old woman. It is hard to believe that the woman being described in the first and last verse here is the same. Alexander MacDonald tells of a version that is "a sort of rhyming dialogue—the one party praising her good parts, and the other as eloquently pointing out her numerous faults and failings" (1922: 103). William Lamb suggests that fragments of this original dialogue have resulted in a variety of versions that either praise or criticize Cairistiona. Alexander MacDonald provides yet another version (from Lochaber) suggesting that Cairistiona Chaimbeul may not be the most upstanding citizen:

Thog thu taigh aig ceann an rathaid
'Chairistìona Chaimbeul
Thog thu taigh aig ceann an rathaid
'Chairistìona Chaimbeul
Thog thu taigh aig ceann an rathaid
'Chairistìona Chaimbeul
'S bidh na h-uaislean ort a tàmhaich
Fad na h-oidhche geamhraidh.

> You built a house at the end of the road
> Christina Campbell
> You built a house at the end of the road
> Christina Campbell

You built a house at the end of the road
Christina Campbell
And the gentry will dwell with you
All winter night long.

K. N. MacDonald indicates that this port-a-beul is linked to a fiddle tune called "Christina Campbell," otherwise known as "The Miller of Drone." However, the port-a-beul melody transcribed above seems only to share the general melodic shape of K. N. MacDonald's tune (which is pretty much identical with "The Miller of Drone" as documented in various fiddle collections).

"The Miller of Drone" is widely considered to be a composition by Nathaniel Gow (1766-1831), one of Niel Gow's sons. Nathaniel Gow was not a Gaelic speaker. If it is true that he composed this tune and that this was the tune to which the lyrics of "Cairistiona Chaimbeul" were originally sung, then this fact indicates that the tune came first and only later did someone else set Gaelic lyrics to it.

K. N. MacDonald does say in his book that "Cairistiona Chaimbeul" was sung to the (more-or-less) same tune as Gow's (1931 [1901]: 27), although it would not be possible to fit the Gaelic words to the fiddle tune without adjusting the rhythms significantly. However, MacDonald writes:

The way in which the old Highland fiddlers played ["The Miller of Drone"] was quite different from the set in Gow's books: it had a sort of more ancient flavour about it. Nathanial Gow was fully as good a composer as his more famous father, Neil [*sic*], but it has been alleged by some competent judges that some of their tunes at least were "old stories retold" under a different garb.

In other words, it's possible that Gow's composition was based on a pre-existing and older Highland tune, which might explain the differences between the port-a-beul and fiddle settings. However, the differences between the version of "Cairistìona Chaimbeul" I transcribed above and the fiddle tune known as "The Miller of Drone" are so substantial that it seems unlikely that the port-a-

Fig. 6. "Cairistìona Chaimbeul," from Keith Norman MacDonald's Puirt-à-Beul: The Vocal Dance Music of the Scottish Gaels (Lamb 2012: 87).

beul "Cairistìona Chaimbeul" was ever related to the instrumental tune "The Miller of Drone." William Lamb notes that "Miller of Drone" was published by John Pringle in 1801 (the year *before* Nathaniel Gow claimed to have composed it in 1802, although it's possible that Pringle simply published Gow's composition before Gow himself did), and a tune by the same name was also published in Platts' *Eight Cotillons & Six Country Dances for the Year 1789* (Lamb 2013: 163).

In Cape Breton, "The Miller of Drone" and "Christie Campbell" are known as two separate, albeit related, tunes. "The Miller of Drone" refers to Gow's (supposed) composition, whereas "Christie Campbell" refers to a "high bass" tune (a tune that requires the retuning of the two lower strings on the violin to A and E from their more usual G and D; see Fig. 7). Peter MacPhee of Foot Cape once told Allan MacDonald,

I don't think they're the same damn tune. I think that someone who didn't read music tried to play "The Miller of Drone" and came up with ["Christie Campbell"]. And he came up with a better tune, whether he meant to or not! (Qtd. in Wilson and Dunlay 2002: 27).

Interestingly, although both the instrumental tunes "The Miller of Drone" and "Christie Campbell" are associated with the port-a-beul "Cairistìona Chaimbeul," the port-a-beul itself is not well known on the island. Dunlay notes,

Because *Christie Campbell* is an all-time favourite traditional tune in Cape Breton, there are quite a few settings of it. Here the fiddler is freer to put his/her own stamp on the tune, using any of the traditionally accepted old bowings, ornaments, and melodic variations. (Dunlay and Greenberg 1996: 124)

Is it possible that so many fiddle variations have proliferated and are acceptable in part because they are no longer linked to associated puirt-a-beul lyrics (if they ever were)? If the tunes were linked to puirt-a-beul lyrics, the lyrics would presumably constrain the rhythmic variations possible (see Chapter 4 for a discussion of the relationship between lyric and musical rhythms, and Chapter 7 for an analysis of the debate over whether Highland and Cape Breton fiddlers need to speak Gaelic to play in an "authentic" Highland or Cape Breton style).

We can observe a significant difference between the two tunes by looking at the notes used in each. In the case of "Cairistìona Chaimbeul" the port-a-beul (Fig. 5), the range is over a tenth between its lowest and highest notes (a tenth is about as wide a range as one would want for a vernacular or "folk" song; a range of an octave would be more comfortable) whereas "The Miller of Drone" ranges across two full octaves, clearly indicating that it is not just an instrumental tune but a fiddle tune specifically (the bagpipes' full range is only a ninth).

To summarize, this section has illustrated the key characteristics of a strathspey and its differences from a reel: a strathspey is a "jumpier" tune with asymmetrical (dotted) rhythms and frequent melodic leaps. Strathspeys are also played at a different speed from reels, although this is only evident in performance. Although it is not possible to come to incontrovertible conclusions about "Cairistiona Chaimbeul," we can see that the port-a-beul version seems only distantly related to the fiddle tune that shares its name, particularly given that the port-a-beul is limited to a tenth whereas the fiddle tune traverses two octaves. I am unable to

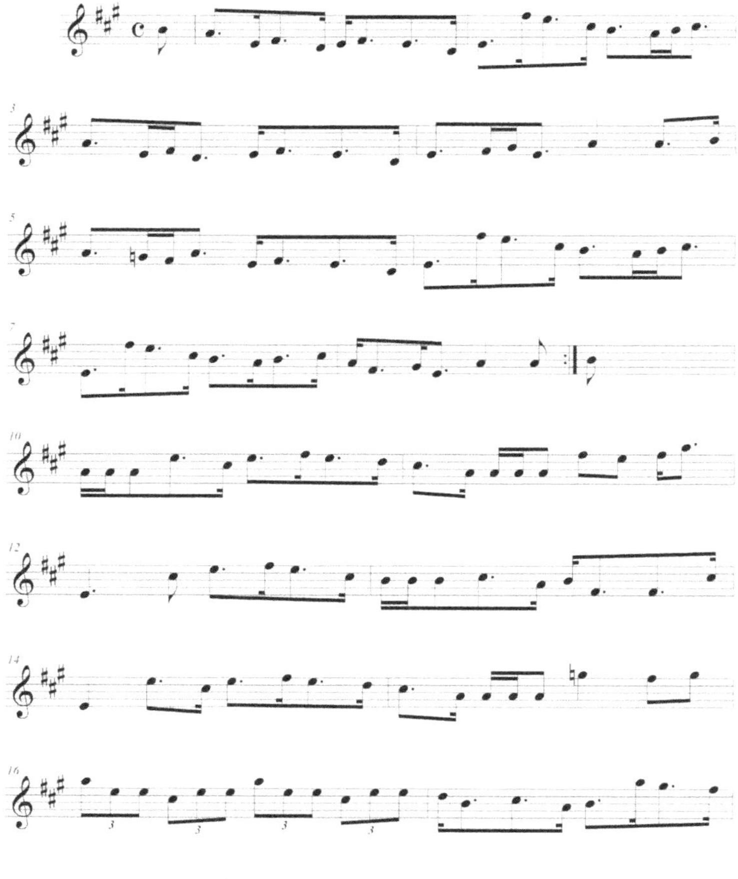

Fig. 7. Transcription by David Greenberg of "Christie Campbell" as played by Carl MacKenzie. From Traditional Celtic Violin Music of Cape Breton *(Dunlay and Greenberg 1996: 123).*

say definitively, however, whether Gow's composition was loosely based on a pre-existing tune (i.e., the port-a-beul tune) or whether the port-a-beul tune was loosely based on Gow's composition.

Jigs

Jigs have been popular throughout England, Scotland and Ireland for several centuries, although they are today especially associated with Ireland. Compared to the reel, strathspey, and other tune types, they have a unique metre: 6/8 (six beats per bar with each beat represented by an eighth note/quaver). The six beats per bar are divided into two groups of three so that, when counting along with a jig, one can say, "one-and-ah, two-and-ah, one-and-ah, two-and-ah" or "jiggity jiggity." The first beat of every bar gets the strongest accent, followed by the fourth beat. These two accents, combined with a quick jig tempo, often give the impression that the music is "in two" rather than "in six." However, the triple sub-division of these primary beats differentiates the jig from other tune types whose beats are subdivided into twos (eighth notes/quavers), as in the case of the strathspey and reel. This triple metre gives jigs a very smooth feel, like a reel, but jigs have a different rhythmic feel than reels due to the triple subdivision of the beat.

A knowledgeable musician might note that jigs and strath-speys are rather closer in rhythm and metre than indicated by the conventions of notation. While it's true that strathspeys are al-most always notated in 4/4 (duple metre) while jigs are notated in 6/8 (triple metre), the strathspey's dotted rhythms, as noted above, tend to be played more like triplets than true dotted rhythms as would be heard in the classical music tradition. Strathspeys also often end with runs of triplets, as illustrated in the transcription of "Cairistìona Chaimbeul" from K. N. MacDonald's book, above, tying them even more closely to jigs. However, the two tune types can still normally be differentiated by ear. Strathspeys rarely have runs of triplets except sometimes at the end, whereas jigs are al-most always characterized by triplet runs throughout. The strath-spey's characteristic "snap" rhythm is defined by a "short–long" pattern whereas jigs are more likely to use the opposite rhythm, "long–short" (a combination of a quarter note/crotchet and eighth note/quaver).

Although there are occasional leaps in jigs—and even some jigs that prominently feature leaps—most melodic movement in jigs tends to be either stepwise (scalar) or by small leaps outlining the harmonic triad.[12] Larger melodic leaps tend to occur at particular points to create rhythmic drive and musical interest. This compound metre often gives jigs a relaxed sound no matter how fast they go. Jigs are typically played in the range of 112-132 beats per minute.[13]

The following jig, "Fear an Dùin Mhòir" ("The Lord of Dunmore"), is well known in Scotland and has been recorded commercially by several singers.[14] Although there are some occasional leaps in the tune, they are not difficult to sing and they provide a striking contrast to the rest of the tune.

As an instrumental tune, it goes under quite a few names, including "Bung Your Eye" and "Lord Dunmore," among others. An Irish variant exists as "The Jolly Old Man" as well as under various other titles. Andrew Kuntz, in his excellent online fiddle tune collection (http://www.ibiblio.org/fiddlers/) traces the tune to the mid-18th century.

> Fear an Dùin Mhòir a' mire ri Mòr
> Fear an Dùin Mhòir 's Mòr a' mire ris
> Fear an Dùin Mhòir a' mire ri Mòr
> Ach cò nì mire ri Màiri a-rithist
>
> Fear an dùin bhig a' mire gu tric
> Fear an dùin bhig gu tric tha mire ri
> Fear an dùin bhig a' mire gu tric
> Gu tric tha mire ri Màiri
>
> Fear an dùin bhig a' mire gu tric
> Fear an dùin bhig gu tric tha mire ri
> Fear an Dùin Mhòir a' mire ri Mòr
> Ach cò nì mire ri Màiri
>
> > The Lord of Dunmore is flirting with Mòr
> > The Lord of Dunmore and Mòr is flirting with him

The Lord of Dunmore is flirting with Mòr
But who will flirt with Mary? (repeat)

The lord of the little fort is flirting frequently
The lord of the little fort frequently is flirting
The lord of the little fort is flirting frequently
Frequently is flirting with Mary.

The lord of the little fort is flirting frequently
The lord of the little fort frequently is flirting
The Lord of Dunmore is flirting with Mòr
But who will flirt with Mary?

This tune is also associated with a set of English/Scots lyrics, which likely gave the instrumental tune yet another name by which it is known, "Brisk Young Lad":

There cam' a young man to my daddie's door,
My daddie's door, my daddie's door,
There cam' a young man to my daddie's door,
Cam' seeking me to woo.

Fig. 8. "Fear an Dùin Mhòir," transcribed by Chris McDonald from the singing of Rachel Walker (2004).

Chorus:
And wow! but he was a braw young lad,
A brisk young lad and a braw young lad!
And wow! but he was a braw young lad,
Cam' seeking me to woo.

But I was baking when he came,
When he came, when he came,
I took him in and gied him a scone,
To thowe his frozen mou'.

I set him in aside the bink;
I ga'e him bread and ale to drink;
But ne'er a blythe styme wad he blink
Until his wame was fu'.

Gae, get you gone, you cauldrife wooer
Ye sour-looking, cauldrife wooer!
I straightway show'd him to the door,
Saying, Come nae mair to woo!

There lay a deuk-dub before the door,
Before the door, before the door,
There lay a deuk-dub before the door,
An' there fell he, I trow!

Out cam' the gudeman, and high he shouted;
Out cam' the guidwife, and laigh she louted;
And a' the toun-neebors were gather'd about it;
An' there lay he, I trow!

Then out cam' I, and sneer'd and smil'd,
Ye cam' to woo, but ye're a' befyled;
Ye've fa'en i' the dirt, and ye're a' beguiled;
We'll ha'e nae mair o' you![15] (Graham 1871: 166)

The English lyrics were first published in Herd's *Scots Songs, Volume 2* (1776) and again with the tune in Johnson's *Scots Musical Museum* (1790). Interestingly, the Gaelic version does not appear in K. N. MacDonald's book of puirt-a-beul. There are several recordings of it on Tobar an Dualchais (http://www. tobarandualchais.co.uk/), including two dating from the 1950s (with slightly different B section melodies), as well as a recording by Joe Neil MacNeil on *Sruth nan Gaidheal* (http://gaelstream.

stfx.ca/). However, there is no way to know when the Gaelic words were initially created, nor whether they were created before or after the English words, or their associated fiddle tune. Although both the Gaelic and English lyrics share the theme of "wooing," they are otherwise quite different. It's certainly interesting to note that instrumental tunes were at one time associated with English as well as Gaelic lyrics, and equally interesting to note that the puirt-a-beul tradition continues whereas English instrumental songs are far less common. Finally, it's worth observing that the English lyrics are not structured like Gaelic puirt-a-beul, a topic I will discuss further in the next chapter.

While the strathspey had four bars per section, the jig has eight. However, the different tempos of the jig and strathspey, along with the fact that each bar of the jig is counted in two whereas each bar of the strathspey is counted in four, means that the overall impression is of sections of similar lengths. Scalar or stepwise melodic motion predominates. The only dotted notes are those appearing in the last bar of each section and in the case of compound metre, these dots are simply used to indicate that the two quarter (crotchet) notes are actually worth three eighth (quaver) notes each, the duration of a beat in compound metre. These longer notes emphasize the end of each section rhythmically. Thus there are no "jagged" rhythms such as we saw in the strathspey. Both the A and B sections start with the same repeated note figure, but the second beat of the first bar of each section differs: in the first section, the melody stays close to the low note on which the melody starts whereas there's an octave leap in the second section. An octave leap is not hard to sing, but it does sound dramatic and creates a melodic contrast between the sections.

This tune seems designed for the bagpipes with its range of a ninth, the maximum range of the bagpipes. However—and now we get into an area that is difficult to describe quickly and easily to those without a musical background—this tune could not be played on the bagpipes. This tune is in the Aeolian mode. For those more familiar with major and minor scales than with modes, the Aeolian mode has the same pitches as the natural minor scale.

A full discussion of modes and scales is beyond the scope of this book, although I discuss them further below. Briefly, however, each note of the Aeolian mode is represented in this tune, plus there's an extra lower note (the mode's pitches are: B, C#, D, E, F#, G, A, B plus the lower A). The bagpipes are capable of playing in the Aeolian mode if it is started from the pipes' third pitch (B). But the pipes would not then be capable of reaching an upper octave (there's only one B on the bagpipes).

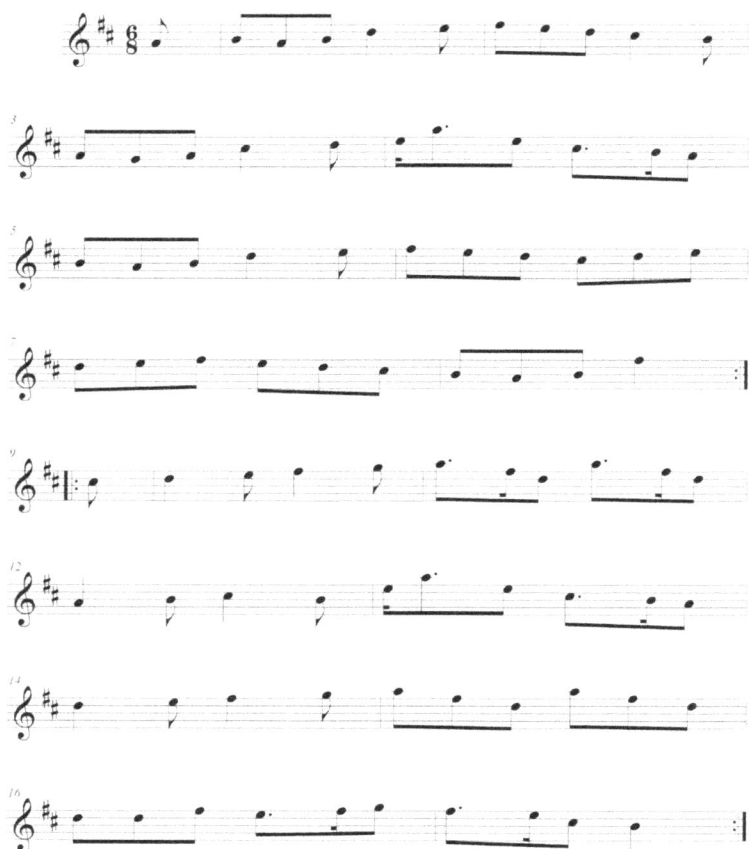

Fig. 9. "Lord Dunmore." This version comes from Kuntz's online Fiddler's Companion (2009). However, the original source is not identified.

But the mystery deepens, for "Lord Dunmore" is known as a Scottish pipe jig in the Aeolian mode of B (the Aeolian mode on the bagpipes). How is this possible? It means that the original pipe tune and the port-a-beul melody notated above are not the same. If we look at a version of the pipe tune "Lord Dunmore" (Fig. 9), it is easy to see that the first section is very similar. However, the B section—where the octave leap not possible on the bagpipes occurs in the port-a-beul—differs. "Lord Dunmore" obviously remains within the pitches possible on the bagpipes whereas the port-a-beul does not.

The unanswered (and so far, unanswerable) question is: which came first? Did the pipe tune come first and get varied when Gaelic lyrics were set to it? Or the other way around? Or perhaps the port-a-beul and pipe melodies were the same at one time and one or the other (or both!) gradually varied in different ways over time.

Other Tune Types

Puirt-a-beul consist mostly of strathspeys and reels with a small number of jigs known in the repertoire. This is true in my personal collection of almost 350 puirt-a-beul, and it is true of K. N. MacDonald's much earlier collection (1931 [1901]). However, one occasionally comes across a tune that doesn't fit any of these tune types. For example, there is a very small number of marches in my collection as well. This is curious to me, as marches are not typically associated with dancing so much as with, well, marching!

Marches are somewhat unusual as tune types in that they can encompass a considerable range of features. There are 2/4 marches and 6/8 marches. There are slow marches and quick marches. Some marches, other than the differences between 2/4 and 4/4 metre, look similar to reels. Other duple metre marches share rhythmic asymmetries and intervalic leaps with strathspeys. For example, here is a transcription of "A Sheana Bhean Bhochd," one of the few puirt-a-beul marches in my collection for which there is

Fig. 10. "A Sheana Bhean Bhochd," transcribed by Heather Sparling and Chris McDonald from the singing of Mary Jane Lamond (1994).

a contemporary, commercial recording (Mary Jane Lamond's *Bho Thìr nan Craobh / From the Land of the Trees*, 1994):

This tune has suggestive Irish connections. There's an Irish song called "The Sean [sometimes spelled phonetically as "Shan"] Bhean Bhocht," or "The Poor Old Woman," which exists in many versions and dates from at least the late 1790s. The "poor old woman" refers to Ireland (H. H. Sparling 2005 [1887]: 11; Bruford 1978c) but according to Andrew Kuntz's *The Fiddler's Companion*, the air may have originally been Scottish. There is an Irish reel or hornpipe known as "An Seanbhean Bhocht," but its tune has little similarity to the one above.

Despite the strong titular link, the Scottish Gaelic port-a-beul text seems to have little relation to the Irish song lyrics and the "poor old woman" doesn't seem to have any allegorical meaning in the Scottish version:

A sheana-bhean bhochd, chan fhalbh thu a-nochd,
A sheana-bhean bhochd, chan fhalbh thu a-nochd,
A sheana-bhean bhochd, chan fhalbh thu a-nochd,
No idir moch a-màireach.

Thig am fidhleir an nochd, 's bheir i sgrìob air a' phort,
Thig am fidhleir an nochd, 's bheir i sgrìob air a' phort,
Thig am fidhleir an nochd, 's bheir i sgrìob air a' phort,
'S ged a dh'fhalbhadh e an-diugh, thig e màireach.

Poor old woman, you won't leave tonight,
Poor old woman, you won't leave tonight,
Poor old woman, you won't leave tonight,
Or even early tomorrow.

The fiddler will come tonight and she'll scratch out the
tune,
The fiddler will come tonight and she'll scratch out the
tune,
The fiddler will come tonight and she'll scratch out the
tune,
And though he would go today, he'll return tomorrow.

The tune is also closely linked to the Scottish instrumental tune known as "Glengarry's March." Although it looks similar to a strathspey in that it has many dotted, asymmetrical rhythms, there are also some features that distinctly identify it as a march. First, there are many long notes (quarter and half notes) sprinkled throughout and at the end of each section. These longer notes, particularly at the ends of sections, are typical of a march but atypical of a strathspey. Each section also consists of eight bars repeated whereas strathspeys tend to have only four bars in each part. In general, however, these are relatively minor indicators of a march; performance practice, particularly tempo and accents, is really what differentiates a march from other tune types.

The question is, why are there so few puirt-a-beul marches? Any answers to this question can only be purely conjectural at this time. But there are numerous possibilities. First, although most puirt-a-beul are strathspeys, jigs or reels, there's no real reason why a march could not have its own Gaelic lyrics as well. Since it's quite common for Celtic instrumental tunes of various types—not just those used to accompany dance—to be associated with lyrics, it's not surprising that this association would exist for a range of tune types, even if some are more common than others.

Second, it's possible that there were more march puirt-a-beul at one time and they have simply not been documented or continued in oral tradition. One might guess that march puirt-a-beul could at one time have been associated with dance forms no longer practised. As the dances disappeared, perhaps the associated songs and tunes did as well. However, it seems relatively clear that pipe marches began to be developed specifically for military—not dance—purposes in the late 18th century (G. F. Graham 1871: 166).[16]

Third, it is possible that some strathspeys were turned into marches or vice versa. So it's conceivable that puirt-a-beul today known as marches were once strathspeys. For example, "The Haughs of Cromdale" is a well-known march among both pipers and fiddlers but it exists in the puirt-a-beul repertoire as a strathspey, "Siud Mar Chaidh an Càl a Dholaidh" ("That's how the cabbage/kale was ruined").[16]

It's also worth noting that many slow airs played instrumentally are associated with Gaelic lyrics. However, these are not known as puirt-a-beul probably because they lack so many of the characteristics of other types of puirt-a-beul: they are not generally in binary form; the lyrics tend to involve less repetition and longer texts (see the next chapter for an in-depth discussion of puirt-a-beul lyrics); and their performance challenges are quite different from those of puirt-a-beul (an issue I discuss further below).

Another interesting type of song associated with instrumental music is the pibroch song.[17] Pibrochs consist of a "ground" (ùrlar in Gaelic), or theme, which is then repeated in increasingly difficult variations. The ùrlar is often associated with a Gaelic song and its lyrics can look quite similar to those of puirt-a-beul: short and repetitive. However, pibroch grounds are not normally in binary form and, more importantly, are sung extremely slowly. They are not intended for dancing. Significantly, in the Gaelic musical community, these songs are known as "pibroch songs," never as puirt-a-beul. But if you saw pibroch lyrics without knowing their associated tune, you could be forgiven for thinking they were a port-a-beul.

It's also worth noting that some puirt-a-beul do not conform to any of the standard forms discussed so far. In Mary Ann Kennedy's thesis about puirt-a-beul (1995), she gives the example of "Meal do bhrògan" ("Your Shoes Are Deceiving"), which has several bars of only three beats (instead of four) in the second half, as though those bars had lost a beat each. This port has all the qualities of a reel, but the "missing" beats makes it unsuitable for accompanying any known dances. It's possible that it once accompanied a specific dance that is now lost (see Chapter 5 for a more detailed discussion of the relationship between puirt-a-beul and dance) but Kennedy argues that its very complicated second part suggests that it was always designed as a means of showing off vocally. I discuss the challenges of performing puirt-a-beul further below.

Sets

In Celtic traditional music, tunes are joined together in performance to create "sets," or "groups," as they are known in Cape Breton. Sets can consist of only two or three tunes, or they can consist of more, perhaps as many as six or eight. Set lengths are usually only dictated by the desire of the musicians or, if they are accompanying dancers, the length of the dance. Sets provide a means of extending a performance without boring the audience (or the musicians) with the same piece repeated over and over.

Although musicians tend to be overtly appreciated most often for the creativity they bring to individual tunes (through their ornamentation, rhythmic variations, bowing techniques and so on), some creativity can be exhibited in the selection of tunes brought together in a set. One Irish music scholar has even suggested that sets be considered a kind of composition (Meade 1999). While there are some "fixed" sets that typically aren't modified, musicians are generally free to link most tunes with any other tunes they wish. However, there are a few rules that musicians must follow when creating sets.

First, only certain kinds of tunes can be linked together and they can only be linked in a particular order, an order that overall creates an accelerating set. Strathspeys are almost never performed on their own (except when used to accompany Scottish country dancing); they must generally be followed by one or more reels. They also always precede reels; they never follow them, largely because reels are faster than strathspeys. Meanwhile, sets of reels and jigs can each be heard on their own and only rarely in combination with each other, no doubt in part because they involve different metres. Marches, strathspeys and reels are all in duple metre (2/4 or 4/4), making it easier to combine them. Typically, there are either equal numbers of each tune type in a set (e.g., a single march, a single strathspey and a single reel) or there is an increasing number of each tune type as one progresses through the set (e.g., a single strathspey followed by two reels). However, this is not a hard and fast rule; exceptions occur.

Where marches are involved, they usually precede strathspeys, followed by reels, again following the principle of increasing tempos through a set. However, pipers, who have a significant march repertoire compared to other Celtic instrumental traditions, can and often do play stand-alone sets of marches. Although I mention this point here, it is not overly relevant to this particular discussion since pipe marches seem to be only infrequently associated with puirt-a-beul, as discussed earlier. Other tune types can also be combined into instrumental sets, including hornpipes, clogs, slip jigs and so on. But because these types of tunes are not associated with puirt-a-beul, I do not discuss them here (for a discussion of typical and atypical tune types in Cape Breton fiddle sets, see Doherty 1996: 244; Doherty identifies a list of ten tune types found in the Cape Breton instrumental repertoire; see Dohety 1996: 202).

Of course, set construction depends on the purpose of the set. If a set of puirt-a-beul is intended to accompany dance—or even if it's simply conceived as dance accompaniment, whether it actually accompanies dance or not—only the tune types required for the dance will be incorporated (see Chapter 5 for further discussion of the relationship between puirt-a-beul and dance). But if a set of puirt-a-beul is intended to be used without reference to dance and more as entertainment, or even as a competition piece, then singers may be much more creative with the kinds of tunes they link (see Chapter 6 for a discussion of puirt-a-beul's functions beyond dance accompaniment).

In Scotland, one can find quite a few examples of puirt-a-beul sets that do not conform to the general rules I have set out above, although it's exceedingly rare in Cape Breton.[18] Exceptions are particularly evident on recordings by the Campbell family (including Kenna Campbell, Wilma Kennedy and Mary Ann Kennedy, all of whom I cite at various points in this book), widely regarded as the best living performers of puirt-a-beul. For example, the Gaelic group Cliar, which includes Mary Ann Kennedy, performs puirt-a-beul sets that are frequently unusual, both in terms of the types of tunes included, as well as the tunes themselves. On their album *Grinn Grinn* (2005), two sets of puirt-a-beul move from strathspeys to jigs, something that Mary Ann Kennedy repeats on her own album, *Strings Attached* (1991). The repertoire itself often consists of songs that have not otherwise been recorded and which are atypical in various ways, such as irregular puirt-a-beul, as discussed earlier. Many other commercial recordings and artists also feature unusual sets. These unusual combinations are appropriate for a commercial recording context in which experimentation, originality and innovation are highly valued, and in which dance accompaniment is no longer the primary purpose of puirt-a-beul. Expectations of puirt-a-beul singers could also be said to be higher in Scotland where the prestigious Royal National Mod competition includes a popular puirt-a-beul category (see Chapter 6 for more about puirt-a-beul at the Mod) and so it is no surprise that Scottish puirt-a-beul singers have put together some challenging and unusual sets.

Archival recordings, such as those that can be found on the websites Tobar an Dualchais (http://www.tobarandualchais. co.uk/) or Gael stream (http://gaelstream.stfx.ca/) tend to have recordings of individual puirt-a-beul rather than of sets, so they do not offer many clues about how these tunes would be put together. However, in those cases where two or more puirt-a-beul are performed together, they tend to consist of strathspeys and reels. In general, the following set combinations of tune types associated with puirt-a-beul are most common:

Stand-alone reels
Stand-alone jigs
Strathspeys and reels

To a lesser extent, the following combinations are possible and occasionally heard:

Jigs and reels
Marches and reels
Marches, strathspeys and reels

In fiddle sets, the number of times a tune is played before moving on to the next tune in a set varies somewhat by region. In Ireland, for example, tunes are repeated two or more times with the player creating different variations each time through. In Cape Breton, fiddle tunes are usually repeated once, or sometimes not at all, in part because there isn't the same emphasis on variant ornamentation each time through. In the case of puirt-a-beul, however, there is no particular expectation of ornamentation. Rather, performance emphasizes the clear enunciation of lyrics at a very quick tempo. Therefore, the number of times a particular port-a-beul is repeated depends somewhat on the lyrics: the more "verses" there are, the more the port is repeated. However, in cases where there are only two sections (the "chorus" and the "verse," or the A and B sections), the tune is often repeated only once before moving on.

Another "rule" governing the tunes that can be combined in sets is the key or modality of the tunes (better known as "scale" when referring to classical art music). The key or mode refers to the set of pitches used in a tune and the intervals or relationships between them. There are Celtic tunes in modes that correspond to the major and minor scales (Ionian and Aeolian modes), but they are also frequently set in the Dorian or Mixolydian modes. These are modes not generally used in the best-known or most widely recognized classical art music but are common in Western European "folk" musics. The difference between the Ionian, Aeolian, Dorian and Mixolydian modes is the pattern of distances (called "intervals") between notes in their respective "scales."

In a case where a piece is based on seven notes (sometimes pieces are based only on six or five notes), there will be a pattern of "half step" and "whole step" intervals between each note. In the Ionian mode, for example, there is a very short distance between the seventh note of the scale and the return to the tonic (the repeat of the first note of the mode an octave higher). This small distance is called a "half step" (as opposed to a "whole step") and would be recognizable to most people in the song "Do-Re-Mi" (also known as "doe, a deer"): "tea ["ti," as it is usually spelled in solfege], a drink with jam and bread" is the seventh note and it pulls strongly back to "do." It is one of the most characteristic aspects of the Ionian mode. Although half-step intervals exist in the other modes, they occur at different points in the note series, and this gives each a distinct sonic quality. In the other three modes, the final interval of the mode is a whole tone rather than a half step (although the Aeolian mode can vary; sometimes the seventh is raised in order to create a half step between it and the tonic, creating the same sense of pull that occurs in the Ionian mode). Tunes set in different modes offer sonic variety and contrast, and Dunlay and Greenberg provide an excellent description of how modes work in Celtic music (1996). It is not necessary to provide a music theory lesson in this book, but a good set of puirt-a-beul is linked through relationships in mode, and a singer or musician must at least have an instinctual understanding of which tunes work together well, whether due to the fact that they are in the same mode or because there are different modes with a clear relationship to each other, such as when different modes share a key signature (e.g., A Aeolian, C Ionian, D Dorian, and G Mixolydian all share the same key signature).

Performing Puirt-a-Beul

So far, my discussion of the musical characteristics of puirt-a-beul has focused on those features that can be perceived on a page of notation. I would now like to consider those features that make puirt-a-beul unique in performance since those features surely contribute to their popularity, whether in language classrooms, competitions, concert programs or simply informal contexts. Although puirt-a-beul are often considered simple, due in no small part to their repetitive musical and lyrical features (see the next chapter for a discussion of puirt-a-beul lyrics), and therefore appropriate repertoire for language learners and children but perhaps not for "serious" singers, puirt-a-beul are actually quite challenging to sing well.

First, there's the issue of breathing. Given the strong connection between puirt-a-beul and fiddle and bagpipe tunes, we should pay attention to the performance characteristics of these instruments. A fiddler obviously doesn't need to breathe in order to play and can therefore play quite continuous streams of notes without a break. Likewise, although pipers do need to breathe, the sound is continuous because their breath is not sent directly through the chanter but rather stored in the airbag and squeezed out in continuous pressure. Puirt-a-beul are often very difficult to sing because they offer little opportunity to breathe, particularly when the tune is sung at full tempo. Longer note values at the ends of sections (visible in the scores above) technically offer the singer the opportunity to grab a breath by shortening the last note

Fig. 11: *Tha Mis' air Uisg' an Lònain Duibh, transcribed by Heather Sparling from the singing of Arthur Cormack on* Nuair Bha Mi Òg *(2008).*

without really changing the rhythm in any substantial way, but in reality there is no real time to do this, especially if the tune has "pick-up" notes (introductory notes that appear before the first full bar of music, as in Fig. 11) since these notes take up the space that might otherwise be used for breathing.

The best singers avoid "dropping" a note or syllable in order to take a breath, although the practice of replacing notes with breaths is quite common, as one can hear on many archival recordings of puirt-a-beul. Thus puirt-a-beul become an excellent test of breath control, requiring singers to perform long stretches of music with limited opportunities to refill the lungs. Mary Ann Kennedy explains how singers can address the challenge of breathing:

> Where there is not enough time to breathe at the end of a line, a lone singer can choose to drop a word at the beginning of, or half-way through a line. There is still a gap, but it occurs on the beat, and adds to the rhythmic variation of the performance. Sometimes more than one word is dropped, sometimes as little as a single syllable. The Campbell family, when singing together, adopt this technique, often using

"staggered breathing," taking turns to drop words to ensure an unbroken line. (M. A. Kennedy 1995: 16-17)

As I will discuss in Chapters 5, 6 and 7, and as I hinted in the first chapter, puirt-a-beul have many functions and often enable "something else" to happen, whether that be dance or instrumental performance. However, puirt-a-beul can also be said to have value in and of themselves, not least because they demonstrate a singer's vocal abilities. Celticist Alan Bruford acknowledges that puirt-a-beul may have accompanied dance but:

> in practice they were probably always predominantly what they are today, songs designed to exhibit the singer's vocal agility—a few puirt-a-beul have five or six verses, but most have only one or two, and it would need not only a good memory but double-ended lungs and a rubber tongue to keep up the words for the length, say, of an eightsome reel; though supplemented with a bit of diddling and missing a beat now and then to draw breath, as singers have to, it might just be possible. (Bruford 1978a: 7)

Jackie Dunn agrees that puirt-a-beul are "not only used for dancing but as solo music, displaying the singer's vocal and rhythmic expertise" (J. A. Dunn 1991: 17).

Ethnomusicologist Thomas Turino has argued that we can generally divide music into two types: music predominantly for listening, and music predominantly for participation (2008). Participation can include many musicians playing together (such as at a session), but can also include dancing to music. Participatory music is evaluated based on the how effectively it enables people to participate, rather than on how "impressive" the musicians or dancers are technically. The focus on participation does not, however, mean that the music, dance or performers are not technically accomplished; rather, it means that there is room for a range of abilities in performance. In the case of puirt-a-beul, as I discuss in Chapter 6, they are often sung by and for children—to accompany their dancing, to teach them instrumental tunes and to entertain them—as well as by and for accomplished adults. Emphasis on participation does not mean that all participants are tolerated equally—too many beginners or inept performers can disrupt the "flow" of participatory music—nor does it mean that performance is not judged for its quality. However, in the case of participatory music, "quality" is less important than participation.

Turino points out that the function of the music will dictate many of the music's formal and structural features. In particular, he points out that participatory music tends to be based on short, simple, predictable forms and is highly repetitive (to make it easier for people to join in) and open-ended (to allow the music to extend as long as needed or desired by the participants). "Heightened repetition" means that repetition can be heard at multiple levels, including melodic motives, phrases, sections and the overall form (Turino 2008: 38).

As described in this chapter, puirt-a-beul exhibit many of the characteristics of participatory music. As explained, the form itself is highly repetitive (AABB AABB), and there is repetition within each section (such that melodic material from the A turn is repeated in the B turn to create coherence across the sections). Repetition no doubt helped musicians to learn and recall tunes orally, without the benefit of notation. The basic form is very short and highly predictable: virtually every port-a-beul has the same basic structure based on phrases of four or eight bars in each turn. The overall structure is open-ended in that any number of puirt-a-beul can be strung together into a set. Although puirt-a-beul tend to be performed by solo singers, rather than by groups, it is still participatory in that people of all ages and degree of language fluency tend to sing puirt-a-beul (see Chapter 6), and in that it accompanies dancers of varying abilities.

But puirt-a-beul are increasingly becoming a more presentational genre, and are being judged accordingly (see Chapter 7 for a discussion of varying attitudes toward puirt-a-beul, including negative ones). Presentational music is meant to entertain a listening audience and, as such, performance tends to emphasize virtuosity and contrast in order to keep the audience's attention. Consequently, the music tends to involve longer forms, unpredictable elements, more contrast than repetition, and carefully pre-planned arrangements and "closed" structures (structures that are not designed to be extended or repeated indefinitely). Puirt-a-beul are today rarely performed to accompany dance; instead, they are generally performed on their own as a presentational genre. Recorded music is almost always presentational as it is generally meant to be listened to, rather than participated in, and this is why traditional participatory music does not often transfer well to a recording context unless it is made more presentational through careful arrangements and varied instrumentation. The focus today tends to be on a singer's agility and technical prowess, including his or her ability to sing quickly but accurately, to maintain breath control in a challenging context, and to sustain these technical skills for a relatively lengthy period of time.

The showy nature of puirt-a-beul performance, together with the novelty factor (something I discuss more in Chapter 6), is no doubt a good part of the reason that they are so popular with audiences. Singers and performers of course recognize this aspect of puirt-a-beul too, and therefore many Gaelic song recordings and concerts wind up with puirt-a-beul as the grand finale. I discuss the place of puirt-a-beul in singers' repertoire at greater length in Chapter 6. But having now provided an overview of the musical features of puirt-a-beul, in the next chapter I turn my attention to describing their typical lyrical features.

Chapter 4
Nonsense, Innuendo and Twisted Tongues: Puirt-a-Beul Lyrics

As noted earlier, the lyrics of puirt-a-beul almost always consist of real words in complete sentences, despite their reputation for consisting of "nonsense" words and vocables. Indeed, puirt-a-beul are often denigrated for their lyrics. As I mentioned in the introduction, many would not even consider them "songs" so much as tunes. So what's the problem with their lyrics? Some possible answers emerge in this chapter, but I also suggest why puirt-a-beul ought to be valued despite their lyrics. In this chapter, I describe typical lyrical features, explore why puirt-a-beul are composed and by whom, and discuss common subject matter.

To begin, though, it is helpful to have a sense of what puirt-a-beul lyrics look like. There are three key features that can help to identify a set of lyrics as a port-a-beul by sight: form, length and extent of textual repetition. Alliteration is a fourth characteristic that is sometimes present. Puirt-a-beul lyrics follow the musical form that provides their musical accompaniment, as described in the previous chapter. In general, puirt-a-beul lyrics appear in four-line verses, sometimes called "turns." Each line of text corresponds to one or two bars of music. There are usually at least two turns, corresponding with the two melodic sections of the tune. Just as each section of the associated instrumental tune is repeated during performance, so it is that each lyrical turn is also repeated and then the entire tune is repeated. This results in the overall form of AABB AABB, with A representing both a melodic and lyrical turn. See the example opposite for an illustration of how this form works in an actual port-a-beul.

If there are more than two lyric turns in a given port-a-beul, one usually acts as a chorus so that the same set of lyrics keeps getting repeated with one melodic turn whereas the other melodic turn is repeated with a different text each time. Although the melodic form would continue to be AABB AABB, the lyrical form would look something like AABB AACC.

As indicated, puirt-a-beul tend to be short, especially compared to other genres of Gaelic song, which almost all tend to be much longer. This is the second indicator of puirt-a-beul lyrics. It would be rare to find any Gaelic song other than a port-a-beul with only two or three verses. Of course, there are exceptions: some puirt-a-beul have many verses. For example, "Sid Mar Chaidh an Càl a Dholaidh" ("That is How the Kale Broth was Ruined") appears in Helen Creighton's book, *Gaelic Songs in Nova Scotia*, with eight verses plus a chorus. But the vast majority tend to be significantly shorter.

The third characteristic to note is extensive lyrical repetition. Not only do the same words appear throughout a song, but entire lines also tend to be repeated. Although repetitive lyrics may seem boring when seen on the printed page, they are ideal in performance. Since puirt-a-beul are usually sung quite quickly, repetition gives the listener a chance to hear the lyrics clearly. Repetition also makes it easier for the singer to remember the words, especially since there is so little time to remember them when singing at full tempo.

A good example illustrating all three lyric characteristics is "Fear a Bhios Fada gun Phòsadh" ("A Man Will Go Long Without Marrying"):

Fear a bhios fada gun phòsadh	a
Fàsaidh feur is fraoch is fireach air	b
Fear a bhios fada gun phòsadh	a
Fàsaidh feusag mhòr air.	c

A (section/turn repeated)

Fàsaidh feur air fàsaidh fraoch air	d
Fàsaidh feur is fraoch is fireach air	b
Fàsaidh feur air fàsaidh fraoch air	d
Fàsaidh feusag mhòr air.	c

B (section/turn repeated)

A man will go long without marrying
Grass and heather and moorland will grow on him
A man will go long without marrying
A big beard will grow on him.

Grass will grow on him, heather will grow on him
Grass and heather and moorland will grow on him
Grass will grow on him, heather will grow on him
A big beard will grow on him.

As a typical port-a-beul, this jig consists of only two 4-line turns with several lines repeated. If we refer to the letters labelling each line, we can see that not only is there repetition of lines within each turn, but there is line repetition across the turns, which helps the song to cohere. In addition, as is the case with some puirt-a-beul, when the second turn is sung for the second time, the last two lines (and melody) of the *first* turn are substituted for the last two lines of the second turn (so that the second turn ends "dc" the first time through but "ac" the second time through). Thus the entire lyrical form (including repetitions) looks like this:

Turn 1: abac
Turn 1: abac
Turn 2: dbdc
Turn 2: dbac

This particular song is also a good example of a trait found in many puirt-a-beul: the use of alliteration. In this case, an "f" sound is prevalent, which can easily be seen even by the non-Gaelic speaker: *fear* (man), *fada* (long), *fàsaidh* (will grow), *feur* (grass), *fraoch* (heather), *fireach* (moorland) and *feusag* (beard).

In addition, "ph" in Gaelic sounds like an English "f," so *phòsadh* (marrying) starts with an "f" sound too. "Bh" and "mh" in Gaelic both sound like "v" in English, which is simply a voiced "f" sound. Thus *bhios* (will be) and *mhòr* (big) also contribute to the alliteration. This alliteration creates some of the allure of this song. Compare the use of alliteration here with this silly English-language children's song:

> Great green globs of greasy, grimy gopher guts
> Mutilated monkey meat
> Roasted, toasted parakeet
> Great green globs of greasy, grimy gopher guts
> And me without my spoon.

Some of the humour and pleasure of such a song is generated by the many similar sounds. They challenge comprehension when heard at full speed. Listeners appreciate a singer's ability to perform tongue-twister-like lyrics. One only has to think of all the English-language tongue twisters whose effectiveness rests upon alliteration: "lemon liniment" is a good example, as is "rubber baby buggy bumpers." Based on the characteristics of form, length, repetition and alliteration—all of which can be readily identified by ear or by eye—one can generally make a reasonable guess as to whether a song is a port-a-beul or not. No Gaelic required!

Composition, Creation and Circulation

So we know what a port-a-beul looks like lyrically; now, where can we find them? Aside from K. N. MacDonald's book, *Puirt-a-beul* (1931), which was revised, edited, corrected and republished in 2012 by Gaelic scholar William Lamb, there are no published collections devoted exclusively to puirt-a-beul. However, most Gaelic song collections, whether in print or online, as well as commercial recordings, include a few. Over the years, I have personally compiled a list of over 350 puirt-a-beul from various sources. And yet this number is likely only a fraction of the puirt-a-beul that have existed over the past couple of centuries. As I wrote in the introduction, readers can find many puirt-a-beul online or use the recordings listed in this book as a starting point for exploring the sounds of puirt-a-beul. However, more and more Gaelic song recordings are being released every year, so I would encourage readers to explore and support new singers and albums too.

Since many puirt-a-beul feature humorous representations of local people or events, it seems clear that they are intended for a local audience who will understand the references. Most were never meant to be preserved over time or sung outside of a local context. We can therefore assume that many puirt-a-beul created over the years disappeared once they were no longer relevant to the communities who created and sang them. This conclusion is supported if one compares the puirt-a-beul contained in the St. Francis Xavier University Gaelic song collection (available online at http://gaelstream.stfx.ca) and those contained in published song collections from Scotland and on recordings. The Gael Stream collection includes more than one hundred puirt-a-beul recorded by numerous Cape Breton tradition-bearers, with significant numbers contributed by Joe Neil MacNeil, Lauchie MacLellan, Joe Allan MacLean and Isabelle MacIsaac, recorded primarily ca. 1978-1981 and mostly by ethnologist John Shaw. I have not been able to find many of their puirt-a-beul in any other sources, printed or recorded. This could suggest that the Gael Stream repertoire represents puirt-a-beul once sung in Scotland but now only remembered in Cape Breton. Alternatively, it's possible that the Gael Stream puirt-a-beul were newly created in Cape Breton. Regardless of their provenance, the fact that most of the Gael Stream examples are no longer sung even in Cape Breton speaks to their ephemeral nature.

It also happens that a significant number of tunes have more than one set of puirt-a-beul lyrics associated with them. Given that it is quite common for new lyrics to be set to borrowed melodies in all genres of Gaelic song, it is not really surprising that so many puirt-a-beul share the same tunes. But it does suggest the localized nature of puirt-a-beul, with different communities creating different sets of lyrics at different times for their own reasons. Here are two examples that share the same melody:

Seallaibh curraigh Eòghainn
Seallaibh curraigh Eòghainn
Is còig ràimh fhichead oirre
Seallaibh curraigh Eòghainn
'S i seachad air a' Rubha Bhàn.

Bidh Eòghainn, bidh Eòghainn
Bidh Eòghainn na sgiobair oirre
Bidh Eòghainn, bidh Eòghainn
'S i seachad air a' Rubha Bhàn.

> **Look at Ewen's corracle**
> Look at Ewen's corracle
> There are twenty-five oars on her
> Look at Ewen's corracle
> She's going past White Point.
>
> Ewen will be, Ewen will be
> Ewen will be the skipper of her
> Ewen will be, Ewen will be
> She's going past White Point.

Fire faire Mhòrag
Fire faire Mhòrag
Gaol mòr aig na gillean ort
Fire faire Mhòrag
Càite nis an robh thu raoir?

A Mhòrag, a Mhòrag
Gaol mòr aig na gillean ort
A Mhòrag, a Mhòrag
Càite nis an robh thu raoir?

> **What a fuss Morag**
> What a fuss Morag
> The boys love you
> What a fuss Mora
> Where were you last night?
>
> Morag, Morag
> The boys love you
> Morag, Morag
> Where were you last night?

The first example, "Seallaibh Curraigh Eòghainn," is very well known in both Scotland and Cape Breton, although it seems to have been introduced to Cape Breton relatively recently due to its inclusion on a CD released by the University of Edinburgh's School of Scottish Studies as part of their Scottish Tradition series (Various artists, *Music from the Western Isles*, 1992 [1971]). The singer on the Scottish Tradition CD, Annie Arnott, was from Skye. Given the widespread popularity of "Seallaibh" today, it's interesting to note that Annie Arnott's version is the only one to be found in Tobar an Dualchais. In other words, it seems to be more popular today than it was in the past. Meanwhile, the only version of "Fire Faire Mhòrag" in Tobar an Dualchais is one by Alasdair Boyd from South Uist. I was unfamiliar with it until I heard it on Gillebrìde MacMillan's CD, *Thogainn Ort Fonn* (2006). It's not clear which may have been created first, or even if these two songs were once associated specifically with Skye and South Uist. But these puirt do illustrate how commercial recordings can help in spreading a port-a-beul beyond its initial locality. And the fact that there are two different sets of lyrics set to the same tune also suggests how easily puirt-a-beul lyrics could be created in different locales.[1]

If we look at puirt-a-beul published or recorded over the years, we also get a sense of how the repertoire has changed, another indicator of its ephemerality. Commercial Gaelic song recordings generally include puirt-a-beul, often examples not appearing in earlier printed collections. Even as the number of Gaelic song recordings released in any given year seems to be increasing, singers still manage to find puirt-a-beul not previously documented in print or on recordings. There is thus a sizeable body of documented puirt-a-beul at this point, but it seems to have changed over a century: many of the puirt-a-beul documented by Mackintosh (ca. 1910, 1916), for example, do not seem to be in oral circulation today, while a number of the puirt-a-beul recently recorded do not seem to have been documented by earlier collectors. While it is technically possible that all these puirt-a-beul existed simultaneously at one time (we can't expect that collectors managed to collect every example extant), it is more likely the case that the repertoire has changed over time, once again indicating that puirt-a-beul tend to have a relatively short and/or local lifespan.

There are few puirt-a-beul that we can trace over time, but a particularly excellent and interesting exception is "Calum Crùbach," the strathspey known by instrumentalists as "Miss Drummond of Perth." This port-a-beul is known in both Scotland and Cape Breton and its lyrics have been documented in multiple sources over the years, allowing us to observe changes that occurred at different times and in different places. The lyrics have altered considerably, which, although understandable in any oral tradition, runs counter to Gaelic aesthetics, which require that one learn a song *exactly* as it was sung by one's source. It's also somewhat unusual given that so many versions have been documented; usually, the more often a version has been documented, the less it changes. It becomes "fixed" since the printed versions often come to be seen as the "authentic" versions and are used by signers to "correct" their own versions. I have included some of the various versions of this song in Appendix A. It is easy to see that verses have been added, dropped and completely changed in the various versions. Although one could say that this port-a-beul has remained in the active Gaelic repertoire in both Scotland and Cape Breton, it is not really the same song. The significant changes suggest that puirt-a-beul are not held to the same kinds of aesthetic requirements as other Gaelic songs; they can be moulded to suit the needs and interests of different individuals and communities.

Having emphasized puirt-a-beul's ephemerality and changeability, one could reasonably point to a significant number of puirt-a-beul found in MacDonald's book that are still found in oral tradition today and ask why they have been remembered rather than forgotten. Why do they persist outside of small, circumscribed communities and beyond particular time periods? It is difficult to answer with certainty. Perhaps the lyrics are flexible or vague enough to apply to multiple contexts. Or perhaps the words themselves have a pleasing effect, making them worth preserving. Of course, given that MacDonald published his book with tune transcriptions, it is entirely possible that some puirt-a-beul were revived after a period during which they were not sung. MacDonald also published *Puirt-a-Beul* after his very well-known fiddle tune book, *The Skye Collection*, which continues to be used by fiddlers today. Many of the tunes in *Puirt-a-Beul* are connected to tunes in *The Skye Collection*, which means that they are linked to well-known melodies in the active instrumental repertoire. If the tunes are well known, it may be easier to keep associated texts in circulation or to reintroduce texts at a later time.

With today's audio technologies, including recordings, radios and digital music software and hardware, it is hard to see the local and ephemeral nature of puirt-a-beul. Although the songs recorded on a CD may be highly local in nature, the CD itself can circulate far beyond a particular community. Moreover, although today's liner notes often (but not always) provide considerable detail about the songs on a recording, earlier Gaelic song recordings tend to have few liner notes describing song sources, information that is traditionally provided in face-to-face song contexts. Furthermore, songs accessed from programs like iTunes lack any liner notes at all. Puirt-a-beul consequently seem free of any local associations.

Published song collections likewise contribute to this sense. Although *Eilean Fraoich* (Comunn Gaidhealach Leodhais 1998 [1982]) provides a collection of songs specific to Lewis, including quite a few puirt-a-beul, and Tolmie's collection (1910-1913) is from Skye, most popular song collections do not specify localities associated with the puirt-a-beul included in their pages. MacDonald provides only the briefest descriptions of each port-a-beul in his book; he does not name his sources and does not even indicate the communities with which his puirt-a-beul are associated. In Lamb's updated and annotated version of MacDonald's book (2012), there is information about the history of each tune and port-a-beul, whenever possible. But many are still of unknown origins. Ultimately, commercial recordings and publications have not given the impression that puirt-a-beul are tied to particular communities. And because singers from any community at any time can use these recordings and publications to learn puirt-a-beul, some puirt wind up having lengthy lives and currency across wide terrains.

The frequent claim that puirt-a-beul lyrics are "nonsensical" may well be the result of lyrics being sung out of their original context so that the humorous references are no longer recognized and understood. As an example, let's consider this specimen collected by Rosemary McCormack from Joe Lawrence MacDonald of Boisdale (Cape Breton) and composed by Malcolm MacNeil of Ironville (Cape Breton):

Aig ceann an rathaid iaruinn,
Bidh h-uile fear, bidh h-uile fear,
Aig ceann an rathaid iaruinn,
Bidh h-uile fear, bidh h-uile fear,
Aig ceann an rathaid iaruinn,
Bidh h-uile fear, bidh h-uile fear,
'S bidh Iain Peatain cuideachd ann,
Am buin a bhuideal 's gheibh sinn dram.

Bi bodach Chalum Mhór ann,
'S am bodach ad aig Neillie ann,
Bi bodach Chalum Mhór ann,
'S am bodach ad aig Neillie ann,
Bi bodach Chalum Mhór ann,
'S am bodach ad aig Neillie ann,
'S bi Iain Peatain cuideachd ann,
Am buin a bhuideal 's gheibh sinn dram.

    At the end of the railway
    They'll all be there,
    At the end of the railway
    They'll all be there,
    At the end of the railway
    They'll all be there,
    Ian Beaton will be there too
    Handling the bottle and we'll get a drink.

Old Calum Mor will be there
And Neillie's old man,
Old Calum Mor will be there
And Neillie's old man,

Old Calum Mor will be there
And Neillie's old man,
Ian Beaton will be there too
Handling the bottle and we'll get a drink.

In a song workshop led by Rosemary McCormack, she surmised that this port-a-beul was composed around the time that the railway was first introduced to Cape Breton. She suggested that it probably had more verses at one time, each of which would have named and described a different person. She also suggested that it was made during Prohibition (essentially the late 1910s through the 1920s in Nova Scotia), describing the illegal activity of drinking outside a private dwelling or licensed building, which may be part of the reason why the lyrics do not appear in writing anywhere. The lyrics are rather banal to anyone who does not know the people named, the place where the drinking occurred, or the circumstances governing alcohol at the time of the song's creation. But the lyrics could have been highly amusing to those who knew the people named.

This song also attests to the composition of puirt-a-beul in Cape Breton. Ethnomusicologist and Cape Breton fiddle scholar Liz Doherty claims that "there is no evidence to indicate that new puirt-a-beul versions of tunes were constructed in Cape Breton, and so it seems likely that all the tunes derived from this source are of Highland Scottish origin" (Doherty 1996: 180). While it is true that most puirt-a-beul commonly remembered and circulated today appear to have originated in Scotland, the example above suggests that at least some Cape Bretoners tried their hands at making puirt-a-beul. Indeed, Cape Breton piper and Gaelic learner Paul MacNeil has told me of puirt-a-beul he has created to sing to his young daughters. Andrew McFayden, a Gaelic learner from British Columbia who regularly visits Cape Breton, has also included his own puirt-a-beul compositions on his independent albums. Although puirt-a-beul may be denigrated by some fluent Gaelic speakers (a topic I discuss in more detail in Chapter 7), it is worth considering that puirt-a-beul may be an ideal genre through which learners could experiment with Gaelic poetry and song composition. Many English speakers, to provide a parallel, have likely created a haiku or limerick in their lives. Puirt-a-beul composition may provide a bridge to more complex poetry, allowing learners to play with rhyme and rhythm in a genre that celebrates silliness, simplicity and repetition. This seems to be the case for McFayden, who has spent a lot of time learning Gaelic from Cape Bretoners. He wrote this reel, which he recorded on his album *An Rathad Cam 's an Rathad Dìreach* (2004), when he was frustrated looking for his friend's phone number:

> C'àit' an do chuir mi an number aig Aonghas?
> C'àit' an do chuir mi an number aig Aonghas?
> C'àit' an do chuir mi an number aig Aonghas?
> Sin agam a-seo, 's e an number aig Aonghas!
>
> 'S ann ri taobh mo phàipeir-naidheachd, pàipeir-
>   naidheachd, pàipeir ùir',
> 'S ann ri taobh mo phàipeir-naidheachd, c'àit' a'bheil mo
>   phàipear ùir?
> 'S ann ri taobh mo phàipeir-naidheachd, pàipeir-
>   naidheachd, paipeir ùir',
> Sin agam a-seo, 's e an number aig Aonghas!

> > Where did I put Angus's number?
> > Where did I put Angus's number?
> > Where did I put Angus's number?
> > Here it is, it's Angus's number!
> >
> > It's beside my newspaper, newspaper, new paper,
> > It's beside my newspaper, where's my new paper?,
> > It's beside my newspaper, newspaper, new paper,
> > Here it is, it's Angus's number!

There are also a few people currently creating and recording puirt-a-beul in Scotland. A good example is "Màiri Ruadh a' Dannsadh A-Nochd" ("Red-Haired Mary will be Dancing Tonight") by Blair Douglas. Blair Douglas is a well-known composer of traditional tunes and was a founding member and accordionist for Scottish supergroup Runrig. Arthur Cormack describes this song as a "contemporary [port] a beul" on his album *Ruith na Gaoith* (1989).

Bidh Màiri Ruadh a' dannsadh a-nochd
Dannsa gu madainn mhoch
Bidh Màiri Ruadh a' dannsadh a-nochd
Nuair chluinneas i 'n druma bualadh

Di-luain, Di-mairt, Di-ciadain, Diardaoin
Obair-thràilleil, 's obair chruaidh
Ach nuair a thig oidhche Dihaoin'
Bidh Màiri Ruadh a' dannsa

Coma leat leabaidh, 's coma leat sìth
Tha ceòl near anam 's ceòl nar crídh'
'S leanaidh sinn dlùth tro' shràidean Phort-Rìgh
Cas-cheum a' chòmhlain

Gleus a' phìob, 's gleus an fhidheall
Caismeachd, 's ruibhle, 's piurt chrídheil
Sios tro'n bhaile bidh sinn a' trial
Is Màiri Ruadh a'dannsa

Di-luain, Di-mairt, Di-ciadain, Diardaoin
Obair-thràilleil, 's obair chruaidh
Ach nuair a thig oidhche Dihaoin'
Bidh Màiri Ruadh a' dannsa

> Red-haired Mary will be dancing tonight
> Dancing until early morning
> Red-haired Mary will be dancing tonight
> When she hears the drum beating

> Monday, Tuesday, Wednesday, Thursday
> Slavish work, hard work
> But when Friday comes 'round
> Red-haired Mary will be dancing

> You care nothing for bedtime nor for peace
> The music in our souls and the music in our hearts
> And we'll follow closely through the streets of Portree
> The footsteps of the band

> Tune the pipes, tune the fiddle
> A march and a reel and a lively tune
> Down through the town we'll go
> And red-haired Mary dancing

Monday, Tuesday, Wednesday, Thursday
Slavish work, hard work
But when Friday comes 'round
Red-haired Mary will be dancing

This port-a-beul is unusual given its three verses and limited repetition. However, the theme of dancing is common in puirt-a-beul and the subject matter is light-hearted rather than deep, serious or literary. Despite the lack of repetition, the lyrics involve relatively basic vocabulary and straightforward grammar, which help to mark it lyrically as a port-a-beul, a conclusion supported by the musical form and quick tempo.

Although not identified explicitly as a port-a-beul, Eilidh MacKenzie's "Hai-O Eadaraibh O" might also be considered a contemporary example. Eilidh MacKenzie is a native Gaelic speaker from the Isle of Lewis who sings with her two sisters in a group called MacKenzie. She is well known as a Gaelic songwriter. This particular example appears on MacKenzie's album *Camhanach* (1997).

Hai o eadaraibh o
Hai o eadaraibh o-ro
Hai o eadaraibh o
Lodaraibh eadaraibh o-ro

Bàrd an-diugh, beiridh mi bàrdachd
Bàrd an-dè, 's rug mi bàrdachd
Bàrd an-diugh, beiridh mi bàrdachd
Èistibh ri dàn mo bheatha

Deilbhear an-diugh, deasaichidh mi dealbh
Deilbhear an-dè, 's dheasaich mi dealbh
Deilbhear an-diugh, deasaichidh mi dealbh
Seallaibh air ealan mo bheatha

Cleasaich' an-diugh, cuimhnichidh mi cuideigin
Cleasaich' an-dè, 's chuimhnich mi cuideign
Cleasaich' an-diugh, cuimhnichidh mi cuideigin
Dèanaibh gàir' ri luchd mo bheatha.

Dannsair an-diugh, ceumaidh mi cearcall
Dannsair an-dè, 's cheum mi cearcall

Dannsair an-diugh, ceumaidh mi cearcall
'S coinnichidh mi am bàrd air earball.

> A bard today, I'll bear a poem
> A bard yesterday and I bore a poem
> A bard today, I'll bear a poem
> Listen to the poetry of my life.

> A painter today, I'll prepare a painting
> A painter yesterday and I prepared a painting
> A painter today, I'll prepare a painting
> Look at the art of my life

> An actor today, I'll remember someone
> An actor yesterday and I remembered someone
> An actor today, I'll remember someone
> Smile on the characters in my life

> A dancer today, I'll step a circle
> A dancer yesterday and I stepped a circle
> A dancer today, I'll step a circle
> And meet the bard on its tail.

The repetition within verses, the pattern followed across the verses, the general brevity of the song and the vocable chorus are consistent with puirt-a-beul. The jig metre also suggests that this is a port-a-beul, although the extremely fast tempo and cross-rhythms are not as typical.

Although we know the identity of the composers of these recently composed puirt-a-beul, the creators of puirt-a-beul are more often unknown. Unlike other genres of Gaelic song, most of which were authored by recognized bards (composers known for their exceptional poetic abilities), puirt-a-beul tend to be created by laypeople, a fact suggested by their brevity and lyrical repetition. It is possible that repetition may once have been the result of lyrics being extemporized in the moment rather than carefully constructed beforehand. Repetition obviously makes it easier to fill a melody and it also buys a composer time to come up with the next new line.

Although it is hard to say anything with certainty about the authorship of puirt-a-beul since we have so little evidence, in all probability most puirt-a-beul composers created one or two, or perhaps a small handful of puirt-a-beul in their lifetimes. Without having a body of poetry associated with them, as with Gaelic bards, their names are forgotten, particularly as puirt-a-beul move out of their original contexts. It is also possible that puirt-a-beul composers did not want to be associated with their creations. For one, it would doubtless be in the composer's best interest if the people named in a given port-a-beul did not know who had written a humorous account of them and their activities. For another, the composers are presumably under no delusions about the poetic value of their creations and would not aspire to be remembered as a song creator on par with more respected Gaelic bards.

Although repetition and brevity are hallmarks of most puirt-a-beul, there are exceptions. The exceptions call into question standard definitions of the genre as simple, silly dance songs. Or, since they certainly form only a small percentage of the overall puirt-a-beul repertoire, perhaps they're the exceptions that prove the rule. For example, note the limited repetition and extended number of verses in this strathspey, "An Dotair Leòdach 's Biodag Air" ("The MacLeod Doctor Wearing a Dagger"; K. N. MacDonald 1931[1901]: 14):

Thugaibh thugaibh òb òb
An Dotair Leòdach 's biodag air
Faicill oirbh an taobh sin thall
Mu'n toir e 'n ceann a thiota dhibh.

Biodag 's an deach an gath-seirg,
An crios seilg an luidealaich;
Bha seachd òirlich oirre 'mheirg,
'S gur mairg an rachadh bruideadh dh' i.

Bha thu na do bhasbair còrr
'S claidheamh mòr an tarruing ort,
An saighdear is mios' aig Rìgh Deòrsa
Chòmhraigeadh e Alasdair.

Claidheamh agus sgàbard dearg,
'S cearbach sud air amadan,

'Ghearradh amhaichean nan sgarbh,
A dh'fhàgadh marbh gun anail iad.

Gu'm biodh sud ort air do thaobh,
Claidheamh caol 's a' ghliocartaich
Chan eil faoileag thig o'n tràigh
Nach cuir thu bàrr nan itean d' i.

> Thugaibh thugaibh oh, oh
> The MacLeod Doctor wearing a dagger
> Watch out over there
> In case he suddenly takes your head off.

> A dirk, and the shrivelled dart's movement
> The hunting belt of the lazy lout
> Seven of its inches were rusted
> It would be foolish to stab with it.

> You were a notable swordsman
> A great sword you drew
> The worst of King George's soldiers
> Would fight Alasdair.

> A sword and a red scabbard
> That would be awkward on a fool
> Cutting the necks of cormorants
> Leaving them for dead without breath.

> If you were wearing that by your side
> A slim sword tinkling
> A seagull wouldn't come from the beach
> So you couldn't take off the ends of her feathers

The MacLeod doctor was apparently the son of the Rev. Mr. MacLeod of St. Kilda. St. Kilda is a collection of islands located on the most western edge of Scotland's Outer Hebrides. In 1930, all thirty-six remaining residents were moved to the Scottish mainland at their own request. Much of the islanders' diet came from birds, which probably explains the bird references in the song. The MacLeod Doctor was a surgeon in the army known for strutting about in his Highland garb (K. N. MacDonald 1929 [1900]: 41).

The atypical features of these lyrics are no doubt explained by the fact that this song was composed by a comic North Uist bard, Archibald MacDonald (ca. 1750-ca. 1815), rather than by a layperson (K. N. MacDonald 1931 [1901]: 14). Just as bards sometimes tried their hands at creating women's work songs known as "waulking" songs[2] (such as esteemed bard Duncan Bàn MacIntyre's song "Horo Gun Togainn"), a genre not normally associated with named composers, so they sometimes wrote humorous songs in the style of puirt-a-beul.

If we think of puirt-a-beul as a continuum, apparent exceptions make more sense. Most puirt-a-beul would be positioned in the middle of the continuum, a position filled by songs that share most or all of puirt-a-beul's typical and defining features. At one end of the continuum, however, we might find more carefully constructed examples with longer texts, sophisticated vocabulary and grammar, and less repetition, blurring the boundary between puirt-a-beul and other types of Gaelic song. At the other end we might find more and more vocables, blurring the boundary between puirt-a-beul and vocabelized mouth music. Take another example from K. N. MacDonald's book, *Puirt-a-Beul*:

> E ho rithill àill, hi rithill ù
> Se do bheath' a Raonaill, hi rithill ù
> E ho rithill àill, hi rithill ù
> Do bheath' 'us do shlàinte, hi rithill ù
> E ho rithill à, earum hi, rithill ù
> An nochd a bhios a' bhanais ann
> Ho ro um bo
> E ho rithill aire-rum hi rithill ù
> An nochd a bhios i 'm banaraig
> Ho ro um bò
> E ho rithill i rum hi rithill ù
> No cheisd air an t-saighdear, hi rithill ù
> E ho rithill ir-um, hi rithill ù

>> E ho rithill aill, hi rithill u
>> It's your life, Ronald, hi rithill u
>> E ho rithill aill, hi rithill u
>> Your life and your health, hi rithill u
>> E ho rithill a, earum hi, rithill u
>> Tonight is the wedding

Ho ro um bo
E ho rithill aire rum hi rithill u
Tonight she will be a fool (?)
Ho ro um bo
E ho rithill i rum hi rithill u
Or his question to the soldier, hi rithill u
E ho rithill ir um hi rithill u

This example consists primarily of vocables with only a few scattered phrases of "real" words. K. N. MacDonald notes that this "is one of the most uncommon dance songs" (1931 [1901]: 34), suggesting that this example was atypical of puirt-a-beul even at the time MacDonald published his collection. As a matter of interest, MacDonald also explains that this song would be sung by two people alternating lines and that the beginning of each line would be marked with a clap of the hands. The method of performance described is unique in my research and I have certainly never witnessed puirt-a-beul performed in this manner.

Although puirt-a-beul are often associated with vocables, I have yet to find any examples in my personal collection that consist of vocables alone, presumably because such an example would not be considered a port-a-beul. Aside from anything else, an exclusively vocable text would make it very difficult to remember. One likely reason why vocabelized mouth music is extemporized (rather than composed with a fixed text) is that it can be challenging to remember long lists of vocables. And while vocables can render a tune as easily as words, their lack of semantic meaning eliminates their potential to make pointed commentary about specific people, places or events.

But while I have never found an example consisting exclusively of vocables, vocables are reasonably common in puirt-a-beul. The appearance of vocables in puirt-a-beul is entirely consistent with the frequent appearance of vocables in other Gaelic song genres, especially work songs. Waulking songs, for example, often have choruses made entirely of vocables. In the case of both puirt-a-beul and waulking songs, it is important to note that the vocables are fixed and must be sung as learned; singers are not free to improvise whatever vocables come to mind. The fixed nature of the vocables is part of what makes puirt-a-beul distinct from other types of mouth music, as described in Chapter 1.

Other examples of puirt-a-beul with vocables illustrate how puirt-a-beul lie on a continuum since they have fewer vocables than the one I have just discussed. Generally, when vocables occur in puirt-a-beul, they tend to be restricted to one section (what might be considered the chorus) whereas the verses will consist of texts, as in this well-known example:

I bhì à da, ù a idal ana,
I bhì à da, ad al ad al u a.
I bhì à da, ù a idal ana,
I bhì à da, ad al ad al u a.

Ciamar a ruidhleas mo nighean
'S dithis anns an rathad oirre?
Ciamar a ruidhleas mo nighean
'S ceathrar air an ùrlar?

'S iomadh rud a chunna mi,
'S iomadh rud a rinn mi,
'S iomadh rud a chunna mi
A-muigh air feadh na h-oidhche.

Chunna mi na piseagan,
Na piseagan, na piseagan,
Chunna mi na piseagan
Air spiris fad' an t-saighdeir.

> I bhì à da, ù a idal ana,
> I bhì à da, ad al ad al u a.
> I bhì à da, ù a idal ana,
> I bhì à da, ad al ad al u a.

> How does my daughter reel
> Alongside the two on her road?
> How does my daughter reel
> Alongside the four on the ground?

> I saw various things,
> I did various things,
> I saw various things
> Outside throughout the night.

I saw the kittens,
The kittens, the kittens,
I saw the kittens
On a hen-roost high as the soldier.[3]

Ultimately, the majority of puirt-a-beul have few, if any, vocables. Meanwhile, vocables are common in other Gaelic song genres such as waulking songs. The presence of vocables is therefore not a reliable indication of a port-a-beul, even though they are often defined in casual conversation as consisting of vocables. Puirt-a-beul are also often described as nonsensical. There is a tendency to conflate "vocables" with "nonsensicality" but these terms should not be treated as the same in the context of puirt-a-beul. It is true that vocables are, as non-semantic sounds, nonsensical. But, as I have suggested in this section, the nonsensical aspect of puirt-a-beul more likely (and more often) arises from references and meanings no longer understood by audiences. In other words, the nonsensicality attributed to puirt-a-beul by many Gaelic singers may be better understood as pertaining to "real" words that make no sense to an uninformed listener than to the presence of vocables. Many puirt-a-beul likely made sense within their initial contexts but became nonsensical as they moved outside their original communities. After having studied puirt-a-beul for many years, I would not use the term "nonsensical" to describe their texts at all. Given that virtually all puirt-a-beul have "real" words, that the words appear to have had significance at one time and for at least some people, and that vocables appear in only a small number of puirt-a-beul, to label puirt-a-beul as "nonsensical" would perpetuate a misunderstanding about the lyrics of puirt-a-beul.

In this section, I have discussed how puirt-a-beul are typically composed by average people, rather than bards, and are designed for small, local, circumscribed audiences. Many were never intended to be heard outside their immediate communities or beyond the lifetimes of people who would recognize the references within the lyrics. And yet there are exceptions: the composers of some puirt-a-beul are known, especially newly composed examples. And thanks to commercial recordings and publications, some puirt-a-beul circulate well beyond their original localities and for lengthy periods of time.

Humour

Puirt-a-beul can be about almost anything. I have already described one port about a ridiculous, twenty-five oared coracle; one about looking for someone's phone number; one about working in various occupations; one about dancing; and one about drinking. Clearly, the range of topics is large. There are, however, common themes, including descriptions of dancing, drinking and drunkenness; weddings and events; animals; work; hunting; and especially romantic relationships. But rather than focus on specific topics in this chapter, I want to focus on other key features of puirt-a-beul lyrics, such as their form, composition, vocables and humour. It would be easy to get caught up in listing and describing various themes—something I indeed did as I prepared to write this chapter—but I am generally more interested in understanding what makes puirt-a-beul lyrics distinct and why they are the way they are. So in this section, I focus on humour since so many puirt-a-beul are meant to be funny in some way or other.

The work of humour scholars can help us to understand both *what* is funny about puirt-a-beul and *why* it is funny. Several scholars suggest that theories of humour can generally be grouped in three types: relief theories, incongruity theories, and superiority theories (Meyer 2000: 312-15; Long and Graesser 1988: 36; Berger 1993: 2-4). Theories of relief posit that humour arises as a means of dispelling tension. Theories of incongruity argue that humour arises from surprise, the unexpected, or from some noticeable break with an accepted pattern or social norm. Superiority theories suggest that humour arises when someone (or a group of people) feels superior to someone or something else.

In light of these three types of humour theories, we see that there are several ways to understand how and why "The MacLeod Doctor," discussed above, is funny. First, given that the MacLeod

Doctor was a real person, we can imagine that he might have engendered some tension in his community that may have been partly dispelled by this song. The doctor is portrayed as having a dirk or sword that he doesn't seem to know how to use properly. The bard warns listeners to watch out for fear that they might be inadvertently beheaded. The rusty sword has obviously not been cared for. The doctor is described as being a brave—even a vicious—hunter of an innocuous seabird. Although we do not know what the real Doctor MacLeod was like, the song suggests that he may have been somewhat absent-minded, even eccentric. Unusual people may be tolerated socially, but they can cause apprehension when they ignore—deliberately or not—social conventions and norms. Alternatively, the lyrics could be more metaphorical with the dirk standing in for the surgeon's knife, or there might even be sexual innuendo (I discuss bawdry further below). Perhaps Doctor MacLeod was somewhat incompetent in his practice, ineffectively wielding his medical tools and not caring for them properly. In either case, we can imagine that singing about Doctor MacLeod would help to release communal tension about these unpopular aspects of the Doctor. This would be especially important in a situation in which the Doctor could not be directly confronted with complaints or concerns due to social norms or fear of reprisal, or perhaps because there was no other doctor available locally.[4]

Second, we can see how the description of Doctor MacLeod is incongruous. What is a doctor doing with a dirk? Why would someone wear a weapon that he couldn't control and that therefore threatened those around him? What kind of person goes about with a rusty sword? Why would anyone waste his or her time killing cormorants? Each verse contributes another incongruous image.

Third, Doctor MacLeod is clearly being made fun of, suggesting the superiority of the composer at the very least and probably of all those who would sing this song. Doctor MacLeod is inferior not only due to his inability to handle a dirk well, but because he insists on trying to handle it anyway. This putting of Doctor MacLeod "in his place" is all the more interesting given the standing that he would have enjoyed as a doctor. In many cultures, there are checks and balances that are designed to prevent any particular individual from acquiring too much power. Historically, for example, the Gaelic bard's role was to celebrate his clan cief in verse, contributing to the chief's power and status. However, if the chief abused that power, the bard could critique him in verse, causing potentially significant consequences:

> [In pre-Christian times,] it was seriously believed that a satirical poem ... could not only make people laugh at a man but actually hurt him, say by raising a boil on his face; and since, in theory at least, a king with such a blemish was not fit to rule, a competent poet could get a king deposed. (Bruford 1978a: 5)

Michael Newton explains that "poets were not just sycophantic flatterers. They could withhold their approval or explicitly disapprove of actions and policies, and wielded considerable influence over the nobility" (2009: 99). The bard himself enjoyed considerable prestige as a person of knowledge and as a verbal artist. However, if he abused his station, he could lose the chief's patronage and therefore his means of livelihood. Thus both the chief and bard have prestige and status, but there are social systems in place to prevent their abuse. We may likewise consider this song as a means of mediating Doctor MacLeod's status.

Folklorist and Gaelic scholar Tom McKean has documented the life and songs of a Skye bard, Iain MacNeacail (1921-2003). He explains how songs and singing provided the means for people to engage in community debates indirectly. Community members could indicate their position within a debate by the songs they chose to sing, and by the songs they chose not to sing. Others indicated approval through laughter and applause, or indicated opposition by withholding support. If someone criticized the position expressed in a song, the singer could scapegoat the composer, claiming that he or she didn't make the song and is only singing it, absolving the singer of guilt (McKean 1997: 142). Thus, a song such as this one about the MacLeod doctor can be sung as a means of indirect criticism.[5] Moreover, although not the case in this particular instance (the composer is known), the anonymous creation of most puirt-a-beul means that no particular composer can be accused of any wrongdoing either.

Several humour scholars have generated categorization systems of humour types to help organize and understand the substance of humour (e.g., Long and Graesser 1988; Berger 1993). Long and Graesser (1988) propose a taxonomy of jokes:

1. Nonsense
2. Social satire
3. Philosophical
4. Sexual
5. Hostile
6. Demeaning to men
7. Demeaning to women
8. Ethnic
9. Sick
10. Scatological

They also propose a taxonomy of wit:

1. Irony
2. Satire
3. Sarcasm and hostility
4. Overstatement and understatement
5. Self-deprecation
6. Teasing
7. Replies to rhetorical questions
8. Clever replies to serious statements
9. Double entendres
10. Transformations of frozen expressions
11. Puns

By drawing on these categories and labels, we get a sense of the kinds of humour typical in puirt-a-beul. For example, many puirt-a-beul involve teasing or making fun of an individual, often as a result of their appearance, as in the case of the MacLeod Doctor example above. Sometimes greater attention is paid to a particular item of clothing rather than to a particular person, as in this example (James Graham, *Siubhal* 2005):

Leis a' bhriogas uallaich, horo-o hì
Leis a' bhriogais uallaich, ho ri ho rò
Briogais an duin' uasail, horo-o hì
'S iomadh duine chual i nach robh na còir

Siod a' bhriogais fhasanta, horo-o hì
Bhriogais a bha agamsa, ho ri ho rò
Bha i muthas fada dhomh, horo-o hi
'S gad a chanainn farsaing air a h-uile dòigh

'S chaidh mi chun an tàilleir, horo-o hì
'S gun gearradh e pàirt dhi, ho ri ho rò
Thuirt e airson pàigheadh, horo-o hì
Gun dèanadh e dhà air na bh' innte chlò

Cha robh innt ach diùbhaidh, horo-o hì
B' fharsuing anns a' chùl i, ho ri ho rò
Gad a rachadh triùir innt', horo-o hì
Ghabhadh i co-dhiù 'ad, gu brith an còrr

Saoil nach robh i cunnartach, horo-o hì
Nuair a chuir mi umam i, ho ri ho rò
Shaoil iad nach robh duin' innte, horo-o hì
Gus an cual 'ad bruidhinn agus thuirt iad "ò"

> With the fantastic breeks [trousers], horo-o hi
> With the fantastic breeks, ho ri ho ro
> The gentleman's breeks, horo-o hi
> Many a person heard of them that was not near them
>
> These were the trendy breeks, horo-o hì
> The breeks that I had, ho ri ho rò
> They were rather long, horo-o hì
> And I would say wide in every way
>
> I went to the tailor, horo-o hì
> That he would cut some of it, ho ri ho rò
> He said that for payment, horo-o hì
> He would make two from the amount of cloth

> They were worthless, horo-o hì
> They were wide in the back, ho ri ho rò
> Though three people would go in them, horo-o hì
> They would take them and more
>
> Don't you think they were dangerous, horo-o hì?
> When I put them on, ho ri ho rò
> People thought there was no one in them, horo-o hì
> 'Til they heard talking and said, "Oh"[6]

In both "The MacLeod Doctor" and "The Fantastic Breeks," humour arises in part from exaggeration and overstatement, which is common in puirt-a-beul.

As already discussed, one of the most common descriptions of puirt-a-beul is that they are silly or nonsensical. Absurdity of this type can be funny because it makes light "of the 'demands' of logic and rationality as we traditionally know them" (Berger 1993: 19). Here is a short example from Gillebrìde MacMillan's album, *Thogainn Ort Fonn* (2006):

> Cuiridh 'ad do chas air fàd
> 'S do chas eil air caoran
> Do cheann ann an Tobar Mhoire
> 'S do cholann sa Chrianan
>
> > They will put your leg on a peat
> > And your other on a small peat
> > Your head in Tobermory
> > And your body in Crinan.

Although set to the relatively well-known tune of "Brochan Lom" ("Thin Porridge"), these lyrics are not themselves well known. There may well have been a story at one point that would have explained the lyrics but, in its absence, the lyrics are nonsensical when taken literally.

One more example will suffice to represent absurd lyrics. This longer example comes from Margaret Fay Shaw's book, *Folksongs and Folklore of South Uist*:

> Danns' a bhrigi, danns' a bhocai,
> Danns' a bhrigi, a chait bhàin!

Danns' a bhrigi, danns' a bhocai,
Bha thu 'n raoir an taigh Iain Bhàin!

Danns' a bhrigi
Danns' a bhrigi
Ù a hu a
'S geal do shùilean

Danns' a bhrigi, danns' a bhocai,
Danns' a bhrigi, a chait bhàin!
Danns' a bhrigi, danns' a bhocai,
Bidh thu nochd an taigh Iain Bhàin!

> Dance the breeks, dance the bucks
> Dance the breeks, white cat!
> Dance the breeks! dance the bucks!
> Last evening you were at fair John's house.
>
> Dance the breeks
> Dance the breeks
> U a hu a
> Bright are your eyes
>
> Dance the breeks, dance the bucks,
> Dance the breeks, white cat!
> Dance the breeks, dance the bucks,
> Tonight you will be at fair John's house.

Although there are understandable, translatable words in each of the above two cases, it is not really clear what is being described or why. Individual words make sense, but the overall song does not.

Freud's work on humour has been very influential in humour scholarship. He suggested that humour results from the release of what is normally suppressed by society. Folklorists Abrahams and Dundes draw on Freud to suggest the reasons for the popularity of nonsensical jokes:

> The veil of nonsense is so opaque that the serious nature of the underlying rationale of the humor is effectively concealed. This is as it should be, or rather as it always is. The release, the safety-valve function of oral humor, would be less effective if one knew what he was saying or was laughing at. This veiling from consciousness is one way of duping so-

ciety into the casual acceptance of argument. As an escape from the psychological pressures of the human condition we must translate or transmute reality into an unrecognizable form. (1969: 228)

For these authors, then, the "hidden" aspect of nonsensical humour is to be expected and even necessary. But even without complete understanding, it still serves as a "release valve," enabling participants to release tension and anxiety through laughter. They also suggest that nonsensical humour provides a socially acceptable means to "regress" to childhood, to act immature (which apparently we all need and want to do but rarely, as adults, have licence to do) (1969: 227).

In addition to the nonsensical aspect of this song, there is also a play on words, for "boc" means not just "buck" but also "fop." Double-entendres are another feature of puirt-a-beul, which makes them difficult to translate and challenging to appreciate for a Gaelic learner, even a very fluent one. But the witty use of words is a favourite technique of humour in Gaelic culture and its use in puirt-a-beul suggests that the lyrics may sometimes be more sophisticated than they appear at first glance.

A great example of a double-entendre is "A' Chaora Chrom" ("The Crooked-Horned Ewe") in which the "caora chrom" refers to a whisky still (M. F. Shaw 1977[1955]: 174-75):

A' chaora chrom a bh'air an leacaidh,
A' chaora chrom a bh'air an leacaidh,
Air an leacaidh, air an leacaidh,
Cha lig i duine 'na gaoth.

Chuireadh i le séid a stròineadh,
Chuireadh i le séid a stròineadh,
Séid a stròineadh, séid a stròineadh,
A' chaora smògach air a druim.

Tha bainn' aig na caoirich uile,
Tha bainn' aig na caoirich uile,
Caoirich uile, caoirich uile,
Galan aig a' chaora chruim.

Tha uan aice urad ri gamhain,
Tha uan aice urad ri gamhain,
Urad ri gamhain, urad ri gamhain,
'S e cho sleamhain ris an ìm.

> The crooked-horned ewe was on the flat rock
> The crooked-horned ewe was on the flat rock
> On the flat rock, on the flat rock
> She will not let anyone near her.
>
> She would put with a snort from her nose
> She would put with a snout from her nose
> Snort from her nose, snort from her nose
> The clumsy-footed ewe on her back.
>
> All the sheep have milk,
> All the sheep have milk,
> All the sheep, all the sheep,
> But the crooked-horned ewe has a gallon!
>
> She has a lamb as big as a stirk [a year-old bull or cow],
> She has a lamb as big as a stirk,
> Big as a stirk, big as a stirk,
> And as slippery as butter.

Illegal whisky stills generated quite a bit of humour of different types. For example, there's a beautiful, sad lament, "Cha Tig Mòr Mo Bhean Dhachaigh" ("My Wife Will Never Again Come Home"), which I know best from Mary Jane Lamond's album, *Làn Dùil* (*Full of Hope*, 1999), but which was also made famous as "A Dunvegan Dirge" by Marjory Kennedy-Fraser. Although it may certainly have been created as an expression of grief, I also heard a story that it was used by a man who was told that the Royal Canadian Mounted Police were on their way to his home to check for illegal whisky. The man barely had time to hide some of his collection in a cradle. When the police arrived, he was singing this sad lament and rocking the cradle of his "motherless child." The police were so moved by the man's grief that they left him alone. Or so the story goes!

In Canada, 19th-century federal acts gave individual counties and municipalities the right to prohibit the sale of alcohol by majority vote. During the First World War, most provinces enacted Prohibition partly in support of war efforts but also in response to the Temperance Movement. The latter hit its zenith in the 1920s but throughout that decade, provinces rejected Prohibition laws and returned to being "wet" provinces. Nova Scotia repealed Prohibition in 1930; Prince Edward Island was the last province to do so in 1948.

In Scotland, the situation was somewhat different. In the late 1700s, whisky was heavily taxed, which drove much whisky production underground, which in turn caused thousands of illegal stills to be seized and destroyed. One humorous printed broadside from 1795 gives the "last words" of a whisky still facing execution, a parody of popular broadsides that published the final words of condemned criminals (available from the National Library of Scotland's digital collection of broadsides at http://www.nls.uk/broadsides/broadside.cfm/id/16656). With the reaction to illegal alcohol expressed in so many different ways, it is not surprising to find puirt-a-beul referencing illegal stills too. Humour scholars might label this kind of humour as "social satire" which targets social institutions and policies (Long and Graesser 1988: 39).

It is clear that different types of humour are at play in puirt-a-beul. I have shown in this section how one example, "The MacLeod Doctor," can be understood in humour terms as releasing tension, presenting an incongruous image, and suggesting the superiority of the singer (and his or her listeners) over the character portrayed in the song. I have also offered examples of puirt-a-beul illustrating several categories of humour, including teasing, exaggeration, nonsense (with particular attention to the importance of opacity or incomprehensibility), and double entendres. I encourage readers to watch for wit and humour in the other examples of puirt-a-beul in this book.

Bawdry

One particular kind of humour is bawdry. When conducting my research, several people suggested that puirt-a-beul are predominantly bawdy. Gaelic song scholar Alan Bruford also notes this tendency among puirt-a-beul:

> The words are mostly either untranslatable or unprintable: some are more or less nonsense, more may look that way because written about some long-forgotten local incident, many are scurrilous about individuals (for instance the well-known reel tune "Tha biodag air MacThòmais," "Thomson's got a dirk" is one of several songs mocking commoners for wearing swords like gentlemen), and a great many, like Scots mouth music, are extremely bawdy. The bawdiness may be hidden in a tongue-twister, as in early English catches, or it may be so well disguised by the Idiom of the People that it is quite common to hear groups of girls singing a song whose refrain threatens to exhaust a man's sexual powers without a blush between them. (Bruford 1978b: 7)

Despite the claim that there are a great many bawdy puirt-a-beul, I have very few examples. Of course, that's not particularly surprising. People would be especially circumspect about singing bawdy examples in public or sharing them with others. Bawdry tends to be passed along in very particular circumstances to very particular people; the clinical collection of puirt-a-beul texts by an outside scholar does not readily create the conditions in which bawdy puirt-a-beul might be shared.[7] This caution would also make it less likely for bawdy puirt-a-beul to be passed on to enough people and to be practised often enough to be remembered over a long period of time, especially when the overall number of Gaelic speakers has been declining steadily for some time in both Scotland and Cape Breton. Collectors are certainly at a disadvantage for few people would be willing to go on the record being associated with a bawdy song.

But despite the limited number of examples in my collection, it is not hard to believe that bawdy puirt-a-beul have long existed since the genre is well-suited to lewd humour in the same way as, say, a dirty limerick in English. A Scottish Gael who wishes to remain nameless did volunteer the following example:

O, na miolan 's na dearagadan air a' chaillich mhòr
Shuas air a' manachain, shios air a' manachain
O, na miolan 's na deargadan air a' chaillich mhòr
Shuas air a' manachain an còmhnaidh

> Oh, the lice and the fleas on the large old lady
> Up the crotch and down the crotch
> Oh, the lice and the fleas on the large old lady
> Always up the crotch.

William Lamb refers to the rather "blue" connotations of a port-a-beul still popular today:

Dhiùlt am bodach fodar dhomh
Gun d' dhiùlt am bodach feur dhomh   } x2
Dhiùlt am bodach fodar dhomh
Chuirinn fo mo shliasaid.

Dhiùlt am bodach fodar dhomh
Gun d' dhiùlt am bodach feur dhomh
Dhiùlt am bodach fodar dhomh
Gun d' dhiùlt am bodach feur dhomh
Dhiùlt am bodach fodar dhomh
Gun d' dhiùlt am bodach feur dhomh
Gun d' dhiùlt am bodach luideach odhar
Anns an t-sabhal feur dhomh

> The old man refused me fodder
> The old man refused me hay
> The old man refused me fodder
> For me to put beneath my thigh.

> The old man refused me fodder
> The old man refused me hay
> The old man refused me fodder
> The old man refused me hay
> The old man refused me fodder
> The old man refused me hay
> The silly, sallow old man
> Refused me hay in the stable.

Lamb explains that the common interpretation is that "the gentleman referred to in the song did not offer the lady soft-padding during their dalliance" (2012: 161-62).

171

The association of dance tunes with bawdy lyrics is not restricted to Gaelic culture and puirt-a-beul. Folklorist Colin Quigley observes that "the predominant theme among [Newfoundland] dance rhymes ... is sexuality" (Quigley 1985: 87). Two of Quigley's examples demonstrate:

Chase me Charlie I got Barley
Up the leg of me drawers
If you don't believe it come and see it
Up the leg of me drawers.

Some like the girls who are pretty in the face
Some like the girls who are neat around the waist
But I love the girls with a wriggle and a twist
In the bottom of her belly is the cuckoo's nest.

These lyrics were so well known that even if people heard the associated tunes without the words, the words automatically came to mind (Quigley 1985: 88). Quigley reports that one person became embarrassed just hearing the tunes! This parallel English-language tradition occurring in Newfoundland—which is geographically quite close to Cape Breton and the closest part of Canada to Scotland and Ireland—suggests that bawdy puirt-a-beul cannot be considered unusual or even unexpected.

Because there are social constraints upon bawdry, it would not be surprising to find that the nonsensical aspect of some puirt-a-beul is a deliberate effort to mask socially inappropriate language or themes. Turning again to the Newfoundland context, Quigley tells us, "crucial lines are often omitted or obscured in performances, yet the audience still responds with gales of laughter and appreciative howls. Obviously, they recognized and knew the rhyme" (1985: 88). It's possible that some puirt-a-beul lyrics known today are actually edited and censored versions of more explicitly bawdy originals. This could explain why some puirt-a-beul lyrics seem to make no logical sense.

Charlotte Frisbie, an ethnomusicologist who studies Navajo music, recounts how one interviewee laughed when listening to the recording of a Moccasin Game Song, saying, "He's singing that song with no words; it has dirty words. He must have changed it because he was being recorded" (Frisbie 1980: 354). The singer substituted vocables for words to mask the obscenities. Quigley likewise describes the deliberate obfuscation of bawdy English-language dance rhymes. It is not inconceivable that puirt-a-beul vocables, at least in some cases, function in a similar way.

Puirt-a-beul provide other means to mask obscenities or lewd topics. It is possible that puirt-a-beul are the medium of choice for bawdy texts because their quick tempos and syllabically dense lyrics make words difficult to comprehend. Thus, it may not always be necessary to make the words nonsensical, for in performance they will still come across as nonsensical to the uninitiated. Moreover, if a singer were to suspect that a bawdy song was about to be heard by an inappropriate party, it would be easy to stop singing the lyrics and continue vocabelizing the tune, which has enough musical merit to warrant singing even in the absence of lyrics. Singing such a wordless tune might not, in this case, arouse suspicion.

Communication professor Ed Cray is one of the few scholars to have studied bawdry, arguing that if we don't acknowledge bawdy songs then we are ignoring a substantial segment of folksong and we wind up with an incomplete image of folksong in any given culture or community (see also Dundes and Georges 1962; Halpert 1962; Goldstein 1967). Cray first published *The Erotic Muse: American Bawdy Songs* in 1969. He writes that despite the social inappropriateness of bawdry, and despite its absence from print and scholarship, it is alive and well, at least in the U.S. Indeed, bawdry has perhaps had better staying power than almost any other type of folksong, at least in English. Despite bawdry's association with tastelessness and people of a (presumed) lower social order, Cray reveals that the examples from his book come from a broad cross-section of society, including highly educated middle and upper class professionals. Moreover, he suggests that many samples indicate that they were created by literate authors. Indeed, he lists prominent and respected writers who have been known to turn their pens to bawdry, including Rudyard Kipling, Gilbert and Sullivan, Robert Service, Gene Fowler, Ogden Nash,

James Joyce, and even Alfred Lord Tennyson (1992: xi-xii). William Shakespeare is himself known for weaving bawdry and sexual innuendo into his plays.

Established Gaelic bards likewise tried their hands at bawdy puirt-a-beul. A good example comes from Lachlan MacPherson (ca. 1723-ca. 1795) of Strathmashie, a well-known humorous song-maker and tacksman, a tacksman being a landholder of intermediate social status in Highland society. One of his songs is included in K. N. MacDonald's *Puirt-a-Beul*, although its length of ten verses and lack of lyric repetition clearly mark it as a bardic rather than lay composition. "A' Bhanais Bhàin" ("The White Wedding") is about a bunch of aging men who make various threats against a bard should he write about their greying hair. One verse in particular is bawdy (Thomson 1993: 134-35):

Thuirt am Maighstir-sgoile liath
"Mas e gleus air mhàs a mhiann,
Mo roghainn-s' e thar seachd caid
'S i 'cheàird bha riamh cur ann da."

The grey-haired schoolmaster said,
"If it's buttocking he wants
He's better than seven hundred at it,
It's a job he was always promoting."

Despite the apparent ubiquity of bawdy puirt-a-beul, it is very difficult to find examples. Regardless of the number of bawdy puirt-a-beul or their popularity, they are still considered risqué. In mainstream North American and British society, there have long been rules that so constrained obscenity and lewdness that even those few folklorists who collected and published bawdry often had to omit words or rewrite texts to make them conform to social norms of appropriateness. For example, Gaelic song collector Thomas Sinton omits Lachlan MacPherson's verse above in his 1906 book, *The Poetry of Badenoch*, due to "suggestive overtones" (Lamb 2012: 151). It, along with five other verses, are also absent from K. N. MacDonald's book, *Puirt-a-Beul*. Another port-a-beul, "An Gunna Dubh" ("The Black Gun"), composed by highly accomplished and respected North Uist bard, John MacCodrum (ca. 1693-1779), apparently consisted of a number of verses not suitable for print (Lamb 2012: 152). The Rev. William Matheson writes:

> MacCodrum composed one or two pieces of a Rabelaisian nature.... Though this does not justify such compositions, it must not be forgotten that in the society in which MacCodrum lived coarse lampoons of this kind often had a salutary effect.... Another formerly well-known port-a-beul, "*Tha meirg air a' gunna dhubh*" ["There's Rust on the Black Gun"], ascribed (evidently correctly) to him, has not this justification, and the best that can be said is that the excellent strathspey air to which it is sung deserves better words. (Matheson and MacCodrum 1938: xxxiii-xxxiv)

The Rev. Aeneas Macdonald writes similarly:

> Quite a number of MacCodrum's ditties have been forgotten in my own time—some of them, no doubt, not very fit for polite ears. "*Meirg air a' Ghunna Dhubh*" was certainly never intended for a drawingroom [*sic*]." (Qtd. in Lamb 2012: 152)

Interviewees must completely trust that their interviewers will not impugn them or judge their character upon being sung a bawdy lyric. To be sure, it is not just the interviewer with whom the singer must be concerned, but rather the interviewer's entire potential audience.

The situation is further complicated with Gaelic. The declining number of speakers means that there are fewer people to hear, share and learn bawdy rhymes and songs in the first place. More importantly, perhaps, is that all Gaelic speakers at this point are bilingual and therefore have absorbed the cultural rules that govern English speech and conversation. But Gaelic bawdry is likely different from English bawdry. Two Cape Breton interviewees with whom I spoke (both very fluent learners comfortable with idiomatic and regional Gaelic) suggested that the themes of bawdy puirt-a-beul would seem impossibly harsh to anyone unfamiliar with Gaelic language and culture. The problem here is not simply one of literal translation of the words, but of translating cultural humour. These two interviewees were not just worried about what I or anyone else would think of them as individuals, but how we might judge the culture as a whole. Thus, while English-language bawdry tends most often to deal with sex or excretion (Cray 1992: xxiv), Gaels may well have traditionally found different themes, such as body parts or gender relations, funny, which seem unfunny when translated into English for an English-speaking audience. Although not writing specifically about bawdry, Gaelic scholar Derick Thomson has described the difficulties of translation, particularly with respect to humour:

> There is no complete substitute for appreciation of poetry in a particular language short of learning that language and learning it well. In particular there are many examples of verbal wit that can hardly be fully translated, for they may often depend on the whole range of a word's connotations, and there is only one kind of computer, to date, that can be programmed in the right way to appreciate this [i.e., the human brain]. In similar fashion, humour of situation and humour of character often depend for their effect on a knowledge of the culture's stereos [sic], and an intimate knowledge at that. (Thomson 1990: 15)

Given the threat of censure from both cultural insiders and outsiders, what enables bawdry to survive? Cray argues: "The immodest ballad has only one overt function, that of entertainment. Titillation is incompatible with humor; the man doubled over in belly-aching laughter is not one intent upon copulation" (Cray 1969: 263n3). In other words, bawdry survives because it is funny. Moreover, not least because it falls outside the rules of social acceptability, bawdry also provides an important social release, as humour often does:

> Bawdy songs are remembered and sung as adults because they ... feel a need to "rebel." The prevailing public opinion, or what the singers feel is the prevailing public opinion, that somehow bawdy songs are "dirty" or not fit for polite society permits the bawdy songster to thumb his nose at convention

even as he relieves his own fears and guilt with laughter. Further, he must confine his songs to the stag smoker or the fraternity party, far from prying ears. The very locale of the presentation lends a cover, "underground" sense of group identification. (Cray 1969: xxiii)

Humour in general, not just bawdry, contributes to a sense of community. People sharing the joke often feel that they share more than just the joke: they share a common sense of what counts as funny. Contexts and joke content can also help to reinforce differences between the joke tellers and some other group. Thus jokes about men or women serve to unite particular gender groups and to differentiate them from the opposite gender. Ethnic jokes project a sense of "us" vs. "them." As a teacher, I have had to endure laughter in the classroom that no one will explain to me, unifying the students against the teacher.

But a shared sense of humour is crucial: "If the song is not humorous, the listener is left with fear and guilt unassuaged by amusement" (Cray 1969: xxiv). As the number of Gaelic speakers declines, and given that every Gaelic speaker is enculturated within Western mainstream English-language cultural norms, it is possible that Gaels' senses of humour are changing. Change, of course, is inevitable, regardless of the reason. Cray reminds us that many words and topics considered obscene today have not always been so: "Times change and peoples' attitudes change with them" (Cray 1969: xiii). But the shift from an older Gaelic sense of humour to an English sense of humour may have resulted in the loss of bawdy puirt-a-beul. They may no longer reflect what people today find funny, and since other avenues for expressing bawdry are available, old ones are no longer sung and new ones are no longer created. This assumes, however, that I am correct in my assumption that there are few bawdy puirt-a-beul in existence today, that those that do survive tend not to be performed very often, and that many more existed at one time. There is another possibility: as a Gaelic learner and a cultural interloper, I may simply have been excluded from today's bawdy puirt-a-beul.

Language Learning and Group Identity

Humour is social. For humour to work, there must be a shared understanding of what is funny. A person offering something humorous to others assumes that others will likewise find it funny and laugh. Indeed, research shows that people laugh more in groups than when alone (Meyer 2000: 310-11). Humour thus helps to reinforce a sense of community. It also serves to differentiate one group from another: there are those who "get" the humour and those who do not. Thus, humour can simultaneously unify and divide (Meyer 2000: 311). Obviously some people will not "get" puirt-a-beul humour simply because the people or events referenced in the lyrics are no longer known. This is almost inevitable for those puirt-a-beul that are passed down over time, or those that travel beyond a local community. But another group of people who will be quite unlikely to "get" puirt-a-beul jokes is language learners. Thus puirt-a-beul divides fluent speakers (who have the cultural knowledge to make sense of culturally specific references) from cultural outsiders.

At the same time, puirt-a-beul have the potential not just to reinforce existing Gaelic community boundaries, but to be used to create new communities elsewhere. Puirt-a-beul can and do function in this way in the language classroom. As I discuss in Chapter 6, language instructors often use puirt-a-beul in their teaching. They are useful pedagogical tools in part because they provide students with new vocabulary, examples of grammatical rules in action, and pronunciation practice. But they also work in the classroom because, performed at full speed, learners inevitably make mistakes and laugh. They forget the words. They say the wrong words. Their tongues get tied in knots. They gasp for breath. These "mistakes" are part of the fun of performance, in the same ways that making a mistake when reciting a tongue twister might make a casual group of English speakers laugh. These performance mistakes unite the class in their efforts to master the language as a whole, and a given song in particular.

Sociologists Gary Alan Fine and Michaela De Soucey note that almost every group develops its own humour:

> A salient part of [group] culture—found in almost every group—is a set of repeated humorous and joking references.... Over time this comic discourse comes to characterize the group to its members and can subsequently be used to identify the group. The joking becomes historicized. Sarcastic remarks, gaffes, prank[s], or jokes are capable of being referred back to by group members. They have what Erving Goffman (1981: 46) describes as a "referential afterlife" and can provoke fond or upsetting reflection, even after group activities have terminated. (Fine and Soucey 2005: 2)

In other words, humour serves to unite people not simply in the moment that something humorous is said or performed, but in the recollections of that moment afterward. The light-hearted nature of puirt-a-beul lyrics makes them particularly suited to this kind of humorous bonding; it is hard to imagine the same sort of bonding over mistakes made when reciting a more serious form of Gaelic poetry. In this case, the humour arises from the imperfect performance of a song, rather than from the meaning of the lyrics. Regardless, it still serves to create and reinforce a sense of community among learners in a given classroom. Laughter puts learners at ease, lessens the formality of the classroom, and makes learning more fun.

But the humour inherent in the lyrics themselves is also relevant in the language classroom. John Schmitz argues for the introduction of humorous materials in the language classroom from very early on:

> It is important for students of foreign languages to know what types of discourse native speakers consider to be humorous or "funny" or downright hilarious. It is important also to identify appropriate texts that provoke laughter or at least a smile on the part of native speakers. The earlier students are introduced to authentic language input, to different styles of speech and to speakers of different ages,

sex, socio-cultural level and from different regions, the less artificial or "classroom-like" their output will be. I would disagree ... that humor [should] be deferred until students have the necessary linguistic competence to understand and appreciate humor. Bearing in mind that there is so much to learn about specific languages and their respective cultures and so little time in most courses, it would not be wise to hold humor entirely ... in abeyance until later stages. (Schmitz 2002: 95-96)

Most language learners are eager to learn about the cultural context associated with the language they are learning. They are keen to learn more than just vocabulary and grammar; they want to know how to engage with the language in ways consistent with native and fluent speakers. Puirt-a-beul lyrics help learners to develop an appreciation of what counts as funny among Gaelic speakers.

The learner's developing awareness of cultural humour is arguably even more important in the case of Gaelic given the low numbers of speakers remaining, particularly in Nova Scotia. If there are fewer daily contexts in which native and fluent speakers can interact in Gaelic, then there are presumably fewer contexts in which cultural humour can be shared and learned. At the same time, it is hard for learners not only to understand the humour in another language and culture (Schmitz 2002), but to develop an appreciation for it too so that the learner finds the same kinds of language, jokes and references funny that a native speaker does.

Conclusions

I have known many people who have dismissed puirt-a-beul as inconsequential, largely due to their lyrics. After all, puirt-a-beul lyrics are often short, repetitive, frequently silly or nonsensical, and sometimes riddled with vocables. They are certainly not literary masterpieces. But the persistence of puirt-a-beul as a genre over time and the sheer number of puirt-a-beul in existence suggests that these songs *are* significant. For one, they document local events and characters from the perspective of average, everyday people. For another, they're funny—and they illustrate what constitutes humour in Gaelic culture. Their humorous and nonsensical lyrics also provide a socially appropriate means of dispelling social tensions. Finally, they help to define and bond communities together, whether those communities consist of native Gaelic speakers or learners. Drawing on Ed Cray's arguments regarding the importance of acknowledging, collecting and studying bawdry, I would argue that to ignore puirt-a-beul when studying Gaelic song is to ignore a substantial body of music and an important expressive genre. Without an understanding of puirt-a-beul, we have an incomplete picture of Gaelic culture and society.

Chapter 5
From the Tip of the Tongue to the Tips of the Toes: Puirt-a-Beul and Dance

Part of the fascination with puirt-a-beul has to do with the ways in which they are used. Various song genres, such as labour songs and lullabies, may be attractive and intriguing but they are common in many world cultures. There's nothing particularly unusual about them that might attract special attention. Songs equated with an instrumental tradition, however, are not familiar to most North American or British English speakers, despite the use of mouth musics throughout the world, as described in Chapter 1. Puirt-a-beul therefore fascinate on a different level. In this and the next two chapters, I examine the various functions that puirt-a-beul have—functions that have long fascinated audiences.

The definition of puirt-a-beul as dance accompaniment is not quite as straightforward as it might first appear. After all, the kind of dancing that it accompanies in Cape Breton (step dancing) was unknown in Scotland for many years, and not everyone agrees that it originally came from Scotland. Since puirt-a-beul originated in Scotland and continue to be sung there, the question is then what kinds of dancing did and do puirt-a-beul accompany there?

I must emphasize that this chapter focuses on dance forms for which there is a clear connection to puirt-a-beul and it is therefore not a comprehensive history of Scottish dance and its derivations in Cape Breton. Histories of Scottish and Cape Breton dance review many dance forms not mentioned here, and describe in greater depth those dances that I do discuss here. But if we are to understand puirt-a-beul as dance accompaniment, it makes sense to explore in at least a cursory manner the kinds of dances that it once accompanied.

Scottish Dance Types

The significance of dance within Celtic cultures is reflected in the variety of dance types, as well as in the number of particular dances, within various "Celtic" regions, including Scotland, Ireland, and Cape Breton. In general, we can differentiate between social dances involving multiple people, such as Scottish country dancing or Cape Breton square sets, and solo dancing, such as Scottish Highland dancing or Cape Breton step dancing. There is a tendency to romanticize Celtic dance forms as expressive arts that have existed largely unchanged for centuries, originating in rural areas among the lower classes, and transmitted through informal performance contexts such as barn dances, weddings and kitchen parties. The reality is that urban and continental European influences, formal instruction, and upper class contexts have all influenced these dance forms to varying degrees. Despite the popular belief that the traditional Celtic dance forms still practised today have remained untouched for centuries, none of them existed in its current form prior to the 18th century. There are four different types of dances which are today defined as distinctly Scottish: Scottish country dance, Highland dance, step dance and ceilidh dance. I focus on the first three because at some point or other they have all been connected to puirt-a-beul. Ceilidh dance can be understood in a couple of different ways. It is arguably best understood as an informal form of vernacular (or "folk") dance that occurred spontaneously in the homes and villages of Scottish Gaelic speakers, and puirt-a-beul was indeed used in such contexts. But today, particularly outside Gaelic communities, the term "ceilidh dance" has come to refer to a formal dance event in an urban assembly hall or other public venue with a relatively fixed dance repertoire (e.g., Strip the Willow, Dashing White Sergeant, The Gay Gordons, etc.). The ceilidh band provides the expected accompaniment; puirt-a-beul have never, to my knowledge, played a role at these dances since they began to emerge around the 1970s (Morrison 2003: 18). Therefore, while I address puirt-a-beul within their traditional ceilidh contexts, I will not be discussing puirt-a-beul in relation to the more modern, urban understanding of ceilidh dance.

To begin, it is important to note that we really know nothing about music or dance in Scotland before approximately 1500. We can safely assume that music and dance existed before this time, but we have virtually no descriptions or even references to music and dance prior to this date. As I described with respect to music in Chapter 2, people simply did not consider it important to "collect" or describe dances, particularly vernacular dances, prior to the 18th century.

Most of what we know about dance in the Highlands, which would have the strongest connections to puirt-a-beul, comes from descriptions of dancing that are usually brief and vague. More often than not, they appear in the travel diaries of non-Highlanders, so we must take their descriptions with a grain of salt. There are also some images of dancers (such as in artworks) and some references to dancing in Gaelic poetry, which sometimes provide information about where and when dances were held, the names of dances, and something about the people who danced. They might even say something general about the quality of the dancing, describe the figures or characterize body postures or limb movements. They rarely, if ever, however, describe the actual footwork. Dance steps are notoriously difficult to describe in words and, until the relatively recent development of Labanotation,[1] there was no notation system—such as exists for music—designed for dance. Scholars try to correlate the tidbits of information that do exist in order to build a sense of what particular dances looked like and when they were performed, but there are many large gaps in our knowledge of historical dance practices.

Prior to the 18th century, social dances were practised across Europe. The upper and lower classes danced the same dances, although not necessarily together in the same place at the same time. During the Renaissance (roughly the 14th to 17th centuries), class-differentiated social dances first emerged: the upper classes began dancing different dances than the lower classes. The process of differentiating dances into dances of two distinct classes would have been slow, and there would have remained many similarities at first. Dance steps and patterns became increasingly complex, requiring training and choreography, both of which were provided by the dancing master who became increasingly important through the 18th century. The growing skill of dancers resulted in such a dramatic rise in new dances that the 18th century is known in Scotland as the "Golden Age of Dance" (Morrison 2003).

Newton has traced the development of vernacular (or "folk") dance in the Scottish Highlands (2009: 279ff; 2013). He makes a strong argument that Scottish dances we today consider to be "traditional" came to the Scottish Highlands from continental Europe by way of France during the 18th century, replacing whatever forms of dance had previously existed there (2013). The reel is first mentioned in Scottish sources in the 16th century and seems directly related to the figure-of-eight movement featured in the French *hay d'Alemaigne* (Emmerson 1972: 40, Brennan 1999: 21, Newton 2009: 279). A reel originally referred to a figure rather than to a dance or a step: a weaving or figure-of-eight figure involving three or four people, and although it was a linear figure throughout the Lowlands and the eastern Highlands (clearly seen in today's Scottish country dancing), in the western Highlands the reel was danced in a circle. Newton speculates that the circular formation was the result of the legacy of choral dancing (also known as circular or chain dancing) that had once been popular throughout Renaissance Europe (2009: 279).

Gaelic terms like *dannsa* (dance) are clearly borrowed from French and such terms apparently replaced whatever Gaelic terms existed prior to the introduction of French (Newton 2013: 63). In Scotland, the newly arrived Renaissance European court dances "were social—not ritual or dramatic—in nature. They were increasingly governed by the rhythm of the music rather than just reflecting its mood or enacting the story conveyed by the words of a song" (Newton 2009: 280).

In analyzing 18th-century Gaelic song and poetry, Newton discovered a recurring stock phrase referring to dance ("*dannsair air ùrlar-déile thu*" / [you are] a dancer on a wood-plank floor) (2013: 56-57). Newton argues that wood-plank floors would have been found only in élite homes, as peasant homes had dirt floors, stone walls and thatched roofs. They contained little, if any, wood. Moreover, Gaelic poems of the period tend to emphasize dancers' refinement, manners, learning and stateliness—all characteristics of the nobility. Newton also argues, based on references found in Gaelic poems, that percussive footwork was an 18th-century innovation in the Highlands that came part and parcel with the importation from France of new (binary) dance tunes and the fiddle (2013: 69). In other words, according to Newton's research and theory, percussive footwork in the Highlands would have begun in the 18th century in the homes of the Gaelic aristocracy, where wood floors provided a surface upon which percussive footwork could be heard. Newton argues that these French fashions were subsequently adapted by the peasant classes and vernacularized (2013: 66). Emmerson agrees that percussive stepping within social dances likely developed in the 18th century, although he is not as certain about solo percussive dance:

> The employment of beating techniques [percussive footwork] in social dance must derive from dancing in hard shoes on a resounding surface, and hence can hardly predate the use of wooden flooring in dancing places (to say nothing of the hard shoes). Not many barns or inns in Scotland—or Ireland—had suitable wooden floors prior to the 18th century. (Emmerson 1972: 159-60)

What Newton's and Emmerson's comments indicate is that percussive footwork was not a timeless Highland folk tradition, but rather an 18th-century innovation that emerged among the Gaelic aristocracy as they adapted French dance fashions. Only later did the peasant "folk" adapt such dancing for themselves.

Newton's case contradicts earlier beliefs about the origins of percussive footwork in Highland dance. The Fletts argue that although soft Highland dancing shoes are common footwear today, only professional dancers would have worn them in earlier times. Dancing students from among the peasant classes would have worn their "kirk-shoon" or church shoes, which had hard soles and heels, making them suitable for beating out a dance's rhythms (Flett and Flett 1996: 8). Thus, from the Fletts' perspective, percussive footwork began among the peasant classes, since they were the ones wearing hard-soled shoes. Newton is the first scholar to offer evidence from 18th-century Gaelic sources on the origins of percussive footwork in Highland dance and his new perspective is therefore worth considering.

During the 18th century's "golden age of dance," every major community in Scotland and elsewhere in the U.K. had at least one resident dancing master. Smaller communities were visited by itinerant dancing masters who taught for a few weeks before moving on to another community. We know that dancing masters operated in Gaelic-speaking areas as well as elsewhere in Scotland thanks to references in Gaelic poems (see Newton 2013). The dancing masters themselves trained with other dancing masters, the more prominent ones travelling to London and France to study with major figures in the European dance world. For example, in 1764, David Strange, an Edinburgh teacher, advertised that he

> last season studied Dancing, under the celebrated Signor GALLINI at London: he is now returned from Paris, where, for some time past, he has been improving himself in the MINUET; and learned, at the same time, several NEW DANCES under the first two Masters in France, Monsieur MALTERE, Teacher to the Royal Family of France, and Monsieur VESTRES first Dancer in the Royal Academy of

> Dancing at Paris. From these Gentlemen he has acquired the
> latest improvements in the Minuet. (Flett and Flett 1996: 5)

Other dancing masters travelled to major cultural centres during summer vacations to learn the latest dancing fashions. Still others were influenced by continental dance instructors who moved to London. It would seem that dancing masters learned dances with a significant amount of classical stage influence drawn especially from character dances and ballet. Thus the dances that Scottish dancing masters taught were not purely Scottish, nor were they exclusively "folk" but rather they were dances with cosmopolitan and stage influences.

As the church's influence waned in Britain, dance increased in popularity and moved into public dance halls. The first public dance hall in Edinburgh opened in 1723. Wanting to keep abreast of London's fashions, the Scottish upper classes began dancing mostly minuets and English country dances at public balls. Scottish figures were added to some dances based on reels, which themselves were once highly fashionable dances. Although these dances were first popular among the upper classes, itinerant dancing teachers taught them to the lower classes so that they were danced throughout Scotland by about 1880 (Flett and Flett 1964: 4). Social dancing continued to evolve throughout the 18th and 19th centuries. Old and new dances were performed together without concern. There was no anxiety about "preserving" older dances and no worry that new dances were somehow less authentic or threatening to the older dances. It was not until the late 19th and early 20th centuries that a desire arose to locate authentic forms of Scottish dance and, once found, they were fixed forever through transcription, institutionalization and publication.

Eighteenth- and 19th-century dance masters held "finishing balls" at the conclusion of lessons—what we might call recitals today—to enable students to demonstrate their dancing skills. The instructors created new solo dances for their best students, based mostly on 18th-century stage character dances with some influence from vernacular dance (Moore 1995; Morrison 2003: 10). These became the basis for Highland dance. Most of these solo dances were known only to the dancer and his or her im-mediate social circle. But some became popular and circulated throughout the country with itinerant dancing masters (Flett and Flett 1996: 7). The dancing masters modified steps and added their own so that many variations exist of each dance. The peak period for these solo dances was ca. 1750-1850, when dancing masters taught them alongside social dances. A letter written by a Major Edward Topham in Edinburgh in the 1770s describes them: "The motion of the feet is indeed the only thing that is considered in these dances, as they rather neglect than pay any attention to the other parts of the body" (Letters from Edinburgh written in the years 1774 and 1775; qtd. in Flett and Flett 1996: 4). This description is consistent with solo step dance, such as that danced in Cape Breton today, in which the upper body remains relaxed but relatively still, and emphasis is on the footwork.

Scottish Highland dancing evolved in part from these cus-tom-choreographed solo student dances and in part from "High dances," the performances of 19th-century dancing masters themselves. Eighteenth-century dancing masters first performed High dances to break up the tedium of student finishing balls (Flett and Flett 1996: 4). But when these dances began to be performed regularly in competition at Highland Games, which themselves emerged in the early 19th century, the movements became larger and more balletic, perhaps to make it easier for the audience (and the judges) to see (Moore 1995). Some of today's most popular Highland dances such as the Sword Dance and Highland Fling had their roots in earlier solo and High dances.[2]

By the end of the First World War, traditional Scottish dances were fast losing popularity in the face of newer styles of dance, such as jazz and swing. But at the same time, nationalism dictated the need for nations to define themselves through the everyday culture of the average citizen, particularly from the past. Defining distinctive forms of national dance became an important project. In 1923, Jean Milligan and Ysobel Stewart founded the Scottish Country Dance Society (SCDS, in 1951 renamed the Royal Scottish Country Dance Society, or RSCDS). Milligan and Stewart turned not to the dances that were still at the time being danced in various parts of Scotland, nor to the dances recently popular, but instead to select dance movements from more than a century prior:

> Scottish Country Dance movement and set arrangements draw upon the elite style of eighteenth-century ballroom dance. The movements, although fast at times, remain graceful. The back is held upright, and the feet are pointed and turned out. The hands, when held, are done so elegantly, just below the shoulder. (Morrison 2003: 12)

Part of the mandate of RSCDS was to document dances. RSCDS publications carefully name dances, describe steps, and provide diagrams of dance figures. These publications have served to fix the dances, with any variations to be avoided as corruptions of an authentic original. New dances are acceptable as long as they are based on "authentic" movements, but once a dance is published, it cannot be changed (Morrison 2003, 2004). The RSCDS has become a significant cultural institution and wields considerable influence through its teacher training, certification and professional development; its dance publications; its official events, including balls and courses; and its graded testing to motivate young dancers. Not surprisingly, some people resent and resist the authority and restrictions of the RSCDS. The relatively recent rise of urban "ceilidh dances" is an example of anti-establishment dancing, for ceilidh dances often include Scottish country dances, but ceilidh dance participants are not required to conform to RSCDS standards when dancing them (see, for example, Shoupe 2001: 135-36). However, the RSCDS's continued existence demonstrates that many other dancers support its principles and aims. Emmerson, for example, believes that the RSCDS saved Scottish country dancing, and the music that accompanied it, from extinction (1972: 284).

Although a centralizing institution did not emerge in Highland dance until 1952 with the creation of the Scottish Official Board of Highland Dance (SOBHD), the Highland games in which Highland dance was performed had already contributed to the fixing and formalization of the dances.[3] Dancers emulated successful competitors, ultimately limiting the steps and dances used in competition, and fixing the style of their presentation. In response to complaints about unfair judging, the SOBHD published a textbook of approved dances and steps selected from the repertoire of famous dancers. As with the RSCDS publications, the textbook served to further limit any potential innovation or variation within Highland dance (Morrison 2003, 2004).

Cecily Morrison (2003, 2004) argues that the four main types of dance labelled today as Scottish (Scottish country dance, Highland dance, step dance and ceilidh dance) were all codified in the 20th century and that none except step dance was even based on dances that pre-existed the 18th century. Michael Newton would argue that even step dance, which I discuss in greater detail below, does not pre-date the 18th century (2013). This history means that these dances were not self-consciously recognized as "Scottish" until the 20th century; they were just dances that people happened to learn and enjoy. Until the 20th century, there was no particular concern for maintaining specific dance traditions, just like today we do not worry about preserving particular clothing or hair fashions after they have gone out of style. But during the 19th and 20th centuries, people throughout Europe became increasingly interested in identifying national culture (including music and dance), and this national culture was generally believed to exist in rural areas that had supposedly remained untouched by the forces of industrialization, immigration and globalization that had so obviously and dramatically affected urban centres. Anxieties also began to arise that traditional forms of national culture were endangered, even in rural areas, by the pressures of modernization. Collectors began documenting traditional culture for both nationalistic and preservationist reasons. Although it may be true that rural areas were generally affected by external and modernizing influences to a lesser extent than urban areas, they were not, as people often still like to believe, immune. We have already seen, for example, how dancing masters spread

European dance trends throughout Britain and Ireland so that both upper and lower classes danced the same dances, marked only by some stylistic differences.

Moreover, as we have also seen, dances labelled today as "Scottish" were often based on forms of dance originally from outside Scotland, such as English country dance in the case of Scottish country dancing, and stage dance in the case of Highland dancing. Nevertheless, certain dances began to be self-consciously identified as uniquely Scottish and began to be collected and preserved. Once they were written down, they tended not to change very much since dancers continually referred to these "correct" versions. An emphasis on older dance forms, steps and sources helps to convey the impression that these dances have remained unchanged until the present day, and are only now threatened with extinction.

Scottish Dances in Cape Breton

Given that the majority of Scottish immigration to Cape Breton occurred from the late 18th to mid-19th centuries, it is not surprising that urban ceilidh dancing, which became popular in Scotland in the 1970s, is not known on the Canadian island. Neither is Scottish country dancing, which was not formally recognized and defined until 1923, although it was heavily promoted for a time at Cape Breton's Gaelic College (Kennedy 2001: 221). Even social country dancing, prior to its institutionalization by the (Royal) Scottish Country Dance Society, didn't reach the western Highlands and Hebrides until the 1850s, after most emigrants for Nova Scotia had left (Emmerson 1972: 282). However, social square dances, based on 18th-century continental European quadrilles, are well known and popular, although it seems that they came to Cape Breton in the 1890s by way of the United States rather than Scotland (Kennedy 2001: 221; see also Rhodes 1964: 274). Strong ties between Cape Breton and Boston—resulting from Cape Bretoners seeking work in the "Boston States" and regularly returning home for visits—ensured plenty of American influence and content. But while square dances came to Cape Breton via the U.S., they were "indigenized" with the integration of stepping in various figures. Percussive footwork—particularly in the style used in Cape Breton—is not typical of most quadrilles and square dances in other parts of North America, the U.K. or Ireland.[4]

The dance form currently most associated with Cape Breton is its extemporized solo step dancing, and despite obvious differences today, it was once closely linked to Highland dance. Celtic scholar Michael Kennedy argues that 19th-century precursors to today's Highland dance looked much more like contemporary step dance, with hard-soled shoes and quick, neat footwork (Kennedy 2001: 210-11). According to Kennedy, the primary difference between Highland dance and step dance was that the former consisted of fixed choreographies whereas step dance was extemporized. Many traditional dancers interviewed in Allister MacGillivray's *Cape Breton Ceilidh* (1988) recall seeing or dancing dances that are no longer in evidence today, except in formal Highland dancing circles, including the Irish Washerwoman, Jacky Tar, Seann Triubhas and the Highland Fling. The Flowers of Edinburgh seems to have been particularly popular at one time, as it was recalled by numerous dancers. Kennedy argues that "in Cape Breton, traditional Highland dancing and step dancing continued to exist side by side and interact for at least the first hundred years of settlement, but the more formalized style of dancing eventually went into steep decline" (Kennedy 2001: 211). Kennedy has mapped Nova Scotian areas where Highland dancing is currently concentrated, and it dramatically demonstrates that, today, Highland dance almost invariably happens outside the Gaelic cultural strongholds where the language, fiddling, piping and—most significantly for our purposes—step dance are still concentrated. In Cape Breton, the majority of Highland dancers are found in the Cape Breton Regional Municipality, the urban area of the island, as well as in a couple of areas on the east side of the island. Meanwhile, there are no concentrated numbers of Highland dancers in any of the historically Gaelic-speaking areas. On the mainland, Highland dancers are concentrated in areas such as Antigonish, New Glasgow, and Halifax, as well as in a few other places, but again, there are no significant numbers where Gaelic-speakers settled. It's not that there were no Highland dancers in Gaelic-speaking areas; rather, the point is that there is no concentration of Highland dancers in these areas. Note that Highland dance, in this case, refers to the institutionalized form that can be seen at Highland Games and similar events.

It is not entirely clear why the early Highland dances went into decline. Since their sophisticated choreographies were associated with dancing masters, perhaps the dances went into decline as the number of dancing masters diminished. Or perhaps increasing interest in newer dances, such as quadrilles, eventually displaced the older Highland dances. It's also possible that as formal and institutionalized Highland dance regulations made their way to Canada after being developed in Scotland in the 1950s, Highland dance became increasingly suited to competitive stages, such as those found at Highland games, and less suited to informal Gaelic cultural contexts, such as ceilidhs.

Whereas Highland dance in Nova Scotia is today largely restricted to formal instruction and performance, step dance is still widely practised in Cape Breton in both informal contexts (ceilidhs and kitchen parties) and more formal ones (concerts and square dances). Particular families are known for dancing, with younger generations learning to dance by observing their parents or older siblings. For some, informal observation was reinforced with formal instruction from dancing masters. Today, formal step dance classes and workshops are held throughout the island.

Solo, extemporized step dance seems to have developed from reels, social dances that were popular throughout the western Highlands and islands in Scotland at the time of immigration. Reels involved the alternation of setting and travelling steps. Setting steps were not necessarily prescribed; they could be extemporized on the spot. Frank Rhodes, who conducted dance research in Cape Breton in the late 1950s, argues that "when the solo dances taught by the dancing-teachers began to be forgotten, extemporized stepping of a form similar to that used in the Cape

Breton island Reels came to be used in place of the solo dances"
(Rhodes 1964: 272).

Most Cape Bretoners today firmly believe that their step
dancing originated in Scotland and was handed down through
the generations (see, for example, MacGillivray 1988). But because
solo step dancing could not generally be found in Scotland by the
early 20th century, claims for the Scottish origins of Cape Breton
step dance have often been disputed (this dispute is documented
in S. MacInnes 1994, 1996; Rhodes 1964: 273; and Rhodes 1996:
190). Some have suggested that the relatively motionless upper
bodies and rhythmic footwork are more indicative of Irish dance
influence than Scottish. While it is true that there has long been
a small Irish community in Cape Breton which had contact with
Scots and their descendants, the Scottish Cape Breton community
has argued that any Irish influence was negligible, if existent at all.
Documents such as Topham's letter (cited above) lend credence to
the claims that Cape Breton step dance has its roots in Scotland.
Research on traditional dancing and step dancing of Scotland
has also helped to support claims for the Scottish origins of Cape
Breton step dancing.

We know that there were dancing masters among the earliest Scottish settlers, and that they established dancing schools
in Cape Breton, teaching the dances that they had learned in the
"old country" (MacDougall 1922: 259; MacGillivray 1988; Rhodes
1996: 190). During the 19th century, Scottish immigrant communities in Cape Breton primarily danced four-hand and eight-hand
reels:

> A true Reel consists of setting steps danced on the spot,
> alternated with a travelling figure—the setting steps can be
> as varied as the dancers please, while the travelling figure
> is usually the same throughout the dance. In many Reels
> there is also a change in musical rhythm in the course of
> the dance, an unusual feature in social dances. A typical ex-
> ample of a true Reel is the Scotch or Highland Reel, a dance
> now more commonly known as the Foursome Reel; in this,
> the setting steps are performed with the dancers in line, and

the travelling figure is in the form of a figure 8 with a third loop added. This particular Reel also displays the change in rhythm, for it is usually begun to a strathspey, and in the course of the dance the music changes to a reel. (Flett and Flett 1964: 1)

These reels were social dances for either two or four couples. They provided the opportunity to show off an individual's stepping ability as well as his or her ability to match footwork to the music. Scotch Eights and Scotch Fours were regularly and socially danced in Cape Breton within living memory, and the Scotch Four is sometimes still danced on festival stages as a demonstration dance. Dance scholar Mats Melin notes that the travelling figure would originally have been a *chassé* (gliding) step, but from about 1950 on, percussive, rhythmic steps were used during the travelling as well as the setting step portions of the dance (2012: 41).

Gradually, over the course of the 20th century, the Scotch Eight and Scotch Four were superseded by square sets based on the quadrilles imported from the American northeast around the 1890s and danced socially in public dance halls (Rhodes 1964; Moore 1995; Kennedy 2001: 221). However, in the same way that stepping had formed part of the reels, Cape Bretoners incorporated step dancing into some figures of the square sets, particularly in the Gaelic strongholds on the western side of the island. Most famously, perhaps, and still readily apparent, is the improvised step dancing integrated into the final figure of the West Mabou set.

The earliest settlers also brought fixed (as opposed to extemporized) solo dances with them, including the Fling (the Highland Fling in Scotland), the Swords (the Sword Dance in Scotland), Seann Triubhas (Gaelic for "Old Trousers" and transliterated to "Shan Trews"), and the Flowers of Edinburgh (Rhodes 1996). However, because these dances were complex with prescribed steps for particular parts of the tune, they fell out of favour in the New World (Moore 1995).[5] This may have partly resulted from a lack of dancing instructors available to teach the dances. Although dancing masters and formal dance instruction had existed earlier in Cape Breton, it is unclear how many people would have had access to these instructors or for how long. The lack of interest in prescribed solo dances may also have resulted from a growing interest in having the freedom to choose one's own steps, a desire in keeping with the reasons many immigrants moved to the New World in the first place.

The old Scottish solo step dances and reels eventually came together in today's solo step dance tradition in Cape Breton. Although Cape Breton step dance is still performed as part of some square set figures, it is more famously danced alone for an appreciative audience. At many square dances, the musicians will strike up a set of strathspeys and reels during a break between square sets. Since square set figures are all set to jigs and reels, the distinctive sound of the strathspeys functions as a musical invitation to all step dancers to demonstrate their abilities. Depending on who is in attendance, a string of volunteers will take turns performing briefly, much to the enjoyment of the rest of the attendees. Step dancers also perform in other venues, such as at informal ceilidhs and more formal concerts.

Vocal Dance Music in Scotland

The majority of today's dance music is provided by instruments. Different instruments are popular for different kinds of dances in different places. Thus, for example, the bagpipes are *de rigueur* for Highland dance, the accordion for Scottish ceilidh dance, and the fiddle for Cape Breton square sets and step dance. Instruments are ideal since they can provide more volume than a single voice, or even multiple voices, especially in a dance hall filled with shouting dancers and stomping feet. However, instrumental music didn't always accompany dancing in the past. Social dancing in Scotland during medieval times was executed with extemporized vocal music as accompaniment (Emmerson 1972: 31-32; Morrison 2003: 8; Newton 2004: 229). There is a long history in Scotland of accompanying dance with song.

Celticist Michael Newton has documented a Scottish funeral tradition in which the deceased's closest relatives—usually the widow or widower and his or her children—would lead a dance at the wake. These "wake dances," which were performed in the style of a ring or choral dance (ring dances were popular in Medieval Europe and involved a chain of dancers in a circle, accompanied by a song whose verses were sung by the leader while its choruses were sung by the entire group), began to be documented in the late 18th century and seem to have survived until the early 19th. This period coincides with the rise of puirt-a-beul. Drawing on various sources, Newton argues that these dances were originally performed to song and only later to instrumental accompaniment (2004: 226). Unfortunately, we do not know what kind of song would have been used in this context although it is unlikely that the satirical or bawdy lyrics of puirt-a-beul would have been appropriate in such a context. Then again, Newton's research reveals that the church repeatedly enacted prohibitions against "bawdrie songis" at wakes, suggesting that an erotic component to the dance existed and continued for some time despite the prohibitions (2004: 230). Still, puirt-a-beul were not likely used in this context because of their binary form (see Chapter 3). There is also no indication in references to the origins of puirt-a-beul that they emerged or were ever associated with funerals. It is, however, useful to note the relatively recent co-existence of Scottish dancing traditions accompanied by song.

Although there are certainly dance traditions that were always meant to be accompanied by song, it is also possible that puirt-a-beul would have been used as an exception, performed only if instrumental accompaniment were not available. Some have suggested that puirt-a-beul first emerged in response to the church's efforts to eliminate social dancing (see Chapter 2). Whether or not dancers were trying to dance undetected by priests or ministers, it would certainly have been easier to get an impromptu dance started with a singer than with an instrumentalist since singers don't require any special equipment. In the case of these dances, instrumental accompaniment may have been the norm, but puirt-a-beul became a viable alternative in its absence.

A more mundane (but perhaps more likely) scenario is one in which the musicians have been delayed by inclement weather or unable to come due to illness or personal circumstance. Cape Breton Margaree bard, Malcolm Gillis, wrote a song about the lack of a fiddler at a local ball:

> Chruinnich còmhlan cridheil, ùrail,
> Fonnmhor, farumach, glan, cùirteil,
> 'S gur e dh' fhàg mi trom fo chùram
> An luchd-ciùil bhith bhuapa.
>
> Cha robh bhuainn an sin ach fìdhlear
> Leis an gluaiseamaid 's an ruìdhle,
> 'S e bhith cur earbsa á trì dhiubh
> Chuir mi fhìn cho luaineach.
>
> Labhair Donnchadh le guth àrd ruin
> "O' n a tha luchd-ciùil anns a' Bhràighe
> Falbhaidh mise leis an làir,
> 'S thig Peadar Dhaibhidh nuas leam.

> A fresh, merry company gathered
> Tuneful, loud, fine and courteous.
> The thing that has left me disturbed
> Is that we have no musicians.
>
> All we needed then was a fiddler,
> To whom we would move in a reel,
> Waiting for the three we expected
> Made me anxious (for music).
>
> Duncan called out in loud voice
> "Since we have musicians in Margaree
> I will go with the mare,
> And Peter David will come back with me."[6]

This was clearly a significant matter for it inspired a bard to write a song about the event. It is also possible that puirt-a-beul would have been sung while waiting for the fiddler to arrive. Indeed, one Cape Bretoner recounted a situation in which the dance fiddler was delayed and puirt-a-beul saved the day:

> [A woman] went to a dance in a schoolhouse and the fiddler
> couldn't make it because of a snow storm so she got up on
> a chair and sang puirt-a-beul for the first figure of the set.
> And then [someone else] on the side, she stood up and sang
> puirt-a-beul for the second figure. (Interview July 22, 1998)

Mats Melin told me of a similar and relatively recent situation in
Scotland:

> Running a ceilidh dance on the Island on Barra (Northbay
> Hall) about ten years ago we suffered a power cut which
> meant that the musicians' amplification went dead, but
> without losing a beat the crowd started singing in Gaelic and
> continued their social dance (a waltz). We then got candles
> out and placed the musicians in the centre of the floor and
> the dancing continued around them, with the dancers often
> singing along to the tunes played. Great moment indeed.
> Not puirt-a-beul in the strict sense but Gaelic song for dance
> though. (Personal communication, December 11, 2013)

Ethnomusicologist Katherine Campbell provides a similar
example from a 1905 Scots song, "Mrs. MacIntyre's Tea Pairty"
by Jamie McQueen (Campbell 2007: 90). In the song, the fiddler has pawned his instrument, resulting in a woman having
to "diddle" for the dance. Campbell argues that because she's a
Highland woman, she was probably actually singing puirt-a-beul.
Apparently, though, it was not deemed as good as instrumental
accompaniment:

> The howdie jumpit tae her feet,
> An' Heilan' Kate began tae diddle,
> And muckle fash they gaed tae me
> Because I hadna got my fiddle.

> The handy woman jumped to her feet
> And Highland Kate began to diddle
> And much grief they gave to me
> Because I didn't have my fiddle. [7]

It is also possible that dancing to puirt-a-beul occurred for
the novelty of it, which is certainly the reason in the majority of

cases that dance is accompanied by puirt-a-beul today. The novelty factor arises from seeing a traditional dance performed to an appropriate and well-known tune but rendered in a manner not normally practised. Because today's audience knows that there is no actual need to accompany a dancer with puirt-a-beul—after all, even in the absence of a musician today, we have ready access to recordings, radio and the Internet—any performance in this way is interpreted as a curiosity, often an anachronistic one.

Unfortunately but not surprisingly, given the limited information we have about puirt-a-beul in general, we have little documentary evidence of what kinds of dance would have been accompanied by puirt-a-beul and when. As described in Chapter 2, the earliest example of a port-a-beul-like song dates from 1770, although the word "port-a-beul" itself was not used until 1815: Alexander Campbell describes it as singing for dance accompaniment ("Slight Sketch,"qtd. in Dickson 2006: 18; see Chapter 2 for full quotation). What little evidence exists about the relationship between puirt-a-beul and dance comes mostly from the 20th century. These references indicate that puirt-a-beul continued to be used for dance accompaniment for more than two hundred years:

> The music [for Highland dances] was played by a piper or fiddler or sung as a port-a-beul mouth-tune, by a looker-on or by the performers themselves. (Carmichael 1928 [1900], vol. 1: 207)

> [Puirt-a-beul are] vocal tunes for dancing or quick movement. (Tolmie 1910-1913: 147)

> [Puirt-a-beul are] ancient dancing songs ... [which are] evidently the first attempts at applying music to the art of dancing. (K. N. MacDonald 1931 [1901]: iv)

Another indication that puirt-a-beul have long been used as dance accompaniment is their lyrics, some of which themselves refer to dancing. In this Lewis example, an individual is teased for being something of a ladies' man on the dance floor, at least in his own mind (Comunn Gaidhealach Leodhais 1998[1982]: 118-19, translated by Heather Sparling):

'S math a dhannsadh Uisdean Hiortach,
Lùdagan an cùl na h-iosgaid,
'S math a dhannsadh Uisdean Hiortach,
Leis an fhichead maighdinn.

Ceathrar roimhe 's as a dheidhidh,
Ceathrar roimhe 's as a dheidhidh,
Ceathrar roimhe 's as a dheidhidh,
Seisear air gach làimh dheth.

> Hugh of St. Kilda is good at dancing,
> Twisting behind her kneecap,
> Hugh of St. Kilda is good at dancing,
> With twenty maidens.

> Four people before and behind,
> Four people before and behind,
> Four people before and behind,
> Six people on either side of him.

This next example, a jig from Barra singer Catherine-Ann MacPhee, which appears on her album *Sùil Air Ais* (Looking Back), is also known in reel form. The lyrics are typically simple, repetitive and rather inane, describing an old woman dancing. A humorous image is portrayed: either the old woman was unexpectedly nimble on her feet given her advanced age, or the dance is rendered ridiculous as the woman hobbles her way through it. Regardless, dancing is certainly central:

Ruidhleadh cailleach sheatadh cailleach
Ruidhleadh cailleach ris a' bhalg;
Ruidhleadh cailleach sheatadh cailleach
Ruidhleadh cailleach ris a' bhalg;
Ruidhleadh cailleach sheatadh cailleach
Ruidhleadh cailleach ris a' bhalg;
Dhannsadh cailleach ri caillich,
'S sheatadh cailleach ris a' bhalg.

Ruidhleadh cailleach ri caillich,
Dhannsadh cailleach ri caillich;

Ruidhleadh cailleach ri caillich,
'S shetadh cailleach ris a' bhalg. (a-rithist)

> An old woman would reel, an old woman would set
> An old woman would reel to the bellows
> An old woman would reel, an old woman would set
> An old woman would reel to the bellows
> An old woman would reel, an old woman would set
> An old woman would reel to the bellows
> An old woman would dance with old women
> And an old woman would set with the belly.
>
> An old woman would reel with old women
> An old woman would dance with old women
> An old woman would reel with old women
> And an old woman would set to the bellows. (repeat)[8]

Given that the majority of early references to dance accompanied by puirt-a-beul describe social dancing contexts, it would be easy to overlook the role of puirt-a-beul in learning contexts. Although 18th- and 19th-century dancing masters may well have travelled in the company of a musician who could provide dance accompaniment (Sawyers 2000: 57) and some were able fiddlers themselves, it would have been cheaper and easier for the teacher to provide his own vocal accompaniment, or to ask one of his students to provide it. The Fletts provide a provocative example. They cite Felix MacDonough, writing in 1824, some twenty years after the death of a famous Edinburgh dance teacher:

> For how many years did the grotesque Mr Strange lead on his capering legions in the high dance, minuet and highland fling, not without grace and agility. How many mothers' hearts beat high with tender feeling, as Bell or Ellen was taken out to figure on the boards! What crowding, what squeezing, to get a peep at a favourite at these prac-ti-sings! (Qtd. in Flett and Flett 1996: 5)

The Fletts explain that the unusual hyphenation in the last word referred to Mr. Strange's introduction of vocal parts into the music of slow dances. Although not a direct reference to puirt-a-beul, it does suggest the ongoing practice of singing for dance accompaniment. Mats Melin says that his research indicates that Irish dancing masters were more likely to travel with an accompanying musician whereas the majority of Scottish dancing masters provided their own musical accompaniment (personal communication, December 11, 2013).

Robert Craig MacLagan, an Edinburgh physician who took an interest in traditional Scottish lore (see Chapter 2 for his unusual theory regarding the origins of puirt-a-beul), wrote almost a hundred years after MacDonough's reminiscence:

> [A "port"] is the substitute in the case of the absence of pipes, fiddle, or Jew's harp—the so-called trump. These ports are single verses, generally fitted to a specific tune suitable for the dance proposed, and are sung by one of the girls present who has the necessary talent, or by one or more in succession according to their capabilities. If the young men have to be the musicians, they generally fulfil that duty by whistling. (MacLagan 1901: 105)

The numerous references to puirt-a-beul as dance song indicate that puirt-a-beul were well established as dance accompaniment by the early 20th century. The fact that these various authors made the point of referring to it also indicates that the practice was somewhat unusual elsewhere by that time.

Thinking back to the ballet classes I attended as a young girl, I remember the instructor having to give the accompanist instructions about the kind of music to play for particular steps, movements and exercises. Sometimes the instructor wanted to rehearse or correct a particular aspect of the dance that only required a few bars of music. How much easier it would have been if she herself could have sung a line or two of a suitable song. That would have been far easier than instructing the musician on what and how much to play, or cueing up a recording. Although not referring to puirt-a-beul specifically, Chambers makes this same point:

> Vocables are still used by some dance teachers today, often combined with (much abbreviated) instructions interpo-

lated between vocable phrases; it seems likely that this was done traditionally as well. (1980: 226)

The ease of using the voice for dance accompaniment is also reflected in the many stories of step dancers who learned to dance at home to the accompaniment of puirt-a-beul.

Types of Dances Accompanied by Puirt-a-Beul

Most references to the relationship between dance and puirt-a-beul, especially earlier ones, do not specify the kind of dancing that puirt-a-beul would accompany or the particular contexts in which dance would be accompanied by puirt-a-beul. However, some more recent sources do. The Fletts, for example, who are respected scholars of Scottish dance, describe the mid-century use of puirt-a-beul:

> When young people were present at [an informal house] ceilidh there would generally be some dancing toward the end of the evening. Sometimes there would be a fiddler or piper to supply the music, or perhaps a melodeon-player. If no instrument were available, then someone would deedle the tune, or sing puirt-a-beul, the old Gaelic dancing-songs, often to the accompaniment of a Jew's harp or paper-and-comb. (Flett and Flett 1964: 38)

Likewise, Thomas A. ("Tommy Peggy") MacDonald of Cape Breton's North Shore recalled:

> When there'd be weddings they'd always have a reel [in] some part of the house, perhaps 15 or 20 of the people—the ones that weren't dancing would sing. The elderly people. They were great scouts [sic]. Some of the elderly people, they'd get in a reel and they'd sing all night ... something lively—and the younger people would dance. (Qtd. in Caplan 1978: 45)

In Cape Breton today, puirt-a-beul is most often associated with extemporized solo step dance. But in Scotland, it is sometimes associated with Scottish country dance. Christine Chambers describes the case in the 1970s:

> Vocabelising (and sometimes singing of puirt-a-beul) are used by some Scottish Country Dance groups today in public performances to add variety to a programme and to demonstrate traditional, non-instrumental accompaniment for dancing. (Chambers 1980: 226)

Mats Melin, a Scottish and Cape Breton dance scholar, recalls that when he took Scottish country dance lessons in his native Sweden, his instructor sometimes used commercial recordings of puirt-a-beul to demonstrate different forms of dance music available as accompaniment. He also encountered puirt-a-beul sung by a dance instructor from the Isle of Lewis who taught at the Royal Scottish Country Dance Society's summer school in St. Andrew's (interview, August 26, 2009).

Melin recounts a fascinating story in which a Scandinavian dance was "reinvented" as a Hebridean dance and subsequently accompanied by puirt-a-beul:

> One dance in particular that was popular with the RSCDS and done to puirt a beul was the "Hebridean Weaving Lilt" which was said to be from North Uist. It is ironic that the dance is actually "Väva Vadmal" from Sweden/Norway and was learnt by Mary Isdale MacNab in Vancouver from a Norwegian dancer—Thurston wrote about this [see Thurston 1954]—but when MacNab was invited to teach at the St Andrew's Summer School in the 1950s/60s she introduced [this dance] under its new name and new background and the original tune it was danced to in Vancouver was replaced with "Brochan Lom" and "Caristiona Chaimbeul!" [Both puirt-a-beul.] And since then numerous Scottish Country Dance dancers and teachers have passed on the dance as something from the Hebrides. (Personal communication, December 11, 2013)

By the time MacNab taught the dance in Scotland, there was obviously not only an awareness throughout Scotland that puirt-a-beul could be used as dance accompaniment, but that it *ought* to accompany dances from Gaelic-speaking communities such as the Hebrides. Of course, once puirt-a-beul began to be used to accompany MacNab's dance, the puirt-a-beul accompaniment ensured that the dance would be accepted as a Scottish dance.

Melin also indicates that puirt-a-beul were sometimes associated with Highland dance in Scotland: "there was nothing like step dancing or that going on. It would've been fairly much the competitive style Highland dancing that would've been done to puirt-a-beul." It is not particularly surprising that puirt-a-beul would not be associated with step dance in Scotland since it had more or less ceased to exist there from the 1920s until the 1990s. At the same time, puirt-a-beul would not have been ideal accompaniment for either Scottish Country dance or Highland dance. In the case of the former, the singer would need to compete with the sounds of four couples dancing, and often more than one group of four couples danced at a time. In the case of the latter, a singer would have to be heard not just by the dancer but by the judges and audience at a competition.

Of all the dance forms with which puirt-a-beul are associated, they are particularly well suited to accompany step dancing, as would seem to have been the case in Cape Breton and likely Scotland too. First, step dance is a solo dance form and it is easier to hear a singer over one set of feet than many. Although this limitation could perhaps be overcome by a group singing puirt-a-beul, there is little evidence to suggest that puirt-a-beul were traditionally performed in this way and it is rare to see a group performance even today. When a group performance of puirt-a-beul does occur, it is even more rarely performed to accompany dancers; rather, it is performed for its own sake and entertainment value.[9] Because puirt-a-beul are so challenging to sing, they are difficult to sing well with others.

Second, the vast majority of puirt-a-beul are in the form of either reels or strathspeys, and step dancing is likewise based on strathspey and reel steps. In my own collection of over 350 puirt-a-beul, less than 10 per cent are jigs and there are only five marches. If puirt-a-beul were at one time typically used to accompany other kinds of dances, such as the jig figures in Cape

Breton's square dances, we might expect to see more examples of these forms of puirt-a-beul. On the other hand, the fact that there *are* puirt-a-beul jigs and marches raises the question: what kind of dance *did* they accompany? Various folklore collectors and dance scholars have identified the names of countless dances once known in the Scottish Gàidhealtachd, although very little is known about their steps or music. It's possible that some of these would have been danced to jigs.[10] Perhaps puirt-a-beul jigs are the result of cultural connections and interactions between Scotland and Ireland, where jigs are favoured.

Several Cape Breton step dancers in MacGillivray's book of interviews with step dancers, *A Cape Breton Ceilidh*, including Danny "Dougald" Campbell (1988: 40), Margaret Gillis (60), Mary Janet MacDonald (86) and Sadie MacMullin MacNeil (128), mention having jig steps. It is not clear, however, whether they danced improvised solo step dances in jig time, or whether the steps belonged to particular types of fixed dances. Kimberley Fraser, a Cape Breton fiddler and step dancer, recalled seeing Jennifer Roland step dance to jigs before moving on to reels on *Up Home Tonight*, a television show produced in the Canadian Maritimes in the 1980s (personal communication, August 9, 2014). I was recently surprised to see a rather extended step dance routine danced to jigs in an Acadian variety show, *Les Noces… Gelas II*, in Cheticamp (August 11, 2014). One of the dancers later told me that they learned some of the jig steps from their dance instructor, and others they had made up. But these exceptions prove the rule; by and large, it is rare to see extemporized step dancing in jig time. More often, a couple of basic jig steps may be seen during a square set when a figure is set to jigs.

Although no one in *A Cape Breton Ceilidh* mentions march steps, the Fletts and Emmerson do refer to a few dances set to marches, although these would seem to be far less numerous than dances set to other types of tunes. I do, however, start the next section with the discussion of a dance and tune named "King Sweden's March." It is possible that many more puirt-a-beul jigs and marches once existed but have been forgotten as a result of disuse. Their lack should therefore not be taken to infer that they never really existed in the first place.

To counter my own argument that puirt-a-beul are best suited to accompany solo step dancing, it is worth noting the absence of references to puirt-a-beul in *A Cape Breton Ceilidh* (MacGillivray 1988). The majority of the dancers refer to instrumental music accompaniment. A handful mention dancing to jigging. Jigging could refer to puirt-a-beul since terminology is not always consistent (see Chapter 1), but it is just as likely that it was true jigging: the singing of an instrumental tune using improvised vocables. Only a couple of dancers, such as Willie Fraser, refer to puirt-a-beul by name. The lack of references to puirt-a-beul suggests that puirt were not typically or widely sung as dance accompaniment within living memory. It's possible that they were once common but declined over time. Or perhaps they simply were never popular as dance accompaniment in Cape Breton. They may have played other roles on the island, as I describe in the next chapter.

Specific Dances Associated with Puirt-a-Beul

Early in my research, I assumed that when puirt-a-beul accompanied dance, the dance involved was extemporized solo step dance, since that is what I observed in Cape Breton and what Cape Bretoners described to me in interviews. Because the dance is extemporized, any strathspey or reel would do (although some are considered better for accompanying step dancing than others). Any references to puirt-a-beul accompanying other types of dance in Scotland, such as Scottish country dance and Highland dance, struck me as having resulted from the loss of step dance there, rather than because there had been a traditional association of puirt-a-beul with these dance forms. I was surprised, therefore, by a story recounted by Wilma Kennedy, daughter of Kenna Campbell and a highly respected Gaelic singer in her own right. In a 2003 interview in Scotland, she told me about a discovery that linked a particular port-a-beul with a specific dance, a dance that had a fixed set of steps in a fixed order, and the port-a-beul was not a reel or a strathspey, but a march.

It was a personal revelation to discover that dance scholars have recorded quite a few fixed step dances that would seem to be no longer practised in either Scotland or Cape Breton. Take, for example, Rhodes's list of Cape Breton dances associated with puirt-a-beul:

> Puirt-a-beul, rather than fiddle music, seems to have been used for dance games such as Marbadh [Marbhadh] na Beiste Duibhe (The Killing of the Otter), Cailleach an Dùdain (The Old Woman of the Milldust) and Tri Croidhan Caorach (Three Sheep's Trotters).... Some special reels such as Ruidhleadh nan Caraid (The Married Couple's Reel) were also danced to puirt-a-beul. The puirt-a-beul for Ruidhleadh nan Coileach Dubha (The Reel of the Blackcocks) was sometimes used for Dannsa na Tunnag (The Duck's Dance), in which the dancers go down on their hunkers and throw their legs forward alternately.... The Duck's Dance seems most often to have been danced by children individually, but a lady of ninety-three who demonstrated it in 1957, recalled seeing it performed at a picnic by a ring of grown-ups holding hands. (Rhodes 1996: 189)

As I quickly discovered in reading histories of Scottish dance, particularly by the Fletts and Emmerson, dances with fixed steps and step order were once common in Gaelic-speaking areas of Scotland. Unfortunately, although we know many by name and some were described in general terms, few have been documented in detail. We often do not know the tunes to which these dances were performed, although some are explicitly linked to puirt-a-beul. What follows is the description of four different dances of this type, each associated with puirt-a-beul.

First of August and King of Sweden's March

Here is the story Wilma Kennedy told me about a discovery that links a particular port-a-beul with a specific dance:

It was in the first Ceòlas in South Uist, the first festival—adult festival—which was really examining the links between piping, song, fiddle and step-dancing and looking at all the links between them, with language being the backbone of it all. And I did a set of puirt at a ceilidh on a Wednesday night. We'd been at a ceilidh on the Tuesday night.... And Mats [Melin] was at the one I was at. And [there were] no instrumentalists that could play for him to dance. So I said, "Oh, I'll just do some dance music for you." And he says, "Well, I've got this dance from South Uist. Just sing...." I think [he wanted] a slow reel or something. And it just so didn't fit. But I kept going and that was fine. And he says, "I don't know what the [proper] music for it is." Well, I think he knew that it was meant to be "The White Cockade," I found out afterwards.

[So then] I sang a [different] set [of puirt-a-beul] at the cei-lidh the next night. And the next morning, Mats just kind of stopped me in the canteen and he said, "What was that set you sang last night?" And I said, "a set of puirt." He said, "No, *what* was it you sang?" So I started [singing a port-a-beul]. He said, "Stop, stop!" He says, "One, two, three, go" and he started dancing the dance and I started singing puirt. And the hairs on the back of our necks just went rigid because it fitted like a glove. And he says, "That's the White Cockade." But if you sang it like "The White Cockade" [as performed in] the English way, it didn't fit. You had to sing the Gaelic words to get the proper rhythms for it to fit the rhythms of the feet. He says, "Where did you get that piece of mouth music?" I said, "Obviously, my Mum." I said, "Wait a minute, I'll go and phone my mother." So I phoned my mother and I said, "Where's this port [from]" and she said, "Oh, it was in the family. Your great uncle"— or was it great-great-uncle?—"was a stone mason in South Uist for a while and he'd come back with a piece of mouth music." Our family only had one verse of it and then she'd learned a second verse from Catriona Garbett, who sings from Benbecula. And that's where it came from. So it was one these really huge buzz moments when you think, "Wow." And he danced it on Friday night and I sang it and it was just tremendous. And the dance is called "Latha Lùnasdal" (the First of August) and the dance is split into quarters. (Interview, April 30, 2003)

Here is a case where a particular port-a-beul was apparently designed to accompany a particular fixed set of dance steps. This is quite a different scenario from typical Cape Breton step dance, where a dancer improvises steps in response to the music he or she hears, regardless of the tunes involved. The Fletts discuss the dance Wilma mentioned, "First of August," briefly (1996). There is a tune known as "First of August," a tune that is also known as "Charles, Twelfth King of Sweden's March" (generally simplified to "King of Sweden's March"), which is, in turn, itself associated with a dance by the same name. The dance known as "King of Sweden's March" was common in Scotland by the end of the 18th century and many popular songs were written to its tune. It is likely that the "First of August" came to be distinguished from "King of Sweden's March," both as a tune and as a dance, due to two separate sets of lyrics.

The Fletts suggest that the "King of Sweden's March" tune takes its name from a Jacobite song honouring Charles XII of Sweden. After the first Jacobite uprising of 1715, James Francis Edward Stuart (Bonnie Prince Charlie's father) persuaded Charles XII to invade Britain with the assistance of Jacobite troops. The British government, however, learned of the plot and arrested the Swedish representative in London which, together with the Stuarts' military difficulties, brought the plot to naught. Because the Jacobites were primarily Catholic, "King of Sweden's March" has Catholic associations. Meanwhile, the tune "First of August" has distinctly Protestant connotations. The date refers to August 1, 1714, the day Queen Anne died and George I ascended the throne. Protestants saw this as a victory over the pro-Stuart Catholics and wrote a song to celebrate the event. Since the two songs refer to events that occurred so close in time, it is hard to know which came first.

Oddly, when the Fletts later describe the steps of the "First of August" dance, they note that their informant danced to the tune known as "The White Cockade" rather than to the tune known as "First of August." They do not explain how the dance came to be associated with this different tune rather than the one by the same name as the dance. A "cockade" is a ribbon rosette that was especially fashionable to wear in the 18th century either on a man's or woman's hat, a man's lapel or in a woman's hair. Distinctive colours could represent allegiance to a particular political faction, a person's status, or it could function as part of a uniform. In Scotland, the white cockade represented a Jacobite supporter in contrast to the black cockade of the Hanoverians. There is a port-a-beul that is sung to the tune of "The White Cockade":

Mo Thasdan Bòidheach
Mo thasdan bòidheach, mo thasdan geal
Mo thasdan bòidheach, dhachaidh gu mo bhean
Sgillinn anns an t-òl dheth, sgillinn anns an danns'
'S bheir mi deich sgillinn bhòidheach, dhachaidh gu mo
    bhean.

Mo dheich sgillinn bhòidheach, mo dheich sgillinn mhaith
Mo dheich sgillinn bhòidheach, dhachaidh gu mo bhean
Sgillinn anns an t-òl dheth, sgillinn anns an danns'
'S bheir mi ochd sgillinn bhòidheach, dhachaidh gu mo
    bhean.

Mo ochd sgillinn bhòidheach, mo ochd sgillinn mhaith
Mo ochd sgillinn bhòidheach, dhachaidh gu mo bhean
Sgillinn anns an t-òl dheth, sgillinn anns an danns'
'S bheir mi sia sgillinn bhòidheach, dhachaidh gu mo
    bhean.

Mo shia sgillinn bhòidheach, mo shia sgillinn gheal
Mo shia sgillinn bhòidheach, dhachaidh gu mo bhean
Sgillinn anns an t-òl dheth, sgillinn anns an danns'
'S bheir mi ceithir sgillinn bhòidheach, dhachaidh gu mo
    bhean.

Mo ghròtan bòidheach, mo ghròtan galan
Mo ghròtan bòidheach, dhachaidh gu mo bhean
Sgillinn anns an t-òl dheth, sgillinn anns an danns'
'S bheir mi dà sgillinn bhòidheach, dhachaidh gu mo
    bhean.

Mo dhà sgillinn bhòidheach, mo dhà sgillinn mhaith
Mo dhà sgillinn bhòidheach, dhachaidh gu mo bhean
Sgillinn anns an t-òl dheth, sgillinn anns an danns'
'S thèid mi-fhìn nam aonar dhachaidh gu mo bhean.

The White Cockade
My lovely shilling, my gleaming shilling
My lovely shilling, home to my wife
A penny of it on the drink, a penny on the dance
And I'll take ten lovely pennies home to my wife

My ten lovely pennies, my ten good pennies
My ten lovely pennies, home to my wife
A penny of it on the drink, a penny on the dance
And I'll take eight lovely pennies home to my wife

My eight lovely pennies, my eight good pennies
My eight lovely pennies, home to my wife
A penny of it on the drink, a penny on the dance
And I'll take six lovely pennies home to my wife

My six lovely pennies, my six gleaming pennies
My six lovely pennies, home to my wife
A penny of it on the drink, a penny on the dance
And I'll take four lovely pennies home to my wife

My lovely wee groat, my pure wee groad
My lovely wee groat, home to my wife
A penny of it on the drink, a penny on the dance
And I'll take two lovely pennies home to my wife

My two lovely pennies, my two good pennies
My two lovely pennies, home to my wife
A penny of it on the drink, a penny on the dance
And I myself will go alone home to my wife.
(K. N. MacDonald 1931 [1901]: 38)

K. N. MacDonald describes the social dance that this port-a-beul was known to have accompanied:

> A bonnet was thrown on the floor, when a young swain took it up and danced with the lady of his choice, who, in her turn, danced to another favourite partner, and so on until the whole company had a turn on the floor.... In modern times, "the bonnet dance" has been performed to instrumental music, to the air of "The White Cockade," and generally for the last dance at a wedding or ball. (1931 [1901]: 38)

Note that MacDonald describes a social dance, not a solo step dance of the sort that Mats Melin performed to Wilma Kennedy's accompaniment.

To complicate matters, "The White Cockade" is not just a tune name but is *also* the name of a dance. However, it is a Scottish country dance, whereas "First of August," at least as recorded by the Fletts, is a solo step dance. It is interesting to note that "The White Cockade," as with the tune known as both "King of Sweden's March" and "First of August," still has associations with the Jacobite era. Part of the tune's fame results from its associated lyrics written by Robbie Burns:

> My love was born in Aberdeen,
> The bonniest lad that e'er was seen;
> But now he makes our hearts fu' sad,
> He's taen the field wi' his white cockade.
>
> Chorus:
> O he's a rantin, rovin blade,
> He's a brisk and a bonny lad,
> Betide what may, my heart is glad,
> To see my lad wi his white cockade.
>
> Oh leeze me on the philabeg [small kilt]
> The hairy hough and garten'd leg;
> But aye the thing that blinds my ee,
> The white cockade aboun the bree.

I'll sell my rock, I'll sell my reel,
My rippling-kame and spinning wheel,
To buy my lad a tartan plaid,
A braidsword, dirk, and white cockade.

I'll sell my rokelay and my tow,
My good grey mare and hawkit cow,
That every loyal Buchan lad
May tak the field wi' the white cockade.

Although the Fletts indicate that there are lyrics associated with the tune known as both "King of Sweden's March" and "First of August," I could not readily find them. Neither do I have words for the pipe tune, "An Coc Ard" (*coc* is Gaelic for "stiffening" as found in a Highland bonnet; the title might be translated as "The High Bonnet"), apparently played in South Uist in the place of "The White Cockade," according to Mats Melin's research. However, Wilma Kennedy did furnish me with the port-a-beul that she sang to accompany Melin's performance of "First of August," and which Melin says has some similarity to the pipe tune, "An Coc Ard." Wilma knows the song as "An Tàillear Mòr" (The Big Tailor):

Tha nighean Dhomhnuill 'ic Dhonnachaidh gu tromasan-
    ach tinn
'S mòr a tha chràdh ann an cràmhan a cinn
Na faighinn an ùir i sa mùig as a cinn
Rachinn fhìn a phòsadh le m' òg nighean duinn

Dh'fhalbhainn fhìn leis an tàilleir mhòr
Shiùbhlainn fhìn leis an tàilleir mhòr
Dh'fhalbhainn fhìn leis an tàilleir, fhìdhleir
Rachainn a phòsadh ri m' òg nighean duinn

'S mise bha gòrach a phòsadh ri mnaoi
Air a modha sòd agus breòite san druim
Na faighinn air dòigh i sa seòl air a chìll
Rachainn fhìn a phòsadh le m' òg nighean duinn

Dh'fhalbhainn fhìn leis an tàilleir mhòr
Shiùbhlainn fhìn leis an tàilleir mhòr
Dh'fhalbhainn fhìn leis an tàilleir, fhìdhleir
Rachainn a phòsadh ri m' òg nighean duinn

Daughter of Donald son of Duncan, surly and sickly
There was much pain in the bones of her head
If I could put her in the ground and her scowl from her
    head
I would go to marry my young brown-haired girl.

I would go with the big tailor
I would travel with the big tailor
I would go with the big tailor, fiddler
I would go to marry my young brown-haired girl.

I was foolish to marry a woman
Who is easily angered, and has a sore back
If I could get her "sorted," covered by a sheet
I would go to marry my young brown-haired girl.

I would go with the big tailor
I would travel with the big tailor
I would go with the big tailor, fiddler
I would go to marry my young brown-haired girl.[11]

This kind of fixed step dance was likely a descendant of the dances performed at 18th- and 19th-century finishing balls and of the High dances that eventually evolved into Highland dancing. As Moore (1995) suggests, these choreographed dances existed among the earliest Scottish settlers in Cape Breton too, although they gradually fell out of favour in both Scotland and Cape Breton due to the need for dancing masters to teach the complex choreographies and steps.

Gillie Callum: The Sword Dance

Other examples of particular dances associated with specific puirt-a-beul appear in the publications of a handful of dance scholars, who mostly conducted research in the mid-20th century (Flett and Flett 1953; Flett and Flett 1964, 1996; Rhodes 1964, 1996; Thurston 1954; Emmerson 1972). The most famous of these dances, perhaps, is the Sword Dance, which has been associated with the pipe strathspey, "Gillie Callum" (this dance is consequently also known by this name), a tune that has associated puirt-a-beul lyrics. The Sword Dance is best known today as a competitive Highland dance, but it was once a step dance, and it was known in Cape Breton as well as Scotland. Neil MacNeil, an editor of the *New York Times* and author of *The Highland Heart of Nova Scotia*, describes how a piper visiting his home in Washabuck, Cape Breton, would always start by playing "Callum Gille," to which his grandfather would perform the Sword Dance (N. MacNeil 1958: 149-50). Frank Rhodes also found three people in Cape Breton in 1957 who "had recollections of a Sword Dance from before the introduction of the modern Highland Games Sword Dance to Cape Breton Island," including one person in her 80s and another over 100 years old (Rhodes 1996: 192-93).

There are a number of historical accounts of Scottish dances involving swords or dirks, and these are sometimes confused. The solo Sword Dance that came to be known as a competitive Highland dance first appeared at an Edinburgh competition in 1832 (Flett and Flett 1996: 21) and it probably originated in its current form not long before that (C. M. Scott 2005: 105, 107). Although there are earlier references to sword dances, they seem to describe one or more different dances, such as one involving brandishing a sword rather than dancing over one laid on the ground, or two dancers involved in a mock battle. The most popular understanding of today's Highland Sword Dance is that it originated as a war dance:

> As all know, the Scottish Sword-dance, called *Danns' a' Chaidheimh* [sic] and *Gille Calum*, is danced over two swords or a sword and a scabbard, which are laid across each other on the ground. But few know that, though the dancer turns on his own axis sunwise, he goes round the sword *widdershins* [counter-clockwise]. As a Highlander would never dance ill-luck to his own clan, the conclusion is that the Highland sword-dance is a war-dance, which sought to bring about ill-luck to another clan and good-luck to the dancer's clan. That it was once a war-dance is clear from the fact that it was at one time danced with a sword in each hand. (J. G. MacKay, "Widdershins," Folk-Lore, 1928, qtd. in Flett and Flett 1996: 23)

The first known manuscript of a tune labelled "Gilliam Callum" is John Walsh's *Caledonian Country Dances* published between 1730 and 1765. It was also published as "Kheellum khallum taa fein" (a phonetic rendition of the Gaelic lyrics) in Robert Bremner's *For the Year 1769: A Collection of Scots Reels and Country Dances* (Flett and Flett 1996: 28). However, as the collection titles suggest, the tune is associated in both publications with a country dance, rather than with a solo dance, and both pre-date by quite a span the appearance of the competitive Highland sword dance in 1832.[12]

The Fletts refer to the puirt-a-beul lyrics associated with this tune, describing them as "nonsense rhymes to fit the rhythm of the dance" (1996: 25):

Gille Callum dà pheighinn (x2)
Dà pheighinn, dà pheighinn
Gille Callum bonn-a-sia.

Gheibhinn bean air dà pheighinn (x2)
Dà pheighinn, dà pheighinn
'S té ach phiach air bonn-a-sia.

Gheibhinn leannan gun dad idir (x2)
Gun dad idir, gun dad idir,
'S rogha 's tagha air bonn-a-sia.

> Gille Callum two pennies
> Two pennies, two pennies
> Gillie Callum one bodle.

> I shall get a wife for twopence
> Twopence, twopence
> A useless one for one bodle.

> I shall get a sweetheart for nothing
> For nothing, for nothing
> My pick and choice for one bodle. (Thurston 1954: 62)[13]

A *bodle* was a copper coin of very small value in the 18th century, worth only a fraction of an English penny.

These sarcastic and "nonsense" lyrics seem to have little to do with the dramatic and serious Sword Dance and its grandiose associations with battle and victory. Emmerson wonders if this particular port-a-beul, given its lyrics, actually originally accompanied the Kissing Reel, a dance that often concluded a social event in which dancers took turns handing a handkerchief to attendees, followed by a kiss. Indeed, the Fletts note that the Kissing Reel dance was musically accompanied by either "Gillie Callum" or "The White Cockade" or both (1953). While Gaelic scholar John MacInnes agrees that the Sword Dance ("Dannsa a' Chlaidhimh") is an indigenous Gaelic solo dance, he is not quite so sure that its associated port-a-beul is as old or that its tune did not come from beyond Scotland (2006: 252-53).

One legend, however, does provide a link between the lyrics and the sword dance. Francis O'Neill (1848-1936), the famous Irish-born police chief of Chicago who documented thousands of Irish tunes in numerous publications, says that the name "Gillie Callum" is a corruption of "Callum a chinn mhóir" ("Calum of the Big Head") and was used to accompany a dance performed in celebration of Scottish King Malcolm of Canmore's victory at the Battle of Dunsinane in 1054. Malcolm ("Calum") supposedly slew his opponent, placed his enemy's sword on the ground, crossed it with his own, and danced over them. O'Neill says that Malcolm "incurred the displeasure of the highlanders by marrying a Saxon princess which involved many unpopular changes. Gillie Callum, or Callum's tax-gatherer (an odious official everywhere) has been immortalized in melody, while the traditional story is well nigh forgotten" (O'Neill 1922 qtd. in Kuntz 2009; see also Thurston 1954: 62; Emmerson 1972: 190; K. N. MacDonald 1931 [1901]: 20). While it's almost certain that the melody and lyrics of "Gillie Callum" were composed long after this historical moment, it's en-tirely possible that the story was developed much more recently as a means of explaining the otherwise unclear association between the port-a-beul and the dance.[14]

In short, the story of "Gillie Callum" is a confusing one. It is today known as a competitive Highland dance but it was originally a solo step dance. Although there are multiple histori-cal references to sword dances, they do not all refer to the same dance. It is difficult to say, therefore, whether the Sword Dance currently performed to the tune "Gillie Callum" is a descendant of the dance originally accompanied by this tune. And then there is the fact that the earliest versions of the tune itself appear more than 50 years before the first recorded instance of the competitive Highland dance form of the Sword Dance and they appear in collections of *country* (i.e., social, not solo) dance tunes. Finally, the satirical port-a-beul lyrics seem at odds with the grandiose war associations of the Sword Dance, especially since they make no reference to any movements that would demonstrate their connection to the Sword Dance, unlike many other puirt-a-beul lyrics linked to particular dances, as will become obvious in the accounts of the next two dances. O'Neill's story explaining the lyrics does help to link the lyrics with war and royalty, although it is rather far-fetched. Ultimately, we have a port-a-beul that is today associated with the competitive Highland Sword Dance, but because we have to rely on different histories and sources to trace the evolution of the dance, the tune, and the Gaelic lyrics, it is very difficult to see how and when exactly the three came together.

Dirk Dances

A separate dance that is sometimes confused with the Sword Dance is a Dirk Dance. The Fletts tell us that there are many references to dirk dances in the literature but it is often unclear whether they refer to a dance in which two men simulate a fight, or to a solo dance (1996: 44). D. G. MacLellan, an Edinburgh dancing teacher and author of *Highland and Traditional Scottish Dances* (1950), told the Fletts that he and his brother had danced the Dirk Dance together to either of two tunes, both of which have associated puirt-a-beul: "Biodag air MacThomais" ("MacThomas's Dirk") or "Biodag air MacAlasdair" ("MacAlastair's Dirk"; Flett and Flett 1996: 45). An earlier account describes the involvement of two people, but the focus is clearly on only one dancer:

> A sort of tragi-comic *savage dance*, called the Dirk Dance, was exhibited as of native origin, for the first time, at the [Edinburgh?] competition of 1841. Whether it has been transmitted from earlier times or is merely of modern—very

recent contrivance, as some assert—may be questioned. Here a dancer appears brandishing a dirk or poniard, lays it on the stage and dances round it. While he is describing [marking out, as in physically] a wide circuit another coming forth snatches up the weapon. The owner having a second in reserve they fight: one is stabbed, and falls; the victor, dragging him to a suitable place, dances round this body in a very savage style, then slaps one foot which begins to quiver, next a hand, which quivers also, after this the other hand, which quivers—and as all three members quiver a further slap on the other foot produces symptoms of animation. Whiskey is now offered to the resuscitant, who proving incapable of the draught, most of it is swallowed by the victor himself. He raises the wounded man, then able to share the proffered beverage, restoration follows, and both dance together. (John Graham Dalyell, Musical Memoirs of Scotland, 1849, qtd. in Flett and Flett 1996: 45)

For the Fletts, this description seemed very similar to another dance described by a Canadian. Mrs. Mary Isdale MacNab was born in Glasgow but had emigrated with her family to Vancouver in 1907 when she was ten years old. She took lessons from a Mr. Mather, an accomplished piper, composer and dancer from Scotland who himself emigrated to Canada in 1899, and later to the U.S. in 1914. Mrs. MacNab described learning one dance that involved brandishing a dirk, dancing around it on the floor, and holding it in the teeth. However, Mrs. MacNab also recast a Swedish dance as a Hebridean dance, as described earlier, so we must take her recollections with a grain of salt. D. G. MacLennan knew Mr. Mather in Scotland and suggested that he had worked up his own version of the Dirk Dance after seeing him and his brother dancing it as a duet. This is certainly possible since dancing masters often modified existing dances.

Frank Rhodes records a couple of references to a Dirk Dance in Cape Breton as well:

Hugh MacKenzie had heard his father and Alan Quinn speak about Dannsaidh na Biodag, which he called the Dagger Dance in English. It was said to be a dance in which a dagger was stuck in the ground, point upwards, and the dancer danced round and over it without looking down. It is not clear whether his father has seen such a dance, or whether the story derived from printed references to dancing among upturned swords and spears which are misapplied to "Caledonians." Hugh MacKenzie had not heard of a Dirk Dance in which a dirk was held in the hand, but Archie Kennedy had heard old men talk about a Dirk Dance whose Gaelic name he gave as Dannsa no Pitock ["pitock" sounds quite close to the Gaelic word "biodag"]. In this dance a dirk was held and thrown down and picked up again. It was danced to either of the tunes "Thompson's Dirk" or "MacAllister's Dirk," for each of which his grandfather had canntaireachd. The description of the Dirk Dance fits one of the steps of the dance [as described by the Fletts]. (Rhodes 1996: 192)

It is quite probable that this is another instance of confusing "canntaireachd" with "puirt-a-beul" as the two tunes mentioned are the same as the ones associated with the Dirk Dance by D. G. MacLennan, above. Although it is notable that at least two Cape Bretoners had heard of the Dirk Dance, it is also significant that neither had actually *seen* it, but had instead only heard it talked about. The two accounts also differ in description, so it is hard to know how much credit to put into the existence of such a dance in Cape Breton.

K. N. MacDonald provides the lyrics for both tunes. He provides the following for "Tha Biodag air Mac Alasdair" (K. N. MacDonald 1931[1901]: 18-19; see also Mackintosh ca. 1910: 303-304):

Sud an rud a thogadh fonn
Féile beag 'is sporan donn
Còta goirid os a chionn
Biodag Dhomhnaill 'ic Alasdair

Biodag Dhomhnaill 'ic Alasadair
Biodag Dhomhnaill 'ic Alasadair
Biodag Dhomhnaill 'ic Alasadair
'Ga bhualadh ris na ballaichean.

> Yonder is the thing that would inspire a tune
> A little kilt[15] and a brown sporran
> A short coat above
> [And] Donald MacAlastair's dirk.

> Donald MacAlastair's dirk
> Donald MacAlastair's dirk
> Donald MacAlastair's dirk
> Hitting the walls.[16]

The lyrics poke fun at someone who is dressed to the nines, probably inappropriately either due to the context or his personal status. The dirk is hitting the walls, suggesting a few possibilities. Perhaps the space is so small or crowded that it cannot accommodate a dirk. Or perhaps the dirk is unusually large or perhaps being worn in a way that makes it more obvious to onlookers but also more awkward. A third possibility is that Donald MacAlastair is a relatively incompetent dancer.

The lyrics for "Biodag air MacThòmais" are similar. K. N. MacDonald transcribes a version in his book, and recent commercial recordings also include it. Particularly noteworthy is Kenna Campbell's version on *Guth a Shnìomhas* (1999), where it is part of a set of puirt-a-beul in which each port describes people's appearances. Cape Breton Gaelic tradition-bearer Joe Neil MacNeil recorded a version (available on the Gael Stream website, http://gaelstream.stfx.ca/), as well as a version of "Tha Biodag air Mac Alasdair." However, since he was a widely read Gaelic scholar, some Nova Scotians have suggested that we cannot be sure whether his repertoire is representative of that in circulation in Cape Breton or whether he learned it from published sources. On the other hand, John Shaw indicated that he is certain that Joe Neil's repertoire was not influenced by outside sources; he believes that Joe Neil's repertoire was completely Cape Breton in nature (personal communication, July 30, 1999). I believe him. In

William Lamb's republication of K. N. MacDonald's *Puirt-a-Beul*
(2012), Lamb provides notes about the history of each tune and set
of lyrics in print and on recordings. There are many puirt-a-beul
in MacDonald's collection that can be found nowhere else *except*
in Joe Neil MacNeil's repertoire, so unless Joe Neil had access to
K. N. MacDonald's book and could read the musical notation, he
could not have learned them from any source other than the oral
traditions of his home community. While it's true that Joe Neil
was well read, it seems unlikely that he had access to MacDonald's
book given that it was out of print and difficult to access until
William Lamb republished it in 2012.

Here is a version of the lyrics from an article by Andrew
Mackintosh (ca. 1910: 321-22):

Tha biodag air MacThòmais
Tha biodag fhada, mhòr air
Tha biodag air MacThòmais
'S ro mhaith dh 'fhòghnadh sgian dha.

Tha biodag anns a' gliogarsaich
Air mac a' bhodaich leibidich
Na'm faiceadh e mar thigeadh i
Gur math a dh'fhòghnadh sgian dha.

Tha breacan gorm is dearg air
Tha breacan gorm is dearg air
Tha breacan gorm is dearg air
'S ro mhath dh' fhòghnadh cainb air.

Tha crios dhe leathar ròin air
Tha crios dhe leathar ròin air
Tha crios dhe leathar ròin air
'S ro mhath dh' fhòghnadh sioman.

Tha bucaillean na bhrogan
Tha bucaillean na bhrogan
Tha bucaillean na bhrogan
'S gur math a dh' fhòghnadh iallan.

MacThomas has a dirk
A long, large dirk

MacThomas has a dirk
And well would a knife suffice him

A clattering dirk
On the son of an awkward old man
If he looked as he ought
Well would a knife suffice him.

He wears a blue and red plaid
He wears a blue and red plaid
He wears a blue and red plaid
But very well would canvas suffice him.

He wears a belt of seal leather
He wears a belt of seal leather
He wears a belt of seal leather
But very well would a straw rope suffice.

He has buckles on his shoes
He has buckles on his shoes
He has buckles on his shoes
But well would straps suffice.

The lyrics contextualize the dirk as part of an outfit. They quite clearly indicate that Thomson is wearing clothes inappropriate to his social status. It is significant, I think, that the dirk is described first, since it also sets up a bawdy double-entendre, at least for the duration of the first verse. The form of the song then changes after the dirk verses (whereas the first two verses have four different lines each, all the subsequent verses involve repetition of the first three lines), suggesting that this may have originally been two separate songs. The term *leibidich* in the second verse, which I have translated as "awkward" is a lovely choice because it has so many meanings, all of which are suitable translations in the context of this song: worthless, contemptible, shabby, annoying and long-legged.

To summarize, there seem to have been several dirk dances in existence at one time, although it is hard to know today what they actually looked like. How many different dirk dances existed? Were they variants of each other? Did they involve two dancers or one? Were dirks brandished or laid on the ground?

Were the dances known in Cape Breton as well as Scotland? In this case, two different puirt-a-beul—"Biodag air MacThomais" and "Biodag air MacAlasdair"—bear striking similarities not just in their lyrical themes but also in their very titles. They remain relatively well known today, whereas the dirk dances they apparently once accompanied exist only in scattered and incomplete historical descriptions.

Ruidhleadh nan Coileach Dubha (The Dance of the Blackcocks)
I will conclude this section with one final dance, although there are other solo step dances described in various sources, some of which have particular puirt-a-beul associated with them. The Fletts recorded memories of "Ruidhleadh nan Coileach Dubha" ("The Dance of the Blackcocks") in Barra, although it hadn't been danced there for about sixty years at the time of their interview (in the early 1950s), while Rhodes found evidence of it in Cape Breton. An 89-year-old Barra piper described the dance to the Fletts:

> The dance is a Reel for two couples. To begin, the two couples face each other, the men on the left of their partners. The man and the lady of one couple go down on one knee while the other couple set to them with "any Reel steps" for 8 bars. Then the second couple kneel while the first couple rise to their feet and set to them for 8 bars. The second couple then rise and all four join hands in a ring and dance round to the left for 8 bars. This was repeated as often as the dancers pleased. (Flett and Flett 1953: 118)

Although this suggests a fairly simple dance, it would have been awkward for adults to rise up from one knee, which may be one of the reasons that this particular dance has not continued in the active repertoire. Dancers could make a performance more challenging through their choice of steps. A 70-year-old Barra resident remembered dancing a slightly different version as a child:

Two boys and two girls took part, the boys playing the part of the cocks and the girls that of the ducks. The four children stood in couples facing each other. They then danced a continuous Reel of Four until they were exhausted. There was no setting. The boys danced with a normal travelling step, but the girls crouched on their hunkers, with hands held just in front of their mouths, palms together, to form the ducks' beaks. They waddled and hopped around, the "beaks" waggling from side to side. (Flett and Flett 1953: 119)

One can imagine children learning the associated port-a-beul and wanting to participate in the social activities of their parents and so creating their own dance.

This dance is no longer practised, and Gaelic scholar Michael Newton suggests that the dance's marginalization may have to do with its association with animals:

The growing psychological distance between the aristocracy and the animal world brought disfavour upon dances which imitated animals or were associated with them; ritual dances associated with the harvest, fertility, or other aspects of the crude life of the peasantry were also scorned by the elite. (Newton 2009: 279)

Eventually, even the peasantry moved on to different dances. Interestingly, although the dance is no longer practised, its associated port-a-beul is one of the better known today, especially in Scotland. It has been commercially recorded by numerous artists and is popular with Gaelic choirs.[17]

Ruidhlidh na coilich dhubha
'S dannsaidh na tunnagan
Ruidhlidh na coilich dhubha
Air a' bhruthaich bhòidheach.

Gheibh thu aran agus ìm
'S càise na banaraich
Gheibh thu aran agus ìm
Agus bainne bhò ann.

Ma phòsas Annag an nochd
Pòsaidh gach uile tè
Ma phòsas Annag an nochd
Sgaradh air an t-seana bhean.

Air a' bhruthach againn fhèin
Air a' bhruthach uthard ud
Air a' bhruthach againn fhèin
Air a' bhruthach bhòidheach.

> The black cocks will reel
> And the ducks will dance
> The black cocks will reel
> On the beautiful brae [hillside].

> You will get bread and butter
> And the milkmaid's cheese
> You will get bread and butter
> And cow's milk there.

> If Anna marries tonight
> Every woman will marry
> If Anna marries tonight
> Curses on the old wife.

> On our own brae
> On yonder high brae
> On our own brae
> On the beautiful brae.

> (See K. N. MacDonald 1931[1901]: 17; Mhàrtainn 1994:
>   59-60)

Rhodes also recorded accounts of this dance in Cape Breton:

> I also met one form of the four-handed Reel in which the
> dancers swung each other instead of setting and in which
> the travelling figure was performed by the diagonal pairs
> changing places. This last form, which is very similar to
> the South Uist version of Ruidhleadh nan Coileach Dubha,
> was described to me by the oldest of my informants, Mrs
> Jack MacDonald of Scotch Lake (she was over 100 at the
> time when I visited her, and she put aside the painting of
> her garden shed in order to dance for me). Another of my

informants, Mrs Archie Kennedy of Dunvegan, had actually
performed a dance called Ruidhleadh nan Coileach Dubha
to her mother's canntaireachd as a very young child, and
although Mrs Kennedy could not remember this dance in
full detail, her memories of it fitted Mrs MacDonald's form
of the four-handed Reel. It seems very likely, therefore, that
Mrs MacDonald's four-handed Reel was in fact Ruidhleadh
nan Coileach Dubha. (Rhodes 1964: 270)

However, while the dance was known in Cape Breton, the only
example of the associated port-a-beul in Cape Breton comes once
again from Joe Neil MacNeil, whose source is unknown. In the
end, although it seems clear that some puirt-a-beul were designed
to accompany particular dances, I don't think we should assume
that this was the case for all puirt-a-beul. Puirt-a-beul play too
many roles in addition to that of dance accompaniment, and
these roles are the subjects of the next two chapters. Moreover,
puirt-a-beul's association with an extemporized solo step dance
tradition suggests that at least some, if not most, puirt-a-beul were
not tied directly to specific dances. However, I did find a number
of other traditional dances that are either definitely or likely associated with puirt-a-beul, for any readers inclined to pursue the
subject further, including "Cailleach an Dùdain" (which is perhaps better described as a pantomime than a dance), "Ruidhleadh
nam Pòg" ("The Kissing Reel"), "Ruidhle Thullachain" ("Reel of
Tulloch"), "Croit an Droighinn" ("The Thorny Croft"), "Dannsa
na Tunnag" ("The Ducks' Dance"), "An Dannsa Mòr" ("The
Great Dance"), "Marbhadh na Beiste Duibhe" ("The Killing of
the Otter"), "Tullochgorm" (Tulloch is a place name and "gorm"
means "blue-green"), "Trì Croidhan Caorach" ("Three Sheep's
Trotters"), "Ruidhleadh nan Caraidh" ("The Couple's Reel"),
"Seann Triubhas" (better known in English as "Shan Trews"),
"Dannsa nan Flurs" ("Flowers of Edinburgh"), "Jacky Tar," "Duke
of Fife" and "The Irish Washerman." Many of these dances are
simply mentioned in traditional dance or music scholarship;
clearly, much more research remains to be done.

Puirt-a-Beul and Step Dancing

Although the particular solo step dances described above no longer appear to be known or practised in Cape Breton (except, of course, the Sword Dance, which is performed by Highland dancers in Cape Breton), extemporized solo step dancing still is. Numerous oral accounts suggest that step dancing has often been accompanied vocally, and I will start this section with a review of some of the diverse descriptions of puirt-a-beul's use to accompany dancing in Highland immigrant communities in Canada. To start, around a quarter of the dancers interviewed in Allister MacGillivray's book, *The Cape Breton Ceilidh*, mention vocal accompaniment. However, most refer to jigging rather than puirt-a-beul:

> Myself and my brother used to jig the tunes and my father would get up and dance, even when he was an old man.... [My aunt] was the one that could jig all the good old tunes. My mother used to tell me that they used to have spinning frolics and that my Aunt Katie would be jigging every single one of the very special tunes. She'd have those ladies on the floor stepdancing the Scotch Four. (Margaret Ann Cameron Beaton qtd. in MacGillivray 1988: 36)

> [My mother] used to jig tunes; she was a really good jigger and still is! (Minnie Beaton MacMaster qtd. in MacGillivray 1988: 122)

> My mother used to jig tunes and we'd dance. (Kay MacPherson Handrahan qtd. in MacGillivray 1988: 78)

Given the tendency to conflate puirt-a-beul and jigging, however, it is possible that puirt-a-beul proper were sometimes used. Willie Fraser, a well-known step dancer and puirt-a-beul singer, for example, illustrates the tendency to equate the terms "jigging" and "puirt-a-beul":

> I tried the violin myself but I didn't have the fingers; I only had the feet! But I have the Gaelic of all those old-time

tunes.... When I used to work in the woods, when we'd cut
down a big tree I'd jump up on the stump and dance with
the old gumboots on! They only slowed me down a little.
Someone would always be around who could jig a tune....
When I was jigging a tune, [my daughter Maureen] had four
or five steps just like that! She's dancing all the time and
she's teaching the little ones. Kathleen can dance too. And
I'd jig a tune—a tune like *Calum Cròbach*—and our little
Roddy used to jump up in the crib. (Qtd. in MacGillivray
1988: 57)

Willie talks about having the Gaelic for those tunes, suggesting
that he would sing Gaelic lyrics rather than simply vocables—i.e.,
that he was singing puirt-a-beul rather than jigging. He also refers
specifically to "Calum Cròbach," one of the more well-known
puirt-a-beul in Cape Breton (see Chapter 4). But when I spoke
to Willie Fraser, he told me that jigging was all that was needed;
puirt-a-beul themselves were not necessary. A month later, I saw
Willie Fraser at a concert singing his own dance accompaniment.
He started with some puirt-a-beul but it quickly morphed into
vocabelization (no doubt because it was very difficult to perform
the puirt-a-beul properly while executing his steps; he was also
of an advanced age at the time). Willie seems to treat jigging and
puirt-a-beul as largely interchangeable, something I have not witnessed or heard among other jiggers and singers of puirt-a-beul.

Celtic ethnologist John Shaw's work with the respected Cape
Breton tradition-bearer Joe Neil MacNeil also supports the under-
standing of puirt-a-beul as step dance accompaniment in Cape
Breton:

In Cape Breton, it was common for people to step-dance
to puirt-a-beul as well as instrumental music; in Joe Neil's
words, "chuireadh iad feadhainn a dhannsa le puirt-a-beul,"
"They would get people dancing with mouth music." (Shaw
1992-1993: 44)

Indeed, although not a singer himself, Joe Neil recorded more
than one hundred puirt-a-beul for John Shaw in the late 1970s.

Lauchie MacLellan, a singer from Dunvegan, Cape Breton, recorded more than twenty-five. These can be accessed online from St. Francis Xavier University's site Gael Stream. The fact that these two well-respected singers and tradition-bearers knew so many puirt-a-beul implies that puirt-a-beul once abounded in Cape Breton, as do the many other examples of puirt-a-beul to be found on the Gael Stream site.

Shaw went on to document the unusual use of puirt-a-beul in nearby Prince Edward Island, where puirt-a-beul were regularly heard at weddings and dances (two singers would sing puirt-a-beul while a fiddler between them played their tunes), and they were also used to accompany children's dancing in the home (Shaw 1992-1993: 44).

Virginia Garrison, who documented fiddle transmission processes in Cape Breton for her PhD dissertation, writes:

> Cape Breton fiddlers have a great love and respect for the "old tunes," their favorite types including (a) slow airs; (b) jigs; (c) reels; (d) marches; and (e) strathspeys. Appreciation was also expressed for the performance medium of "mouth music," the vocal renditions of these fiddle tunes performed in the absence of violin or bagpipes at a dance or house party. (Garrison 1985: 192)

As we shall see in the next chapter, references to jigging and puirt-a-beul in Garrison's dissertation are mostly restricted to discussions about their use in the learning and remembering of fiddle repertoire, but she notes here their use in dance contexts. The Highland Village Museum in Iona, Cape Breton, has a "virtual museum exhibit," authored by respected Gaelic speakers from the local community, about traditional life of Scottish settlers and their descendants in which puirt-a-beul are mentioned:

> Our dancing has always been to the music of the violin and of the pipes. But not having a musician at the time did not prevent people from dancing. They simply made their own music by "jigging" tunes or by singing puirt à beul, which

are Gaelic songs set to dance tunes (Nova Scotia Highland Village Society 2006).

While puirt-a-beul are most often associated with extemporized step dancing in Cape Breton, and, as I described earlier in this chapter, some puirt-a-beul apparently accompanied a handful of "fixed" or formal step dances, some have noted their use as accompaniment for other forms of dancing, particularly "tricks" that allowed dancers to show off their abilities:

> Not all puirt-a-beul are in the rhythms of reel, strathspey or jig, and some of them would seem as if they must have been devised for dances which have become forgotten. In Nova Scotia the writer has seen the descendants of Scottish Highland stock perform step-dances around a row of lighted candles, which they extinguish one by one in the course of the dance with the sole of their foot, without if possible knocking the candle over. (Collinson 1966: 98-99)

Frank Rhodes also heard references to *smàladh na coinnle* ("snuffing of the candle") in Cape Breton, although he did not witness it himself (1996: 192). In MacGillivray's *A Cape Breton Ceilidh* (1988), Finlay "Philip" MacDonald's 91-year-old grandson recalled that his grandfather could perform this candle trick. MacDonald was a dancing teacher in Mabou. Donald "the Mason" Rankin's grandchildren likewise recalled that their grandfather, who died in 1924, could snuff out a candle while dancing. Although they did not know of anyone else who could perform this trick, they did note that he was from Mabou and had taken dancing lessons in the area, perhaps from Finlay "Philip" MacDonald.

Given that few Cape Breton step dancers recalled seeing this dance trick, and given that both Rhodes and Collinson wrote about their experiences at approximately the same time, it is likely that this candle-snuffing dance was a novelty step limited to specific people rather than a long-lost Scottish traditional dance maintained in Cape Breton, as Collinson suggests. The Fletts do report one reference to *smàladh na coinnle* in Scotland found in the notes of folk collector John Francis Campbell:

There is a dancing master without arms who is now in Barra and who has hundreds of Sgeulachd [stories].... One of his best steps is to leap up and extinguish a lamp with his heel without spilling a drop of the oil. (Qtd. in Flett and Flett 1996: 17)

The Fletts suggest that the reference is to dancing master Ewen MacLachlan from Renfrewshire who moved to South Uist sometime prior to 1840. They report that several people recalled seeing MacLachlan perform this trick, but there is no indication that it was known by anyone else. It is possible that MacLachlan specialized in the trick and taught it to his best students. It's possible that one of his students emigrated to Cape Breton and it circulated there for a brief while. On the other hand, MacLachlan would have been active in South Uist after the main emigration to Cape Breton occurred. Regardless, the candle-snuffing trick does not seem to be known or practised by anybody in Cape Breton today. It is also not clear whether puirt-a-beul would have been used to accompany this particular trick, although this is what Collinson implies when he suggests that some puirt-a-beul were meant to accompany very particular dances. It's certainly possible that the candle trick was accompanied by puirt-a-beul, just as it may well have been accompanied by fiddle or pipes, depending on the availability of musicians.

Up to this point, I have identified quite an array of sources that refer to the use of puirt-a-beul as dance accompaniment. However, it's also worthwhile noting the number of people who never experienced or witnessed it as such. In 1986, ethnologist Barbara Leblanc, commissioned by Canada's Museum of Civilization in Ottawa, researched dance in Inverness County (the western side of Cape Breton Island, including strong Gaelic communities such as Judique, Mabou, Inverness and Broad Cove, but also strong Acadian communities, such as Chéticamp and Grand Étang, as well as Margaree, where both cultural groups lived). She conducted interviews with dozens of people, some quite elderly at the time they were interviewed, involved in Acadian and Scottish dance: dancers, callers, teachers and musicians. In almost every interview, she specifically asked about what she called "dance songs," asking if the interviewee knew of songs used to accompany dance. In some cases, puirt-a-beul are mentioned, but in several other cases, the interviewee—including some of Scottish descent—flatly denied that there were any dance songs. It is possible that Leblanc's terminology did not call puirt-a-beul to mind, but it is also possible that puirt-a-beul simply were not widely performed as dance accompaniment. Indeed, a few people noted that fiddlers had always been available so vocal accompaniment was never required as dance accompaniment. The mix of references to puirt-a-beul and denials of dance songs could mean that puirt-a-beul as dance accompaniment was known only in certain regions and not in others, or perhaps that puirt-a-beul were used as dance accompaniment at some point in the past but decreasingly so by the 1980s. It is certainly true since I began researching puirt-a-beul in Cape Breton in 1998 that I have only rarely seen puirt-a-beul used as dance accompaniment (even though they are frequently described in conversation as dance accompaniment).

At about the same time that Barbara Leblanc was conducting her research, two Scots fell in love with Cape Breton music: Hamish Moore, a piper, and Alasdair Fraser, a fiddler. They felt that Cape Breton had retained an integrated form of Scottish music, dance and Gaelic language that had been lost in Scotland. They began inviting Cape Bretoners to teach their style of music and dance at summer programs at Sabhal Mòr Ostaig (the Gaelic university on the Isle of Skye) and Ceòlas (in South Uist). As anthropologist Jonathan Dembling notes (2005), not everyone in Scotland was interested in "returning to" or "reclaiming" the Cape Breton style. But a significant minority of Scottish performers did take up Cape Breton step dancing and took instruction from Cape Breton fiddlers, especially during the 1990s. However, Mats Melin has observed that the trend seems now to be on the wane as there are very few Cape Breton–style step dancers active in Scotland as of the late 2000s (interview, August 26, 2009).

The Cape Breton trend in Scottish cultural circles introduced (or reintroduced, depending on your perspective) the use of puirt-a-beul as step dancing accompaniment. In his Master's thesis about step dancing in Scotland, Melin reports that many of today's step dancers enjoy performing to puirt-a-beul: "The preferred instruments to step dance to comes down to personal choice, but among many step dancers there is a strong preference for fiddle, pipes and Gaelic song" (Melin 2005: 41). Melin circulated an anonymous questionnaire in which he asked, among other questions, how important the relationship is between the Gaelic language and step dance (I discuss the relationship between language, music and dance in greater depth in Chapter 7). The responses were strongly divided, but I include two positive responses here that reference puirt-a-beul directly:

> Puirt a beul adds another line of complexity to the dance.... It can add another slice of subtlety to the way you dance a step as the word will influence the way you dance the step, so that it matches the internal rhythm of the word or phrase. When I started practising steps it would be to the accompaniment of my mother ... singing puirt a beul. It was as if it was the most natural thing in the world to put the two things together. As my knowledge of steps increase[d], we could hear what ones suited best to certain puirt. You would try and find ways of putting "the words on the floor." (Qtd. in Melin 2005: 81)

> I admire step dancing which is closest to the form which is performed to accompanying Gaelic mouth music. Maybe, partly because in this format there are 2 natural physical limitations (and therefore objective standards) to the tempo, namely the dancers [sic] capacity to dance at a particular tempo and the singers [sic] ability to sing the words in a comprehensible way. (Qtd. in Melin 2005, 80)

Maggie Moore, another Scottish scholar of step dancing (and once married to Hamish Moore), has noted that both fiddlers and step dancers seem to prefer pipe tunes, whether played in the pipes or fiddle, for dance accompaniment, and most of the tunes she specifies are also known to have puirt-a-beul lyrics:

Well-known tunes like "Calum Crubach" and "The High Road to Linton" are played alongside tunes that are rarely heard in Scotland today, like "Moulin Dubh" and "Put Me in the Big Chest"; and tunes which in Cape Breton are still being played in their original simple two-parted state, like "Pretty Marion" and "Caberfeidh," have in Scotland been turned into complex competition tunes by the addition of a further 2, 4 or even 6 parts [the puirt-a-beul lyrics for these tunes are provided below]. But why pipe tunes, when the instrumentation today is almost always fiddle and piano? The answer is, of course, that both in Scotland and Cape Breton, it was pipers who traditionally played for dancing. (Moore 1995)

Moore argues that while step dancing is often today danced to fiddle accompaniment, the tunes preferred suggest that it was originally performed to pipe music. I would extend her argument and suggest that the preferred tunes indicate not just a preference for piping accompaniment, but also the possibility that step dancers were at least occasionally accompanied by puirt-a-beul, the lyrics of which are known in Cape Breton as well as Scotland.

Calum Crùbach

Calum Crùbach as a' ghleann,
Cum thall na caoraich uile,
Calum Crùbach as a' ghleann,
Cum thall na caoraich.

Cum thall, na toir a-nall,
Cum thall na caoraich uile,
Cum thall, na toir a-nall,
Cum thall na caoraich.

Calum Crùbach

Lame Malcolm from the glen,
Keep all the sheep over there,
Lame Malcolm from the glen,
Keep the sheep over there.

Keep over there, don't take over here,
Keep all the sheep over there,

Keep over there, don't take over here,
Keep the sheep over there.[18]
(Lamond, liner notes ca. 1994)

Bodachan a' mhìrein
Bodachan a' mhìrein,
A' mhìrein, a' mhìrein;
Bodachan a' mhìrein,
A' bhonnaich bhig 's a' ghràinnein.

Bodachan a ri ar o,
A ri ar o, a ri ar o
Bodachan a ri ar o,
A' bhonnaich bhig 's a' ghràinnein.

> **High Road to Linton**
> Little old man with the piece
> The piece, the piece,
> Little old man with the piece
> The little bannock and the grain.
>
> Old man a ri ar o,
> A ri ar o a ri ar o
> Old man a ri ar o
> The little bannock and the grain.
> (Carruthers, liner notes 1998)[19]

Am Muileann Dubh/Moulin Dubh (See Chapter 3)

Cuir sa Chiste Mhóir Mi
Cuir sa Chiste Mhóir Mi
'S cóig bonnaich fo mo cheann;
Cuir sa chiste-mhine mi
Is beag is miste mi bhith ann.

Cuir sa chiste mhine mi,
Cuir sa chiste mhine mi,
Cuir sa chiste mhine mi,
Is beag is miste mi bhith ann.

> **Put Me in the Big Chest**
> Put Me in the Big Chest
> With five bannocks under my head;
> Put me in the meal chest
> I will be none the worse for being there.

Put me in the meal chest
Put me in the meal chest
Put me in the meal chest
I will be none the worse for being there.
(K. N. MacDonald 1931[1901]: 23)

Cabar Fèidh[20]
Deoch-slàinte 'chabair fèidh seo
Gur h-èibhinn 's gur h-aighearach
Ge fada bho thìr fèin e
Mhic Dhè greas ga fhearann e

Mo chrochadh i 's mo cheusadh
Is m' èideadh nar mhealladh mi
Mur àit' leam thu bhi 'g èirigh
Le treun neart gach caraide.

Gur mise chunna' sibh gu gunnach
Ealamh, ullamh, acainneach
Ruith nan Rothach 's math 'ur gnothach
Thug sibh sothadh maidne dhaibh.

Cha deach Cataich air an tapadh
Dh' fhàg an neart le eagal iad
Ri faicinn ceann an fhèidh ort
Nuair dh'èirich do chabar ort.

A toast to this MacKenzie clan
That is funny and that is gay
However long from their own country it is,
O Son of God hurry it to its land.

Let me be hanged and crucified
And may I not enjoy my clothes
If I do not I rejoice in your rising
With the mighty power of each clansman.

It was I who saw you armed
Agile, mature, capable
The Munroes ran, your business is good
You repelled them in the morning.

No Sutherlander was successful
Strength left when their fear rose

> Seeing the head of the deer on you
> When your antlers arose.
> (K. N. MacDonald 1931[1901]: 21)[21]

Clearly, puirt-a-beul were sung to accompany dancing in areas of Canada settled by Scottish Highlanders (especially Cape Breton). In the New World, puirt-a-beul are particularly linked to extemporized step dancing but also possibly with "trick" dances such as *smàladh na coinnle*. And even though step dancing had long been absent from Scotland, Cape Breton step dancing—and the puirt-a-beul associated with it—is being accepted and revived in Scotland once again.

It is worth noting one other context for puirt-a-beul in relation to dance: transmission. As we shall see in the next chapter, and as I discussed in Chapter 1, mouth music is often used to transmit instrumental tunes. This is true of Gaelic puirt-a-beul as well as of vocabelization traditions in other cultures. However, while there is ample evidence to indicate that puirt-a-beul accompanied various forms of dancing in Scotland and in Cape Breton, it is far less clear how or whether puirt-a-beul may have been used to transmit or convey aspects of *dancing* itself from one person to another. In his PhD dissertation on Cape Breton step dance, Mats Melin documents the shift from informal dance transmission (e.g., learning through observation and exposure to the dance such as at house ceilidhs) to formal dance transmission (e.g., organized, structured dance classes), a phenomenon that really only started in the 1970s in tandem with a resurgence in fiddling (Melin 2012: 110). Puirt-a-beul seems absent from most of these formal classes. However, Willie Fraser

> would not teach a class a single step until they had learned to "jig" the strathspey "Calum Crubach" and the reel "Muilean Dubh" along with Willie singing the song in Gaelic and [until the students] reached the standard he was happy with. The process was to enable the class to internalize the rhythm of the tunes. (Melin 2012: 153)

It is clear that, for Willie Fraser at least, something about puirt-a-beul informs the dance and affects the dancer's movements, and isn't merely a form of convenient accompaniment.

The problem that scholars of Gaelic creative expressions have is that there is often an absence of information about what performers have felt was important about their art form and why. In many cultures, scholars turn to language and vocabulary, noting indigenous words relating to the creative arts. The assumption is that those words tell us something about what is deemed most important in the art form. That is to say, if there's a word for something, that "something" must be significant. But in Gaelic, the same logic doesn't work, because there's a remarkable lack of vocabulary pertaining to the various expressive arts. For example, Joshua Dickson notes a limited Gaelic vocabulary pertaining to the piping tradition in North Uist (2006: 224). Dance scholars have long puzzled over the fact that there appears to be no indigenous term for "dance" in Gaelic. The common term *dannsa* comes from the English, which in turn came from a French word (*danser*) and, before that, from old high German (*dansón*) (Emmerson 1972: 10; Breathnach 1983: 14; Thomson 1983: 56). Scholars often assume that activities and ideas enter a community at the same time as their associated vocabulary does, but it's quite impossible to believe that Gaels have not always danced. It *is* possible, perhaps, that the borrowed terms replaced the previous indigenous terms, although it's quite remarkable that the borrowed term should almost immediately start appearing in documents while the previous indigenous term or terms somehow never did.

The point here is that we don't really have any idea what earlier Scottish and Cape Breton dancers thought was important about their dances and about their dancing. We don't know whether puirt-a-beul was used simply as a convenient form of accompaniment or whether it was believed to shape the act of dancing in some way. It is possible too, of course, that there was no conscious belief about the relationship between puirt-a-beul and dance, but that it nonetheless affected dancers in unarticulated ways. Part of our problem stems from the fact that it was not possible to document dance except through language or still images until the development of audio-visual recording technologies in the 20th century. Just as great a problem arises from the fact that the study of cultures, including anthropology and folklore, did not develop until the 19th century and even once they developed, only certain kinds of information were sought. For much of the early 20th century, dances and tunes were documented, and performances observed and described, with very little effort made to document how the practitioners and audiences themselves would describe them and what they felt was important about them.

Unfortunately, this means that we really don't know how Scottish and Cape Breton Gaels historically conceived the relationship between puirt-a-beul and dance. Nor do we have any information about how puirt-a-beul may have affected dancing, such as in the development of timing, rhythm or individual style. We can guess that it did, but it's just a guess. Mary Ann Kennedy suggest thinking of dance as accompanying puirt-a-beul instead of the other way around, which completely shifts the way we think of the relationship between puirt-a-beul and dance (personal communication, Sept 9, 2014). Returning to Willie Fraser, was his insistence that dance students learn puirt-a-beul indicative of a broader cultural belief at one time that puirt-a-beul inform the dance? Or is his method of teaching idiosyncratic and unique to him? These questions indicate just one of the areas that is in need of further research and investigation. Due to a lack of sources, it is also possible that such questions will remain unanswered.

Conclusions

I have covered a lot of ground in this chapter. I started with a history of dances considered traditionally "Scottish" today to set up a discussion about what kinds of dance puirt-a-beul typically accompany. Despite only scattered references to puirt-a-beul in various books, I have demonstrated that puirt-a-beul have likely accompanied a range of dances, both social and solo, which have largely disappeared from the active repertoire in Scotland and

Cape Breton. One of these dances, the "Gillie Callum," also known as the Sword Dance, is now known as a competitive Highland dance. Twentieth-century references to puirt-a-beul in Scotland link them to Scottish country dance whereas they are linked to solo extemporized step dance in Cape Breton (and, with the revival of step dancing in Scotland, now there as well). Puirt-a-beul is therefore associated with ta range of "Scottish" dance types.

There is no reason to think that puirt-a-beul ever accompanied a single form of dance, although it is quite possible that particular tunes and songs were designed to accompany specific types of dance or even specific, individual dances. Just as fiddles and pipes can—and do—accompany all these dance types today, there is every reason to believe that puirt-a-beul has also always done the same. Puirt-a-beul are convenient and could provide an easy form of accompaniment for a spontaneous dance. One Cape Breton Gaelic learner recently recounted to me that she sang puirt-a-beul to accompany family members performing a Highland dance at a family reunion, not because it was in any way traditional to do so, but because the opportunity arose to showcase a dance, and a musician was needed. Puirt-a-beul lyrics provide a form of entertainment not possible with instrumental music. Particular lyrics could be selected or even created to humorously describe the company present or the dance being performed. Dance's ability to reinforce community bonds is thus reinforced through socially understood lyrics.

But just as puirt-a-beul are not associated with just one dance form, neither are they limited to dance accompaniment in general. Puirt-a-beul have been used as a tool in other contexts as well, and I turn to those uses of puirt-a-beul in the next chapter.

Chapter 6
Quit Fiddling Around!
Puirt-a-Beul's Other Functions

Puirt-a-beul are almost invariably associated with dance. However, there is no reason to believe that they were *only* used to accompany dance. In fact, Scottish musicologist Francis Collinson suggests that dance accompaniment was never even their primary function:

> Most people [in Scotland] will have heard on the radio of the Gaelic songs [puirt-a-beul] for providing, by vocal means, music for dancing; for the spectacle of dancing to mouth-music is now a common one on television. Few however even among folk-song collectors will have seen them used for this purpose in a true folk background, for though the singing of them for their own sake is widely popular, the use of puirt-a-beul for dancing, though it is a genuine enough tradition, seems always to have been a kind of marginal one. Puirt-a-beul never seems to have been used *extensively* for the dance, and the music of an instrument has always been preferred when it is available. (Collinson 1966: 93)

Puirt-a-beul are challenging to sing under the best of circumstances (see Chapter 3). They are even more difficult to sing as dance accompaniment. To ensure that the dancer is able to perform adequately, the tempo of the accompanying puirt-a-beul must be fast and sustained, and breathing must be adjusted so that it doesn't interfere with the rhythm or metre.

But if puirt-a-beul did not accompany dance, or if that is not all they did, what other purposes have they served? Quite a lot, it turns out.

Transmitting and Learning Instrumental Tunes

As I explained in the chapter about their origins (Chapter 2), puirt-a-beul are often believed to have evolved to maintain instrumental traditions when particular instruments were prohibited or proscribed for various reasons. Given the strong link between puirt-a-beul and instrumental music, it should not therefore be surprising that puirt-a-beul are often used in learning or transmitting tunes among instrumentalists.

Although not referring specifically to puirt-a-beul, Kim Chambers writes, "one of the most important and widespread use of vocables throughout the world as well as in Scotland is for teaching" (1980: 37). This is evident from the brief survey of global vocable traditions described in Chapter 1. A vocal means of transmitting and learning tunes is particularly suitable, and sometimes essential, in traditions without a standard written notation system or in cases where the musician (either student or teacher) does not read written music. Even in cases where both teacher and student are musically literate, puirt-a-beul and other oral means of performing a tune can provide insights not possible from sheet music. Kim Chambers enumerates several ways in which vocabelizing can assist during musical instruction:

> The list of ways in which vocabelising aids the teaching process includes: a) enabling the teacher to mark the accented beats dynamically; b) allowing for variation of attack by selection from a range of sounds; c) showing stress or lack of stress by the use of certain vocables; d) marking cadences or phrases which are constantly repeated by attaching vocable "words" or "phrases" to them, and thus clarifying

the overall structure of a piece; and e) enabling the teaching to highlight the placement of grace notes and ornaments by the interpolation of associative vocables. (1980: 42)

The need to accent a note vocally is particularly relevant to piping, since bagpipes are incapable of dynamics. Instead, a note on the bagpipes is accented by changing its length or ornamentation, but this can be difficult for a learner to recognize and emulate. Vocabelizing and puirt-a-beul enable a singer to accent a note dynamically. But Chambers also observes that when singing, a teacher's hands and body are freed from the instrument and can therefore be used to physically indicate an accented note (e.g., tapping a foot or finger, punching a fist into an open palm, etc.).

Chambers's second point about how the selection of particular sounds (particular combinations of consonants and vowels, such as "ta" vs. "ill") can indicate variations in attack is less relevant to puirt-a-beul because of its prescribed lyrics. The singer cannot choose particular vocables to illustrate specific musical features. However, it is possible that the lyrics themselves are already designed to do this. In a line such as *"Calum Crùbach às a' ghleann"* ("Lame Malcolm from the glen"), the hard "C's" of Malcolm's name contrast with the sounds of the latter half of the line and work to emphasize the "jagged" nature of the strathspey rhythm. These sounds contrast considerably with a line such as *"Tha am muileann dubh air thuraman"* ("The black mill is moving"). The sounds here are much softer and contribute to the smooth-flowing feel of the reel.

Scottish Gaelic speaker and singer Mary Ann Kennedy suggests that, while the sounds of puirt-a-beul cannot be tied to particular pitches as is the case with canntaireachd (see Chapter 1), they may indicate the approximate melodic range (e.g., high, medium, or low pitches):

The choice of the words and where they are placed in some examples of puirt a beul—especially the tongue-twister variety where the order of words is shuffled around from line to line—could show a natural inclination to place certain syllables and sounds at different levels of the scale, similar to canntaireachd. (Kennedy 1995: 37)

She analyzes "Fosgail an Dorus dhan Taillear Fhidhleir" ("Open the Door for the Tailor Fiddler") to illustrate, observing that the word *fidhlear* (fiddler) "is always placed at a higher pitch than 'taillear'" (tailor; 37-38). The Gaelic language divides vowels into two types: slender (i, e) and broad (a, o, u). Kennedy's point is not so much that particular words are associated with particular pitch areas, but rather that slender vowels are associated with higher pitches than broad vowels. However, an extensive phonetic analysis such as the one performed by Chambers would be required to determine whether this syllable–pitch relationship is consistent across most puirt-a-beul.[1]

Drawing on Scottish Gaelic singer Eilidh MacKenzie's study of some two hundred Gaelic songs of various types (not just puirt-a-beul), Kennedy also notes that there is a tendency for words with a svarabhakhti vowel (essentially the addition of a vowel sound that is not evident in the word's spelling) to remain on a single pitch (Kennedy 1995: 39). For example, the word *gorm*, meaning "blue-green," is pronounced as though it has two syllables, something like "gore-um." According to MacKenzie's research, both the initial and svarabhakhti vowels would normally be set to the same pitch, although Kennedy identifies at least one exception: in the port-a-beul "Ciamar a nì mi an dannsa dìreach" or "How will I do the dance correctly?" the svarabhakhti vowel in "*dh'fhalbh*" is at a higher pitch than the initial vowel sound (1995: 39). It's possible, however, that this is the exception that proves the rule.

Chambers's third point is that vocable selection can reinforce the difference between stressed and unstressed (or accented and unaccented) notes. This is in fact the argument that some have made about the need for traditional Cape Breton musicians to know puirt-a-beul lyrics (along with the Gaelic fluency to pronounce them correctly). Those who argue the importance of puirt-a-beul to the instrumental tradition say that puirt-a-beul texts indicate the (appropriate) rhythm of the associated tune. Since vowel length is significant to meaning in the Gaelic language, words can indicate whether notes are meant to be lengthened or shortened. For example, Danny Graham, a fluent Cape Breton Gaelic speaker whose son, Glenn Graham, is a fiddler, explained:

> The rhythm and accent of the language has had an effect on the music. This makes it more easily produced by one who speaks Gaelic or who speaks English with a Gaelic accent which is often the case in Cape Breton.... I think this sound comes from the rhythm, accent and throaty sound of Cape Breton Gaelic and English speakers whose parents and grandparents spoke the language. (Qtd. in Graham 2006: 62-63)

I discuss the connection between the instrumental and puirt-a-beul traditions at greater length in Chapter 7.

Finally, Chambers's fourth point is that patterns or "phrases" of vocables can be repeated at strategic points to clarify the overall structure of a piece. The same can be said of puirt-a-beul, which, as we have already seen numerous times, tends to be highly repetitive. The repetitive lines in puirt-a-beul need not be seen as a lack of creativity on the part of their composer, but rather an appropriate textual means of reinforcing musical form. As we saw in Chapter 3, it's quite common to find internal melodic repetition within a section or across sections of a port-a-beul tune. Repeated lines in a port-a-beul can likewise indicate this melodic repetition lyrically. For example, in the well-known port-a-beul "'S ann an

Fig. 12. "'S ann an Ìle" (see Mhàrtainn 1994: 18)

Ìle" ("It's in Islay"), melodic repetition of the first and third lines in each section is mirrored in lyric structure:[2]

'S ann an Ìle, 'n Ìle, 'n Ìle
'S ann an Ìle rugadh mi
'S ann an Ìle, 'n Ìle, 'n Ìle
'S ann an Ìle bhoidhich

'S ann an Ìle ghuirm an fheòir
A' rugadh mi 's a' thogadh mi
'S ann an Ìle ghuirm an fheòir
A' rugadh mi 's a bha mi

> It's in Islay, in Islay, in Islay
> It's in Islay that I was born
> It's in Islay, in Islay, in Islay
> It's in the beautiful Islay.
>
> It's in Islay of the green grass
> that I was born and raised
> It's in Islay of the green grass
> That I was born and where I was.[3]

Vocabelizing's ability to indicate particular musical ornaments also makes it useful in teaching contexts. At least one Cape Breton Gaelic speaker has indicated that puirt-a-beul has this ability as well:

> Lauchie MacLellan observes that the information contained in puirt-a-beul may occasionally go as far as to include [bowing] ornaments, remarking that in the reel "*Còta Mór Ealasaid*" "Elizabeth's Big Coat" a verbal rhythm involving three rapid syllables in the middle of the first turn corresponds precisely to where the fiddler is required to insert a bowing ornament called a cut (gearradh). (Shaw 1992-1993: 46)

This can be seen in Fig. 13 in the next chapter (the line "Tha Anna nighean an fhìdhleir"). Cape Breton fiddler Jackie Dunn likewise argues that puirt-a-beul can convey note values and accentuation necessary for the correct performance of a fiddle tune (1991: 27-28). Mary Ann Kennedy argues the same for pipe ornaments:

Certainly the choice of words appropriate to the rhythms of the tune and even its ornamentation can be shown, e.g. the words in the final line of "Pog 'o Leannan an Fhidhleir" (A Kiss from the Fiddler's Sweetheart) imitate very well the effect produced by the ornamentation that a piper would use on the repeated notes. The similar sounds in the words "gum bu leam," which produce an effect like "<u>gum</u>-bullum," are a good imitation of the effect produced by the "G, D, E" graces on the Low "G's." (1995: 38)

Some Cape Breton fiddlers and pipers have stressed that they would not attempt to play a tune without first knowing the associated port-a-beul. For example, Mark Wilson and Kate Dunlay describe Father Angus Morris's approach to fiddling:

Fr. Morris believes that the best way to learn Scottish music is to perfect its strains initially as mouth music before transferring the tune to the violin, for such preparation allows its delicate details to become fully internalized while injecting an important measure of self-expression: "It puts your own flavour into a melody if you tune it to yourself first. When I teach students the violin, I tell them, 'Repeat on the fiddle the way you jig it to yourself.' I think I've gotten pretty good results that way. Or that's the way I tell the story at least." (Wilson and Dunlay 2002: 13-14)

Piper Barry Shears notes that famed Cape Breton piper and Gaelic speaker Alex Currie generally learned the associated Gaelic lyrics whenever he learned a tune (2008: 104). Virginia Garrison, who wrote her PhD dissertation about how Cape Breton fiddlers learn to play, found that the vast majority of the twenty-three fiddlers she interviewed in 1979 and 1980

reported that as a beginning fiddler they were totally dependent on their aural skills—their ear—for learning. Opportunities for these young players to develop their aural skills were many. Those reported included ... listening to relatives and non-relatives sing Gaelic songs, or sing nonsense syllables in vocal renditions of fiddle tunes, a practice known in Cape Breton as "jigging," and making "mouth-music." (1985: 185)

However, Garrison observed a shift occurring at the time of her research which resulted in some fiddlers learning how to play and acquire repertoire in informal, predominantly aural, contexts, while other fiddlers were learning in more formal environments such as private lessons and fiddle classes. Concomitant with this shift came a change in the use of puirt-a-beul and jigging. Aside from differences in motivation for learning to play the fiddle and "pre-fiddling" experiences (music-related experiences occurring before learning the fiddle), she found that "no fiddle class student, in describing how he or she remembered tunes, mentioned 'jigging' them" (1985: 235). It is possible that the fiddlers Garrison interviewed simply didn't think to mention jigging tunes in the classroom context. However, Garrison's observations suggest that puirt-a-beul are primarily used for learning tunes in informal contexts, and that as formal learning increases, puirt-a-beul may be used less and less for tune transmission.

Although fiddlers and pipers without Gaelic fluency often argue that puirt-a-beul may be helpful but not essential to the ability to render a tune properly, it is clear that vocabelizing and puirt-a-beul can sometimes clarify performance aspects, including rhythm, pitch, ornamentation and emphasis, not at first understood or perceived by the student.

Puirt-a-beul may be used not just to teach a tune, but to transmit and share tunes among musicians. Cape Breton fiddler Jackie Dunn writes, "it is common knowledge among the older generations that the first fiddlers in Cape Breton learned their tunes from puirt-a-beul versions" (1991: 16). For Dunn (who is, after all, a fiddler), the primary role of puirt-a-beul is to transmit and identify fiddle tunes. The lyrics help a fiddler to remember a new tune perhaps heard only once before. The lyrics additionally help fiddlers to remember a particular tune within a large repertoire. For Dunn, then, puirt-a-beul are less important as songs sung in the absence of instruments for the purpose of dancing. Rather, they are sung, often in the presence of instruments, as teaching and memory aids. Piping scholar John Gibson makes the same point with respect to the piping tradition in Scotland:

> "Dance and Song" pipe tunes and many other tunes for the violin were transmitted by the playing or singing of the melody as well as the words.... Words were the equivalent of canntaireachd for the passing on of dance-music pipe tunes. Anyone with the grasp of piping "rules" that Joseph MacDonald set down in his "Compleat Theory" (allowing readers to believe such a grasp was common to all competent players) would have all the information required from a song with words, and the same is true of the less intellectual piper who had only his own imagination. Words were also a powerful *aide memoire*. (1998: 87)

When I presented a paper on the subject of puirt-a-beul to a Celtic Studies conference in Cork, Ireland, in 1999, several scholars argued that puirt-a-beul have relatively low status as songs because they are not true songs. These scholars argued that they are, in fact, fiddle tunes and therefore have far more importance to fiddlers than to singers. They suggested that, as with canntaireachd, fiddlers taught other fiddlers new tunes by singing puirt-a-beul. Of course, even if puirt-a-beul have been used among fiddlers, this does not preclude them from having been used for other purposes and in other contexts as well, as this and the previous chapter clearly show. Their argument, however, does indicate that puirt-a-beul are well known as a means for transmitting tunes among musicians.

Vocal transmission of tunes also allows non-instrumentalists to transmit tunes to instrumentalists. This has been particularly evident in cases where women, especially mothers, have transmitted tunes to men. Scottish-derived piping and fiddle traditions in both Scotland and Cape Breton were strongly male-dominated until quite recently. If women played an instrument at all, it was usually the piano as accompaniment. But even if women didn't know how to perform a tune on a melody instrument, they often still knew the repertoire, as we saw in the previous chapter when we read about Cape Bretoners who learned to dance to the accompaniment of jigging and puirt-a-beul, often sung by female relatives. Scottish ethnologist John Shaw records how famed Cape Breton fiddler Bill Lamey first learned to play:

> In the 30s [*sic*] the well-known fiddler Bill Lamey, raised by Gaelic-speaking parents as an English-speaking monoglot in River Denys, Inverness Co., wished to learn fiddle. His mother was not a musician but introduced him to the "correct" style, along with a large number of tunes, through puirt-a-beul—that is, by oral transmission. (Shaw 1992-1993: 44)

Liz Doherty likewise recounts that "Kyle MacNeil [of The Barra MacNeils fame] acknowledges puirt-a-beul, as practiced by his mother, Jean MacNeil, as his initial source of tunes—'she would jig them to me'" (1996: 177). Cape Breton fiddler Natalie MacMaster's grandmother, Maggie Ann Beaton, used to encourage Natalie to dance by jigging tunes for her (see Melhuish 1998: 132).

There are also stories of the supernatural that link song with fiddling. Katherine Campbell cites one story of the Trows, the Shetland name for the fairies. In this account collected by Shetland folklorist Jessie (Edmondston) Saxby, a well-known legend is made somewhat unusual by transmitting a fiddle tune via a fairy song:

> An auld man sitting oot ae simmer nicht saw a murge o' Trows come lichtly ower da mires close by whaur he stüd. Der feet never made a mark upo da weet mires, an' as they skippit alang dey sang "Hupp holes handokes, we'll ride on bulmints." The man cried oot upon da moment: "I'll ride wi' ye." Upon dat they carried him aff and dey keepit him for a twalmonth, and dan dey pat him back upon his ain rüf. But he never telled what he heard or saw as lang as he bed we' da Trows. Dey were an awebaund upon him. But the tune dey sang when he gaed riding wi' them he minded weel, and the fiddlers got it frae him. (Saxby 1932: 65-66)

Although this story locates the origin of a tune with the fairies, and although it is a Shetland rather than Highland tale, it suggests that there was nothing remarkable about learning an instrumental tune from a song, nor was it a practice limited to the Highlands of Scotland. There are also many Highland tales of fiddlers getting their musical talents from the fairies.

More than simply providing a means of sharing a tune, puirt-a-beul can also serve as a memory aid, or mnemonic, for someone who has already learned a tune. Jackie Dunn notes, "[Puirt-a-beul] syllables seem to have a mnemonic, quasi-notational function of enabling the singer to recall the melody" (1991: 17). Virginia Garrison's dissertation documents how fiddlers who learned primarily by ear used puirt-a-beul, among other methods, to recall tunes (1985: 186). Finally, John Shaw cites tradition-bearer Joe Neil MacNeil:

> Certainly they (the puirt-a-beul) would be quite suitable for [musicians]; when they [musicians] knew the words, these [words] would be a help to them. It would be easier for them than to go by the tune (alone). So all this was just running through their mind as they played. (Qtd. in Shaw 1992-1993: 47)

Although puirt-a-beul apparently once played an important role in tune transmission, they do not generally play the same role today. One likely reason is that, since the 1940s, there has been a marked increase in the musical literacy of fiddlers, at least in Cape Breton (Doherty 1996: 167-68). Consequently, there is less need for oral sources of tunes, including puirt-a-beul. Even when fiddlers do still turn to aural tune sources, the ready availability of fiddle recordings, both commercial and archival, means that fiddlers can learn their tunes from other fiddlers rather than from singers. Women have also begun playing melody instruments, allowing women to transmit tunes instrumentally rather than orally.

Another reason puirt-a-beul no longer has much of a role to play in tune transmission is the decline of Gaelic speakers. The decline has been relatively constant in Scotland and dramatic in

Cape Breton. However, there are those who would argue that a fiddler cannot play a tune "properly" without knowing its associated puirt-a-beul lyrics, and I will discuss this debate in the next chapter.

Instrumental or Vocal Genre?

Puirt-a-beul are challenging to sing. Puirt-a-beul singers are often admired for their technical dexterity, including breath control, pitch control, and enunciation. The increasing number of performances of puirt-a-beul by singers in public contexts (whether live performances or commercial recordings) is indicative of a general trend in which puirt-a-beul is becoming increasingly associated with singers rather than with instrumentalists. As noted earlier, puirt-a-beul may once have formed a part of fiddlers' and pipers' repertoires, functioning largely as a means of learning or transmitting tunes, but that no longer seems to be the case in the majority of instances. When puirt-a-beul still *are* part of an instrumentalist's repertoire, they tend to be viewed as something for private use rather than public performance. For instrumentalists, puirt-a-beul are a means to an end: they provide a means of learning, transmitting, or remembering a tune, rather than exist as a performance genre in and of themselves.

It is rare today to hear an instrumentalist sing puirt-a-beul on a public stage or on a recording, whereas I have heard many singers perform them publicly (a notable exception is piper Rona Lightfoot, who includes both canntaireachd and puirt-a-beul on her album, *Eadarainn*, 2004). Commercial recordings of puirt-a-beul are almost invariably by singers. Even where puirt-a-beul are explicitly linked to the instrumental tradition, as in the case of the two recordings released by Margaret Stewart and Allan MacDonald (*Fhuair Mi Pòg*, 1998, and *Colla Mo Rùn: A Blend of Traditional Singing and Piping from Gaelic Scotland*, 2001), a singer performs them. Part of the reason for this, no doubt, stems from the fact that instrumentalists do not claim to be singers, and so might not choose to sing publicly. But if puirt-a-beul's role were limited to certain functions within instrumental traditions, we would not expect to hear them from singers either. Clearly, there has been a shift in the tradition.

Evidence suggests that puirt-a-beul have historically been understood as an instrumental genre, rather than a song genre. This is evident from the very term *puirt*, which refers to instrumental—not vocal—tunes. It is also evident in the stories of their originating as substitutions for instrumental music, and in accounts of instrumentalists transmitting tunes to one another using puirt-a-beul. Their absence from song collections further indicates that they were not part of the standard repertoire of respected Gaelic singers. It therefore seems reasonable to consider puirt-a-beul to have been sung primarily by instrumentalists or by people who were not generally recognized as singers by the broader community.

And yet, when I first began researching puirt-a-beul, Cape Bretoners regularly suggested that I speak to singers rather than instrumentalists. A question arises: how did puirt-a-beul shift from the repertoire of instrumentalists to the repertoire of singers? Gender may provide at least part of the answer. Because women were often discouraged from fiddling or piping until quite recently, they found other ways to participate in these traditions. One way was to learn the instrumental repertoire as puirt-a-beul. Many fiddlers recount learning tunes from women in their families, especially when first learning to play their instrument (see, for example, MacGillivray 1981). Women also sang puirt-a-beul to accompany their children's dancing efforts at home, and several people recalled hearing their mothers sing puirt-a-beul around the house, accompanying domestic chores. Women may have provided a means of shifting puirt-a-beul from an instrumental to a singing tradition. It is perhaps no coincidence that the majority of recordings of puirt-a-beul, whether archival or commercial, are of female performers.

Another reason for puirt-a-beul's current popularity as a vocal genre may have resulted from its inclusion as a category in Scotland's annual Royal National Mod. The Mod, a Gaelic culture competition, was established in 1892 by An Comunn Gaidhealach (The Gaelic Society), itself established in 1891. The Mod was based on the Welsh equivalent, the *Eisteddfod* (established 1880), which also spawned a Gaelic song competition in Ireland, the *Oireachtas* (established 1897). The Mod, created to help preserve Gaelic language and culture, emerged at the height of Highlandism when tartan and Gaelic became symbols of Scotland as a whole (see Chapter 2 for an expanded discussion of Highlandism).

Today, the Royal National Mod is an eight-day affair that includes events in recitation, storytelling, drama, music arranging and instrumental performance, although the largest and most prestigious events are song competitions (solo, small ensembles, and choirs). The most prestigious solo awards are the Gold and Traditional Medals, while choirs vie for the Lovat and Tullibardine and Margrat Duncan Memorial Trophies. Singers and choirs may choose to compete in various categories, including puirt-a-beul. The Mod is a major event, receiving national news coverage and attracting hundreds of competitors and thousands of attendees.

The Mod is a somewhat contentious event in the Gaelic community. Some criticize it for formalizing an informal culture, and for rewarding a non-traditional, "classical" singing style at the expense of a more traditional style. Others, however, value the Mod because its popularity raises the visibility of Gaelic language and culture, it increases the status of Gaelic culture and competitors, it maintains repertoire in circulation through prescribed song requirements, and it establishes standards for performance.

At the risk of overstating the case, I would argue that the puirt-a-beul competition illustrates this controversy. One problem is that a significant number of Gaelic speakers and activists do not feel that puirt-a-beul is a genre worthy of a competitive category. Aside from the fact that it encourages competitors to learn puirt-a-beul, perhaps at the expense of other Gaelic song genres, it also suggests that puirt-a-beul are valued as songs by Gaels. The only other genre-specific competition centres on *òrain mhòra* ("great songs"), the most prestigious song genre within Gaelic culture. By contrast, other competitions are generally either "open choice" or require a prescribed song (often from a particular song collection or affiliated with a particular geographical region). Does the fact that there are only two genre-specific competitions suggest to the general public that puirt-a-beul are in some way equivalent to òrain mhòra?

A second problem is that the solo puirt-a-beul category used to be limited to fluent Gaelic speakers but, due to its popularity with Gaelic learners, it was recently re-designated as an open category. When the competition was limited to fluent speakers, it suggested that puirt-a-beul require fluency to be performed properly and to be appreciated. With the opening of the category to Gaelic learners as well, the implication is that puirt-a-beul do not require the same level of fluency that other genres do. By contrast, the "great song" competition remains limited to fluent speakers. I will discuss this issue at greater length in the next chapter.

However it may have happened, the puirt-a-beul repertoire is now almost always maintained and transmitted through singers rather than instrumentalists. In Cape Breton, I know of no living Gaelic-speaking fiddler who also performs puirt-a-beul. Part of the reason that puirt-a-beul have become popular among singers is that the genre is distinct from others and therefore enables singers to incorporate more variety into a concert program or commercial recording. One singer and Gaelic learner told me that puirt-a-beul "are fun and they break up a night of singing a lot of long, difficult songs." When she sings puirt-a-beul, she focuses on the music, whereas in other songs she concerns herself with the lyrics: both remembering them and pronouncing them correctly. She also observed that puirt-a-beul have the ability to release the singer's tension as much as the audience's, preparing him or her to sing the next serious song. Puirt-a-beul break the tension of more involved, serious songs. Their upbeat melodies and humorous lyrics provide the audience with an emotional release. Puirt-a-beul invite the audience to laugh, to clap and to respond to the music.

Christine Primrose, a native Gaelic speaker from the Isle of Lewis in Scotland with several Gaelic song recordings to her name, likewise uses puirt-a-beul to vary her performances of

Gaelic song:

> My own personal preference is to sing slow, highly emotion-
> ally charged songs. That is when I get the most satisfaction
> from singing. However, nowadays, in a concert situation
> where invariably there are people in the audience who don›t
> have knowledge of either the language or the culture, I vary
> the types of song because it gives the audience an overall
> experience of the richness of material that we do have in
> the Gaelic song repertoire. In the past it wasn't so necessary
> to do this as your audience would have the language and
> there would be more of an opportunity to sing the slower
> songs. And then you take them back into the "real" stuff, the
> real heavy music, the big music of the Gaelic song tradition.
> (Interview with author, July 13, 1998 and personal commu-
> nication, January 8, 2014)

Primrose's differentiation between "the real stuff" and puirt-a-
beul was a trope that returned in several interviews on both sides
of the Atlantic. I address differing attitudes toward puirt-a-beul
in the next chapter. But for now, it is useful to consider whether
puirt-a-beul—as a genre not considered equal to other Gaelic song
genres—may offer singers and recording artists the opportunity
to be more creative in their musical arrangements than they could
otherwise be.

Taking Cape Breton Gaelic singer Mary Jane Lamond's album,
Suas e! (a traditional cry of encouragement, loosely translated as
"up with it"; released in 1997) as an example, it is clear that puirt-a-
beul are arranged quite differently from other songs on the album.
The three milling songs (known as "waulking songs" in Scotland),
for example, which are songs that were traditionally used to accompany the beating of woven wool to shrink it and thereby make
the cloth warmer and more weather resistant, are all arranged
with limited or no accompaniment. Meanwhile, the three puirt-
a-beul tracks have dramatic instrumental arrangements. Whereas
the accompaniment of other songs is made to sound secondary to
the lyrics, which are rendered vocally in a traditional manner, the

puirt-a-beul lyrics are almost always modified substantially. For example, vocal harmonies, the layering of two or more different lyrics simultaneously, tempo shifts, the addition of new lyrics, divided lyrics and the addition of extra lyric repetitions are some of the alterations made to puirt-a-beul on this album. Lamond has acknowledged that she consciously arranges puirt-a-beul differently from other songs: "I try to avoid harmonies except in 'puirt-a-beul (mouth music—unaccompanied acoustic vocal dance music)' songs. I have fun with those" (qtd. in Roden 1998).

While puirt-a-beul are often intermingled with other Gaelic songs to provide variety, both of sound and of genre, they are also used to conclude recordings and concerts. Their quick tempos and tongue-twister-like lyrics make them ideal as flashy finales. For example, according to a 1990 concert program, Oranaiche Cheap Breatuinn (the Cape Breton [Gaelic] Choir) performed in Massachusetts at the invitation of the Boston Branch of the Cape Breton Island Gaelic Foundation for a "Golden Jubilee" celebration. The choir's program was divided into three sections. Both the first and second sections concluded with puirt-a-beul (unnamed), and the final section included puirt-a-beul as the penultimate selection, followed only by "Oidhche Mhath Leibh" ("Good Night"), a traditional farewell song.

Some recordings also conclude with a flourish of puirt-a-beul. The Barra MacNeils conclude both *Until Now* (a "best of" album released in 1997) and *Closer to Paradise* (1993) with the song, "Am Pige Ruadh" ("The Red Jar"). In fact, *Until Now* includes two versions of the song, with the second being a "bonus extended version":

Am Pige Ruadh
Fhuaras am pige ruadh,
Fhuaras na glainneachean,
Fhuaras am pige ruadh
Ann an crò nan eireagan.

U goraidh giridh goraidh,
U goraidh giridh goraidh
U goraidh chè goraidh
Ann an crò nan eireagan.

Làn taighe dh'fhìdhleirean,
Làn taighe chaileagan,
Làn taighe luba dubha
'S làn a' mhuidhe mharagan.

Thàinig 's gun tàinig
'S ma thàinig na maraichean,
Thàinig 's gun tàinig
'S ma thàinig cha d' fhairich mi.

Am Pige Ruadh
The red jug was found
The (drinking) glasses were found
The red jug was found
In the hen-house

U goraidh giridh goraidh,
U goraidh giridh goraidh
U goraidh chè goraidh
In the hen-house.

House full of fiddlers
House full of girls
House full of black pudding
And full of churned pudding.

Came or didn't come
And if the sailors came
Came or didn't come
And if [they] came, I didn't hear.
(see The Barra MacNeils, liner notes, 1993)[4]

The Rankin Family also finished their self-titled debut album with the "Jigging Medley," which concludes with the port-a-beul "Bodachan a' Mhìrein" ("Little Old Man of the Wee Piece"; see Chapter 5 for the lyrics).

Including puirt-a-beul in a concert or recording can be especially important when attempting to appeal to non-Gaelic speakers or learners. Christine Primrose explained how her changing audience necessitated a change in her repertoire:

I would hear puirt when I was growing up but only around people's houses and they didn't seem to be taken very seriously. I cannot recall singing them, nor being asked to sing them. It was always the big songs that people wanted. Later on when I started going to festivals and such where people didn't have the language, that was when I began to look at them and incorporate them in my repertoire. I had to become aware of the format of the program that I was doing. I had to make sure that the tempo of the songs varied in the concert performance I was doing. So that's when I started becoming very aware of puirt-a-beul and seeking them out. Ones that I would know maybe the first part of the tune and wee bits of the second part of the tune, wee bits of the lyric and I started then to learn them properly so that I could actually perform them. (Interview with author July 12, 1998 and personal communication, January 8, 2014)

Some singers feel that it is crucial that Gaelic song reach a broad audience. Obviously, a performer needs at least to recoup recording and concert costs. But there are broader cultural considerations as well. One Gaelic learner and singer explained:

If Gaelic music is to reach a modern audience, that music must be accessible to modern ears or they won't listen. They won't buy it. They won't learn any Gaelic song. If the business fails to make this music accessible, the business not only fails itself but the culture as well. (Personal communication, May 12, 1999)

For this singer, as for others, it's okay to arrange Gaelic songs such as puirt-a-beul with non-traditional instrumentation and to otherwise modify puirt-a-beul in order to appeal to a broad audience.

Puirt-a-beul are ideal for non-Gaelic speakers because their musical characteristics are highly appealing and more significant than their lyrics. The idea of "mouth music" is appealing as a novel genre and it sounds flashy and impressive. As one Gaelic learner and singer observed,

People like things that are fast and loud and high.... Sometimes [puirt-a-beul] sounds harder than it is and sometimes it sounds as hard as it is and people think, "Wow! How can you get all those words out?" And then maybe because it's in a foreign tongue, people who aren't Gaelic speakers are even more wowed by the mystery of it. (Interview, March 24, 1998)

Kim Chambers explains why audiences interpret the performance of mouth music as novel:

> Instrumental tunes are not usually suited to the capabilities of the human voice; they have large jumps at frequent intervals, the note density is often very high and there are seldom spaces for breathing. So to be a performance diddler one needs an agile voice, capable of making large leaps in quick succession; well controlled breathing, and an instrumental musician's intimate knowledge of a tune, which may be exceedingly difficult or complex. These requirements rather rarely combine in one individual, hence the infrequency of vocable performances (in comparison to fiddle, pipe or accordion performances) and hence the novelty or specialty effect when they do appear. (Chambers 1980: 214)

One doesn't need to speak Gaelic to appreciate puirt-a-beul. In fact, the constant repetition means that a careful non-Gaelic-speaking listener might even be able to sing along, especially if the song includes vocables. Celtic scholar Michael Kennedy observes:

> Puirt a beul is proving particularly popular with Gaelic learners, because it is based on a lively instrumental music that is still easily accessible and, therefore, relatively easily learned; because the songs are generally very short, holding the attention of the learner/performer and the non-Gaelic speaking audience; and because it does not make the same heavy demands of linguistic competence and understanding made by the "big songs." (Kennedy 2001: 132)

"Big songs" in Gaelic tend to be lengthy, grammatically complex, involve esoteric and unusual vocabulary, and make use of sophisticated rhyme and rhythmic patterns. They are not particularly accessible to Gaelic-language learners and non-speakers, whereas the lively tempos and short, repetitive lyricsof puirt-a-beul are.

Historically, of course, there were no Gaelic song concerts or recordings, so these are not traditional song contexts in the same way that ceilidhs are, for example. Their development, and the inclusion of puirt-a-beul as part of them, is just one indication of how puirt-a-beul have changed over time to adapt to new circumstances. Perhaps puirt-a-beul were once used to accompany dance in the absence of instruments. But that scenario rarely, if ever, occurs today. There are plenty of musicians and recordings to accompany dancers at the present time. Instead, puirt-a-beul have a new purpose that has resulted in its move to new venues of performance. This kind of change in a tradition can be unsettling. One Cape Breton singer and Gaelic speaker explained why he feels ambivalently about puirt-a-beul: "Years ago, I don't remember hearing anybody singing puirt-a-beul at a concert. I can't remember any 50 years ago." It bothered him that puirt-a-beul were being sung in a non-traditional context and for a non-traditional purpose. And yet it seems likely that puirt-a-beul would disappear if they were not adapted to new contexts, for there is no longer any need to, for example, maintain instrumental repertoire or accompany dance in the absence of instruments.

Another Gaelic speaker and singer worried that efforts to appeal to a broad audience might actually do more harm than good. In response to one particular commercial puirt-a-beul arrangement, she noted:

> I think [some puirt-a-beul arrangements] ... become something quite radically different from the tradition that they originated in. I mean, this stepping song thing with all the overdubbing of this sort of whispery stuff and the timing changes and that sort of thing: to me, they have very little connection with Gaelic tradition. And to say that people are learning and coming into Gaelic tradition from hearing that kind of thing, I really doubt very much if they are. Or if they're coming at anything terribly real in the culture from that sort of pop facsimile of mouth music. (Interview, June 13, 1998)

As noted earlier, it does indeed seem to be the case that some singers take liberties with puirt-a-beul, particularly on recordings and
in concerts, that they don't with other types of Gaelic songs.

There is reason to be concerned, as Rosemary McCormack
discovered. Rosemary is a Gaelic speaker originally from South
Uist in Scotland who lived in Cape Breton for a number of years.
She established an organization, B&R Heritage Enterprises, which
released a number of traditional Cape Breton music recordings
in the 1990s. She recounted an incident that suggests that some
recordings may give the wrong impression of Gaelic song culture:

> We had our *Gaelic Gold* recording. We had somebody from
> Alaska just recently called up. They had seen our descrip-
> tion of *Gaelic Gold* in a paper which was sent to them, so we
> weren't hiding anything. They called us. They wanted two
> copies. We sent them the copies. We got them back in the
> mail about two weeks later and they said "this isn't Celtic
> music! I wanted Celtic music! Could you please send me
> some Celtic music instead?" So, that's really hard. So they
> got a letter back saying, "Celtic music is what comes out
> of the culture and experience and character and history of
> the people who speak the Celtic languages. You could not
> find anything more Celtic music than traditional Gaelic
> singing from Cape Breton." ... That is the downside of the
> sort of poppy stuff that some groups are doing because that
> becomes the standard by which Gaelic stuff is judged. The
> music industry and the majority of the listening public out
> there doesn't realize that, to people within the culture, that
> stuff is not acceptable or is just barely acceptable as Gaelic
> stuff. (Interview, June 13, 1998)

Although I do not know exactly what kind of music the Alaskan
customer expected to receive, Rosemary told this story at a time
when Celtic artists such as Enya, Capercaillie, Ashley MacIsaac
and Loreena McKennitt were extremely popular, and while Anúna
and Riverdance were touring the world.

Another concern with recordings is that they make repertoire available for anyone, anywhere to hear and learn. Singers no longer need to seek out a tradition-bearer or singer to learn a song. This means that songs like puirt-a-beul can be learned out of context, without relevant information (except whatever might be provided in the liner notes), and without the benefit of instruction and correction that would come from personal interaction. Gaelic learners and song enthusiasts may not differentiate between singers they hear on commercial recordings. They may not know the difference between a recording by a well-respected Gaelic speaker and one made by someone who may not know much more than the learner him- or herself. A learner who acquires a port-a-beul from a recording can inadvertently repeat mistakes made by the recording artist.

The Rankin Family provide a useful case study. The Rankin Family consists of siblings who grew up in a Gaelic-speaking area of Cape Breton, but they themselves did not grow up speaking the language. They have used Gaelic-speaking coaches to help them learn Gaelic song lyrics phonetically. Their international success as recording artists has resulted in Gaelic enthusiasts and learners everywhere learning Gaelic songs from their albums. The following review of the Rankin Family's album, *North Country* (1995), appeared on Amazon.com:

> I too was given the gift of a tape of Gaelic singers. One being the Rankin Family. It's great, uplifting music, and some of it's in Gaelic, only the greatest language created by God!! And if I was fortunate enough to afford college this year, I'd be learning Gaelic with one of the lady Rankins. (Customer 1998).

Another telling comment was posted on YouTube under a video of the Rankin Family performing a Gaelic song ("Ho Ro Mo Nighean Donn Bhòidheach" / "Ho Ro My Beautiful Brown-Haired Maiden") at the 1994 Junos:

> Wow. All you Gaelic speakers rock my socks off! Where did you learn? I've loved to sing this song since I was 13, but it

was just sounds I was imitating. Now I'm trying to learn it to perform it, and I have no Gaelic speakers or a pronunciation guide in sight. Any ideas? (Anon. 2008)

These fans seem to be unaware that The Rankin Family singers are not fluent Gaelic speakers. The YouTube contributor indicates that he or she is learning Gaelic songs phonetically from recordings, which already has its limitations, but the situation is even more problematic because the YouTube fan is learning from learners and won't know which sounds are well executed and which ones might not be recognized by a fluent Gaelic speaker. Craig Cockburn, creator and developer of Silicon Glen, "Scotland's Internet guide," has a page about traditional Gaelic song in which he warns language learners and aspiring singers about Gaelic pronunciation:

> Assume your audience knows Gaelic, even if they don't. Therefore you have to be authentic in your pronunciation and respect the stresses and syllable lengths of the words despite what the music says. Assuming the audience knows Gaelic (even though they usually don't) means that you can't be careless with pronunciation. Karen Matheson in Capercaillie (an advanced learner) does an excellent job of delivering the vocabulary authentically, as does Mairi Sine [Mary Jane] Lamond (also a learner). The Rankin Family on the other hand do not. I suspect the Rankins would sell fewer records if more people spoke Gaelic. (Cockburn 2010)

Recordings also make repertoire available in areas where it might never have been known previously. For example, because Cape Breton Gaelic speakers, especially learners, are highly conscious of Gaelic's connection to Scotland, they will sometimes assume that anything in the Gaelic language is appropriate in both Scotland and Cape Breton. For example, one Cape Breton Gaelic learner and singer explained why she uses Scottish recordings as sources for puirt-a-beul repertoire:

> [Puirt-a-beul's] gotten so sparse with the [Cape Breton] native speakers and that. And I think that probably the only

way to keep the puirt-a-beul really going here is, like I say, what comes out of Scotland because I don't think you're going to find too much of it here. (Interview, July 22, 1998)

In Nova Scotia, however, many Gaelic singers are proud of the local repertoire and prefer to sing songs that have been part of the tradition for generations, or songs newly composed by Nova Scotians, rather than adopt new repertoire from Scotland.

Recordings also make it possible for puirt-a-beul once known only in Scotland to begin circulating in Cape Breton. A well-known example is "Seallaibh Curraigh Eòghainn" ("Look at Ewen's Corracle"; see Chapter 4 for a discussion of the lyrics). I am aware of at least six commercial recordings of this song, including two from Cape Breton. It can also be found on an influential archival recording made by the University of Edinburgh's School of Scottish Studies, *Music from the Western Isles* (1992 [1971]), which is likely responsible for the current popularity of "Seallaibh Curraigh Eòghainn" in both Scotland and Cape Breton. One of the Cape Breton artists who recorded "Seallaibh Curraigh Eòghainn" is the Barra MacNeils, although, as indicated in their liner notes, they learned it from Fiona Moore of Scotland rather than from the Scottish Tradition CD. They recorded a version of it on their album *The Question* (1995). Gaelic learners subsequently learned this port-a-beul from the Barra MacNeils' album and may therefore easily make the logical but incorrect assumption that it has had a long history of circulation in Cape Breton.

There is nothing inherently wrong, of course, with acquiring repertoire from a variety of sources, including recordings. Nor is there anything particularly wrong with learning Scottish repertoire and then circulating it in Cape Breton. A healthy musical tradition is always changing. Newer technologies, such as recordings, provide new means of musical exchange, and musical exchange has always occurred as people travelled, migrated or sent music books back and forth. As with Gaelic singers, Cape Breton and Scottish fiddlers also draw upon the tunes found in each other's traditions. It is part of a vibrant and acceptable cultural exchange. However, anxiety in the Gaelic community can arise if repertoire borrowing occurs without awareness, without knowledge of the existing local repertoires and their histories, and without understanding its impact. When a tune like "Seallaibh Curraigh Eòghainn" becomes popular in Cape Breton, it can mean that puirt-a-beul that were once sung in Cape Breton are ignored and eventually forgotten. Some in the Gaelic community are also anxious about who decides what repertoire to introduce and how. I discuss this more in the next chapter.

On the flip side, if you'll pardon the pun, recordings offer a means to preserve and maintain the Gaelic song tradition in the face of declining numbers of Gaelic speakers on both sides of the Atlantic. With fewer Gaelic speakers, there are fewer people capable of, or interested in, maintaining particular traditions, including song. Even where tradition-bearers do exist, they have fewer opportunities to share their repertoire or acquire new material. Not only does the decline of ceilidh culture and other traditional contexts for song sharing mean that tradition-bearers are unable to transmit their knowledge to a new generation, it also means that tradition-bearers forget some of their repertoire simply because of lack of use and repetition. Without constant exposure and practice, they may also lose their ability to learn new songs quickly by ear. Recordings provide a means of documenting and preserving repertoire in these challenging circumstances and enable its transmission into the future. Mary Jane Lamond, for example, has learned her repertoire from a variety of sources, including archival recordings held in various locations. She has thus been able to learn Gaelic songs directly from native Cape Breton Gaelic speakers and respected tradition-bearers, even though they are long dead. Lamond's recordings, in turn, re-introduce the repertoire to the Cape Breton community that would otherwise have difficulty accessing some archival recordings.

But even as archival recordings provide us with access to forgotten songs and to singers of the past, ethnomusicologist Stephanie Conn reminds us that listening to recordings held in archives in institutions are "most unlike the experience of a live performance because they are unmediated by the social interaction and cultural context with which Gaelic singing is so connected" (Conn 2011: 180; see also Conn 2012, 2013). Archival collections also remain inaccessible to most people because of their location and hours. It is true that archives offer access to songs not otherwise available today, but because archival recordings are dissociated from the living contexts in which they were made, we are left to make of them what we can, without access to the people who made, sang and listened to them or to those people's stories and ideas about them. It's true that archives offer a means of preserving songs in challenging circumstances. However, while learning songs from an archival recording may be necessary, it's not necessarily ideal.

Learning Gaelic, Learning Puirt-a-Beul

Puirt-a-beul are also popular in Gaelic-language classrooms. They are ideal for Gaelic learners because of their simple vocabulary and grammar, repetitive lyrics, overall brevity and amusing topics. They are relatively easy to learn and remember, and they provide a fun way to practise pronunciation and enunciation. Learning any song can also give students a sense of accomplishment. One Gaelic learner and teacher from Halifax explains why puirt-a-beul are so useful in the classroom:

> Puirt are excellent learning tools not only because of repetitive vowels, consonants, words or phrases but also for breaking down barriers between students in a classroom setting. Mistakes are inevitable and equal. These mistakes lead to laughter which relaxes the class so that they are free from self-consciousness very quickly. (Personal communication, May 12, 1999)

The humorous or silly nature of the lyrics is also important, since the genre is fun rather than overly serious. Students can make mistakes and they become part of the silliness of puirt-a-beul, rather than committing a cultural faux pas. Other types of Gaelic songs, especially when they tell sombre tales of lost lives or other tragedies, can be daunting for learners who may feel that they cannot do them justice. Because most other Gaelic songs are much longer and more lyrically complex than puirt-a-beul, the almost inevitable mistakes made when performing them can seem to diminish their importance or even seem disrespectful. One native Gaelic speaker and singer from Scotland describes how learners seem more comfortable singing puirt-a-beul than other types of Gaelic song:

> [Puirt-a-beul] comes across as this throwaway type song. So people don't feel so self-conscious when they're singing it. I feel that people who wouldn't consider themselves normally as "singers," they feel they can get off with singing a wee rhyme, [this] sort of a ditty. A wee port, you know. A verse. (Interview, July 13, 1998)

Puirt-a-beul offer students the means of using their Gaelic language skills within an "authentic" context, not simply an exercise created by the teacher. Students thus engage with the culture without having to be fluent. A Gaelic teacher in Toronto explained why he uses puirt-a-beul in the classroom:

> I feel that as adult learners, we're playing a little bit of catch-up. The children's songs are songs that children know so it's good to know them.... So we do silly songs like, "'S ann an Ìle" ["In Islay"] and "Brochan Lom" ["Thin Porridge"]. Partly because they're part of that children's musical vocabulary but also because they're simple and easy to learn.

In other words, language learners would do well to learn children's song repertoire partly because children's songs offer one way in which young native speakers acquire their language skills (and they are therefore presumably suited to adult language learners as well), and partly because most if not all native Gaelic speakers know these songs and it therefore makes cultural sense for learners to acquire them too.

Brochan lom
Brochan lom, tana lom,   } x 3
Brochan lom sùghain.

Brochan lom 'se tana lom,
'Se brochan lom sùghain

Brochan tana, tana, tana,   } x 3
Brochan lom sùghain,
Brochan lom 'se tana lom,
'Se brochan lom sùghain.

Thugaibh aran do na balaich   } x 3
Leis a' bhrochan sùghain
Brochan lom 'se tana lom,
'Se brochan lom sùghain.

Brochan lom
Plain gruel, thin, plain   } x 3
Plain sowans[5] gruel.
Plain gruel, it's thin, plain
It's plain sowans gruel.

Thin, thin, thin gruel,   } x 3
Plain sowans gruel,
Plain gruel, thin, plain
It's plain sowans gruel.

Give bread to the boys   } x 3
With the sowans gruel
Plain gruel, thin, plain
It's plain sowans gruel.[6]

Some consider puirt-a-beul to be the equivalent of English nursery rhymes. Children's songs and rhymes evolved in part to introduce children to the rhythms and sounds of a language, which is why they are then suitable for an adult language-learning context. I have already discussed in Chapter 1 the association of jigging with children, particularly when it was used to accompany children dancing. So not surprisingly, some people such as Christine Primrose also remember hearing puirt-a-beul used with children:

[Puirt-a-beul] started, or developed, in the home, a lot of them, making up wee ditty songs, you know, sort of using— especially when they have children on their knee. I know that they're called dandling songs, officially, but I remember my Granny, she'd have wee kids on her knee and she'd be singing to them. Maybe a verse or two of [sings a verse of a port-a-beul], things like that. That's the kind of song that I always remember being associated with children, being ... dandled on their knee. (Interviews, July 12-13, 1998)

There are two reasons that puirt-a-beul may be particularly strongly associated with children. The first is that puirt-a-beul are attractive to children for all the same reasons that they are attractive in the adult language classroom: they are short, silly and simple. The second reason has to do more with what kinds of music some adults are willing to sing. As a parent, I have observed and heard many parents sing for their children at playgroups or other child-centred activities when it is clear that they are uncomfortable singing. In other words, adults who otherwise might not sing can sometimes be enticed to sing children's songs. Perhaps they feel it is expected of them or they do it for the sake of their child. Or, perhaps because they once sang nursery rhymes as children themselves, they feel capable of singing them as adults. I would argue that puirt-a-beul may have become associated with children in part because it is the kind of repertoire non-singers are prepared to sing for their children, which then, regardless of whether puirt-a-beul was ever originally intended for children or not, creates its association with children's repertoire.

A question then emerges: Given that some puirt-a-beul are known to be bawdy (see Chapter 4), how could they be children's songs? It turns out that bawdry is actually quite typical of children's song repertoires: "we must expect some earthiness, not to say ribaldry—not to say plain vulgarity—in the earliest versions of some of the rhymes. In the seventeenth and eighteenth centuries, adults were far less squeamish about what was fit for children's ears than they are today" (Baring-Gould and Baring-Gould 1962: 12n2). We know that many folklore and folksong collectors of the late 19th and early 20th centuries carefully avoided anything considered to be of questionable taste. Even if collectors were willing to collect bawdry, editors were unwilling to publish it unless it was edited to conform to Victorian standards of taste. Consequently, when we look at collections of children's lore from this time, they generally appear innocent and wholesome:

> Trusting the collectanea in print—the exceptions are very few—one could only conclude that the youngsters are quite as sexless as their elders. But as much as parents may wish this were the case, the fact is that children learn a good deal about sex and excretion quite early in life. (Cray 1969: xx)

Thus the absence of bawdry could be the result of the collector's (or publisher's) interference rather than an accurate and complete reflection of children's lore. There is therefore no reason to think that Gaelic-speaking children might not have had a substantial collection of bawdy puirt-a-beul at one time, nor that its existence was in any way odd or indicative of poor moral judgement or parenting skills on the part of Gaels. For one thing, bawdry often involves the use of euphemisms, which children might not have fully understood.

In an ethnomusicological survey of studies pertaining to children's song and music, Amanda Minks notes that children's music is learned and created partly through interaction with adults, and that it provides an opportunity for children to experiment with appropriate language and to explore boundaries, including social rules governing appropriate and inappropriate language (2002: 398). Bawdry can actually be understood as a means of teaching children about taboos and reinforcing social standards of acceptability:

> A child who actually uses a taboo word in a song is thereby also affirming the rule against using it. To mention such words casually, without recognizing anything unusual about them, would weaken the power of the taboo, but to introduce them in the formal context of a song that is meant to be shocking affirms that the taboo still exists—and is worth violating. Moreover, children need to know what words are forbidden—reserved, that is, for moments of stress—in polite society. (Knapp and Knapp 1976: 183-84)

Folklorists Opie and Opie argue that children are usually incapable of creating a memorable rhyme on their own and therefore "it is, perhaps, only to be expected that the most memorable verses should turn out to be the work of professional humorists and song-writers" (Opie and Opie 1959: 13-14). In other words, puirt-a-beul may not have been intended for children when first created, but children came to learn and perform them themselves. Such a conclusion reconciles evidence that puirt-a-beul are created by (adult) laypeople and even the occasional bard and yet still wind up as children's songs. Australian oral historian Wendy Lowenstein suggests that "it is ... tempting to see children's rhymes as being passed on independently of adults.... In fact ... parents frequently play an important role" (Lowenstein 1974: 4).

On the other hand, recent scholarship criticizes the assumption that children's culture is a watered-down version of adult culture (e.g., Emberly 2004). Instead, scholars are suggesting that we study children as a unique group in the same way that feminists have argued that we ought to study women separately from men (Chin 2001). Children are perfectly capable of creating their own song texts, and they may not all be sweet and innocent! Indeed, I can remember laughing with a friend as we created a humorous song highly critical of one of our teachers, a song whose lyrics I can still recite today. Although I am not suggesting that children were the primary composers of most puirt-a-beul, it is entirely possible that they created at least some of them.

Conclusions

Ultimately, there is no reason that we must determine whether puirt-a-beul was a genre originally intended for children or adults, for dancers or musicians. It is entirely possible that puirt-a-beul emerged and evolved in response to multiple needs all at once. Indeed, part of the reason that puirt-a-beul remains popular today is no doubt its ability to be used in a variety of contexts for many different purposes. There is much to suggest that they have played, and continue to play, many other roles in Gaelic culture.

This is not really surprising: it is a good indication of a healthy and creative society when it uses materials at hand to fulfill a variety of functions. Just as I used a large book as a practice step for my son to develop climbing skills when the stairs were still too big, or just as I turn my jacket into a pillow on a long plane ride, puirt-a-beul are used creatively among Gaels to meet a variety of needs.

Still, in spite of puirt-a-beul's range of functions, these functions are nevertheless related to one another. After all, if puirt-a-beul were originally created as dance tunes when instruments were not available, then they have a close relationship to instruments, sharing their dance repertoire. It is easy to understand how puirt-a-beul could then be used to teach, share and remember instrumental tunes quite apart from their use in a dance context. Neither is there any surprise that puirt-a-beul, as a dance genre, should be used not just in public dance contexts, but in the more informal home environment as well as entertainment for children. It is not hard to believe that some singers would be attracted to the musical qualities of puirt-a-beul and perform them for their own sake, linking puirt-a-beul to the singing tradition as much as to the dance and instrumental traditions.

We can also understand the many functions fulfilled by puirt-a-beul as part of the inevitable and constant changes that take place in any community and its cultural practices. Even assuming that puirt-a-beul did indeed start as a vocal dance genre in the absence of instruments, there are few occasions today when instrumental music, whether live or recorded, could not be procured. If puirt-a-beul had remained only a substitute for instrumental music, it would have stopped being performed long ago. The changing circumstances of a community yield adjustments to the way traditions are practised, together with shifts in the reasons they are practised. Puirt-a-beul can still be heard today because they are still relevant to the Gaelic community, although perhaps for different reasons than one or two hundred years ago.

At the same time, puirt-a-beul seem to be on the wane in Nova Scotia, even as commercial Gaelic song recordings (which almost invariably include puirt-a-beul) increase in Scotland. In

Scotland, a newly devolved parliament elected in 1999 has resulted in substantial funding for Gaelic language and culture initiatives, augmented by the European Union's interest in supporting minority languages. The build-up to a referendum on Scottish independence in 2014 also fuelled the flames of nationalism, which includes supporting Gaelic language and culture. The political circumstances are very different in Nova Scotia. Although there were frequent puirt-a-beul workshops when I first began researching puirt-a-beul in Cape Breton in the late 1990s, I rarely see them anymore. There are few Gaelic song recordings being released. B&R Heritage Enterprises, which produced a significant number of CDs featuring traditional Nova Scotia Gaelic songs and stories, has closed. The last native Gaelic-speaking fiddler, Joe Peter MacLean, died in 2013. Not incidentally, he had a robust repertoire of puirt-a-beul. Puirt-a-beul are still around, but are far less visible than they were just ten years ago, when global mania for all things Celtic, especially music, brought them to the fore.

Before concluding this chapter, I would like to address the fact that I have drawn quite heavily on literature pertaining to Cape Breton. Part of the reason for this, of course, is that I know the Cape Breton context much better than the Scottish one. But it is also because I am simply not aware of Scottish equivalents to Cape Breton studies like those conducted by Liz Doherty, Virginia Garrison or Jackie Dunn. Although I would love to see a study focusing in particular on puirt-a-beul, there is also a need for more studies contextualizing fiddling practices of the recent past and present: understanding how fiddling and piping styles have developed and changed, how tunes are created and circulated, the contexts in which fiddling and piping are used. Although such studies would not necessarily focus on puirt-a-beul, they would likely address any role that puirt-a-beul might play within them. There is certainly more to learn and say about the history and function of puirt-a-beul.

Chapter 7
Keeping Things in Line: The Role of Puirt-a-Beul in Gaelic Society

In the last two chapters, I have documented a number of functions of puirt-a-beul, including its role in accompanying dance (in both formal and informal contexts); its usefulness in teaching, sharing and remembering instrumental tunes; its place in the song tradition; and its function in language acquisition. In this chapter, I consider yet more of puirt-a-beul's functions, but ones that are less obvious, explicit or overt. As an ethnomusicologist, I am interested not just in studying what music is or what it does within a particular community, but also why it is significant and what it tells us about the community involved. In the previous two chapters, I have examined the dance, music and language roles of puirt-a-beul. In this chapter, I will consider its social functions. I start with a description of an ongoing Cape Breton controversy about whether fiddlers must speak Gaelic in order to play "correctly." After reviewing the positions of people both for and against, I explain why I think this debate has emerged, leading to the suggestion that puirt-a-beul has a cultural gate-keeping function, providing a kind of check point that helps to control access to Gaelic culture. This theory helps to explain why puirt-a-beul continue to have a relatively high profile in Gaelic culture despite their low value among many native and fluent Gaelic speakers.

Speaking Gaelic with the Fiddle

Liz Doherty, in her comprehensive study of the Cape Breton fiddle style, writes, "One of the greatest compliments that can be paid to the Cape Breton fiddler is having 'the Gaelic' in their music" (1996: 303). It was a common response as she asked her consultants what made Cape Breton fiddlers excellent: "throughout my fieldwork, the phrase came up again and again in descriptions of style" (1996: 305). For example, she quotes Sheldon MacInnes, the son of the respected Cape Breton fiddler Dan Joe MacInnis, and a musician in his own right:

> I hear it in so many of the old-time violinists, a certain sound, a certain lilt, a certain style, a certain format that appears to have been influenced to a large extent by the language and the Gaelic singing.... the difference I hear in the music among contemporary violinists and I hear in more of the so-called traditional violinists, may well be that absence of the language ... that's not to say that the music is something less, but to my ear it's something different. (Qtd. in Doherty 1996: 304)

Anthropologist Jonathan Dembling likewise encountered the frequent assertion that instrumental music is linked to language: "The assertion of a Gaelic component to the music of Cape Breton essentially boils down to a phrase I heard over and again during my fieldwork: 'You play it as you would sing it'" (2005: 187). Cape Breton fiddler Father Angus Morris explained the relationship between language and music in his own fiddling:

> My mother had words to some of the older tunes and would jig them around the house. You'd listen to the old people jigging tunes to themselves and it'd be very Scotchy. So you'd try to jig it that way yourself and then repeat yourself on the violin. (Qtd. in Wilson and Dunlay 2002: 13)

Puirt-a-beul are central to the belief that the fiddle style is linked to the Gaelic language, since the lyrics are said to provide key information about rhythm, ornamentation and other musical features.

Doug MacPhee, a well-known Cape Breton piano accompanist, described Mary MacDonald's fiddling: "She could play a strathspey and you could cut the Gaelic, you could feel the Gaelic accent in her playing, just as it was in her speaking voice ... her voice was up and down with the Gaelic" (qtd. in Doherty 1996: 305). MacPhee refers to Mary MacDonald's Gaelic "accent" in her fiddling. In language, "accent" refers to the prominence of a syllable. Languages have accented and unaccented syllables, and words sound incorrect if the wrong syllable is accented. Just think, for example, of the difference between saying "AC-cent" and "ac-CENT"; the latter just doesn't sound right in North America. The word "accent" is also used when talking about music when referring to a note that has special emphasis and stands out for listeners. Doug MacPhee is therefore connecting linguistic accent with musical accent. He argues that one could hear a distinctly Gaelic accent or rhythm in Mary MacDonald's fiddling.

Alexander MacDonald, an amateur fiddler from Mabou with Gaelic-speaking parents, also frequently heard this compliment (A. MacDonald 1996: 9), as did John Shaw when he spoke to Gaelic speakers in the community. Revered Gaelic tradition-bearer Joe Neil MacNeil was particularly articulate:

> When I hear some people playing [tunes] I'll recognize that they do not speak Gaelic ... they don't have the swing....
> Some of the younger generation [without Gaelic], they're following the style that they acquired from the older people [with Gaelic], but they miss part of it and when it comes to new tunes, they don't achieve the flavour at all. (Qtd. in Shaw 1992-1993: 41)

This quotation is actually a translation of Joe Neil MacNeil's original Gaelic comments. John Shaw has translated one phrase as "they don't have the swing," but the original Gaelic ("*chan eil am blas aca*") could also be translated as "they don't have the accent." However it is translated, the essence remains the same: some people hear a pattern of accents in the instrumental playing of some musicians that they link directly to accent patterns in the Gaelic language.

Although the above quotations were all made by Cape Bretoners about the Cape Breton fiddle tradition, the connection between language and music is significant in Scotland as well. For example, one of the earliest explicit statements about the connection between fiddle style and puirt-a-beul dates from 1884:

> I was much struck by a remark I heard made a few days ago, by one of our very best reel players, to a class of young men who were learning the violin, and which was to this effect: "Every old reel and strathspey, being originally a 'port-a-beul,' has its own words. Now, if you wish to play with genuine taste, keep singing the words in your mind when you are playing the tune. (Charles Stewart, *The Killin Collection of Gaelic Songs*, 1884: x; qtd. in Newton 2009: 272)

Much more recently, the Ceòlas summer school in South Uist was started in 1996 with the goal of providing a context in which music, song and language would be studied holistically, rather than as separate cultural elements. The respected CD *Fhuair Mi Pòg* (I Got a Kiss, 1998) by singer Margaret Stewart and piper Allan MacDonald was created as a means of demonstrating the interconnectedness between song and instrumental music. A number of singers have also arranged puirt-a-beul recordings to feature a fiddle at some point playing the associated tune, emphasizing the connection between song and the instrumental tradition. Jonathan Dembling heard the belief articulated in interviews with Scots:

> One Gaelic-speaking piper who went to Cape Breton in the late 1960s felt an instant recognition when he first heard the fiddle players there: "We were hearing stuff that wasn't being played over here [in Scotland], but was actually being sung over there. You know, stuff that my father would be singing,

tunes like "Caberfeidh." And we had been brought up playing them on the pipes in a different style, yet the fiddlers
over in Cape Breton were playing them as my father would
be singing them." (2005: 188; see Chapter 5 for the lyrics to
"Cabar Fèidh.")

And yet the notion that Cape Breton or Scottish fiddling is
inextricably connected to the Gaelic language is highly controversial. After all, the vast majority of today's Nova Scotian fiddlers
do not speak Gaelic fluently. Quite a number do not speak Gaelic
at all. To suggest that the Gaelic language is necessary to play the
Cape Breton fiddle style properly can be seen as threatening, as
it suggests that the many fiddlers who pride themselves on their
playing are not actually fully competent, or cannot be considered
fiddlers of the "true" Cape Breton style. Worse, it suggests that
they have not done their due diligence to maintain the tradition if
they have not mastered the language. Such a claim also marginal-
izes the contributions of fiddlers associated with other cultures
(and possibly other languages) to the Cape Breton fiddle style,
including French, Mi'kmaq and Irish fiddlers.

Moreover, there simply is no incontrovertible evidence that
there is a direct connection between the Gaelic language and the
Cape Breton fiddle style: "when queried on the exact nature of
this Gaelic influence ... none of my informants were forthcoming
with a satisfactory explanation" (Doherty 1996: 305). Alexander
MacDonald expresses a similar frustration: "I have also lost
patience with those who say there is a link but refuse to or cannot identify it while criticizing today's players for abandoning it"
(MacDonald 1998: 5). Dembling likewise spoke with Scots who
dismissed any connection between Gaelic and the Cape Breton
playing style:

> One Hebridean fiddler said that the Cape Breton style didn't
> sound "remotely Gaelic" to him. He immediately qualified
> this statement by granting that one particular reel, "Am
> Muileann Dubh" (The Black Mill), was linguistically sound,
> but described another tune as "total chaos" because it was

played for step dancing. Another fiddler from the same island described the style as "Scottish music with a French accent," no closer than bluegrass to Scottish music. Another fiddler from the Highlands, who learned Gaelic, also failed to hear any linguistic connection: "It doesn't convey any emotion to me. It's very brittle, and I don't believe that true Highlanders or West Coasters would have played like that. I think we're very soft people. I think that the way we speak is soft and flowing." (Dembling 2005: 188)

This controversy has led to several studies that have attempted to analyze the claims that the Gaelic language and fiddling are connected. They virtually all hinge on puirt-a-beul, given that these combine fiddle tunes and the language in their lyrics. Jackie Dunn, a Cape Breton fiddler, pianist and step dancer (but non-Gaelic speaker), wrote her undergraduate thesis on the topic (1991). She used a Visi-Pitch machine and Yokoeawa 3655E Analyzing Recorder Computer to analyze the frequencies of fiddle tunes played by a fiddler and the corresponding spoken puirt-a-beul lyrics. She anticipated that the pronunciation and stress of the spoken lyrics would correspond to the contour of the fiddle tunes. Her use of spoken rather than sung puirt-a-beul was designed to eliminate musical modifications and result in the "natural pro-nunciation and stress of the Gaelic words" (Dunn 1991: 82).

Dunn did indeed find correlations between peak points in frequency in the fiddle tunes and puirt-a-beul. Since frequency defines pitch, this finding indicates that there are similar pitch contours between fiddle tunes and spoken Gaelic lyrics. However, this is not to say that the frequencies or pitches actually matched, only that they went up and down in the same places. As Dunn has noted, the research is problematic because the tunes and puirt-a-beul could not be aligned precisely in terms of placement in time in their graphic representations since they were not performed at the exact same tempo. Moreover, Dunn does not detail who the fiddler and speaker were, nor their familiarity with Gaelic and puirt-a-beul. Another problem is that Dunn's research considers frequency (pitch) rather than rhythm, accent and duration, which are the elements emphasized in the quotations above about the relationship between music and language. Pitch is not essential to meaning in Gaelic (unlike the case with some other languages, such as Chinese), but rhythm—particularly duration—is. Dunn concludes, "There is great difficulty determining the exact effect the Gaelic language has had on the fiddling style brought from Scotland to Cape Breton. The entire subject seems to be very vague and almost indefinable" (Dunn 1991: 93).

Dunn's study is innovative because it attempts to compare fiddle tunes and puirt-a-beul directly and objectively using computers: a scientific analysis. No one else has tried anything similar before or since. However, by focusing on frequency, the analysis was limited to aspects of pitch, volume and timbre. Meanwhile, those who argue that a knowledge of puirt-a-beul and Gaelic is necessary for the correct rendering of fiddle tunes usually emphasize the role of rhythm, an aspect not addressed in Dunn's study.

Doherty also considered the relationship between the Gaelic language and Cape Breton fiddling style in her ethnomusicological dissertation. Although she does accept that language has some influence on fiddle music, she does not believe that its current influence is direct, immediate or substantial:

> The demise of the Gaelic language in Cape Breton has been responsible for some degree of change in the fiddle style. Gaelic sources of tunes [i.e., *puirt-a-beul*] for instance have largely become redundant, and those tunes initially acquired from Gaelic sources and which have been maintained, are done so without reference to their origins. Musical changes stimulated by the changing fate of the language were never immediate however. The rhythms of the Gaelic language had already become ingrained in the musical sound before there was a threat to the continuation of the language.... Many of the characteristics of the language had already become established and accepted in purely musical terms.

Doherty's suggestion that Gaelic linguistic inflections have long been integrated into the Cape Breton fiddle style—meaning that a "Gaelic style" continues to be transmitted and audible even though fiddlers may not themselves speak the language—would certainly be embraced by non-Gaelic-speaking musicians. She goes on to address whether the decline of the Gaelic language in Cape Breton is the cause of changes to the fiddle style:

> Some confusion surrounds the issue however, since there has been some degree of change in the rhythmic character of the fiddle music in recent times. For instance, the rhythmic figure, the Scots snap, once found in both strathspeys and reels, is now part of the strathspey only. Changes such as this, I would argue, although ironically coinciding with linguistic changes in the community, are not the result of these changes, but rather reflections of changes being instigated from within the music itself. The greatest problem inherent in the language–music relationship is not one of immediate stylistic change.... For the majority of today's fiddlers, the music and the language are perceived as two separate entities, and I would postulate that a resurgence in the language would not invoke a significant musical change at this stage. (1996: 307)

In other words, Doherty suggests that whatever linguistic influence Gaelic may have had on instrumental music in the past has been absorbed into its performance style and now exists independently of the language. Therefore, even if Gaelic is no longer used in Cape Breton, its influence on fiddle performance will continue to be heard and transmitted as part of the fiddle style. Rather than attribute any changes in musical style, such as the loss of the Scotch snap from reels, to the demise of Gaelic, she suggests that they are a result of processes of musical change; such changes result among fiddlers (internally) rather than from a decline in Gaelic-language use. The fact that such musical changes occurred at the same time that Gaelic was declining in Cape Breton is coincidental in Doherty's argument.

Glenn Graham takes a similar position in his book, *The Cape Breton Fiddle: Making and Maintaining Tradition.* His research is based primarily on a survey completed by eighteen people active in the Cape Breton fiddling tradition. Every single one of his respondents believed that Gaelic had an influence on fiddling (G. Graham 2006: 62). However, all but one disagreed that fiddlers have to speak Gaelic to have a Gaelic sound, and the one person who agreed was not absolute in her assertion. Consequently, Graham, a fiddler himself, doesn't believe that a fiddler needs to speak the Gaelic language to have a Gaelic fiddle style:

> While it might be desirable to speak Gaelic, it is still pos-
> sible with something less than fluency to obtain sufficient
> experience of the language to gain a feeling for its distinc-
> tive equivalent violin sounds. For it is the cultivation of an
> intuitive recognition of the language's rhythms and accents
> combined with digital ornamentation [and here "digital"
> refers to the fingers] and bowing applications, that help to
> create a Gaelic sound in the fiddle, not the ability to speak it.
> (G. Graham 2006: 64)

Graham, like Doherty, argues that the Gaelic sound is already embedded in the traditional Cape Breton fiddle style; as long as the Gaelic-inflected playing style is transmitted, the Gaelic sound will continue, regardless of the player's ability to speak Gaelic. Graham suggests that one way the Gaelic retains its influence on the fiddle tradition is through its relationship to the piping tradition, which was more directly influenced by Gaelic. Many traditional fiddle tunes and their performance style seem to be directly linked to traditional piping tunes, scales, and ornaments. Be that as it may, we really do not know whether or how these particular pipe sounds reflect the Gaelic language any more than we really understand how the language may be manifested in fiddle performance. Even if we accept that the traditional piping tradition at one time did reflect the Gaelic language, there is little to prove that Cape Breton fiddlers have adopted Gaelic-inflected piping sounds in a manner that continues to reflect the language's influence.

It is perhaps especially significant that Graham does not indicate how many of his survey respondents speak Gaelic or to what

degree. He himself admits that he knows "a little Gaelic" (2006: 64). It is not entirely surprising that non-Gaelic-speaking fiddlers would defend their playing despite their lack of Gaelic fluency. If they believed that Gaelic fluency was significant to the fiddle style but could not claim it themselves, they would in effect be saying that their playing was deficient. We might also question the extent to which survey respondents are able to evaluate the Gaelic influence on their own and others' playing if they are not themselves Gaelic speakers.

Dembling likewise accepts that Gaelic may have influenced fiddling in the past, but he suggests a different theory to explain the loss of a Gaelic-inflected instrumental performance style. He suggests that it has been appropriated by non-Gaels, just as other markers of Highland identity, including kilts, bagpipes, tartan and Gaelic song, have been (2005: 191). In this argument, non-Gaels are invested in Highland and Highland-derived instrumental music (i.e., Cape Breton music) but are not able, or are unwilling, to learn its linguistic component. They therefore argue that it was never central to the style to begin with. They are consequently able to dismiss any language-based criticisms of their performance style and claim to "know" and be able to perform an "authentic" Highland style without fluency in the language.

On the other hand, Dembling observes that non-Gaelic speakers are often the very ones claiming that there is a relationship between the Gaelic language and instrumental tradition in the first place. For example, he recounts the somewhat controversial origins of the Ceòlas project, a Gaelic music summer school held annually in South Uist, one of the Gaelic-speaking Hebridean islands in Scotland:

> A non-Gaelic-speaker from the Lowlands [Hamish Moore], with significant cultural capital as a respected piper, sets up a school in the heart of the *Gàidhealtachd,* hiring several tutors from Cape Breton to teach a largely non-Gaelic student body music and dance styles that are touted as more Gaelic than those practiced by the locals. (2005: 192)

He also quotes a fiddler on the subject: "I never have heard the strathspeys—Highland Gaelic strathspeys—played with such life, and such Gaelicness in them or something, it's just unbelievable. Even though I don't speak the language" (qtd. in Dembling 2005: 190). It is hard to accept the claims for a Gaelic-inflected instrumental style when the claims are made by those who do not even know what Gaelic inflections might sound like.

Ethnologist John Shaw, however, feels strongly that there has traditionally been a Gaelic-inflected sound in Cape Breton fiddling. He refuses to discount those who claim that it is possible to tell the difference between a fiddler with and without Gaelic. And for good reason, given the significant number of people arguing this position. Based on comparisons with the fiddle and language situations in areas close to Cape Breton, he predicts the loss of the Cape Breton fiddle tradition should the Gaelic language be lost:

> One of the very few remaining mainland Gaelic informants, Donald Cameron of Beaver Meadow, Antigonish County, has observed that in his youth—some eighty years ago—mainland fiddlers played to a standard as high as that maintained in Cape Breton today. Yet after the demise of the language in the district some two generations back, the line of transmission for fiddling has also disappeared. (1992-1993: 43)

In counter-response, some name Buddy MacMaster (one of the most significant and influential Cape Breton fiddlers in recent history), Natalie MacMaster and Ashley MacIsaac, none of whom speak Gaelic, as strong exponents of the Cape Breton fiddling tradition, and who are therefore proof that there is no direct connection between language and music. But Shaw argues:

> The small number of younger musicians regarded as accomplished traditional players by older Gaels have in common an unusual degree of musical ability, Gaelic-speaking parents, and strong family traditions of violin music. If the criterion of Gaelic-speaking parents is the effective one, it

would be surprising for a Gaelic style to be transmitted over more than one post-Gaelic generation. (1992-1993: 43-44)

It's worth observing that Natalie MacMaster's children are getting a very strong exposure to her fiddle and dance style. Even at very young ages, they are demonstrating talent in both areas, easy to see in the online videos of their stage performances. It is clear that her children are immersed in Cape Breton musical and dance styles. It is therefore not at all certain that any Gaelic influence in the music will stop with their mother. On the other hand, their father, Donnell Leahy, is a high-profile fiddler in the Ottawa Valley style. It remains to be seen how the Ottawa Valley style influences the playing and dancing of the MacMaster-Leahy children.

Shaw's prediction echoes one expressed in the Cape Breton Gaelic community:

> Now Michael MacLean, he can give music a flavour that others can't, and so could John Willie Campbell and Alec Francis MacKay and such players. And, well, some of the younger generation, they're following the style that they acquired from the older people, but they miss part of it, and when it comes to new tunes, they don't achieve the flavour at all. And I was saying to Michael MacLean, as I see it, at the end of another fifteen years when the older generation of fiddlers will be gone and the younger ones will have entered into their own new style, it will be just about as difficult for you to hear any more of the old style as it would to get copies of the tunes played by the Pied Piper.... So the net result over time will be that the old Gaelic flavour in the tunes will be lost. No one will know then whether he's close to it or not—whether he's close to it or not—if he doesn't have the word(s) to go with it). (Joe Neil MacNeil, qtd. in Shaw 1992-1993: 41, translated from Gaelic)

Buddy MacMaster did indeed have Gaelic-speaking parents. Natalie MacMaster has spoken about her grandmother, who was known to sing puirt-a-beul as a way of singing or transmitting a tune. According to Shaw, these musicians inherited a Gaelic-flavoured musical style because of their close generational proximity to Gaelic speakers. However, if Shaw's predictions are correct, then their children and grandchildren will be unlikely to inherit a Gaelic-inflected fiddle style.

Glenn Graham responds, however, by noting that recordings can maintain the Gaelic fiddle sound despite the loss of linguistic fluency. Shaw's argument suggests that fiddlers learn directly (face-to-face) from the previous generation. Consequently, as each generation is further removed from Gaelic, the fiddle style will also change to reflect the language less and less. By contrast, Graham's point is that technology now enables fiddlers to learn from a range of musicians from any generation or geographical locale. Fiddlers today are not limited to learning tunes and performance style in a face-to-face context. Thus, even if today's fiddlers do not speak Gaelic, they can still learn to play with a Gaelic-inflected style by listening to the performance styles of fluent Gaelic-speaking fiddlers from the past (G. Graham 2006: 67; see also Dunn 1991: 61, 63).

Regardless of where or how they learned them, fiddlers have historically used puirt-a-beul to identify and remember tunes, as well as to transmit them, as discussed in the previous chapter: "Recently a younger non-Gaelic-speaker, now viewed by Gaels as a successful exponent of the older fiddle style, consulted Lauchie MacLellan for the port-a-beul versions of tunes in order to gain a better understanding of the music" (1992-1993: 44). Certainly the transmission of fiddle tunes via a song genre with Gaelic lyrics suggests that language could influence instrumental style. Shaw argues that puirt-a-beul lyrics embody a tune's rhythm. In the Gaelic language, vowel length is significant since the "same" word spoken with a lengthened and shortened vowel can have two completely different meanings. For example, *sabaid* and *sàbaid*, spelled the same except for the accent above the "a," both sound like "SAH-pitch" except the latter has a longer "AH" sound. The first word means "fight" and the second word means "sabbath." Joe Neil MacNeil explained to Shaw that the natural or linguistic rhythm of the lyrics ought to dictate the tune's rhythm. MacNeil equated "the post-Gaelic renditions [of fiddle tunes] which ignore the long-short contrast to a foreign language" (Shaw 1992-1993: 44). One of Jonathan Dembling's interviewees highlights the value of puirt-a-beul's rhythm:

> In the old recordings of puirt-a-beul, it's not the tune that matters, it's the rhythm, that's the ... important thing. Like the singers might not have a note of music in their head, from what it sounds like, but they're being recorded singing obviously because they're respected in the community for singing it. But what you get is the rhythm, you don't get a tune, you get rhythm. (Qtd. in Dembling 2005: 187)

Although rhythm is key to the relationship between puirt-a-beul and fiddle tunes, puirt-a-beul lyrics can sometimes convey other musical information too, as I have noted in Chapter 4. According to another of Shaw's interviewees, singer Lauchie MacLellan, puirt-a-beul lyrics occasionally also codify appropriate fiddle ornamentation (1992-1993: 46). Author June Skinner Sawyers explains: "The Gaelic language adds another important element to the Cape Breton fiddle style. The ornamentation of the melodies try to emulate as accurately as possible the nuances and inflections of the Gaelic tongue in the form of grace notes or accents of the bow" (2000: 76). Take, for example, "Còta Mòr Ealasaid" ("Elizabeth's Big Coat"), a well-known fiddle tune in both Scotland and Cape Breton. Note that some of the lyrics correspond to a rhythm consisting of two sixteenth notes and an eighth note (e.g., measure 2, beat 2 in Fig. 13).[1] This rhythm is commonly played as a "cut" on the fiddle, a particular kind of ornament.

In the end, I must agree with Alexander MacDonald and Elizabeth Doherty insofar as there is no incontrovertible evidence linking puirt-a-beul (or Gaelic language in general) with fiddle style. An interesting experiment would be to locate recordings of fiddlers with varying degrees of Gaelic fluency, and play them for a number of people, also with varying degrees of Gaelic fluency, to see who could identify the Gaelic-speaking fiddlers. Such an

Fig. 13. "Còta Mòr Ealasaid," transcribed by Chris McDonald from a recording by Cliar (2005).[2]

experiment would assist in determining whether Gaelic speakers can indeed notice a qualitative difference between Gaelic-speaking and non-Gaelic speaking fiddlers. If the fiddle tunes included some associated with puirt-a-beul and others not associated with any Gaelic lyrics, the experiment would also suggest whether all fiddle tunes have the capacity of exhibiting a "Gaelic flavour," or whether such a flavour is restricted to tunes associated with specific words. However, even this experiment could not indicate causality. Just because some musicians might play in a style defined as "Gaelic" doesn't mean that the style came from the Gaelic language. Co-existence doesn't necessarily mean that one caused the other.

Moreover, it is not always clear that everyone is using the term "Gaelic" in the same way. For language activists and Gaelic speakers, it is generally used to refer to how the music reflects the Gaelic language, particularly its rhythms. But for others, the term "Gaelic" may be used more as an adjective that describes a distinctive *cultural* style, rather than a specifically linguistic one. To clarify with a different example, consider how the term "English" can be used to refer to a cultural style affiliated with

England without necessarily referring to the language specifically. "English tea," for example, doesn't mean that a particular tea has some kind of link to the English language. It's possible that some of the speakers quoted above, particularly non-Gaelic speakers, use "Gaelic" in the same way: to refer to a distinctive style associated with Gaelic-speaking areas but not necessarily directly linked to the language.

Whatever the challenges of determining how the term "Gaelic" is being used by different people, I do agree with John Shaw that the importance of the connection between music and language cannot be dismissed. Too many people have argued for the connection to dismiss the claim lightly. However, I myself am less interested in proving the connection than in exploring why some people are so adamant that it exists. Based on my own research and observations, I would argue that such a connection is particularly important as a means of linking the various elements of Gaelic culture, including language, song, music, folklore and dance, so as to maintain and strengthen them all equally.

A Cultural Linchpin

If the Gaelic language is to survive, it must be relevant to the people who learn and speak it. One of the arguments I hear against learning Gaelic is that it is of "no use." By "use," people generally mean economic use: in Canada and, until recently, in Scotland, there have been few jobs that require knowledge of the Gaelic language. Meanwhile, French fluency, for example, can open doors, particularly in Canada. Economic considerations are even more significant for those living in traditional Gaidhealtachds on both sides of the Atlantic, for they have long been economically depressed areas. Cape Breton has a high unemployment rate and a protracted history of out-migration as young people leave to find jobs elsewhere in Canada and the United States. One can understand why people might choose to invest their time and energy in acquiring knowledge and skills that might lead more directly to gainful employment.

For Gaelic language activists (and for minority language activists more generally), however, the language has a value quite apart from economic considerations. For some, Gaelic is important for its heritage value: it connects people to their pasts, to their ancestors, to their homelands, and to their family and community cultures. The Gaelic language is part of their identity, and learning, speaking, or even just hearing Gaelic provides a means of expressing who they are. For others, its value lies in its ability to express a worldview that they believe cannot be articulated as well (or at all) in another language such as English. As a simple example, we might consider colours in English and Gaelic. In traditional Gaelic, one word encompasses both blue and green: *gorm*. Commonly translated as "blue," it is also used to describe the colour of the sea and grass. Meanwhile, Gaelic has two words for red: *ruadh* and *dearg*. "Ruadh," perhaps best translated as "russet" or "copper," is used to describe an orange-red shade and is most often used to refer to hair colour. Meanwhile, "dearg" can also refer to an orange-red shade, such as when it is used to refer to the colour of salmon or a flame, but it can also refer to a more scarlet shade of red. This simple example illustrates how language affects the way that we categorize, perceive, and make sense of the world. To lose the Gaelic language would be to lose a unique way of perceiving the world and all the potential insights inherent in such a worldview.

Gaelic is also valuable because it contributes to a diversity of global cultures. The United Nations Educational, Scientific and Cultural Organization's (UNESCO's) Universal Declaration on Cultural Diversity states:

> Culture takes diverse forms across time and space. This diversity is embodied in the uniqueness and plurality of the identities of the groups and societies making up humankind. As a source of exchange, innovation and creativity, cultural diversity is as necessary for humankind as biodiversity is for

nature. In this sense, it is the common heritage of humanity and should be recognized and affirmed for the benefit of present and future generations. (UNESCO 2001)

Our efforts to protect endangered species stem from our belief that diverse wildlife is needed to maintain a healthy planet. Our laws against monopolies in the corporate world speak to our belief that a variety of businesses work in the best interest of consumers. The pride Canadians take in defining their country as multicultural attests to the value placed on ethnic and cultural diversity. There is a growing body of scholarship identifying the ways in which the sustainability of one part is related to the sustainability of another part, and by extension, the sustainability of the whole. For example, sustainable agricultural practices support both environmental sustainability and sustainable farming business. As another example, culturally specific knowledge about wildlife, such as Indigenous forms of knowledge in North America, contribute to our understanding and maintenance of biological diversity and a healthy environment. From such a perspective, Gaelic does not have to *do* anything to make it worth preserving; it is valuable in and of itself, and perhaps in ways that we cannot yet see or recognize.

But while many might accept that Gaelic is valuable simply because all languages are valuable, not everyone is prepared to spend the considerable time, effort and even money to become fluent. Something must inspire and motivate Gaelic speakers to use their language and non-speakers to learn it. One motivating factor might be the assertion that popular cultural expressions such as music and dance that do not *seem* to be dependent on language actually *are* dependent upon it. The argument that fiddlers cannot play properly without Gaelic fluency could inspire fiddlers to learn the language—or so the hope goes.

I do not want to suggest that the claim that Gaelic fluency is necessary to play the fiddle, or, for that matter, to engage in other cultural activities, is a fabrication resulting from a desire to increase the number of Gaelic learners and speakers. Rather, my point is that it is significant that this claim is being made explicitly and at this particular moment in time, when the Gaelic language is threatened both in Nova Scotia and Scotland. The debate over the relationship between the Gaelic language and musical style is quite recent. As long as no one was concerned with the loss of Gaelic, there was no need to make such a claim. In fact, even assuming that Gaelic fluency is indeed necessary for distinctive styles of fiddling, dancing and other non-linguistic cultural expressions, Gaelic speakers might never even have thought about it simply because there was no need to think about it.

My job as an ethnomusicologist is to consider why this particular claim is being asserted at this particular time. Any number of values and ideas could be significant to, and expressed about, Gaelic language and music. But to my mind it is significant that it is *this* particular issue that is being highlighted and debated. Rather than engage in the debate, I prefer to analyze why the debate exists, and why it has emerged now. In addition to believing that the "Gaelic in the fiddle" debate has emerged in order to encourage more people to learn the language, I would like to suggest that puirt-a-beul remain important in Gaelic culture because they function as a "cultural linchpin" or a nexus point, connecting and integrating diverse strands of expressive culture, including language, music, dance and storytelling. They support an argument in which language and language-related expressive arts are necessary for fiddlers and dancers to learn.

At one point, the various strands of Gaelic culture, including storytelling, song composition, dancing and music, were equally strong, often performed by the same people in the same venues. For example, in *The Cape Breton Ceilidh*, step dancers repeatedly speak of people who combined two or more talents, including fiddling, piping, step dancing, singing and storytelling. Jackie Dunn, the fiddler who wrote her undergraduate thesis about puirt-a-beul and fiddling, is also a pianist and step dancer. Natalie MacMaster and Ashley MacIsaac are also both known as step dancers and pianists as well as fiddlers. Finlay "Philip" MacDonald was a noted step dancer and "a beautiful Gaelic singer" (MacGillivray 1988: 83). Joe Neil MacNeil was primarily known as a storyteller, but had a deep knowledge of songs as well. Rod C. MacNeil is known for his songs, but whenever I visit, he pulls out his fiddle and we play together. At one time, it would have been quite common for fiddlers to be Gaelic singers and storytellers as well as instrumentalists. Traditionally, ceilidhs provided the venues in which these various talents were integrated, and gave an equal opportunity for any and all visitors to share whatever talents they had. As Michael Kennedy notes, they would have provided situations in which fiddlers "rubbed up against Gaelic song, piping, dancing, and a host of other traditions on a regular basis," helping to create a Gaelic-influenced fiddle performance style (Kennedy 2001: 194).

Triskele, a group of young Cape Breton performers, staged weekly shows in Port Hawkesbury in 2000 in order to introduce tourists to Cape Breton Gaelic culture. Their show demonstrates the ways in which various Gaelic cultural forms are interrelated and presented as such. It starts with the MC's dramatic claim that the musical culture does not even require instruments and musicians to survive. To illustrate, Colin Watson sings puirt-a-beul to accompany Melody Cameron's step dancing. Later in the show, Colin tells a story that accompanies a port-a-beul. In the story, a man continually loses his cattle in the woods. One day when looking for them, he hears the most beautiful music he has ever heard and follows it to a fairy mound (a fairy dwelling place). He enters the mound and dances with them all night. But, as a human, he is forbidden to interact with the fairies. When he is discovered in the morning, he is told that he cannot return home for a year and a day unless he can clear all the bracken from a particular hill. Try as he might, he can't clear the bracken. Each time he clears one side and moves to the other, the ferns on the first side grow back. And so he continues to try to clear the ferns for the entire 366 days. He composes and sings a port-a-beul while he works:

Tha Mi Sgìth
Tha mi sgìth, 's mi leam fhìn
Buain na ranaich, buain na ranaich,
Tha mi sgìth, 's mi leam fhìn

Buain na ranaich daonnan.

Cùl an tomain, bràigh an tomain
Cùl an tomain bhòidhich
Cùl an tomain, bràigh an tomain
H-uile latha nam aonar.

> **Cutting Ferns**
> I am tired, and I'm on my own
> Cutting the bracken, cutting the bracken
> I am tired, and I'm on my own
> Forever cutting the bracken.
>
> On the backside of the hill, on the front slope of the hill
> On the backside of the beautiful hill
> On the backside of the hill, on the front slope of the hill
> Every day by myself.[3]

After the story and song, the fiddlers play their instrumental version of the tune, demonstrating the connection between song, story and fiddle tunes.

Interestingly, "Tha Mi Sgìth" does not seem to have circulated much in Nova Scotia until it was recorded by John Allan Cameron on his album *Freeborn Man* (1979). Even in Scotland, it seems to have been a relatively recent addition to the puirt-a-beul repertoire, for it does not appear in any of the early collections of puirt-a-beul, and most recordings of it in the Tobar an Dualchais collection[4] date from the 1970s and later, although there is a recording of Annie Arnott, a key Scottish source of puirt-a-beul, singing this song in 1954. So while this song and story encapsulate traditional relationships between various forms of Gaelic cultural expression, "Tha Mi Sgìth" itself does not seem to have had a long tradition in either Gaelic Scotland or Nova Scotia. However, the instrumental tune, "Cutting Ferns," was documented in the popular tune collection, the *Athole Collection* (1884), in which Stewart-Robertson describes the tune as "very old." Regardless of the history of "Tha Mi Sgìth," Triskele's show, together with various community concerts, suggests that Gaelic culture has historically been integrated and interrelated.

However, whatever past practices may have been, there is at present an imbalance and segregation between Gaelic music, song, language, dance and other cultural expressions. While there currently seems to be a healthy number of fiddlers and step dancers in Cape Breton, there is a steeply declining number of Gaelic speakers, singers and storytellers. Where once it was common for Gaelic speakers to have talents as musicians and singers, as dancers and storytellers, there now appears to be a widening divide: those arts requiring the Gaelic language (song and storytelling) are declining, while those not requiring the Gaelic language (fiddling, piping and step dancing) are at least being maintained, if not strengthening. If the Gaelic culture is to exist holistically, then the language-based components must be bolstered. One way to do that is to emphasize the connections between cultural forms, and to promote their integration as necessary rather than simply ideal. The language is consequently promoted as necessary to musicians and dancers (hence the argument that a "true" Cape Breton fiddler "has the Gaelic"). If every musician and dancer learned Gaelic, the language would perhaps again be viable as a living language.

However, the assertion that Gaelic culture is integrated and holistic seems to have been articulated explicitly only relatively recently. Of course, there would have been no need to draw attention to this aspect of Gaelic culture so long as community members did not feel that it was threatened. This self-conscious claim corresponds with efforts to protect and revive the Gaelic language. For example, there are very few references to puirt-a-beul in *A Cape Breton Ceilidh*, suggesting that puirt-a-beul have not accompanied step dancing for some time—certainly not within living memory for most people. Historically, they appear to have played a limited role in Cape Breton Gaelic culture. Obviously there has been no recent shortage of fiddlers available for dances and ceilidhs that would necessitate puirt-a-beul. But puirt-a-beul have taken on renewed importance in recent years due to their ability to connect music and dancing to language, story and song. They have become a tool used in the efforts to revive the language, and central to the notion that Gaelic culture is integrated and interrelated in nature.

The few times I have seen puirt-a-beul used to accompany step dancing have been in the context of staged concerts or shows, often meant to inform locals and tourists about Gaelic cultural history. Such events construct an ideal vision of the culture: a culture in which dancing, music, language, song and folktales are all interconnected and necessary to each other, and a culture in which people with different talents are all equally heard, seen and encouraged. The fact that puirt-a-beul are carefully included in such events, and that they are explicitly and directly linked to fiddle music and dance (despite the fact that they apparently have not played a significant role in either practice for some time), strongly suggests that puirt-a-beul are important not simply because they provide dance accompaniment, but because they can be presented as providing a point of connection in a network of cultural elements. One fluent Gaelic learner suggested this during an interview:

> [Puirt-a-beul are a] kind of a bridge, I guess. Puirt-a-beul can be a bridge to those interested in music to see ... that there's a language base to the whole tradition. And I think they're very important like that because, as far as I can see, it was all kind of connected. It was all language, song, story, you know, piping, fiddling. (Interview, July 16, 1998)

"Fosgail an Doras": Puirt-a-Beul's Gatekeeping Function

I have been focusing on the social value of puirt-a-beul. They serve to connect various components of Gaelic culture and therefore demonstrate the necessity of the language's survival for the proper maintenance of Gaelic culture as a whole. They also serve to attract people to the culture, drawing tourist dollars and language learners. It is therefore no surprise that puirt-a-beul are readily found in Cape Breton at a range of venues and in a variety of contexts. What surprised me, however, was the vehemence with which some people rejected puirt-a-beul and others denied their existence and role in the community. For example, when I first met Jamie MacNeil, whose parents were Gaelic speakers and who became a fluent Gaelic speaker as an adult, and he heard of my research into puirt-a-beul, he said, "Get some real songs!" Christine Primrose from Lewis in Scotland also differentiated between puirt-a-beul and "real" songs, as discussed in Chapter 6. Hector MacNeil, who also became a fluent Gaelic speaker as an adult and who taught Gaelic language courses at Cape Breton University and was the Gaelic Director of the Gaelic College in St. Ann's, warned me early in my research that I wouldn't find many puirt-a-beul in Cape Breton because people don't like them. He recalled one singer who had said, "The worst thing that ever happened was when words were put to them fiddle tunes!" Again, the implication is that puirt-a-beul are really fiddle tunes dressed up as songs by virtue of their lyrics and by the fact that they are sung rather than played.

I found ample evidence to corroborate that puirt-a-beul have low social value. First, they are almost non-existent in published song collections, such as *An t-Òranaiche* (Mac-na-Ceàrdadh 2004 [1879]) or *Gaelic Songs in Nova Scotia* (Creighton and MacLeod 1964). These two song collections can be found in many Nova Scotia homes. Gaelic singers regularly refer to them to assist them in learning songs thoroughly and accurately. The absence of puirt-a-beul from these published collections implicitly reinforces the notion that puirt-a-beul are something other than songs, as though they have no place among "legitimate" songs.

Second, they are almost non-existent in early Canadian Gaelic song collections, such as those by Helen Creighton and MacEdward Leach. Either the collectors themselves did not think puirt-a-beul were worth collecting and therefore did not ask for them, or their informants did not value them and therefore did not offer them. At other times, informants did offer puirt-a-beul, as in the case of Joe Neil MacNeil, who recorded more than one hundred for the St. Francis Xavier University Gaelic Folklore Project, and Lauchie MacLellan, who provided more than twenty-five for the same project. And yet their puirt-a-beul are not documented in the books that were directly based on this project, *Tales Until Dawn* (J. N. MacNeil 1987) and *Brìgh an Òrain* (Shaw 2000).

Third, although I found many privately owned and created Gaelic song scrapbooks deposited in the Beaton Institute archives at Cape Breton University, they did not include puirt-a-beul. Instead, people carefully cut newspaper clippings of four-line and eight-line songs, or painstakingly hand-wrote them in a journal. Given that these scrapbooks usually contained dozens of Gaelic songs, I believe it is significant that puirt-a-beul are absent. Moreover, newspapers such as *Mac-Talla*, a Gaelic-language newspaper published in Sydney from 1892 to 1904, tended to print songs at readers' requests; readers apparently did not often request or submit puirt-a-beul.

Fourth, they are described as "little," in stark contrast to other genres, such as "heavy" songs, which are sometimes called "òrain mhòra" (great/big songs). For example, John Lorne Campbell writes, "Like her name sake, Annie Johnston on Barra, [Mrs. J. R. Johnston, nee Margaret MacNeil] excelled at 'little songs' and puirt-a-beul" (Campbell 1969-1981: 64). Jeff MacDonald, a fluent Cape Breton Gaelic speaker, called them "light" in an interview with me (interview, July 22, 1998). I have already documented the ambivalence that some Gaelic singers feel about puirt-a-beul. One fluent learner explained that the Gaelic in puirt-a-beul is less "interesting" (interview, January 21, 1998). Christine Primrose likewise explained her view of puirt-a-beul lyrics: "That's why I feel that puirt-a-beul are always essentially a tune.... It's a tune before it's words. The words I don't think will ever be better than the tune" (interview, July 12-13, 1998).

Although it may be easy to label some songs as puirt-a-beul, others may be harder to categorize. Discussions and disagreements about how to categorize songs can be quite revealing about what defines a genre within a community (H. Sparling 2008a). One well-respected Cape Breton Gaelic singer and speaker started an interview by telling me about a time that he travelled to Ontario to compete in the Mod they once held there. A friend encouraged him to sing a particular song about a small Cape Breton community called Canada in which all the local women decide they're "going places" and take on airs. According to the interviewee, the Gaelic-speaking judge from Scotland said, "Well, you'd have no problem winning this only that's a port-a-beul." The singer argued that it *wasn't* a port-a-beul because the song had "real" words and was of known provenance:

> That's not a port-a-beul! That's a song! ... I know the people who composed it and it's got words. The only thing is that it's been beefed up [tempo-wise] and if you want to dance with it ... go ahead and dance! But it's not puirt-a-beul. It's a song! (Interview, June 29, 1998)

He felt that the judge considered it a port-a-beul because of its tempo, while he himself felt that the lyrics and composer determined its genre. According to this particular singer, Cape Breton songs are often sung much faster than songs in Scotland, making it difficult for Scottish Gaelic singers to evaluate Cape Breton Gaelic songs appropriately.

This story is interesting for a number of reasons. It suggests that lyrics and tempo are significant in marking puirt-a-beul, and it also suggests that there may be different definitions of puirt-a-beul in Scotland and Cape Breton. As described earlier, several songs with "real" words and known composers have been labelled puirt-a-beul in Scotland. But this story is also interesting because it suggests that puirt-a-beul cannot be used in contexts suitable for other types of songs. Singing a song that the judge interpreted as a port-a-beul apparently disqualified the singer from the competition. The interviewee's angry insistence that his song was not a port-a-beul intimates that he was insulted by the suggestion that he would sing a port-a-beul.

I struggled to understand the discrepancy I encountered. If puirt-a-beul were not "real" songs, why did I seem to hear them everywhere I went? Why would Hector tell me that I would not find many when, in fact, I had already discovered lots through recordings, workshops, and concerts? At the same time, if they were so popular, why had they not been collected by folklorists and published in song anthologies? I thought a lot about who performed puirt-a-beul and who said what about them. I eventually realized that all the people who dismissed puirt-a-beul or described them in negative terms were either native or fluent Gaelic speakers. But the question still remained: what was it about puirt-a-beul that generated such strong statements? The strong opinions indicated that something was at stake, but what? Ultimately, I concluded that there were two major issues involved. First, unlike other song genres, particularly "heavy" songs, puirt-a-beul do not effectively preserve or record either the Gaelic language or Gaelic history. Second, they may project an inappropriate, potentially superficial or "primitive" image of Gaelic culture to outsiders. Moreover, their popularity may come at the expense of other, "better" song genres.

This negative discourse about puirt-a-beul denies their status as "real songs" based on their lyrics. Language is key. Native speakers and especially fluent learners are deeply invested in the language and are keenly aware of its steep decline. I think they see themselves as having become the tradition-bearers, whether they believe they can bear the tradition well or not. More than one fluent Cape Breton Gaelic learner acknowledged that they hope or expect to be tradition-bearers in the future, that they accept that they are currently tradition-bearers or are identified as tradition-bearers by others.

With the declining number of speakers and contexts in which Gaelic may be sung and shared comes a decline in the range of repertoire that may be "borne" by these remaining speakers. In the past, tradition-bearers recalled extraordinary numbers of songs and folktales when prompted by collectors. However, their capacities as tradition-bearers were surely helped by the Gaelic cultural context of which they were a part and in which they lived: they had the opportunities to hear and recount their songs and stories repeatedly. That cultural context has changed significantly of late. There are fewer and fewer opportunities for today's Gaelic tradition-bearers to hear and share their portions of the culture, and people in general are rarely required to develop their memories in the same manners as in the past. Consequently, I would argue that Gaels must select—consciously or not—what repertoire they will "bear." They must choose what songs to learn and sing at the few remaining venues open to them. Puirt-a-beul are not a priority because their lyrics do not preserve the variety and colour of the Gaelic language, nor do they record significant historical events or cultural values in the same way as other song genres. Of course, no one has ever claimed that puirt-a-beul lyrics are comparable to those of other genres; their value lies in their capacity to record, maintain and transmit instrumental tunes or to facilitate dancing. But fiddle tunes are being more than adequately maintained in the living fiddle repertoire. There just is not the same urgency or need for puirt-a-beul as there is for other kinds of songs. Moreover, because puirt-a-beul are so popular among Gaelic learners and widely recorded (in both Scotland and Cape Breton), there really isn't much need for native and fluent speakers to focus their efforts on them. Ultimately, in terms of internal cultural dynamics, puirt-a-beul are not worth the attention that other song genres are.

A related problem is the manner in which puirt-a-beul "represent" Gaelic culture. While it's true that puirt-a-beul are important for drawing new supporters and learners to the culture, it is also true that they may be misinterpreted by non-speakers and thus misrepresent Gaelic culture. There is a fear that outsiders will take puirt-a-beul as representative of Gaelic song and poetry. For example, the Canada Music Rough Guide CD represents Gaelic Nova Scotia with a track from Mary Jane Lamond's album, *Suas e!* Although there are many kinds of songs on this album from which they could have chosen, the track selected is a port-a-beul. I have read student essays that, in direct response to this particular track, associate Gaelic song and culture with "New Age" music or call it "relaxing." I doubt that any Nova Scotian Gael would find either notion an appropriate response to Gaelic culture generally, or to puirt-a-beul in particular. One Gaelic speaker explained that she worried that commercial puirt-a-beul might attract people to the culture, but not really draw them into it: "To say that people are learning and coming into Gaelic tradition from hearing that kind of thing [i.e., popular renditions of puirt-a-beul], I really doubt very much if they are. Or if they're coming at anything terribly real in the culture from that sort of pop facsimile of mouth music" (interview, June 13, 1998).

French cultural theorist Pierre Bourdieu argues that those without strong cultural knowledge will use their everyday life experiences to make sense of art (1980: 246). In other words, those who do not have Gaelic language fluency and familiarity with other Gaelic songs or expressive art will draw on whatever experiences and knowledge they do have that seem relevant. Those lacking Gaelic cultural knowledge will naturally draw upon their personal cultural experiences and decoding skills. This seems to be the case when people evaluate puirt-a-beul by drawing parallels between them and English-language children's songs or nursery rhymes even though puirt-a-beul are generally defined as dance music in Gaelic culture. For example, one Gaelic learner explained why, in her opinion, puirt-a-beul are not well regarded in Cape Breton:

> Even when you sing a lot of the good ones, a lot of [puirt-a-beul] are kind of almost like nursery rhyme-type things. So, as English-speaking adults, we don't go around singing "Mary Had a Little Lamb." There's all the little tunes and nursery rhyme things you learn as a child and when you get to be an adult, you certainly wouldn't get on stage and sing any one of them. People would really give you an odd look, I think, unless you were specifically there to entertain children.... The [people] here that you talk to, they've only heard [puirt-a-beul] as children so therefore you only sang it as a child.... So I mean, if people in Cape Breton back in the bygone days were learning puirt-a-beul at their mother's knee and as little kids playing around outside—little games or whatever—well, once they wanted to be treated as adults, maybe right away they just dropped the puirt-a-beul. (Interview, July 22, 1998)

Puirt-a-beul may be frequently associated with children because they are highly reminiscent of English-language children's songs, skipping rhymes, and nursery rhymes. The songs I remember from my own childhood were often nonsensical, funny, short and/or repetitive, just like puirt-a-beul. The question is whether this is an accurate understanding of puirt-a-beul. Focusing on the similarities between puirt-a-beul and English nursery rhymes may make it hard to see their differences, and those differences may well be key to understanding the significance of puirt-a-beul within Gaelic culture.

If people lack awareness of other Gaelic song genres, then there is the risk that they will assume that puirt-a-beul represent Gaelic song culture. The problem is that non-Gaels might assume that puirt-a-beul, as the most public, popular and accessible genre of Gaelic song, are representative of Gaelic song culture in general, or that puirt-a-beul represent the best that Gaelic song culture has to offer. This potential is increased by the tendency for the "Other," particularly "the Folk," to be associated with simplicity and a lack of sophistication. As historian Ian McKay makes clear, this tendency continues today: "The Quest of the Folk continues, even in a late-20th-century landscape dotted with factories and warehouses, shopping malls and fast-food franchises" (1994: 275). McKay documents how particular people, including politicians, cultural activists and tourists sought a particular preconceived notion of "the Folk" among Nova Scotians. He capitalizes "Folk" to clarify that he is referring to an imagined group of people who were and are envisaged to embody stereotypical characteristics (e.g., poverty, self-sustaining farming and fishing practices, orally transmitted culture, etc.), rather than to actual people (or "folk") accurately described as complex human beings living complex lives. When looking for "the Folk" and folk culture, people simply ignore signs of modernity and complexity. The danger, then, is not simply that non-Gaels will view puirt-a-beul as "primitive," but that they will interpret them as representative of the entire culture. This is not only an insulting reduction of a complex, diverse culture, but also threatens Gaels' abilities to convincingly

counter typical arguments that diminish the value and significance of Gaelic. If the assumption is that puirt-a-beul is the best
that Gaelic culture has to offer, or the *only* cultural expression to
be found among Gaelic speakers, then it may be enjoyably quaint,
but little would be lost should it disappear.

Puirt-a-beul not only create the possibility of misrepresent-
ing Gaelic culture among cultural outsiders, but also pose a risk
within the culture. Jamie MacNeil, who protested that I ought
to research some "real songs," later explained his position in an
interview:

> I don't hate puirt-a-beul by any means, by any means what-
> soever! What I say about puirt-a-beul is that it's taking the
> place in singing nowadays that it didn't used to have. Years
> ago, I don't remember hearing anybody singing puirt-a-beul
> at a concert. I can't remember any fifty years ago. (Interview,
> July 23, 1998)

Jamie suggests that the growing popularity of puirt-a-beul
comes at the expense of other Gaelic song genres. Puirt-a-beul
are possibly being disproportionately represented whenever the
opportunity to perform or showcase Gaelic arises. Puirt-a-beul,
according to Jamie's observation, have been growing in popularity
while other Gaelic song genres have been decreasing in popularity
(or, at least, opportunities appropriate for singing them have been
decreasing).

Jamie's comments also raise the matter of the changing
nature of Cape Breton concerts. Fifty years ago, concerts tended
to be directed more at local audiences, whereas today they are directed as much at tourists as at locals. Large-scale, annual variety
concerts have been running in Cape Breton since the mid-20th
century. Initially, these were concerts celebrating local events or
fundraising for community concerns. For example, the Broad
Cove concert, which has been held annually since 1957, was first
held to celebrate the hundredth anniversary of St. Margaret of
Scotland parish. Highland Village Day, launched in 1962 when
the Highland Village museum opened in Iona, Nova Scotia, raises

funds for the museum. Historically, these events—and many smaller concert events—drew upon local talent and were aimed at a local audience. With the rise in tourism, audiences have changed. There are still many locals in attendance but also visitors who come with different kinds of knowledge, experience and expectations. Although Gaelic song is generally included on concert programs, audiences are now rarely Gaelic-speaking, whether local or not. Puirt-a-beul, for all the reasons mentioned thus far, are well-suited to a non-Gaelic speaking audience. Jamie's comments, however, highlight how concerts have changed, and consequently their repertoire, resulting in the replacement of other types of Gaelic song and singing with puirt-a-beul.

Part of the problem in this case is that puirt-a-beul are being recontextualized from instrumental tunes used as dance music to stand-alone songs. This concern is evident in the arguments that puirt-a-beul are tunes rather than songs, articulated by several people on both sides of the Atlantic. The terms "tune" and "song" imply not just a different understanding of the role of puirt-a-beul, but also of the significance of their lyrics. Songs generally involve lyrics while tunes generally don't. Puirt-a-beul may have lyrics, but in the minds of some, they are secondary to their musical features and, in fact, even the lyrics are designed to convey musical information (e.g., rhythm, ornamentation) before they are meant to communicate semantic meaning.

In Chapter 3, I introduced Thomas Turino's theory that music can generally be categorized as either participatory or presentational, and that its function will determine its musical characteristics and the appropriate criteria by which it ought to be judged. Turino points out that mainstream Anglo-American society generally privileges presentational music and values and this has resulted in a tendency to dismiss more participatory forms of music as simple, repetitive and "boring." But, Turino argues, participatory music *must* be simple, repetitive and predictable if it's doing its job as a participatory performance. His point is that participatory music is not an amateur, "lesser" version of "real music" made by professionals. Rather, both types of performance are valuable but they must be judged according to their purpose. It is not appropriate to use presentational criteria to judge a participatory performance. If and when this occurs, the participatory performance will, of course, be found lacking, just as a presentational performance would be judged too difficult and ineffective if it were evaluated using participatory criteria.

There are two implications for Gaelic society and puirt-a-beul. First, the reality is that Gaelic culture is constantly being observed and evaluated by non-Gaels who live in a society dominated by presentational music and who therefore use presentational music criteria to judge all forms of music, whether that music is presentational or participatory in orientation. Consequently, participatory puirt-a-beul may be judged poorly for being simple, repetitive, and predictable, and there is a risk that this assessment could extend to all Gaelic culture. Second, all Gaels also operate in mainstream Anglo-American society and many Gaels have therefore absorbed a presentational attitude toward all musics. Gaels themselves, therefore, may dismiss puirt-a-beul based on presentational criteria, even though they may be better evaluated using participatory criteria and, in fact, may have traditionally been evaluated as a participatory music in the past.

Conclusions

Puirt-a-beul have the potential for both good and harm. On the one hand, they draw people to the Gaelic language and its culture. The potential benefits of this are many: new language learners, Gaelic activists and cultural participants who help to justify the production of Gaelic resources and to make such resources financially viable. Puirt-a-beul are also valuable as a cultural linchpin, providing a point at which language, song, storytelling, instrumental music and dance intersect. Puirt-a-beul have become central to the argument that Gaelic fluency is necessary for fiddlers and pipers to play with a "correct" Cape Breton—and even Highland Scottish—musical style, which in turn helps to bolster the language against claims that it has little economic value.

On the other hand, puirt-a-beul can be dangerous. Their popularity among non-Gaels means that they threaten the viability of other, less popular genres, especially in contexts such as recordings and concerts where sales to non-Gaels are important to ensure financial viability. Non-Gaels may get the wrong impression from puirt-a-beul, assuming that Gaelic culture is childish and simple, rather than diverse, complex and sophisticated.

Puirt-a-beul surely have a role to play in Gaelic communities. In fact, they *are* playing a role, although that role is contested by different people. The debate about the value of puirt-a-beul hinges on the social needs for puirt-a-beul, quite apart from their cultural roles that tend to be more clearly and obviously defined. The assertion that fiddlers must learn Gaelic in order to acquire and appropriately use the puirt-a-beul associated with various tunes results as much from the social desire to increase the number of Gaelic speakers and to assert the Gaelic language's value as from any actual link between language and playing style. This is not to say that a link between language and performance style does not exist; it is only to say that the assertion of such a link is as important for social as for cultural reasons.

When I first set out to research puirt-a-beul, I remember hearing through the grapevine that a prominent Gaelic singer felt that I was crazy to try to write a whole thesis on the subject. She felt that I might get one essay out of it but couldn't imagine that I could find much to write about. I am perhaps as surprised as she that I am now at the end of an entire book about puirt-a-beul, having considered their origins, musical features, lyrics and various functions, including accompaniment for various types of dance, transmission of instrumental tunes, teaching the Gaelic language, linking various Gaelic expressive forms, and maintaining the boundaries between insiders and outsiders to Gaelic culture. And yet there is still room for additional research on puirt-a-beul. Their origins, for example, are still largely unknown. My analysis of the social functions of puirt-a-beul are interpretations; a different researcher might present quite different but equally (or even more) valid interpretations. More could be done to investigate the relationship between the Gaelic language and instrumental style, especially how the relationship may have changed over time.

I must also admit that some of the furor over puirt-a-beul seems to have died down of late. When I first began researching puirt-a-beul in the late 1990s, Gaeldom was still riding the wave of the global craze for Celtic pop, and puirt-a-beul was front and centre. Artists such as Enya in Ireland and Mouth Music in Scotland put Gaelic songs on the international music charts. The band Mouth Music was named for the English translation of "puirt-a-beul," and some of their most popular tracks were based on puirt-a-beul. In Canada, Cape Breton fiddler Ashley MacIsaac had a national rock hit in 1995 with "Sleepy Maggie," based on two puirt-a-beul sung by Mary Jane Lamond. It is no wonder that puirt-a-beul were everywhere by the late 1990s and early 2000s. With their dramatic rise in popularity and visibility came increased anxieties about what their presence meant: what kind of message did they send to non-Gaels about Gaelic song culture, and what did their popularity portend for the future of Gaelic song, whether in traditional or popular circles? Puirt-a-beul became a lightning rod for debates about how Gaelic culture is or should be represented to outsiders, how new Gaelic speakers and supporters should be recruited, how Gaelic song is defined and what its most valued features are, and the nature of the relationship between language and music or language and dance. These have been important debates as the Gaelic community—both in Scotland and in its transatlantic diasporas—has struggled to maintain and revitalize the Gaelic language and traditional arts from historically Gaelic-speaking areas.

Today, world music fashions have moved on to other sounds and cultures. However, there are new forces at play in both Nova Scotia and Scotland. In Nova Scotia, the provincial Gaelic Affairs is changing the way that Gaelic language is taught, focusing on community-based instruction that brings older native speakers together with young learners in order to reintroduce the language to such everyday contexts as baking and cooking, gardening, housework, and woodworking and repairs. Meanwhile, in Scotland, the devolution of the Scottish parliament in 1999 brought about recognition of Gaelic as an official language of Scotland in 2005. The 2011 census shows that a steady decline in Gaelic speakers appears to have been halted, although not yet reversed. A historic referendum on Scottish independence, was held September 18, 2014. The role that puirt-a-beul may play in such contexts, if any, is not yet clear.

Gaelic song recordings proliferated in the 1990s and 2000s, particularly in Scotland (as this book's discography amply illustrates), but also in Nova Scotia. It is now standard practice for puirt-a-beul to be recorded on just about every commercial Gaelic song album. However, the desire to record respectful but creative arrangements of traditional Gaelic songs will inevitably shift as new musical fashions develop and once it is felt that most known traditional Gaelic songs have been recorded commercially. Gaelic singers will no doubt find new ways to mark themselves and their music in distinctive ways. Once again, it remains to be seen what role puirt-a-beul may play in the commercial music industry and in traditional music circles.

Compared to some Gaelic songs and genres, puirt-a-beul are relative newcomers. But they have existed for something like 250 years. Moreover, they continue to be a healthy part of living Gaelic culture. Although their silly lyrics and ephemeral nature mean that we have no doubt lost many examples to the vagaries of time, these same characteristics make them easy to create anew for each generation and for each community. Puirt-a-beul are a flexible genre easily accessible to speakers and singers of varying talents and abilities. This flexibility is part of what has ensured their longevity and continuing relevance, and no doubt will play a role in their future as well.

Appendix A
Calum Crùbach
Strathspey
"Miss (Sarah) Drummond of Perth"

Example 1: As it appears in Mackintosh (ca. 1910), Scotland, early 20th century. Note that the first turn also appears in K. N. MacDonald's *Puirt-a-Beul* but without the other turns.

'Ille chrùbaich anns a' ghleann	Oh lame lad in the glen
Cum thall na caoraich uile/agad	Keep yonder all the/your sheep
'Ille chrùbaich anns a' ghleann	Oh lame lad in the glen
Cùm thall na caoraich.	Keep yonder the sheep.
Cùm thall na toir a nall	Keep yonder, don't bring [them] here
Cùm thall na toir a nall	Keep yonder, don't bring [them] here
Cùm thall na toir a nall	Keep yonder, don't bring [them] here
Cùm thall na caoraich	Keep yonder the sheep.
Ged a tha do leth-shùil cam	Although your one eye is blind
Chì thu leis an t-sùil ud eile	You can see with the other eye
Ged a tha do leth-shùil cam	Although your one eye is blind
Chì thu leis an t-aon sùil.	You can see with the one eye.

Example 2: Frank Rhodes (1996: 189; spelling as in the original), Cape Breton, mid-20th century.

Calum crubach anns a' Ghleann	Lame Calum in the glen
Till a null na coraich chusainn [thugainn?]	Return there the sheep to us
Calum crubach anns a' Ghleann	Lame Calum in the glen
Till a null na coraich	Return there the sheep

Ged a tha do leth-shuil dall	Although your one eye is blind
Chi thu leis an t-suil udieile	You can see with the other eye
Ged a tha do leth-shuil dall	Although your one eye is blind
Chi thu lei an aonte	You can see with the one eye.

Calum crubach anns a' Ghleann	Lame Calum in the glen
'Se 'na dheann asiarraidh mna	He's in a hurry looking for a wife
Calum crubach anns a' Ghleann	Lame Calum in the glen
'Se a' bagairt posaidil	And he's threatening to marry.

Example 3: Mary Jane Lamond, *Bho Thìr nan Craobh* (ca. 1994, liner notes), Cape Breton, late 20th century.

Calum Crùbach as a' ghleann,	Lame Malcolm from the glen,
Cum thall na caoraich uile,	Keep all the sheep over there,
Calum Crùbach as a' ghleann,	Lame Malcolm from the glen,
Cum thall na caoraich.	Keep the sheep over there.

Cum thall, na toir a nall,	Keep over there, don't take over here,
Cum thall na caoraich uile,	Keep all the sheep over there,
Cum thall, na toir a nall,	Keep over there, don't take over here,
Cum thall na caoraich.	Keep the sheep over there.

Example 4: Song workshop with Christine Primrose, Scotland, late 20th century.

Cailleach chrùbach as a' ghleann	Bent old woman from the glen
Till a nall na caoraich thugam	Return the sheep over to me
Cailleach chrùbach as a' ghleann	Bent old woman from the glen
Till a nall na h-òisgean.	Return the lambs over here.

| Till a nall thoir a nall | Return over here, take over here |
| Till a nall na caoraich thugam | Return the sheep over to me |

Till a nall thoir a nall	Return over here, take over here
Till a nall na h-òisgean.	Return the lambs over here.

Till a nall thoir a nall	Return over here, take over here
Till a nall na caoraich thugam	Return the sheep over to me
Cailleach chrùbach as a' ghleann	Bent old woman from the glen
Till a nall na h-òisgean.	Return the lambs over here.

Example 5: Learn Gaelic Website (http://learngaelic.net/ underfives/grd-puirt-a-beul.jsp), Scotland, early 21st century.

'Ille chrùbaich anns a' ghleann	Oh lame lad in the glen
Cùm thall do chaoraich agad,	Keep yonder your sheep
'Ille chrùbaich anns a' ghleann	Oh lame lad in the glen
Cùm thall do chaoraich.	Keep yonder your sheep.

'Ille chrùbaich tha thu ann,	Oh lame lad you are there,
Maol an ceann is cam an casan,	Bald of head and crooked of leg,
'Ille chrùbaich tha thu ann,	Oh lame lad you are there,
Cùm thall do chaoraich.	Keep yonder your sheep.

Cùm thall 's na leig a-nall,	Keep yonder and don't let them [come] here,
Cùm thall do chaoraich gheala,	Keep yonder your white sheep
'S ged a tha do leth-shùil dall	And although your one eye is blind
Cùm thall do chaoraich.	Keep yonder your sheep.

Cùm thall 's na bi mall,	Keep yonder and don't be slow
Cùm thall do chaoraich agad,	Keep yonder your sheep
'S ged a tha do chuilean cam	And although your puppy is crooked
Cùm thall do chaoraich.	Keep yonder your sheep.

Cùm thall, na toir a-nall,	Keep yonder, don't bring them [over] here

Cùm thall, na toir a-nall,   Keep yonder, don't bring them [over] here

Cùm thall, na toir a-nall,   Keep yonder, don't bring them [over] here

Cùm thall na caoraich.   Keep yonder your sheep.

Ged a tha do leth-shùil cam,   Although your one eye is blind
Chì thu leis an t-sùil ud eile;   You can see with the other eye
Ged a tha do leth-shùil cam,   Although your one eye is blind
Chì thu leis an aon sùil.   You can see with the one eye.

Glossary

amhrain. Irish Gaelic for "song" (Scottish Gaelic equivalent: *òran*)

binary form. Piece of music whose form is AABB AABB

branle. Popular 16th-century French dance involving movement from side to side and set to binary dance tunes

canntaireachd. Formal oral and written notation system for bagpipe music in which vocables indicate pitch (vowels) and ornamentation (consonants)

cèilidh. Literally means "visit" in Gaelic and traditionally referred to informal house gatherings at which news, stories, dance, songs and music were shared

ceòl beag. Scottish Gaelic for "little music"; refers to binary dance tunes (e.g., jigs, reels, strathspeys)

ceòl mòr. Scottish Gaelic for "big music"; refers to the classical theme and variations music of the Highland bagpipes (also known as *pìobaireachd* in Gaelic, and "pibroch" in English)

clàrsach. Harp common in Scotland and Ireland

dàn. Scottish and Irish Gaelic for "song"

diddling. Term common in Scotland referring to the use of improvised vocables to render an instrumental tune vocally; also known as "lilting" (Ireland) and "jigging" (Nova Scotia), as well as by other terms in other fiddling communities

Dirk Dance, the. Dance involving a real or imaginary dirk, a short sword associated with the Scottish Highlands

eephing. Appalachian tradition in which the voice is used to imitate farm animal sounds

formes fixes. Fourteenth- and 15th-century French poetic and musical forms (the rondeau, the ballade and the virelai)

Gàidhealtachd. Place with an existing or former concentration of Gaelic speakers

High dances. Dances choreographed and performed by dancing masters, primarily in the 19th century

jigging. Term common in Nova Scotia referring to the use of improvised vocables to render an instrumental tune vocally; also known as "lilting" (Ireland) and "diddling" (Scotland), as well as by other terms in other fiddling communities

Kirk Session. Presbyterian Church court; "kirk" is a Scots word for "church"

lilting. Term common in Ireland referring to the use of improvised vocables to render an instrumental tune vocally; also known as "diddling" (Scotland) and "jigging" (Nova Scotia), as well as by other terms in other fiddling communities

òrain mhòra. Literally "great songs" or "big songs," which are lengthy songs with sophisticated lyrics, rhyme schemes and rhythms and usually without a refrain

òran. Scottish Gaelic for "song"

pibroch. Anglicization of the Gaelic word *pìobaireachd*; refers to the classical theme and variations music of the Highland bagpipes (also known as *pìobaireachd* and *ceòl mòr* in Gaelic)

pìobaireachd. Scottish Gaelic for "pipe music," *pìobaireachd* refers to the classical theme and variations music of the Highland bagpipes (also known as *ceòl mòr* in Gaelic, and "pibroch" in English)

pipe major. Non-commissioned officer commanding a pipe band

port mòr. Literally "big tune"; another term for *pìobaireachd* or "pibroch"

port-a-beil. Irish Gaelic equivalent of "puirt-à-beul"

portaireacht. Irish Gaelic term for "lilting," the use of improvised vocables to render an instrumental tune vocally

practice chanter. Double-reed instrument that looks something like an oboe and allows a piper to practice a tune without having to use the full bagpipes; lacking the full pipes' drones and air bag, the practice chanter is much quieter than the full bagpipes

puirt-à-beul. Scottish Gaelic for "tunes from the mouth" but more often translated as "mouth music" (singular spelling: "port-à-beul")

sean-nós. Irish Gaelic for "old manner"; a term used to refer to traditional singing and dancing

shieling. Scottish term for a rough hut used during the summer season while livestock grazed on common lands

strathspey. Binary dance tune developed in Scotland and characterized by asymmetrical rhythms and wide intervals

Sword Dance, the. Originally a step dance, the Sword Dance is today a popular competitive Highland dance performed over crossed swords; associated with the port-a-beul "Gillie Calum"

tradition-bearer. Person recognized as someone with an extensive traditional cultural repertoire (e.g., songs, stories, genealogies) and deep knowledge about traditional practices, beliefs, values and histories

tuning. Term sometimes used instead of "jigging" in Nova Scotia and Prince Edward Island

Notes

Notes to Chapter 1

1. Samuel's article describes music in the social life of aristocrats in Lhasa prior to the 1959 Tibetan uprising against Chinese control. At the time of publishing his article in 1976, the musical practices he describes were still being performed by Tibetan refugees.

2. See, for example, Gina Fatone's article about the use of "intermodal imagery" (the mental transfer of one domain of experience to another, such as the use of singing or physical gestures to convey something about instrumental music) in the context of bagpipe transmission in Atlantic Canada (2010).

3. I am indebted to Chambers (1980) for much of the information in this section.

Notes to Chapter 2

1. "Chuirinn air a' Phìob e," in the title of this chapter, is the name of a port-a-beul and means "I would put it on the pipes."

2. However, John MacInnes speculates that the "foull hieland sang" referred to in the confession of three women accused of witchcraft and documented in the Kirk Session of Elgin in 1596 might even have been an instance of puirt-a-beul (2006: 260). Although it is unlikely that puirt-a-beul as we know them today existed at that point, it is entirely possible that whatever song was sung, given that it was "presumably erotic or perhaps bawdy" (MacInnes 2006: 260), was the precursor of modern puirt-a-beul.

Notes to Chapter 3

1. The title of this chapter, "Ciamar a Nì Mi an Ruidhle Bhòidheach" ("How Will I Make the Beautiful Reel?"), is the title of a port-a-beul.

2. For the history of the reel as a tune type, consult Alburger (1983); Collinson (1966, 2001); Newton (2009); and Lamb (2013).

3. I use the term "syncopation" to refer to any and all accents occurring on normally unaccented notes. Thus, syncopation here refers to accented notes occurring on a normally unaccented beat (in the case of reels, this would include accented notes on beats 2 and 4) as well as to accented notes occurring between beats, sometimes referred to as "off beats."

4. William Lamb, however, argues that reels weren't always so rhythmically smooth and that puirt-a-beul reels often exhibit a more strathspey-like "jumpy" or "pointed" rhythm when slowed down (2013). Kate Dunlay also argues that the extent of "smoothness" depends on the tradition, with some Irish fiddlers playing reels quite smoothly while Cape Breton fiddlers tend to play them less smoothly (personal communication, December 31, 2013).

5. Despite its popularity, there are surprisingly few commercial recordings of this port-a-beul. However, it can be heard on The Campbell's *Tha Mi 'n Dùil* (2011), Mary Jane Lamond's *Bho Thìr nan Craobh / From the Land of the Trees* (ca. 1994), Tannas's *Rù-Rà* (1995) and Andrew McFayden's *An Rathad Cam 's an Rathad Dìreach* (2004). Archival recordings can also be heard at Gael Stream (http://gaelstream.stfx.ca/) and Tobar an Dualchais (http://www.tobarandualchais.co.uk/).

6. "Conjunct" and "disjunct" are musical terms used to refer to melodic motion. "Conjunct" refers to a melody that moves mostly by scale step or by very small leaps. "Disjunct" refers to a melody that moves by larger intervals.

7. For the history of the strathspey as a tune type, consult Alburger (1983); Collinson (1966, 2001); Newton (2009, 2014); and Lamb (2013).

8. In standard Western classical music, a dotted note is worth three times the note with which it is paired. However, in Cape Breton and Scottish fiddling styles, the length of the dotted note is not as exact or as long as in art music practice, although it is still longer than the note with which it is paired.

9. As noted above, instrumental reels tend to have many melodic leaps that are not evident in puirt-a-beul reels, likely due to the difficulty of singing such leaps at reel tempo. Therefore, the melodic contrast be-

tween strathspeys and reels is more pronounced in puirt-a-beul than in instrumental practice.

10. I am aware of only one difficult-to-acquire commercial recording of this port-a-beul by Oranaiche Cheap Breatuinn (the Cape Breton Gaelic Choir, 1988). However, archival recordings can be heard at Gael Stream (http://gaelstream.stfx.ca/) and Tobar an Dualchais (http://www.tobarandualchais.co.uk/).

11. A slightly different version sung by Nan Bryan Buchanan of Barra in 1965 is available from the same site: http://www.tobarandualchais.co.uk/fullrecord/95851/1.

12. The concept of triadic harmony will make sense to most musically literate musicians. However, it would take quite a bit of space and would move this chapter along a fairly significant tangent to explain it to the non-musician. Suffice it to say that leaps between triadic pitches are second only to stepwise motion in terms of creating the impression of a smooth melody.

13. It is worth noting that one can find the occasional slip jig in the puirt-a-beul repertoire, which is like a regular jig except that it is in 9/8 instead of 6/8. One example is "Nead na lach às an luachair," a port-a-beul that can be heard on Mary Ann Kennedy and Charlotte Petersen's *Strings Attached* (1991) and Cliar's *Cliar* (2000). "Nead na lach às an luachair" is also known as an Irish song, "Nead na lachan sa mhúta" and as an instrumental tune, "The Foxhunter's Jig." It is an unusual example of a Scottish port-a-beul that began as an Irish tune. Mary Ann Kennedy says that her mother, Kenna Campbell, together with Na h-Eilthirich, adapted the song after having learned it in Ireland (personal communication, Sept 9, 2014). Another slip jig is "Faca Sibh Màiri Nighean Alasdair," available on Dòchas's self-titled album (2002). Although slip jigs were certainly known in 18th- and 19th-century Scotland, they are rarely played by Scottish and Nova Scotian traditional musicians today, perhaps because any dances that may have been associated with them have not persisted.

14. Recordings of "Fear an Dùin Mhòir" include Christine Primrose's *Àite Mo Ghaoil* (1993), Mary and Kenna Campbell on *Celtic Mouth Music* (1997), Rachel Walker's *Braighe Loch Iall* (2004), the Whistlebinkies' *Timber Timbre* (1999), and, for a Canadian recording, John Allan Cameron's *Here Comes John Allan Cameron* (1969).

15. "Bink" = bench, long seat before the fire; "But ne'er a blythe styme-wad he blink" = Never a cheerful glance would he give; "cauldrife" =

cold, cheerless; "deuk-dub" = duck-pond; "heigh" = high, loud; "laigh she louted" = low she chuckled.

16. Both Doherty (1996: 205ff) and Emmerson (1971: 118) discuss the tendency for tunes to change type in Celtic traditions.

17. Refer to Chapter 1 for a definition of pibroch, pìobaireachd and ceòl mòr.

18. A Cape Breton exception is John Allan Cameron, who follows a recording of the jig "Fear an Dùin Mhòir" with a strathspey, "A-Null Thar nan Eileannan" on his album *Here Comes John Allan Cameron* (1965).

Notes to Chapter 4

1. "Seallaibh Curraigh Eòghainn can be heard on numerous recordings, including Màiri MacInnes's *This Feeling Inside* (1995), Tannas's *Sùilean Dubh* (1999), Talitha MacKenzie's *Sólas* (1994), Anne Martin's *Nighean nan Geug* (2000), as well as on Cape Breton recordings by Mary Jane Lamond (*Làn Dùil*, 1999) and The Barra MacNeils (*The Question*, 1995).

2. A "waulking" (or "milling frolic," in Cape Breton) is an event at which woven wool is beaten in order to shrink the cloth before making it into blankets or clothing. Waulking (or milling) songs were sung to accompany the group labour and to pass the time. For more information about the waulking and milling tradition, see Campbell and Collinson (1969-1981) and H. Sparling (2006: 189-272; 2008b).

3. This song can be found in *Tog Fonn!* (Mhàrtainn 1994) and on the CD *Trì Nithean* by Anna Murray (1999); the eponymously named CD by Mouth Music (1991); Capercaillie's *Beautiful Wasteland* (1998); and Karen Matheson's *Downriver* (2005).

4. Folklorist Michael Taft has written about this function of song in "Of Scoffs, Mounties and Mainlanders: The Popularity of a Sheep-Stealing Ballad in Newfoundland" (I. MacInnes 2007: 228). In country singer Dick Nolan's humorous song, "Aunt Martha's Sheep," a Mountie (Royal Canadian Mounted Police Officer) goes after sheep stealers. The sheep stealers, however, trick him by feeding him the stolen and now roasted sheep, telling him that it is moose. Taft argues that the anti-authoritarian theme has played an important role in the song's local popularity: "Humor at the expense of the RCMP counteracts their threatening and authoritarian role and helps to relieve this point of tension in the community" (93).

5. While the song text itself is overt in its criticism of the MacLeod doctor, the behaviour around the song could be understood as a "hidden transcript" or a "complicit act of coding" (Scott 1990). The choice to sing or not to sing the song, or to applaud or not to applaud, becomes a coded indication of one's opinion of the doctor, while allowing the singer or audience to claim that their behaviour is "merely" an indication of their opinion of the song.

6. This version of "The Fantastic Breeks" comes from James Graham's album *Siubhal* (2004) but others have recorded it as well, including Eilidh MacKenzie (*Eideadh na Sgeulachd*, 1992) and Maeve MacKinnon (*Fo Smuain*, 1995).

7. Herbert Halpert has written about the challenges that folklorists face in collecting and publishing obscenity (1962).

Notes to Chapter 5

1. Labanotation was first developed by Rudolph Laban in the 1920s. Symbols are used to indicate the direction and level of the movement, the part of the body doing the movement, the duration of the movement, and the dynamic quality of the movement (Dance Notation Bureau 2014). Labanotation requires specialized training to read and write.

2. For a history of Highland dance, see C. M. Scott (2005) and Emmerson (1972: 241-54). Scottish and Cape Breton dance scholar Mats Melin told me that in the early 1900s in the Dundee area of Scotland, people would refer to what we today would call a Highland dancing class as "step dancing" (personal communication, December 11, 2013).

3. For more information on the development of today's Highland Dance, see also Newton (2012) and C. M. Scott (2005).

4. Roger Ellis, however, in his excellent history of the quadrille, does say that stepping was introduced into quadrilles danced by the working classes in U.K. industrial cities during the 19th century:

> In the new, crowded industrial towns the adoption of the wooden soled shoe, or clog, by factory workers was general and the rhythmic tapping of the wooden sole on a hard floor was quickly developed into highly skilled and admired art. When the quadrille eventually entered into the repertoire of these factory workers it became the custom to introduce a few clog dance steps while awaiting one's turn to dance the figure. If the space for dancing was very restricted, it frequently happened that a dancer would complete a figure earlier than in-

tended and in such a case the music would be "filled out" with "stepping." This practice of "stepping" the last bar or two of a quadrille figure became particularly common in those parts of England, Scotland and Ireland where, as the 19th century drew to a close, many of the more interesting figures of the quadrille had been forgotten or were impractical in the restricted space available for dancing. Thus, the stepping added interest to an emasculated and over-simplified form of the dance and enabled those proficient in the art to be admired for their skill. (2004: 143)

It is not clear, however, how much of this working-class stepping in the U.K. influenced quadrille dancing in North America.

5. According to Mats Melin, who interviewed Margaret Gillis in Cape Breton in 2007, the order of the steps was not fixed in these solo step dances, but particular steps had to be danced to specific parts of the tune (personal communication, December 11, 2013).

6. Lyrics and translation taken from Mary Jane Lamond's album, *Stòras* (2005).

7. Translation mine.

8. This port-a-beul is available on Catherine Ann MacPhee's *Sùil Air Ais* (2004).

9. An exception to group singing of puirt-a-beul is the Campbell family in Scotland (Na Caimbeulaich). The Campbell family includes, among others, Kenna Campbell and her daughters Mary Ann Kennedy and Wilma Kennedy, all mentioned in this book. The Campbells are very well known for their Gaelic singing—both as individuals and as a group—and perhaps especially for their performances of puirt-a-beul. The Campbells often sing sets of puirt-a-beul together, and occasionally do so to accompany a step dancer. For more about the Campbell family, see NicLeáoid (2013).

10. Although the Fletts published an article called "Dramatic Jigs in Scotland" (1956) and Emmerson has a chapter on the "Folk Jigs of the Highlands and Isles" (1972), the term "jig" in these cases refers to theatrical dances that are not necessarily restricted to music in compound jig time (see Chapter 3 for a description of jig features). In fact, many of the "jigs" referenced by these authors, such as the Reel of the Black Cocks, are danced to reels, not jigs.

11. Gillebride MacMillan recorded this port-a-beul on *Air Fòrladh* (2011).

12. Numerous transcriptions of this tune are available, including a couple easily accessible in ABC notation on Kuntz's *Fiddler's Companion* (http://www.ibiblio.org/fiddlers/) and a transcription of the port-a-beul melody on the Gaelic Resource Database (http://www.gaelicresources. co.uk/index.php/multimedia-pages; look for the puirt-a-beul collection). Interestingly, fiddle tune publications show that "Gillie Callum" has changed somewhat over the years, although it is always recognizably the same tune. In particular, the rhythm varies considerably. None of the fiddle tune versions I have seen have the same rhythm as the port-a-beul rhythm documented on the Gaelic Resource Database. Perhaps the tune preceded the Gaelic words and therefore the Gaelic words have not historically been of significance to the transmission of the tune (see Chapter 7). Otherwise we might expect the linguistic rhythms to be evident in the tune transcriptions.

13. This puirt-a-beul can be heard on Tannas's *Rì-Rà* (1995).

14. There is another very different origin story for the "Gillie Calum" dance: in 1953, Scottish Gaelic scholar John MacInnes recorded Hugh MacRae of Skeabost, Skye telling the story of Noah of the Ark's son, Calum, who volunteered to determine whether land was appearing on the flooded planet or not. When he managed to climb on land and realized that the water levels were going down, he crossed two sticks that he found and began to dance from point to point. Noah was so delighted that he cried out, "Mo ghille Calum!" ("My son Callum!" ca. 1975 Tocher 17: 10-12)

15. *Fèile beag* (sometimes written in English as "phillabeg") literally means "little kilt." It is little compared to the full kilt sometimes known in English as the "belted plaid." Today's modern kilt is a form of the fèile beag.

16. Readers can hear this port-a-beul sung on Kenna Campbell's *Guth a' Shnìomhas* (1999), Dòchas's eponymous album (2005) and Griogair's *Dail-Riata* (2007).

17. Recordings of this port-a-beul can be found on, for example, Mac-Talla's ... *Mairidh Gaol is Ceòl* (1994), Màiri MacInnes's *Orosay* (2001), Talitha MacKenzie's *Sólas* (1994) or Tannas's *Sùilean Dubh* (1999).

18. "Calum Crùbach" is one of the most popular fiddle tunes and best-known puirt-a-beul in Cape Breton. Unusually, it has many variant lyrics (unusual since published lyrics usually limit subsequent changes) although it remains recognizably the same port. I've included a number of variants in Appendix A so that interested readers may consider

how this particular port-a-beul has changed over time and in different regions.

19. This port-a-beul is well known in Cape Breton and is set to the same tune as "Dòmhnall Beag an t-Siùcair," which is better known in Scotland. Recordings of "Bodachan a' Mhìrein" can be found on Anne Martin's *Cò...?* (1998) and Margo Carruthers' *Tàlant nam Bàrd* (1998).

20. According to Dwelly's Gaelic-English dictionary, *cabar fèidh* is the war cry and one of the crests of the Mackenzies.

21. There are many recordings of this tune by pipe bands, but the only commercial Gaelic song CD to include it, as far as I know, is The Choir of the Glasgow Gaelic Musical Association's *Gaelic Galore* (1990).

Notes to Chapter 6

1. One of the more interesting facts to note about the different kinds of mouth music in Scottish Gaelic song culture is that each seems to have its own typical vocables and vocable phrases. Francis Collinson provides a brief analysis of the vocables in forty Gaelic waulking song refrains, ultimately concluding that they provide vague or general guidance on rhythm and pitch, but they function predominantly as mnemonic tools to assist the singer in remembering a particular song and its associated melody ("The Meaningless Refrain Syllables and Their Significance," in Campbell and Collinson 1969-1981: vol. 1, 227-37). Collinson's argument regarding waulking song vocables is similar to the conclusions that Kennedy draws about puirt-a-beul lyrics.

2. Transcription based on that found in *Tog Fonn! Gaelic Songs and Dance Tunes* (Mhàrtainn 1994).

3. A recording of "'S ann an Ìle" can be heard on Sileas's *Harpbreakers* (1990).

4. This port-a-beul shares characteristics with several others. It can be heard on The Barra MacNeils *Closer to Paradise* (1993) and *Until Now* (1997), Capercaillie's *Get Out* (1992) and sung by several youg Gaelic singers on *Mary Ann Kennedy & Na Seòid* (2008).

5. "Sowans" were "the fermented juice of oatmeal husks boiled, in bygone times a favourite article of food in Scotland" (Lamb 2012: 147).

6. A recording of "Brochan Lom" can be heard on Cliar's *Grinn Grinn* (2005).

Notes to Chapter 7

1. Mary Ann Kennedy disagrees with the musical transcription in Fig. 13; she argues that the word "nighean" (approximately "NEE-an" phonetically) is contracted to "nigh'n" ("NEEN" phonetically) in the lyrics. This contraction is quite common in Gaelic conversation and song, and would mean that the musical transcription would be better notated without sixteenth/semi-quavers at all. Instead, consistent with many reels, the tune would consist of almost all eighth/quaver notes. However, in reviewing three different recordings of this port-a-beul by three different singers, Chris McDonald and I agree that we can hear something rhythmically significant wherever "nighean"/"nigh'n" appears in the lyrics. Perhaps the voiced "n" sounds are creating the impression of extra syllables. Regardless, given that this is the spot where fiddlers typically perform cuts, it's clear that they hear it too. Therefore, while I accept that singers may be singing "nigh'n" instead of "nighean," I still believe that the rhythm of the lyrics comes across as transcribed in Fig 13.

2. In addition to Cliar's recording of this port-a-beul, it can be found on Puirt-a-Baroque's *Return of the Wanderer* (1998). It is set to the same tune as "Mo Ghille Mòr Foghaineach," which can be heard on Mary Jane Lamond's album, *Làn Dùil* (1999).

3. This port-a-beul can be heard on Capercaillie's *Beautiful Wasteland* (1998), Tannas's *Suitean Dubh* (1999) and Andrew McFayden's *Sùilean Fosgailte, Fuasgladh Cinn* (2007).

4. This collection can be found online at http://tobarandualchais.co.uk/.

Discography

Barra MacNeils, The. 1993. *Closer to Paradise*. Polydor 314 521 106 2. Compact disc.

———. 1995. *The Question*. Mercury/Polydor 314 529 077-2. Compact disc.

———. 1997. *Until Now*. Celtic Aire Records/Tidemark 02-50731. Compact disc.

Cameron, John Allan. 1969. *Here Comes John Allan Cameron*. Apex AL7 1645. LP.

———. 1979. *Freeborn Man*. Glencoe CSPS 1432. LP.

Campbell, Kenna. 1999. *Guth a' Shniomhas*. Macmeanmna SKYECD 12. Compact disc.

Campbell, Mary and Kenna Campbell. 1997. B' fheàrr mar a bha mi 'n uiridh / Fear an Dùin Mhòir. Track 10 on *Celtic Mouth Music*. Ellipsis Arts… CD4070. Compact disc.

Campbells, The. 2011, *Tha Mi 'n Dùil*. Watercolour Music WCMCD 037. Compact disc.

Capercaillie. 1992. *Get Out*. Survival Records SURCD016. Compact disc.

———. 1998. *Beautiful Wasteland*. Survival Records/Rykodisc RCD 10441. Compact disc.

Carruthers, Margo. 1998. *Tàlant nam Bàrd*. B&R Heritage Enterprises BRCD0010. Compact disc.

Choir of the Glasgow Gaelic Musical Association. 1990. *Gaelic Galore*. Lismore LCOM9037. Compact disc.

Cliar. 2000. *Cliar*. Macmeanmna SKYECD 14. Compact disc.

———. 2005. *Grinn Grinn*. Macmeanmna SKYECD40. Compact disc.

Cormack, Arthur. 1989. *Ruith na Gaoith*. Temple Records COMD 2032. Compact disc.

———. 2008[1984]. *Nuair Bha Mi Òg*. Temple Records COMD 2016. Compact disc.

Dòchas. 2002. *Dòchas*. Macmeanmna SKYECD 23. Compact disc.

Doorley, Éamon, Muireann NicAmhlaoibh, Julie Fowlis and Ross Martin. 2008. *Dual.* Machair Records [no catalogue number]. Compact disc.

Graham, James. 2004. *Siubhal.* Foot Stompin' Records CDFSR1728. Compact disc.

Griogair. 2007. *Dail-Riata.* Dunnach Records DUN 0701. Compact disc.

Kennedy, Mary Ann and Charlotte Petersen. 1991. *Strings Attached.* Macmeanmna SKYECD05. Compact disc.

Kennedy, Mary Ann et al. 2008. *Mary Ann Kennedy & Na Seòd.* Watercolour Music WCMCD033. Compact Disc.

Lamond, Mary Jane. ca. 1994. *Bho Thìr nan Craobh / From the Land of the Trees.* B&R Heritage Enterprises BRCD 0001. Compact disc.

———. 1997. *Suas e.* turtlemusik/A&M Records 268 842 000-2. Compact disc.

———. 1999. *Làn Dùil.* turtlemusik 26884-20042. Compact disc.

———. 2005. *Stòras.* turtlemusik 02 06363. Compact disc.

Lightfoot, Rona. 2004. *Eadarainn.* Macmeanmna SKYECD 28. Compact disc.

MacInnes, Màiri. 1995. *This Feeling Inside.* Greentrax CDTRAX 092. Compact disc.

———. 2001. *Orosay.* Greentrax CDTRAX 209. Compact disc.

MacKenzie. 1997. *Camhanach.* Macmeanmna SKYECD10. Compact disc.

MacKenzie, Eilidh. 1992. *Eideadh na Sgeulachd.* Temple Records COMD 2048. Compact disc.

MacKenzie, Talitha. 1994. *Sólas.* Shanachie 79084. Compact disc.

MacKinnon, Maeve. 1995. *Fo Smuain.* Macmeanmna SKYECD 08. Compact disc.

MacMillan, Gillebrìde. 2006. *Thogainn Ort Fonn.* Macmeanmna SKYECD42. Compact disc.

———. 2011. *Air Fòrladh.* Dealas DEALAS01CD. Compact disc.

MacPhee, Catherine Ann. 1993. *Cànan nan Gaidheal.* Greentrax CDTRAX 009. Compact disc.

———. 2004. *Sùil Air Ais.* Greentrax CDTRAX 258. Compact disc.

Mac-Talla. 1994. ...*Mairidh Gaol is Ceòl*. Temple Records COMD2054. Compact disc.

Martin, Anne. 1998. *Cò...?* Whitewave Music WWAVECD001. Compact disc.

———. 2000. *Nighean nan Geug*. Whitewave Music WWAVECD002. Compact disc.

Matheson, Karen. 2005. *Downriver*. Vertical Records VERTCD075. Compact disc.

McFayden, Andrew. 2004. *An Rathad Cam, 's an Rathad Dìreach*. Grian Culture & Language RCRD2004. Compact disc.

———. 2007. *Sùilean-Fosgailte, Fuasgladh Cinn / Open Eyes, Open Mind*. Grian Culture & Language SFFC2007. Compact disc.

Mouth Music. 1991. *Mouth Music*. Triple Earth Records/Rykodisc RCD 10196. Compact disc.

Murray, Anna. 1996. *Into Indigo*. Lochshore CDLDL1249. Compact disc.

———. 1999. *Trì Nithean—Three Things*. Lochshore CDLDL 1293. Compact disc.

Ó Ceannabháin, Peadar. 1997. *Mo Chuid den t-Saol / Traditional Songs from Connemara*. Cló Iar-Chonnachta CICD 131. Compact disc.

Oranaiche Cheap Breatuinn (Cape Breton Gaelic Choir). 1988. *Gaelic Songs from Oranaiche Cheap Breatuinn*. World Records WRCi-5863. LP.

Primrose, Christine. 1993. *Àite Mo Ghaoil (Place of My Heart)*. Temple Records COMD 1006. Compact disc.

Puirt-a-Baroque. 1998. *Return of the Wanderer*. Marquis Classics MAR223. Compact disc.

Rankin Family, The. 1989. *The Rankin Family*. Capitol Records C2 07777 99995 2 1. Compact disc.

Sileas. 1990. *Harpbreakers*. Lapwing Records LAP 127. Compact disc.

Stewart, Margaret, and Allan MacDonald. 1998. *Fhuair Mi Pòg*. Greentrax CDTRAX 132. Compact disc.

———. 2001. *Colla Mo Rùn: A Blend of Traditional Singing and Piping from Gaelic Scotland*. Greentrax CDTRAX 217. Compact disc.

Tannas. 1995. *Rù-Rà*. Lochshore CDLDL1231-K. Compact disc.

———. 1999. *Sùilean Dubh (Dark Eyes)*. Lochshore CDLDL 1289. Compact disc.

Various artists. 1992 [1971]. *Music from the Western Isles*. Vol. 2 of the Scottish Tradition Series. Greentrax CDTRAX 9002. Compact disc.

Walker, Rachel. 2004. *Braighe Loch Iall*. Skipinnish Records SKIPCD03. Compact disc.

———. 2006. *Fon Reul-Sholus*. Skipinnish Records SKIPCD09. Compact disc.

Whistlebinkies. 1999. *Timber Timbre*. Greentrax CDTRAX 159. Compact disc.

References

Abrahams, Roger D., and Alan Dundes. 1969. On Elephantasy and Elephanticide. *Psychoanalytic Review* 56(2): 225-41.

Alburger, Mary Anne. 1983. *Scottish Fiddlers and their Music*. London: V. Gollancz.

———. 2007. The Fiddle. In *Oral Literature and Performance Culture*, 238-73. Eds. J. Beech, O. Hand, F. MacDonald, M. A. Mulhern and J. Weston. Edinburgh: John Donald.

Anon. 2008. [YouTube comment.] "Ho Ro Mo Nighean Donn Bhòid-heach" / "Ho Ro My Beautiful Brown-Haired Maiden." *YouTube*. http://www.youtube.com/watch?v=ZZX8fr_ijGE (accessed October 15, 2009; offline as of August 2014).

Atherton, Michael. 2007. Rhythm-Speak: Mnemonic, Language-Play or Song? Paper, International Conference on Music Communication, Sydney, Australia. Available online: http://marcs.uws.edu.au/links/ICO-Music/ArchiveCD/Full_Paper_PDF/Atherton.pdf (accessed January 15, 2014).

Baring-Gould, William, and Ceil Baring-Gould. 1962. *The Annotated Mother Goose: Nursery Rhymes Old and New*. New York: Bramhall House.

Bassin, Ethel. 1977. *The Old Songs of Skye: Frances Tolmie and Her Circle*. London: Routledge and Kegan Paul.

Batish, Ashwin. 2003. RagaNet Tabla Lesson 5: Some Basic Tabla Bols (Sounds). http://raganet.com/RagaNet/Issues/5/tabla5.html (accessed May 25, 2009).

Bauer, Michael. 2011. *Blas na Gàidhlig: The Practical Guide to Scottish Gaelic Pronunciation* N.p.: Akerbeltz.

Bennett, Margaret. 1998. *Oatmeal and the Catechism: Scottish Gaelic Settlers in Quebec*. Edinburgh, Kingston and Montreal: John Donald Publishers and McGill-Queen's University Press.

Berger, Arthur Asa. 1993. *An Anatomy of Humor*. New Brunswick, NJ: Transaction.

Berliner, Paul F. 2009. *Thinking in Jazz: The Infinite Art of Improvisation*. Chicago: University of Chicago Press.

Black, Ronald, ed. 1999. *An Tuil: Anthology of 20th Century Scottish Gaelic Verse*. Edinburgh: Polygon.

———, ed. 2001. *An Lasair: Anthology of 18th Century Scottish Gaelic Verse*. Edinburgh: Birlinn.

Bohlman, Philip Vilas. 2004. *The Music of European Nationalism: Cultural Identity and Modern History*. Santa Barbara, CA: ABC-CLIO.

Bourdieu, Pierre. 1980. The Aristocracy of Culture. *Media, Culture and Society* 2:225-54.

Boyden, David Dodge. 1965. *The History of Violin Playing from its Origins to 1761 and its Relationship to the Violin and Violin Music*. London: Oxford University Press.

Breathnach, Breandán. 1983. *Dancing in Ireland*. Miltown-Malbay, Co. Clare: Dal gCais Publications in association with the Folklore and Folk Music Society of Clare.

Bronson, Bertrand Harris. 1976. *The Singing Tradition of Child's Popular Ballads*. Princeton: Princeton University Press.

Bruford, Alan. 1978a. Gaelic Folksong: A Brief Pre-History. *Folk Review* 7(5): 4-7.

———. 1978b. Gaelic Lullabies, Laments and Mouth Music. *Folk Review* 8(1): 4-8.

———. 1978c. Love Songs in Gaelic I. *Folk Review* 7(8): 10-13.

———. 1979. Gaelic Songs. *Folk Review* 8(5): 8-14.

Buchan, David. 1972. *The Ballad and the Folk*. London and Boston: Routledge and Kegan Paul.

Campbell, John Lorne. 1990. *Songs Remembered in Exile*. Aberdeen: Aberdeen University Press.

Campbell, John Lorne, and Francis Collinson. 1969-1981. *Hebridean Folksongs*. 3 vols. Oxford: Clarendon Press.

Campbell, Katherine. 2007. *The Fiddle in Scottish Culture: Aspects of the Tradition*. Edinburgh: John Donald.

Cannon, Roderick. 2002. *The Highland Bagpipe and Its Music*, 2nd ed. Edinburgh: John Donald.

Caplan, Ronald. 1978. A Milling Frolic on the North Shore. *Cape Breton's Magazine*, 39-46. Available online: http://capebretonsmagazine.com/modules/publisher/item.php?itemid=820.

Carmichael, Alexander. 1928 [1900]. *Carmina Gadelica: Hymns and Incantations* 2nd ed. Vol. 1. Edinburgh and London: Oliver and Boyd.

Carolan, Nicholas. 2001. s.v. Ireland: Traditional Music. *New Grove Dictionary of Music and Musicians*, 2nd ed. Oxford: Oxford University Press.

Chambers, Christine Knox. 1980. Non-Lexical Vocables in Scottish Traditional Music. PhD dissertation, Edinburgh University.

Chapman, Malcolm. 1992. *The Celts: The Construction of a Myth*. New York: St. Martin's Press.

Cheape, Hugh. 2000. *The Book of the Bagpipe*. Lincolnwood, IL: Contemporary Books.

———. 2010. Gheibhte Breacain Charnaid (The Scarlet Tartans Would Be Got...): The Re-Invention of Tradition. In *From Tartan to Tartanry: Scottish Culture, History and Myth*, 13-31. Ed. I. Brown. Edinburgh: Edinburgh University Press.

Chin, Elizabeth. 2001. Feminist Theory and the Ethnography of Children's Worlds: Barbie in New Haven, Connecticut. In *Children and Anthropology: Perspectives for the 21st Century*, 129-48. Ed. H. B. Schwartzman. Westport, CT: Bergin and Garvey.

Cockburn, Craig. 2010. Traditional Gaelic Song and Singing Sean-Nós. http://www.siliconglen.com/culture/gaelicsong.html (accessed November 28, 2010).

Collinson, Francis. 1966. *The Traditional and National Music of Scotland*. London: Routledge and Kegan Paul.

———. 1980. s.v. Scotland: Folk Music: Gaelic Song. *The New Grove Dictionary of Music and Musicians*, 2nd ed. London: Macmillan Publishers.

———. 2001. s.v. Reel. *The New Grove Dictionary of Music and Musicians*, 2nd ed. New York: Oxford University Press.

Comunn Gaidhealach Leodhais. 1998 [1982]. *Eilean Fraoich: Lewis Gaelic Songs and Melodies*. Stornaway, Scotland: Acair Earranta.

Conn, Stephanie. 2011. Carn Mor de Chlachan Beaga/A Large Cairn from Small Stones: Multivocality and Memory in Cape Breton Gaelic Singing. PhD dissertation, University of Toronto.

———. 2012. Fitting between Present and Past: Memory and Social Interaction in Cape Breton Gaelic Singing. *Ethnomusicology Forum* 21(3): 354-73.

———. 2013. Peter's Tapes: Private Collections and Mid-Century Cape Breton Musical Culture. Unpublished manuscript.

Craig, K. C. 1949. *Òrain Luaidh Màiri Nighean Alasdair: Air an Cruinneachadh*. Glasgow: Published for the author by A. Matheson.

Cray, Ed. 1969. *The Erotic Muse*. New York: Pyramid Communications.

———. 1992. *The Erotic Muse: American Bawdy Songs*, 2nd ed. Urbana: University of Illinois Press.

Creighton, Helen, and Calum MacLeod. 1964. *Gaelic Songs in Nova Scotia*. Ottawa: National Museum of Canada.

Customer. 1998. Tha i glé mhath!!(It's great!!). *Amazon.com*. http://www.amazon.com/North-Country-Rankin-Family/product-reviews/B000002UK5?pageNumber=2 (accessed October 15, 2009).

Dance Notation Bureau. 2014. http://www.dancenotation.org/lnbasics/ (accessed August 5, 2014).

Dembling, Jonathan. 2005. You Play It as You Would Sing It: Cape Breton, Scottishness, and the Means of Cultural Production. In *Transatlantic Scots*, 180-97. Ed. C. Ray. Tuscaloosa: University of Alabama Press.

Dickson, Joshua. 2006. *When Piping was Strong: Tradition, Change and the Bagpipe in South Uist*. Edinburgh: John Donald.

Doherty, Elizabeth A. 1996. The Paradox of the Periphery: Evolution of the Cape Breton Fiddle Tradition, ca. 1928-1995. PhD dissertation, University of Limerick.

Dolmetsch, Mabel. 1959. *Dances of England and France from 1450 to 1600*, 2nd ed. London: Routledge and Kegan Paul.

Donaldson, William. 2000. *The Highland Pipe and Scottish Society, 1750-1950: Transmission, Change and the Concept of Tradition*. East Linton, East Lothian, Scotland: Tuckwell Press.

Douglas, Katherine. 1971. *Sar-Òrain le Catriona Dhughlas: Na h-Òrain is an Ceòl gu h-uile le Catriona Dhughlas*. Dunvegan, Scotland: D. Budge.

Duesenberry, Peggy, and Francis Collinson. 2001. s.v. Scotland: Traditional Music. *The New Grove Dictionary of Music and Musicians*, 2nd ed. Oxford: Oxford University Press.

Dundes, Alan, and Robert A. Georges. 1962. Some Minor Genres of Obscene Folklore. *The Journal of American Folklore* 75(297): 221-26.

Dunlay, Kate, and David Greenberg. 1996. *Traditional Celtic Violin Music of Cape Breton*. Mississauga: DunGreen Music.

Dunn, Charles. 1991 [1953]. *Highland Settler: A Portrait of the Scottish Gael in Cape Breton and Eastern Nova Scotia*. Wreck Cove, NS: Breton Books.

Dunn, Jacqueline Ann. 1991. Tha Blas na Gàidhlig air a h-uile Fidhleir (The Gaelic Flavour in Every Fiddler). BA Thesis, St. Francis Xavier University.

Edwards, Brent Hayes. 2002. Louis Armstrong and the Syntax of Scat. *Critical Inquiry* 28(3): 618-49.

Emberly, Andrea. 2004. Exploring Children's Musical Culture in Ethnomusicology. http://portal.unesco.org/culture/es/files/21801/10892137393emberly.pdf/emberly.pdf (accessed November 4, 2009).

Emmerson, George S. 1971. *Rantin' Pipe and Tremblin' String: A History of Scottish Dance Music*. Montreal and Kingston: McGill-Queen's University Press.

———. 1972. *A Social History of Scottish Dance*. Montreal and Kingston: McGill-Queen's University Press.

Eydmann, Stuart. 2007. Diversity and Diversification in Scottish Music. In *Oral Literature and Performance Culture*, 193-212. Eds. J. Beech, O. Hand, F. MacDonald, M. A. Mulhern and J. Weston. Edinburgh: John Donald.

Fatone, Gina. 2002. Making Hands Sing: Vocal-to-motor Transfer of Melody Within Classical Scottish Highland Bagpiping and Selected Asian Instrumental Traditions in North America. PhD dissertation, University of California, Los Angeles.

———. 2010. "You'll Break Your Heart Trying to Play It Like You Sing It": Intermodal Imagery and the Transmission of Scottish Classical Bagpiping. *Ethnomusicology* 54(3): 395-424.

Feintuch, Burt. 2004. The Conditions for Cape Breton Fiddle Music: The Social and Economic Setting of a Regional Soundscape. *Ethnomusicology* 48(1): 73-104.

Fergusson, Donald A. 1977. *Fad Air Falbh As Innse Gall: Leis Comh-Chruinneachadh Cheap Breatuinn / Beyond the Hebrides: Including the Cape Breton Collection*. Halifax, NS: D. A. Fergusson.

Fine, Gary Alan, and Michaela de Soucey. 2005. Joking cultures: Humor themes as social regulation in group life. *Humor: International Journal of Humor Research* 18(1): 1-22.

Flett, T. M., and J. F. Flett. 1953. Some Hebridean Folk Dances. *Journal of the English Folk Dance and Song Society* 7(2): 112-27.

———. 1956. Dramatic Jigs in Scotland. *Folklore* 67(2): 84-96.

———. 1964. *Traditional Dancing in Scotland*. London: Routledge and Kegan Paul.

———. 1996. *Traditional Step-Dancing in Scotland*. Edinburgh: Scottish Cultural Press.

Frisbie, Charlotte J. 1980. Vocables in Navajo Ceremonial Music. *Ethnomusicology* 24(3): 347-92.

Garrison, Virginia Hope. 1985. Traditional and Non-Traditional Teaching and Learning Practices in Folk Music: An Ethnographic Field Study of Cape Breton Fiddling. PhD dissertation, University of Wisconsin-Madison.

Gerould, Gordon Hall. 1957 [1932]. *The Ballad of Tradition*. New York: Oxford University Press.

Gibson, John G. 1998. *Traditional Gaelic Bagpiping, 1745-1945*. Montreal and Kingston: McGill-Queen's University Press.

———. 2002. *Old and New World Highland Bagpiping*. Montreal and Kingston: McGill-Queen's University Press.

Goldstein, Kenneth S. 1967. Bowdlerization and Expurgation: Academic and Folk. *The Journal of American Folklore* 80(318): 374-86.

Graham, George Farquhar. 1871. *Songs of Scotland, Chronologically Arranged with Introduction and Notes*. Glasgow: Maurice Ogle and Company.

Graham, Glenn. 2006. *The Cape Breton Fiddle: Making and Maintaining Tradition*. Sydney, NS: Cape Breton University Press.

Greenhill, Pauline. 1989. *True Poetry: Traditional and Popular Verse in Ontario*. Montreal and Kingston: McGill-Queen's University Press.

Halpern, Ida. 1976. On the Interpretation of "Meaningless-Nonsensical Syllables" in the Music of the Pacific Northwest Indians. *Ethnomusicology* 20(2): 253-71.

Halpert, Herbert. 1962. Folklore and Obscenity: Definitions and Problems. *The Journal of American Folklore* 75(297): 190-94.

Haruko, Komoda, and Nogawa Mihoko. 2002. s.v. Theory and Notation in Japan. *The Garland Encyclopedia of World Music*, vol: East Asia: China, Japan and Korea. Eds. Robert C. Province, Yoshiko Tokumaru, J. Lawrence Witzleban. London: Routledge.

Hennessy, Jeffrey. 2008. Fiddle Grooves: Identity, Representation, and the Sound of Cape Breton Fiddle Music in Popular Culture. PhD dissertation, University of Toronto.

Herdman, Jessica. 2008. The Cape Breton Fiddle Narrative: Innovation, Preservation, Dancing. MA thesis, University of British Columbia.

Hinton, Leanne. 1980. Vocables in Havasupai Song. In *Southwestern Indian Ritual Drama*, 275-305. Ed. C. J. Frisbie. Albuquerque: University of New Mexico Press.

James, Clifford. 1988. Identity in Mashpee. In *The Predicament of Culture: Twentieth-Century Ethnography, Literature, and Art*, 277-343. Cambridge, MA: Harvard University Press.

James, Simon. 1999. *The Atlantic Celts: Ancient People or Modern Invention?* Madison: University of Wisconsin Press.

Johnson, Samuel, and Finlay J. Macdonald. 1983. *A Journey to the Western Isles: Johnson's Scottish Journey*. London: Macdonald.

Kassebaum, Gayathri Rajapur. 2000. s.v. Karnatak Raga. *The Garland Encyclopedia of World Music*, vol: South Asia: The Indian Subcontinent. Ed. Alison Arnold. London: Routledge.

Kennedy-Fraser, Marjory, and Kenneth MacLeod. 1909. *Songs of the Hebrides and Other Celtic Songs from the Highlands*. London: Boosey and Co.

Kennedy, Mary Ann. 1995. Puirt-à-Beul, The Mouth Music of the Scottish Gael: A Study of Gaelic Mouth Music, Its Structure, Style, Influence and Historical Background. MMus thesis, University of Manchester.

Kennedy, Michael. 2001. Gaelic Nova Scotia: An Economic, Cultural and Social Impact Study. Report. Halifax, NS: Nova Scotia Museum. Available online: http://gaelic.novascotia.ca/sites/default/files/files/Gaelic-Report.pdf.

Knapp, Mary, and Herbert Knapp. 1976. *One Potato, Two Potato ...: The Secret Education of American Children*. New York: Norton.

Kopka, Matthew. 1997. CD liner notes. *Celtic Mouth Music*. Ellipsis Arts... CD4070.

Kuntz, Andrew. 2009. *The Fiddler's Companion*. http://www.ibiblio.org/fiddlers (accessed September 21, 2009).

Lamb, William. 2012. *Keith Norman MacDonald's Puirt-à-Beul: The Vocal Dance Music of the Scottish Gaels*. Isle of Skye, UK: Taigh na Teud.

———. 2013. Reeling in the Strathspey: The Origins of Scotland's National Music. *Scottish Studies* 36:66-102.

Landin, Anne. 2009. *Guthan Prìseil: Guthan agus Òrain Gàidheil Cheap Breatainn/Precious Voices: Voices and Songs of the Cape Breton Gael.* Sydney, NS: Centre for Cape Breton Studies, Cape Breton University.

Lau, Frederick. 2002. s.v. Transmission of Music in East Asia. *The Garland Encyclopedia of World Music*, vol: East Asia: China, Japan and Korea. Eds. Robert C. Province, Yoshiko Tokumaru, J. Lawrence Witzleban. London: Routledge.

Locke, David. 2007. Dagomba Dance-Drumming: Teaching and Learning. https://wikis.uit.tufts.edu/confluence/display/DagombaDance-Drumming/Teaching+and+Learning (accessed August 25, 2012).

Long, Debra L., and Arthur C. Graesser. 1988. Wit and Humor in Discourse Processing. *Discourse Processes* 11(1): 35-60.

Lowenstein, Wendy. 1974. *Shocking, Shocking, Shocking: The Improper Play Rhymes of Australian Children.* Prahran, Australia: Fish and Chip Press.

Mac-na-Ceàrdadh, Gilleasbuig. 2004 [1879]. *An t-Òranaiche: The Gaelic Songster.* Ed. T. Matheson. St. Andrew's, NS: Sìol Cultural Enterprises.

MacDonald, Alexander. 1922. Fragments of Gaelic Song and Lilt. *Transactions of the Gaelic Society of Inverness* 29:95-118.

MacDonald, Alexander. 1996. Cape Breton Fiddle Music: Is it unique? Yes! Why? *Celtic Heritage*, June/July, 8-9.

———. 1998. Gaelic Music. What is it? *Celtic Heritage*, February/March (5): 32-33.

MacDonald, Allan A. 1995. The Relationship Between Pibroch and Gaelic Song: Its Implications on the Performance Style of the Pibroch Ùrlar. MLitt thesis, University of Edinburgh.

MacDonald, Donald John, and Bill Innes. 1998. *Chì Mi: Bàrdachd Dhòmhnaill Iain Dhonnchaidh / I See: The Poetry of Donald John MacDonald.* Edinburgh: Birlinn.

MacDonald, Keith Norman. 1895. *The Gesto Collection of Highland Music.* Edinburgh: K. N. MacDonald.

———. 1906. *In Defense of Ossian: Being a Summary of the Evidence in Favor of the Authenticity of the Poems.* N.p.: Kessinger Publishing.

———. 1929 [1900]. *MacDonald Bards from Mediaeval Times.* Glasgow: A. MacLaren.

———. 1931 [1901]. *Puirt-a-Beul.* Glasgow: Alex MacLaren and Sons.

———. 1986 [1887]. *The Skye Collection of the Best Reels and Strathspeys Extant.* London, ON: Scott's Highland Services.

MacDonald, Norman. 1863. *Sar-obair nam Bàrd Gaelach, or The Beauties of Gaelic Poetry and Lives of the Highland Bards.* Halifax, NS: James Bowes and Sons.

MacDougall, J. L. 1922. *History of Inverness County, Nova Scotia.* Privately printed.

MacGillivray, Allister. 1981. *The Cape Breton Fiddler.* Sydney, NS: College of Cape Breton Press.

———. 1988. *A Cape Breton Ceilidh.* Sydney, NS: Sea Scape Music.

MacGregor, Gregor. 1900. Am Muileann Dubh. *Celtic Monthly* 8:159-60.

MacInnes, Iain. 2007. Caus Michtilie the Weirlie Nottis Breike, on Hieland Pipes, Scottes and Hybernicke. In *Oral Literature and Performance Culture*, 225-37. Eds. J. Beech, O. Hand, F. MacDonald, M. A. Mulhern and J. Weston. Edinburgh: John Donald.

MacInnes, John. 1969-1970. The Choral Tradition in Scottish Gaelic Songs. *Transactions of the Gaelic Society of Inverness* 46:44-65.

———. 2006. Gaelic Song and the Dance. In *Dùthchas nan Gàidheal: Selected Essays of John MacInnes*, 248-64. Ed. M. S. Newton. Edinburgh: Birlinn.

MacInnes, Sheldon. 1994. Cape Breton Step-Dance: An Irish or Scottish Tradition? http://www.siliconglen.com/celtfaq/3_2.html (accessed June 24, 2009).

———. 1996. Stepdancing: Gach Taobh dhe'n Uisge ("Both Sides of the Water"). In *The Centre of the World at the Edge of a Continent*, 111-18. Eds. C. Corbin and J. A. Rolls. Sydney, NS: University College of Cape Breton Press.

Mackintosh, Andrew. ca. 1910. English and Gaelic Words for Strathspeys and Reels. *Transactions of the Gaelic Society of Inverness* 28:288-326.

———. 1916. Gaelic and English Words for Old Highland Marches, Strathspeys and Reels. *Transactions of the Gaelic Society of Inverness* 20:81-94.

MacLagan, Robert Craig. 1901. *The Games and Diversions of Argyleshire.* London: The Folk-Lore Society.

———. 1905. Additions to "The Games of Argyleshire." *Folk-Lore* 16:208-10.

MacLeod, John. 1996. *Highlanders: A History of the Gaels*. London: Hodder and Stoughton.

MacLeod, Morag. 1984. The Folk Revival in Gaelic Song. In *The Folk Music Revival in Scotland*, 191-204. Ed. A. Munro. London: Kahn and Averill.

MacNeil, Joe Neil. 1987. *Tales Until Dawn: The World of a Cape Breton Gaelic Story-Teller*. Ed. J. Shaw. Kingston and Montreal: McGill-Queen's University Press.

MacNeil, Neil. 1958. *The Highland Heart in Nova Scotia*. Toronto: S. J. Reginald Saunders and Company.

MacNeill, Seumas, and Frank Richardson. 1987. *Piobaireachd and Its Interpretation: Classical Music of the Highland Bagpipe*. Edinburgh: John Donald Publishers.

Matheson, William, and John MacCodrum. 1938. *The Songs of John Maccodrum: Bard to Sir James Macdonald of Sleuth*. Edinburgh: Scottish Gaelic Texts Society.

McDavid, Jodi. 2009. The Fiddle Burning Priest of Mabou. *Ethnologies* 30(2): 115-36.

McKay, Ian. 1994. *The Quest of the Folk: Antimodernism and Cultural Selection in Twentieth-Century Nova Scotia*. Montreal and Kingston: McGill-Queen's University Press.

McKean, Thomas A. 1997. *Hebridean Song-Maker: Iain MacNeacail of the Isle of Skye*. Edinburgh: Polygon.

McKinnon, Ian. 1989. Fiddling to Fortune: The Role of Commercial Recordings Made by Cape Breton Fiddlers in the Fiddle Music Tradition of Cape Breton Island. MA thesis, Memorial University of Newfoundland.

Meade, Don. 1999. The Composition of Irish Traditional Music. *Current Musicology* 67/68:289-98.

Meek, Donald E. 1977. *Màiri Mhòr nan Òran: Taghadh d'a h-Òrain le Eachdraidh a Beatha is Notaichean*. Glasgow: Gairm.

Melhuish, Martin. 1998. *Celtic Tides: Traditional Music in a New Age*. Kingston, ON: Quarry Music Books.

Melin, Mats. 2005. "Putting the Dirt Back In": An Investigation of Step Dancing in Scotland. MA thesis, University of Limerick.

———. 2012. Exploring the Percussive Routes and Shared Commonalities in Cape Breton Step Dancing. PhD dissertation, University of Limerick.

Meyer, John C. 2000. Humor as a Double-Edged Sword: Four Functions of Humor in Communication. *Communication Theory* 10(3): 310-31.

Mhàrtainn, Cairistìona. 1994. *Tog Fonn! Orain is Puirt Dannsaidh.* Isle of Skye, UK: Taigh na Teud.

Minks, Amanda. 2002. From Children's Song to Expressive Practices: Old and New Directions in the Ethnomusicological Study of Children. *Ethnomusicology* 46(3): 379-408.

Moore, Maggie. 1995. Scottish Step Dancing. http://users.bandzoogle. com/johnsikorski/files/Stepdance_History.doc (accessed June 5, 2009).

Morrison, Cecily. 2003. Culture at the Core: Invented Traditions and Imagined Communities Part I: Identity Formation. *International Review of Scottish Studies* 28:3-21.

———. 2004. Culture at the Core: Invented Traditions and Imagined Communities Part II: Community Formation. *International Review of Scottish Studies* 29:49-71.

Nettl, Bruno. 1956. *Music in Primitive Cultures.* Cambridge, MA: Harvard University Press.

Newton, Michael. 2004. "Dancing with the Dead: A Ritual Dance at Wakes in the Scottish Highlands". In *Canan agus Cultar / Language and Culture: Rannsachadh na Gaidhlig 3*, 215-34. Ed. W. McLeod. Edinburgh: Dunedin Academic Press.

———. 2009. *Warriors of the Word: The World of the Scottish Highlanders.* Edinburgh: Birlinn.

———. 2013. "Dannsair air ùrlar-dèile thu": Gaelic Evidence about Dance from the mid-17th to late 18th century Highlands. *International Review of Scottish Studies* 38:49-78.

———. 2014. The Origins of the Strathspey: A Rebuttal. *The Virtual Gael*, January 4. http://virtualgael.wordpress.com/2014/01/04/the-origins-of-the-strathspey-a-rebuttal/ (accessed January 24, 2014).

NicLeáoid, Norma. 2013. *Fonn: The Campbells of Greepe—Music and a Sense of Place in a Gaelic Family Song Tradition.* Stornoway, U.K.: Acair.

Nilsen, Ken. 1996-1997. The Role of the Priest in the Gaelic Folklore of Nova Scotia. *Béaloideas* 64-65:171-94.

Nova Scotia Highland Village Society. 2006. Céilidh air Cheap Brea-tunn/ Cape Breton Ceilidh. www.virtualmuseum.ca/Exhibitions/Ceil-idh/html/dance_readexhibittext.html (accessed August 15, 2013).

Ó Baoill, Colm. 2009. *Maighread Nighean Lachlainn, Song-maker of Mull: An Edition and Study of the Extant Corpus of her Verse in Praise of the Jacobite Maclean Leaders of her Time.* Edinburgh: Scottish Academic Press.

Ó Laoire, Lillis. 2005. Irish Music. In *The Cambridge Companion to Modern Irish Culture*, 267-84. Eds. J. N. Cleary and C. Connolly. Cambridge: Cambridge University Press.

OnMusic Dictionary. 2013. Scat Singing. http://dictionary.onmusic.org/terms/3012-scat_singing (accessed August 16, 2014).

Opie, Iona and Peter Opie. 1959. *The Lore and Language of School-chil-dren*. Oxford: The Clarendon Press.

Perks, Robert and Alistair Thomson, eds. 2006. *The Oral History Reader*. 2nd ed. New York: Routledge.

Perlman, Ken. 1996. *The Fiddle Music of Prince Edward Island: Celtic and Acadian Tunes in Living Tradition.* Pacific, MO: Mel Bay Publications.

Pound, Louise. 1932. On the Dating of the English and Scottish Ballads. *PMLA* 47(1): 10-16.

Purser, John. 1992. *Scotland's Music: A History of the Traditional and Classical Music of Scotland from Early Times to the Present Day*, 2nd ed. Edinburgh: Mainstream Publishing in conjunction with BBC Scotland.

Quigley, Colin. 1985. *Close to the Floor: Folk Dance in Newfoundland.* St. John's, NL: Memorial University of Newfoundland Folklore and Language Publications.

Rankin, Rev. D. J. 1944-1945. Reverend Kenneth J. MacDonald. *Canadian Catholic Historical Association Report* 12:109-16.

Rhodes, Frank. 1964. Dancing in Cape Breton Island, Nova Scotia. In *Traditional Dancing in Scotland*, 267-85. Eds. J. F. Flett and T. M. Flett. Edinburgh: Scottish Cultural Press.

———. 1996. Step-Dancing in Cape Breton Island, Nova Scotia. In *Traditional Step-Dancing in Scotland*, 185-211. Eds. J. F. Flett and T. M. Flett. Edinburgh: Scottish Cultural Press.

Roden, Christina. 1998. Mary Jane Lamond—Cape Breton's Reluctant Gaelic Diva. http://www.rootsworld.com/interview/lamond.html (accessed May 13, 2004).

Rogers, Ellis. 2004. *The Quadrille*. Orpington, UK: Ellis Rogers.

Ross, James. 1957. A Classification of Gaelic Folk-Song. *Scottish Studies* 1:95-151.

Ruckert, George E. 2004. *Music in North India*. Eds. B. C. Wade and P. S. Campbell. New York: Oxford University Press.

Samuel, Geoffrey. 1976. Songs of Lhasa. *Ethnomusicology* 20(3): 407-49.

Sanger, Keith, and Alison Kinnaird. 1992. *Tree of Strings = Crann nan Teud: A History of the Harp in Scotland*. Temple, Midlothian, Scotland: Kinmor Music.

Sawyers, June Skinner. 2000. *Celtic Music: A Complete Guide*. New York: Da Capo Press.

Saxby, Jessie M. E. 1932. *Shetland Traditional Lore*. Edinburgh: Grant and Murray.

Schmitz, John Robert. 2002. Humor as a Pedagogical Tool in Foreign Language and Translation Courses. *Humor: International Journal of Humor Research* 15(1): 89-113.

Scott, Catriona Mairi. 2005. The Scottish Highland Dancing Tradition. PhD dissertation, University of Edinburgh.

Scott, James C. 1990. *Domination and the Arts of Resistance: Hidden Transcripts*. New Haven: Yale University Press.

Sharpe, Jennifer. 2006. Jimmie Riddle and the Lost Art of Eephing. http://www.npr.org/templates/story/story.php?storyId=5259589 (accessed May 25, 2009).

Shaw, John. 1987. Summary and Final Report: Gaelic in Prince Edward Island, A Cultural Remnant (Gaelic Field Recording Project). Introduced and indexed by Michael Kennedy. http://projects.upei.ca/iis/files/2014/07/GAELIC-IN-PRINCE-EDWARD-ISLAND.pdf (accessed July 28, 2014).

———. 1992-1993. Language, Music and Local Aesthetics: Views from Gaeldom and Beyond. *Scottish Language* 11/12:37-64.

———. 2007. *The Blue Mountains and Other Gaelic Stories from Cape Breton*. Montreal and Kingston: McGill-Queen's University Press.

———, ed. 2000. *Brìgh an Òrain*. Montreal and Kingston: McGill-Queen's University Press.

Shaw, Margaret Fay. 1977 [1955]. *Folksongs and Folklore of South Uist*. Oxford: Oxford University Press.

Shears, Barry. 2008. *Dance to the Piper: The Highland Bagpipe in Nova Scotia*. Sydney, NS: Cape Breton University Press.

Shoupe, Catherine A. 2001. Scottish Social Dancing and the Formation of Community. *Western Folklore* 60(2/3):125-48.

Sparling, Heather. 2000. Puirt-a-Beul: An Ethnographic Study of Mouth Music in Cape Breton, Nova Scotia. MA Thesis, York University.

———. 2006. Song Genres, Cultural Capital and Social Distinctions in Gaelic Cape Breton. PhD dissertation, York University.

———. 2008a. Categorically Speaking: Towards a Theory of (Musical) Genre in Cape Breton Gaelic Culture. *Ethnomusicology* 52(3): 401-25.

———. 2008b. Grist for the Tourist Mill: Tourists in Gaelic Milling Frolics in Cape Breton, Nova Scotia. In *Refereed Papers from the Third International Small Islands Culture Conference*, 94-100. Ed. I. Novaczek. Small Island Cultures Research Initiative. Available online: http://sicri-network.org/archives/ISIC3/.

Sparling, Henry Halliday, ed. 2005 [1887]. *Irish Minstrelsy: Being a Selection of Irish Songs, Lyrics and Ballads, Original and Translated*. N.p.: Elibron Classics.

Spielman, Earl V. 1972. The Fiddling Traditions of Cape Breton and Texas: A Study in Parallels and Contrasts. *Anuario Interamericano de Investigacion Musical* 8:39-48.

Taft, Michael. 1986. Of Scoffs, Mounties, and Mainlanders: The Popularity of a Sheep-Stealing Ballad in Newfoundland. In *Media Sense: The Folklore-Popular Culture Continuum*, 77-98. Eds. P. Narváez and M. Laba. Bowling Green, OH: Bowling Green State University Press.

Taylor, Seumas. 1998. ... in which we learn more of Gaelic music. *Celtic Heritage*, December/January, 5-6, 26-28.

Thomson, Derick S. 1951. *The Gaelic Sources of MacPherson's "Ossian."* Edinburgh: Oliver and Boyd.

———, ed. 1983. *The Companion to Gaelic Scotland*. Glasgow: Gairm Publications.

———. 1990. *Introduction to Gaelic Poetry*. Edinburgh: Edinburgh University Press.

———, ed. 1992. *Scottish Gaelic Texts*. Vol. 17 of *The MacDiarmid Manuscript Anthology*. Edinburgh: Scottish Gaelic Texts Society.

———. 1993. *Gaelic Poetry in the Eighteenth Century: A Bilingual Anthology*. Aberdeen: Association for Scottish Literary Studies.

Thurston, Hugh A. 1954. *Scotland's Dances*. London: Bell.

Tolmie, Frances. 1910-1913. Frances Tolmie Collection. *Journal of the Folk-Song Society* 4(16): 143-276.

Trevor-Roper, Hugh. 1983. The Invention of Tradition: The Highland Tradition of Scotland. In *The Invention of Tradition*, 15-41. Eds. E. Hobsbawm and T. Ranger. Cambridge: Cambridge University Press.

Turino, Thomas. 2008. *Music as Social Life: The Politics of Participation*. Chicago: University of Chicago Press.

Uí Ógáin, Ríonach. 1995. Traditional Music and Irish Cultural History. In *Irish Musical Studies*, 77-100. Eds. G. Gillen and H. White. Blackrock, U.K.: Irish Academic Press.

Um, Hae Kyung. 2002. s.v. Korean Vocal Techniques. *The Garland Encyclopedia of World Music*, vol: East Asia: China, Japan and Korea. Eds. Robert C. Province, Yoshiko Tokumaru, J. Lawrence Witzleban. London: Routledge.

UNESCO. 2001. UNESCO Universal Declaration on Cultural Diversity. November 2. http://portal.unesco.org/en/ev.php-URL_ID=13179&URL_DO=DO_TOPIC&URL_SECTION=201.html

Vallely, Fintan. 1999. *The Companion to Irish Traditional Music*. Cork, Ireland: Cork University Press.

Viswanathan, T., and Matthew Harp Allen. 2004. *Music in South India*. Eds. B. C. Wade and P. S. Campbell. New York: Oxford University Press.

Watson, J. Carmichael. 1965. *Gaelic Songs of Mary Macleod*. Edinburgh: Oliver & Boyd for the Scottish Gaelic Texts Society.

Watson, Seósamh. 2005-2006. An Muileann Dubh: Story and Tune. *An Rubha* (winter): 14-15. Available online: http://museum.gov.ns.ca/hv/images/anrubha_9-1.pdf.

Williams, Sean. 2009. *Focus: Irish Traditional Music*. New York: Routledge.

Wilson, Mark, and Kate Dunlay. 2002. CD liner notes. *Mabou Coal Mines*. Vol. 1 of *Traditional Fiddle Music of Cape Breton*. Rounder Records 82161-703725.

Index

Page numbers refer to print edition

Act of Proscription (Scotland) 57-59
alliteration 141-42
archives 271, 303, 347
arrangements 35, 137, 190, 260, 265, 314
attitudes toward Puirt-a-beul 2, 39, 59, 69-70, 72, 311

bagpipes 20, 39, 42, 46-47, 56-60, 65, 75, 88-90, 94-95, 117, 123-25, 197, 233, 247, 288, 319-20
bards 6-7, 88, 95, 153-54, 156, 159, 174
Barra MacNeils, The 2, 254, 261-62, 269, 325, 329, 331
Battle of Culloden *see* Jacobite Rebellion (1745-1745)
bawdry 21, 161, 169, 172-77, 181, 274-75; obfuscation 173
binary form 88-92, 94, 96, 98, 128, 186, 198, 319
body language *see* gestures
Bonnie Prince Charlie *see* Stuart, Charles Edward
brail *see bransle*
bransle 91
breath control 134, 138, 256

Cameron, John Allan 40, 43, 73, 74, 231, 289, 298, 299
Campbell, Kenna 83, 131, 209, 224
canntaireachd 20, 26, 28, 34-37, 46-51, 223, 230, 247-48, 253, 256, 319
Celtic languages 12
Celtic, definition 12
ceòl mòr see pibroch
Ceòlas 211, 236, 282, 288
Child, James Francis 75
children 1, 23, 37, 44-46, 51, 101, 168, 227, 230, 274-75, 307
clàrsach see harp
community ix, xiii, 2, 18, 45, 41, 46, 105, 128, 147, 161-62, 173, 177-79, 187, 195, 225, 233, 242, 244, 257-58, 270, 277, 279, 281, 286, 290, 292, 295, 299-301, 303, 309, 313-14
competition 130-31, 189, 191, 207, 218, 221, 238, 258-59, 304
composition 4, 21, 31, 74, 77, 79, 91, 96, 98, 115, 116, 119, 129, 149-50, 160, 163, 174, 190, 297
concerts 134, 232, 259-63, 265, 309-10
creation, *see* composition
cultural diversity 9, 11, 16-17, 55, 61, 96, 175, 180, 188, 243, 270, 277, 293, 295-301, 307, 309
cultural sustainability 296

dance accompaniment 4, 66, 86,
        90, 94, 96, 130-31, 182-83,
        201, 203-206, 209, 230, 232,
        235-37, 244-45, 301
dance:
    Branle d'Écosse 91;
    Cailleach an Dùdain 210, 230;
    Cape Breton step 41, 43, 183,
        195, 197, 208, 212, 234, 236,
        241
    choral 185, 198;
    dagger see dirk;
    Dannsa Mòr, An 230
    Dannsa na Tunnag 210, 230;
    Dannsa nan Flurs see Flowers of
        Edinburgh;
    dirk 155, 161, 170, 216, 221-27,
        319;
    Duke of Fife 230;
    finishing balls 188-89, 217;
    First of August 210, 212-13, 215-
        16;
    Flowers of Edinburgh 193, 196,
        230;
hay d'Alemaigne 185
    Hebridean weaving lilt 206;
    Highland fling 84, 189-90, 193,
        196, 216-17, 238-39, 320,
    Irish xiv, 12-13, 15-16, 18, 35-37,
        51-54, 61, 76-77, 95, 97-98,
        120, 126, 129, 193, 195, 204,
        220, 230, 283, 319-21;
    Irish washerwoman 193;
    Jacky Tar 193, 230;
    King of Sweden's March 210,
        212, 215-16;
    Kissing Reel see Ruidhleadh nam
        Pòg;
    Marbhadh na Beiste Duibhe
        230;
    percussive footwork 186-87;
    quadrille 73-74;

dance. continued
    reel, eight-hand 195-96;
    reel, four-hand 195;
    Reel of Tulloch 230;
    Ruidhleadh nam Pòg 220, 230;
    Ruidhle Thullachain 230;
    Ruidhleadh nan Caraidh 230;
    Ruidhleadh nan Coileach Dubha
        210, 227, 229-30;
    Scotch Eight see reel, eight-hand;
    Scotch Four see reel, four-hand
        196, 231;
    Scottish country dance 183, 189,
        191-92, 205-207, 209, 215,
        244;
    Scottish Highland dance 183,
        189, 234;
    Seann Triubhas 193, 196, 230;
    setting step 196;
    Shan Trews see Seann Triubhas;
    smàladh na coinnle 234, 241;
    snuffing the candle see smàladh
        na coinnle
    square sets 197, 208;
    step dance 43, 108, 183, 189,
        191, 193-95, 197, 205, 207-
        209, 212, 215, 217, 220, 230,
        232, 237, 241, 244, 321;
    strathspey 44, 84, 88, 100, 108-
        10, 117, 119, 123, 127-30,
        146, 154, 175, 196, 207,
        209-10, 217, 234, 241, 247,
        281-82, 286, 321
    sword 22, 155, 161, 218-20, 319;
    travelling step 228;
    Trì Croidhan Caorach 230;
    Tullochgorm 230;
    wake 20, 55, 75, 198;
    White Cockade 211, 213-16, 220

dance shoes 186-87, 193, 326
dancing master 185, 187, 235

deedling *see* jigging

devil 39, 64-65, 105

diddling *see* jigging

Disarming Act (Scotland) 57, 59

Druids 4, 75, 78, 95

enunciation 132, 256, 271

ephemerality 145-46

ethnomusicology 1, 6-8, 10

fiddle xv, 17, 37-39, 43, 45, 50-51, 56, 61, 63-65, 69, 71-72, 74, 75-76, 81, 84, 87, 92-93, 95, 100-101, 106, 115, 117-18, 120, 123, 130, 132, 134, 147, 149, 151, 186, 197, 200, 204, 210-11, 233, 235, 237-38, 250-51, 252-55, 264, 280-93, 296-99, 301-302, 306

form iv, 8-9, 12, 20, 27, 32, 35, 49-50, 61, 68, 84, 88-91, 96, 98-99, 128, 137, 139-42, 152, 154, 160, 167, 179, 183, 193-94, 196, 198, 202, 207, 218, 221, 226, 228-30, 236-37, 242, 244, 249, 292, 319

formes fixes 91, 319

Fraser, Alasdair 236

Fraser, Willie 43, 45, 209, 231-32, 241-43

Freud, Sigmund 166

Gael Stream 20, 143, 224, 233

gender 6, 176, 177

genre 3, 10, 12, 29, 34, 47, 75, 84, 86, 88, 95-96, 137, 149-50, 154, 156, 170, 180-81, 256-61, 263, 272, 276-77, 291, 303-304, 308, 314

gestures 39, 91

groups of tunes 9, 15-17, 61, 28, 46, 52, 81, 89, 98, 110, 119, 129-32, 137, 143, 145, 170, 177-78, 183, 196-97, 206, 212, 226, 235, 266, 295, 288

group singing 207

harp 61, 88-90, 94, 204-205, 319

Highland dance *see* dance, Scottish Highland

Highlandism 75, 258

humour 21, 95, 142, 160, 163, 165-70, 176-81

identity 13, 16, 21, 153, 288, 295

Indo-European language tree 12

instrumental tunes:

Am Muileann Dubh 101, 103-106, 110, 239, 107;

An Seanbhean Bhocht 126;

Brisk Young Lad *see* Lord of Dunmore;

Brochan Lom 165, 206, 272-73;

Bung Your Eye *see* Lord of Dunmore;

Caberfeidh 238, 283;

Charles, Twelfth King of Sweden's March *see* King of Swweden's March

Lord of Dunmore 120-21;

Christie Campbell, Christina Campbell 112-18;

Coc Ard, An 216;

First of August 210, 212-13, 215-16;

Gillie Callum 217, 219-21, 244;

Glengarry's March 127;

Haughs of Cromdale, The 128;

High Road to Linton, The 238-39;

Jolly Old Man, The *see* Lord of Dunmore;

King of Sweden's March 210, 212, 215-16;

Lord of Dunmore 120, 121;

instrumental tunes, continued
  Miller of Drone, The 115, 116, 117;
  Miss Drummond of Perth 28, 41-42, 146, 232, 238, 247, 315-16, 328 see also Calum Crùbach
  Put Me in the Big Chest 238-39;

intervals 106, 109, 132, 133, 264, 321
Jacobite, Rebellion (1745-1746), Rising (1715); 20, 55-58, 61, 75, 77, 83-84, 96, 104, 212, 213, 215, 345
jigging 18, 20, 26, 34-38, 40-46, 49-51, 61-62, 136, 209, 231-33, 252, 254, 273, 280, 319-21

Kennedy, Wilma xiii, 131, 209-10, 212, 215-16
Kist o Riches see Tobar an Dualchais

Lamond, Mary Jane 2, 30, 125-27, 168, 239, 260-61, 268, 270, 306, 313, 316
leaps, melodic 106-107, 109-11, 118, 120, 125, 264
learners 2, 13-14, 23, 134, 149-50, 175, 178-81, 259, 262, 264-65, 267-69, 271-73, 296, 301, 305-306, 311, 313
learning 1, 7, 19, 21-22, 27-30, 50, 91, 150, 176, 179-80, 186, 194, 203, 222, 228, 233, 241, 246, 251-52, 255-57, 266-69, 271, 273, 282, 291, 294-95, 302, 306-307
learning Gaelic 271
Lhuyd, Edward 16

lilting see jigging
lyrics as code 31, 104, 326

MacDiarmid manuscript 84, 86
MacDonald, Father Kenneth 72-73
MacDonald, Keith Norman 3, 4, 5, 28, 47, 75-80, 82-83, 112, 115-16, 119, 122, 125, 142, 146-47, 155-57, 174, 201, 214-15, 220, 223-25, 229, 240-41, 315
MacIsaac, Ashley 2, 143, 267, 289, 297, 313
MacLachlan, Ewen 235
MacLellan, Lauchie 42, 143, 221, 233, 250, 291, 292, 302
MacMaster, Buddy 42, 289, 290, 297
MacMaster, Natalie 44, 254, 289, 297, 290
MacNab, Mary Isdale 206, 207, 222
MacNeil, Joe Neil 2, 122, 143, 224-25, 230, 232, 255, 281, 290, 297, 302
metre 100, 119-20, 123, 125, 130, 153, 246
milling songs, see waulking songs

mnemonics 31, 67
Mòd, Royal National 3, 131, 257-58
mode 27, 47, 86, 108, 123-25, 132-33, 248, 309
Moore, Hamish 188-89, 196, 217, 236-38, 269, 288

Mouth Music (band) 313, 324
mouth music
  bols, Indian 27, 30, 33
  Dagomba drumming, Ghanaian 29-30

mouth music, continued
  eephing 33, 319
  kuŭm, Korea 28, 32-33
  luogujing, Chinese 31, 285
  nangma, Tibetan 32
  sargam, Indian 27
  scat singing 25, 27, 32-33
  susŏng, karak, Korean 32
  syôga, Japanese 28-29
  vocables, Navajo 26, 33, 79, 172

Newbattle manuscript 92
Newfoundland 172, 325, 343, 345,
  347
nonsense 29, 38, 41, 51, 139, 166,
  169-70, 219, 251
notation, Curwen 27-28
notation, oral 28, 49
ornamentation 28-29, 34, 41, 47,
  129, 132, 247, 251-52, 281,
  287, 292, 310, 319
Ossian 75-78

participatory music 136-37, 310-
  11
pibroch 39, 46-48, 50, 89-90,
  34-35, 47, 49, 90, 128-29,
  319-20
pibroch song 128
pìobaireachd see pibroch
port (harp) 89-90
port-a-beil (Irish) *see portaireacht*
port-a-beul:
  'S Math a Dhannsadh Uisdean
    Hiortach 202;
  'S ann an Ìle 249-50,272, 329;
  Aig Ceann an Rathaid Iaruinn
    148;
  Bhanais Bhàin, 'A 174;
  Biodag air MacAlasdair, Tha
    221, 227;

port-a-beul continued
  Biodag air MacThomais, Tha
    221, 227;
  Bodachan a' Mhìrein 239, 262;
  Brochan Lom 165, 206, 272-73;
  C'àit' an do Chuir Mi an Number
    aig Aonghas 150;
  Cabar Fèidh 240, 283;
  Cairistìona Chaimbeul 112, 115-
    17, 119;
  Calum Crùbach 28, 41-42, 146,
    232, 238, 247, 315-16, 328;
  Chaora Chrom, A' 167;
  Ciamar a Nì Mi an Dannsa Dì-
    reach 248;
  Còta Mòr Ealasaid 292;
  Cuir sa Chiste Mhòir Mi 239
  Cuiridh 'ad Do Chas air Fad
    165;
  Danns' a Bhocai, Danns' a Bhrigi
    165;
  Dhiùlt am Bodach Fodar Dhomh
    171;
  Dotair Leòdach 's Biodag Air, An
    154;
  E ho rithill aill, hi rithill u 156-
    57;
  Fear a Bhios Fada gun Phòsadh
    140;
  Fear an Dùin Mhòir 120-21;
  Fire Faire Mhòrag 145;
  Fosgail an Dorus dhan Taillear
    Fhidhleir 248;
  Gille Callum 219;
  Hai-O Eadaraibh O 152;
  I bhì à da 158;
  Leis a' Bhriogais Uallaich 164;
  Màiri Ruadh a' Dannsadh a-
    Nochd 150,-51;
  Meal do Bhrògan 129;
  Mo Thasdan Bòidheach 213;

port-a-beul continued
  Muileann Dubh, Am 101-107,
    110, 239;
  O, na miolan 's na dearagadan
    171;
  Pige Ruadh, Am 261,-62;
  Pog 'o Leannan an Fhidhleir
    251;
  Ruidhleadh Cailleach, Sheatadh
    Cailleach 202-203;
  Ruidhlidh na Coilich Dhubha
    228;
  Seallaibh Curraigh Eòghainn
    145, 269-70;
  Sheana Bhean Bhochd, A 125-
    26;
  Siud Mar Chaidh an Càl a
    Dholaidh 128;
  Tàillear Mòr, An 216
  Tha Iolairean a' Chaolais 85;
  Tha Mi Sgìth 298-99;
  Tha Mis' air Uisg' an Lònain
    Duibh 135

portaireacht xiv, 18, 51, 52, 53, 54,
  95, 320
portaireacht, Rógaire Dubh 52
Primrose, Christine xiii, 44, 259-
  60, 262, 273, 30-303, 316
Prince Edward Island x, 38, 40, 45,
  51, 87, 169, 233, 321
Prohibition (Canada) 149, 169

Rankin Family, The 2, 262, 267-68
recordings xiv, 1-2, 137, 147-48,
  255-57, 266-68, 270, 278,
  282, 291, 304, 312, 314
recordings, archival 20, 122, 131,
  134, 255-57, 270-71, 255,
  292, 299

recordings, commercial 32, 125,
  131, 142-43, 145, 160, 206,
  224, 255-57, 259, 261-63,
  266
religion 62, 66-71, 75, 94, 212
repetition 38, 53, 99, 108, 110, 112,
  128, 136-37, 139-42, 150,
  152-56, 174, 226, 249-50,
  264, 270
rhythm 27-31, 41, 47, 49, 82, 109-
  10, 119-20, 134, 150, 186,
  195-96, 219, 237, 241, 243,
  246-50, 252, 281, 284-85,
  291-92, 310
rhythm, Scotch snap 109, 286
Royal Scottish Country Dance Society (RSCDS) 189-91, 206

scale see mode
Scotch snap see rhythm, Scotch
  snap
Scottish country dance see dance,
  Scottish country
Scottish Country Dance Society
  (SCDS) 189, 192, 206
Scottish Official Board of Highland
  Dance (SOBHD) 190-91
Scottish Reformation 94
scrapbooks, song 303
sets (of tunes) see groups of tunes
Sharp, Cecil 76
solfa 27-29, 46
solfège see solfa
square dance see dance, square sets
Sruth nan Gàidheal see Gael
  Stream
step dance see dance, step and Cape
  Breton step
smàladh na coinnle 234, 241
Stuart, Charles Edward 56-57, 77,
  84, 96, 212
syncopation 100

teaching *see* transmission

Temperance Act (Canada) 71

tempo 100-101, 107, 119, 127, 132, 134, 140, 152, 1-53, 237, 246, 261, 263, 284, 304

Tobar an Dualchais 20, 111, 122, 131, 145, 299

transmission ix, 10-11, 26-30, 37-38, 46, 48-49, 88, 91, 178, 195, 232-33, 241, 243, 246-47, 250, 252, 253, 254, 255, 270, 275, 279, 289, 291, 312

Triskele 298-99

tune type:

   jig 38, 39, 40-45, 52-53, 84, 87, 98, 101, 119-20, 123, 125, 141, 153, 202, 207-208, 231-32, 234, 241, 251, 254, 280

   march 97, 127, 128, 130, 151, 208, 210

   reel   reel 84, 88, 100-101, 109-12, 117, 119, 125-26, 129-30, 136, 150-51, 158, 170, 185, 196, 199, 202-203, 205, 209-11, 215-16, 229, 234, 241, 247, 250, 282-83;

   strathspey 44, 84, 88, 100, 108-10, 117, 119, 123, 127-30, 146, 154, 175, 196, 207, 209-10, 217, 234, 241, 247, 281-82, 286, 321

turn 34, 43, 46, 54-55, 67, 74, 99, 137,-38, 140-41, 169, 173-74, 212, 215, 242, 244, 250, 255, 270, 276-77, 311, 315

tuning, *see* jigging

vocabelizing 26, 34-35, 37, 39, 44, 173, 246, 252

vocables 25,-26, 34-35, 37, 47-49, 75, 153, 157, 205, 246, 248, 264

waulking songs, milling songs 7, 156-59

About the author

Heather Sparling, PhD, is the Tier 2 Canada Research Chair (Musical Traditions) and an Associate Professor of Ethnomusicology at Cape Breton University. Heather teaches a range of ethnomusicology and Celtic music courses. A Gaelic speaker and teacher, she is actively involved with both local and international Gaelic organizations, sharing her expertise in Cape Breton Gaelic song. Her publications have addressed genre theory, Bourdieu's theories of social distinction, language attitudes, and oral and print transmission. Her current research focuses on disaster songs of Atlantic Canada, including their role in processing grief, nationalism and commemoration.

www.ingramcontent.com/pod-product-compliance
Lightning Source LLC
Chambersburg PA
CBHW031232090426
42742CB00007B/165